Computer and Information Science: Advanced Principles and Practices

Computer and Information Science: Advanced Principles and Practices

Edited by Fiona Hobbs

CLANRYE
INTERNATIONAL
www.clanryeinternational.com

Clanrye International,
750 Third Avenue, 9th Floor,
New York, NY 10017, USA

ISBN: 978-1-63240-674-3

Cataloging-in-Publication Data

Computer and information science : advanced principles and practices / edited by Fiona Hobbs.
    p. cm.
Includes bibliographical references and index.
ISBN 978-1-63240-674-3
1. Computer science. 2. Information science. I. Hobbs, Fiona.
QA76 .C66 2018
004--dc23

For information on all Clanrye International publications
visit our website at www.clanryeinternational.com

Contents

Preface

Computer and information science is a field that has emerged by the integration of the principles of information science and computer science. The primary areas of concern of this field are programming theories, information systems, computational algorithms, etc. This book covers in detail some existent theories and innovative concepts revolving around computer and information science. The various advancements in this field are glanced at and their applications as well as ramifications are looked at in detail. As this field is emerging at a rapid pace, the contents of this book will help the readers understand the modern concepts and applications of the subject.

The researches compiled throughout the book are authentic and of high quality, combining several disciplines and from very diverse regions from around the world. Drawing on the contributions of many researchers from diverse countries, the book's objective is to provide the readers with the latest achievements in the area of research. This book will surely be a source of knowledge to all interested and researching the field.

In the end, I would like to express my deep sense of gratitude to all the authors for meeting the set deadlines in completing and submitting their research chapters. I would also like to thank the publisher for the support offered to us throughout the course of the book. Finally, I extend my sincere thanks to my family for being a constant source of inspiration and encouragement.

Editor

Conceptual Model of Technological Change on Telecentre Effectiveness

Zahurin Mat Aji[1], Nor Iadah Yusop[1], Faudziah Ahmad[2], Azizi Ab. Aziz[2] & Zaid M. Jawad[2]

[1] Public Enterprise Computing Research Platform, School of Computing, Universiti Utara Malaysia, Malaysia

[2] Human Centred Computing Group, Artificial Intelligence Research Platform, School of Computing, Universiti Utara Malaysia, Malaysia

Correspondence: Nor Iadah Yusop, School of Computing, Universiti Utara Malaysia, 06010 UUM Sintok, Kedah, Malaysia. E-mail: noriadah@uum.edu.my

This research is funded by the Universiti Utara Malaysia.

Abstract

Telecentre effectiveness is highly related with involvement of people in the community and has been measured by the socio-economic benefit gained from the telecentre. One of the important aspects that are often overlooked in the assessment of telecentre effectiveness is the technological change. It is referred to as the overall process of continuous invention, innovation and diffusion of technology that aims at improving the quality of telecentre operations. This paper presents a conceptual model of technological change on telecentre effectiveness. In achieving this, extensive reviews of literature on related concepts were performed. Several elements of technological change that are expected to have impact on telecentre effectiveness were identified. These elements were categorized into three dimensions of technological change process, which are in accordance with the Linear Model of Innovation namely invention, innovation and diffusion. This model can be used as a basis towards getting empirical evidence on the impact of technological change on telecentre operations.

Keywords: technological change, ICT, telecentre, effective usage

1. Introduction

Telecentre is commonly associated with Information and Communication Technology (ICT) for development projects (Mishra, 2013). Telecentres are considered as one of the most successful projects of ICT diffusion in developing countries, particularly the poor and people living in remote rural areas (Rajalekshmi, 2007). According to Gomez *et al.* (2012) and Norizan *et al.* (2010), telecentre is a place where ICT facilities such as computers, and Internet services, training, and Internet access are provided to the rural community. Telecentre is a public place where people can find information, create, learn, and communicate with others while developing digital skills through access to information and communication technology (Telecentre.org). The Economic Planning Unit of the Prime Minster Department of Malaysia defines telecentre as a one-stop centre that provides Information and Communication Technology (ICT) and Internet services to various local communities in improving their socio-economic status (EPU, 2007). Telecentres are much like Internet cafés, except that they are placed in underserved communities with the deliberate intention of accelerating their socio-economic growth. Telecentres are often initiated by private or public business initiatives, which provide communities with information and telecommunication services, with the aim of achieving a variety of development objectives (Bailey & Ngwenyama, 2009; Proenza, 2001; Rao, 2008; Bishop & Bruce, 2005).

Telecentres exist in almost every developing country (Harris, 2007) under a variety of names: Internet centre, community centre, community technology centre, online access centre, electronic village halls, communal computing facilities, multipurpose communication centres, and many others. Previous findings showed that communities have opportunities to improve their access to information, job creation, skill development, study opportunities, and increased income, due to effective utilization of telecentre (Bailey & Ngwenyama, 2013; Zamani-Miandashti *et al.*, 2013; Buhigiro, 2012). It was also found that it could enhance information dissemination related to e-government services, e-health as well as e-banking with the aim to improve the targeted community's socio-economic conditions (Huda *et al.*, 2010).

However, a number of studies have reported that telecentres did not live up to their potential as most of the rural community did not foresee the importance of ICT (Doshi & Gollakota, 2011; Sey & Fellows, 2009; Huda *et al.*, 2009). Telecentre can be a mean to accelerate economic growth (Toyama, 2011) provided that the users are able to take advantage of the technological infrastructure and services offered in the telecentre (Bar et al., 2013). This is feasible if the users possess certain ICT skills and must see the needs to use the telecentre (Bar et al., 2013; Wang & Shih, 2009). This is also important to ensure sustainability of telecentre operation (Stoll, 2008). However, as the users are mainly from the rural areas and usually are not techno-savvy, the advancement and changes in technologies do give impact to them and thus affect the usage of the telecentre. This is worsened as technology changes very rapidly. Technology or ICT infrastructure is one of the important elements in ensuring the successful and effective usage of a telecentre (Bar *et al.*, 2013; Lo *et al.*, 2013; Bashir *et al.*, 2011; Toyama, 2011; Norizan, 2009; Wan Rozaini *et al.*, 2007; Rao, 2004). According to Reddi (2011), "the availability of telecommunications infrastructure is a precondition to the use of ICT4D (ICT for development) and must be addressed; while issues of access are based as much on technology factors as they are on the enabling environments (economic, social and regulatory) that has to be planned for". In order to sustain the usage of the telecentre, access only is not enough, the available technology needs to be enhanced and innovated (Bar *et al.*, 2013; Lo *et al.*, 2013; Bashir *et al.*, 2011; Reddi, 2011). At the same time, the selection of appropriate technologies for the rural communities should emphasize on the cost effectiveness for rural connectivity and information processing solutions (Ab-Hamid, 2011; Reddi, 2011; Crabtree, 2006). Technological change has an impact on telecentre in terms of infrastructure, costs, IT services, and information accessibility (Meng et al., 2013; Garrido et al., 2012; Gomez, 2011; Jimoyiannis, 2010). A study conducted by Qureshi and Trumbly-Lamsam (2008) showed that technological change provides easy and affordable access to ICT resources and thus, have assisted individual in acquiring useful information. Hence, to remain in line with the needs of the community, telecentre needs to be innovative in diversifying its services (Lo *et al.*, 2013) and thus provides convenience towards the effective usage of telecentre.

Technological change is defined as an expression used to illustrate the overall process of invention, innovation and diffusion of technology. Rapid improvement of technology contributed to knowledge through engaging people and making new resources accessible and affordable for them. Easy access to IT has created a substantial effect to telecentre environments through the usage of the new technology devices (Kremer & Maskin, 2003). The innovation in technology has helped towards the accomplishment of societal development through user involvement (Qureshi, 2013; Wang & Shih, 2009; Qureshi & Trumbly-Lamsam, 2008; Harris, 2001). However, most studies on telecentre effectiveness have not specifically focused on technological change. Hence, a conceptual model that focuses on technological change on telecentre effectiveness, in particular from the dimensions of invention, innovation, and diffusion is proposed. These dimensions are adopted based on Linear Model of Innovation suggested by Godin (2013), Godin (2006), and Roman (2003).

2. Telecentre Effectiveness

The concept of telecentre was first introduced in the early eighties in the Nordic countries particularly in Denmark where it is known as telecottage. Telecentre later spread to other countries such as Europe, North America and Australia (Proenza, 2001). Telecentre, also known as multi-purpose community telecentres, public Internet access points, or information kiosks, is an avenue for providing ICT services to rural communities (Gomez, 2011; Best & Kumar, 2008). In line with this, this study adopts the definition by Bailey and Ngwenyama (2009) that define a telecentre as a place where public can have access to ICT facilities and services for economic, social and cultural development.

In general, telecentre can be described as a mechanism, which uses ICT to support a community's economic, social and educational development, bridging the digital divide, and empowerment. In a telecentre, Internet and computer services (ICTs) are provided to the rural community enabling the rural populace who are mostly farmers to increase their income through improved productivity and marketing (Doshi & Gollakota, 2011). Global growth in ICTs industry has created an awareness of the ability of ICTs to transform lives and alleviate poverty. Hence, the use of ICT in enhancing socio-economic development of the targeted community has been used as a dimension in determining telecentre effective usage (Bar *et al.*, 2013; Meng *et al.*, 2013; Doshi & Gollakota, 2011; Reddi, 2011; Toyama, 2011; Bailey & Ngwenyama, 2009).

Several frameworks have been developed to assess the effectiveness of telecentres using various factors such as technology infrastructure, services, technology adoption, and information accessibility (Meng *et al.*, 2013; Naik *et al.*, 2012; Bailey & Ngwenyama, 2009). In addition, the deployment of new technologies has vital impact on individuals' utilization and satisfaction of telecentre effectiveness (Doshi & Gollakota, 2011; Abdulwahab & Zulkhairi, 2010). These factors revolve around the issue related to user satisfaction (Huda *et al.*, 2010; Gurstein, 2007), improvement of socio-economic (Garside, 2009; Rothenberg-Aalami & Pal, 2005), sustainability (Avgerou, 2010; Proenza, 2001), impact (Avgerou, 2010; Roman, 2003), best practice (Avgerou, 2010; Roman, 2003), telecentre governance (Zahurin *et al.*, 2009; Hudson, 2001), technological infrastructure (Meng *et al.*, 2013; Cheuk *et al.*, 2012; Bashir *et al.*, 2011; Zahurin *et al.*, 2010), and technology deployment (Lashgarara *et al.*, 2012; Bailey & Ngwenyama, 2009). In addition to these challenges and issues on telecentres effectiveness, issues related to technological change are yet to be explored.

3. Technological Change

Technological change refers to the rapid and radical changes and development in ICT. The concept of technological change, also known as technological progress (Hritonenko & Yatsenko, 2013), connotes "the presence of a self-sustaining mechanism of cumulative productivity growth". The issue related to technological change has gained attention in recent years due to various incidents whereby established organization being left behind and taken over by other organizations that are more innovative in using technologies strategically for the survival of their businesses. The scenario in which new firms replacing old ones is not new, but has been accelerated in recent years and thus made much more apparent, especially in rapidly developing fields such as ICT (Benson & Magee, 2012).

According to Crabtree (2006), technological change is based on continuous improvement of technology in a more cheaper and affordable medium to achieve social and economic development. In the same study, technology has been defined in term of space matrix. The space matrix is made of three dimensions of technology elements namely the average value by technology element unit, types of technology elements, and number of technology element units. Technology element refers to the specific type of goods, services or processes. Technology, at a given point in time, can be represented by the presence of these elements, the extent of the diffusion of those elements in economy and society, and the value contributed by each technology element unit, either individually or in conjunction with other elements. This definition is based on the principle of goods, service and process, which is similar to Jaffe *et al.* (2002).

Technological change, which is used interchangeably with technology development or technology advancement, describes the overall processes of invention, innovation and diffusion of processes or technology (Jaffe *et al.*, 2002). The term is also synonymous with technological achievement, and technological progress. They described technological change as the invention of a technology (or a process), followed by the continuous process of improving a technology, and subsequently its diffusion throughout the industry or society. One of the earlier models used to explain technological change process is the Linear Model of Innovation of Godin (2006). It was developed as a theoretical framework to understand science and technology in relation to the economy. The model suggests that change happens in a linear fashion from invention to innovation to diffusion as shown in the Figure 1. This model was also referred to as the traditional phase gate model because the concept of gates and gatekeeper was used to illustrate it (Rothwell, 1994). It involves series of sequential phases arranged in such a manner that the preceding phase must be completed before moving to the next phase. The project is assumed to pass through a gate (phase change) with the permission of the gatekeeper (task completion check) before moving to the next succeeding phase. Hence, technological change has been represented by the process stages of invention, innovation, and diffusion (Godin, 2006). These processes are described next.

3.1 Invention

Invention denotes the development of new idea that can transform product, process or services. As observed by (Antonelli et al., 2013), inventions and scientific breakthroughs have the capability of making some portions of the stock of knowledge or technologies obsolete. It involves studying the relationship between complementary technologies, knowledge relatedness, and invention outcomes in high technology mergers. Shaista (2006) argued that research and development (R&D) efforts resulted into invention and creation of new ideas. In this paper, invention can be regarded as an act or process of introducing something new or making a significant change to an existing system. Invention is found to be influenced by research and development (R&D), government policy, and technological knowledge. R&D efforts produce new ideas that lead to invention (Ma & Nakamori, 2008; Dawid, 2006). Government policy plays significant moderating roles in technological change process through various policies such as funding, operational or patent (Makri *et al.*, 2010). In addition, Makri *et al.* (2010) and Crabtree (2006) also indicate that technological knowledge is an essential ingredient of invention.

3.2 Innovation

Innovation is an economic undertaking aimed at developing or enhancing the quality of product, process or services that produce novelty, thus it is considered as a very important determinant of technological change (Hekkert *et al.*, 2007). It connotes the ability to blend and weave together several kinds of knowledge to yield completely new, unique and of economic value products or services as knowledge represents a decisive input for innovation (Feldman, 2002). Moreover, the success of any innovation is measured by its success at market place based on the quality of service and societal impact in terms of economic wellbeing, growth and success. Successful innovation requires organizational changes and collaboration at process level as well as conversion of idea into a marketable product (Verloop, 2004). Breakthrough in innovation is highly dependent upon accumulated knowledge in a particular field. Likewise, successful innovation requires organizational changes at process level as well as conversion and collaboration of idea into commercially product adopted in the market (Verloop, 2004). Another factor that can influence innovation is the infrastructural sustainability. Within the context of this study, infrastructure sustainability refers to technological sustainability, as technology is part of infrastructure (Meng *et al.*, 2013; Cheuk *et al.*, 2012; Bashir *et al.*, 2011; Zahurin *et al.*, 2010). The current state of technology, capability and high deployment rate of technology are found to affect innovation (Nor Iadah *et al.*, 2010; Ali & Bailur, 2007). Hence, innovation success is determined by rate of adoption or diffusion.

3.2 Diffusion

Diffusion refers to the number of usage or rate of adoption of an innovation and also serves as a mean of measuring the level of utilization of a particular product or services (Crabtree, 2006). It represents the last and crucial stage in the linear model of technological change. Rogers (1985) described diffusion as a process by which innovation spread across society through communication channels. The rate of service diffusion, which is the dynamism of individual attention to the service being provided, is influenced by the affordability (cost), level of innovation, and satisfaction, derived from such services. Thus, if the level of innovation is high, cost is affordable and the service satisfactory, this may enhance commitment to short-term utilization and if this continues over time, individual commitment grows and thus triggers long-term utilization that aid effectiveness.

4. Technological Change Impacts on Telecentre

Technological change has been recognized as an important driver of effective growth and the emergence of new technologies from which user derive the perceived benefits (Misuraca & Viscusi, 2014; Dillon & Morris, 1996). It depends not only on the work of scientists and engineers, but also on a wider range of technological markets (Sun *et al.*, 2012). A study by Hlungulu (2010) mentioned that technological change presents special opportunities to the social and geographical marginalized communities. It is observed that technologies like wireless communications permit easier integration of marginal areas that could not be connected physically (hard wired). The interactive capacities of these new technologies offer an added advantage of allowing previously marginalized communities to transmit information symmetrically.

The advancement and proliferation of technological products as in many ways affect telecentre effectiveness (Huda *et al.*, 2010). This effectiveness can either be seen between the telecentre management and end-users, in whichever case; there is always an applicable technological device to smoothen the relationship. This suggests that technological change can have direct effect on telecentre utilization (Pick & Nishida, 2014), and user satisfaction (Yen & Lu, 2008), thus telecentre effectiveness. Tidd and Bessant (2011) suggested that technological change is the most influential and vital source for economic development. Technological change has a great influence on user satisfaction and utilization in particular with the innovation of attractive and enjoyable devices (Nusair & Kandampully, 2008; Cyr *et al.*, 2006). Technological change and telecentres can facilitate community access to information for socio-economic development purposes (Nusair & Kandampully, 2008; Cyr *et al.*, 2006).

5. Applying the Linear Model of Innovation in Conceptualizing Technological Change for Telecentre Effectiveness

Roman (2003) emphasized on the importance of evaluating telecentre effectiveness particularly on economic and social as the results will presumably have important policy implications. Telecentre is regarded as an innovation in itself by Cheang (2015), Ghimire (2012), and Roman (2003). In line with that, Chander *et al.* (2014) considered telecentre as an innovation broker whereby local level of R&D activities can stimulate local innovation thereby lead to better quality of life of the community. In this study, Godin's (2006) Linear Model of Innovation (Figure 1) is used as it is found to be appropriate in understanding the impact of technological change on telecentre effectiveness. Based on the literature as mentioned in Section 3.1 – 3.3, the following factors are extracted to measure each phase in the model:

Invention: research and development, government policies, technological knowledge.

Innovation: technological sustainability, collaboration, technological knowledge, and Invention

Diffusion: satisfaction, cost, and innovation.

Figure 1. The Linear Model of Innovation (Godin, 2006)

The relationships of the three processes are illustrated as the conceptual model of technological change for telecentre effectiveness as shown in Figure 2. The relationships are derived based on the Linear Model of Innovation. In relating the involved processes with telecentre effectiveness, Invention exists if there is an improvement in research and development or government policies. In addition, adequate adoption of technological knowledge will also contribute to invention. Apart from Invention, Innovation occurs when there are technological sustainability, collaboration, and technological knowledge. In terms of technological sustainability, adequate provision of technological amenities that support services delivery enhances the rate of effectiveness, also updating technical knowledge on efficient services. This will contribute to the level of invention as well as innovation (Makri *et al.*, 2010). Innovation has the aim to develop or enhance the quality of product, process or services that produce novelty. With respect to telecentre operations, ICT facilities, the current state of technology, and market demand of services can be classified as elements of innovation (Crespi & Pianta, 2008). Diffusion happens when the level of innovation is high, cost is affordable and the service is satisfactory. This may enhance commitment to utilization and if this continues over time, individual commitment grows and this will lead to effectiveness.

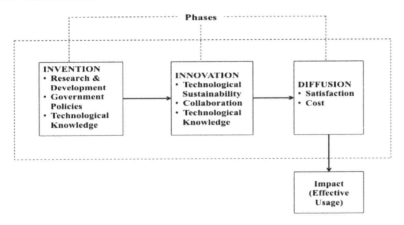

Figure 2. Conceptual Model of Technological Change for Telecentre Effectiveness

4. Conclusion and Recommendations

Research on the impact of technological change on telecentre effectiveness have identified several elements of technological change process that can be classified into three dimensions namely invention, innovation, and diffusion which is in accordance with the Linear Model of Innovation. For the invention dimension, three elements namely research and development, government policy, and technological knowledge have been associated to give impact on it. The innovation dimension is affected by elements such as collaboration, technological knowledge, technological sustainability and invention. The last dimension, diffusion, is affected by the affordability, level of innovation, and satisfaction, gained from the services provided by the telecentre. This clearly reflects the dependency of innovation on invention, and diffusion on innovation. This model is regarded as a contribution in assessing telecentre effectiveness in particular, on the impact of technological change. The model provides a basis for researchers to further explore the relationship of technological change and telecentre effectiveness using various techniques such as simulation or statistical approaches, towards getting more empirical evidence on the issue.

Acknowledgments

We are grateful for the Universiti Utara Malaysia in funding this research work.

References

AbdulWahab, L. (2012). A Modified of the Unified Theory of Acceptance and Use of Technology (UTAUT) from Users' Perspective of Telecentre in Nigeria. Universiti Utara Malaysia.

Abdulwahab, L., & Zulkhairi, M. D. (2010). A Conceptual Model of Unified Theory of Acceptance and Use of Technology (UTAUT) Modification with Management Effectiveness and Program Effectiveness in Context of Telecentre. *African Scientist, 11*(4), 267-275.

Ab-Hamid, K., Tan, C. E., & Lau, S. P. (2011, December). Self-sustainable energy efficient long range WiFi network for rural communities. In GLOBECOM Workshops (GC Wkshps), 2011 IEEE (pp. 1050-1055). IEEE.

Ali, M., & Bailur, S. (2007, May). The challenge of "sustainability" in ICT4D—Is bricolage the answer. In *Proceedings of the 9th international conference on social implications of computers in developing countries.*

Antonelli, C., Crespi, F., & Scellato, G. (2013). Internal and External Factors in Innovation Persistence. *Economics of Innovation and New Technology, 22*(3), 256-280.

Avgerou, C. (2010). Discourses on ICT and Development. *Information Technologies & International Development, 6*(3), 1-18.

Bailey, A., & Ngwenyama, O. (2009). Social Ties, Literacy, Location and the Perception of Economic Opportunity: Factors Influencing Telecentre Success in a Development Context. Proceedings of the 42nd Hawaii International Conference on System Sciences.

Bailey, A., & Ngwenyama, O. (2013). Toward entrepreneurial behavior in underserved communities: An ethnographic decision tree model of telecenter usage. *Information Technology for Development* (ahead-of-print), 1-19.

Bar, F., Coward, C., Koepke, L., Rothschild, C., Sey, A., & Sciadas, G. (2013, December). The impact of public access to ICTs: findings from a five-year, eight-country study. In Proceedings of the Sixth International Conference on Information and Communication Technologies and Development: Full Papers-Volume 1 (pp. 34-42).

Bashir, M. S., Samah, B. A., Emby, Z., Badsar, M., Shaffril, H., & Aliyu, A. (2011). Information and Communication Technology Development in Malaysia: Influence of Competency of Leaders, Location, Infrastructures and Quality of Services on Telecentre Success in Rural Communities of Malaysia. *Australian Journal of Basic and Applied Sciences, 5*(9), 1718-1728.

Benson, C. L., & Magee, C. L. (2012). A framework for analyzing the underlying inventions that drive technical improvements in a specific technological field. *Engineering Management Research, 1*(1), 2.

Best, M. L., & Kumar, R. (2008). Sustainability failures of rural telecenters: Challenges from the sustainable access in rural india (sari) project. *Information Technologies & International Development, 4*(4), 31-45.

Bishop, A. P., & Bruce, B. (2005). Community Informatics: Integrating Action, Research & Learning. *Bulletin of the American Society for Information Science and Technology* (Aug/Sept 2005), 6.

Buhigiro, S. (2012). The Role of Telecentres in Promoting Socio-Economic Development in Rwanda (Master's dissertation), Faculty of Commerce, Law and Management, University of the Witwatersrand, South Africa. http://wiredspace.wits.ac.za/bitstream/handle/10539/12464/BUHIGIRO%20Seth%20-Research%20Report-Final%20300412.pdf?sequence=1.

Chander, M., Rathod, P., & Balaraju, B. L. (2014, September) Rural Telecentres as Innovation Brokers in Livestock Innovation System in India: A Review. *Indian Res. J. Ext. Edu., 14*(3), 14-23.

Cheang, S. (2015). Efficiency and Effectiveness of Telecenters: A Case Study on ICT4D in Cambodia. In Human Centered Computing (pp. 656-669). Springer International Publishing.

Cheuk, S., Atang, A., & Lo, M. C. (2012). Community Attitudes towards the Telecentre in Bario, Borneo Malaysia: 14 Years on. *International Journal of Innovation, Management and Technology, 682-687.*

Crabtree, P. (2006). A Framework for Understanding Technology and Technological Change. *The Innovation Journal: The Public Sector Innovation Journal, 11*(1), 1-16.

Crespi, F., & Pianta, M. (2008). Demand and innovation in productivity growth. *International Review of Applied Economics, 22*(6), 655-672.

Cyr, D., Head, M., & Ivanov, A. (2006). Design aesthetics leading to m-loyalty in mobile commerce. *Information & Management, 43*(8), 950-963.

Dawid, H. (2006). Agent-Based Models of Innovation and Technological Change. *Handbook of Computational Economics, 2*, 1235-1272.

Dillon, A., & Morris, M. G. (1996). User Acceptance of New Information Technology: Theories and Models. Annual review of information science and technology.

Economic Planning Unit (EPU) (2007). Rangka Kerja Strategik Kebangsaan bagi Merapatkan Jurang Digital (NSF-BDD), presented at Bengkel Pusat Perkhidmatan dan Ilmu Komuniti Peringkat Negeri Pulau Pinang, 13 Jun 2007. (in Malay)

Garrido, M., Sey, A., Hart, T., & Santana, L. (2012). Literature Review of How Telecentres Operate and have an Impact on e-inclusion: European Union.

Garside, B. (2009). Village voice: towards inclusive information technologies: IIED.

Godin, B. (2006). The Linear Model of Innovation: The Historical Construction of an Analytical Framework. *Science, Technology & Human Values, 31*(6), 639-667.

Godin, B. (2013). *Invention, Diffusion and Linear Models of Innovation, Project on the Intellectual History of Innovation Working Paper No. 15.* Retrieved from http://www.csiic.ca/PDF/AnthropologyPaper15.pdf.

Gollakota, K., & Doshi, K. (2011). Diffusion of Technological Innovations in Rural Areas. *Journal of Corporate Citizenship, 2011*(41), 69-82.

Gómez, R. (Ed.). (2011). Libraries, Telecentres, Cybercafes and Public Access to ICT: International Comparisons: IGI Global.

Gomez, R., Pather, S., & Dosono, B. (2012). Public access computing in South Africa: Old lessons and new challenges. *The Electronic Journal of Information Systems in Developing Countries, 52.*

Gurstein, M. (2007). What is Community Informatics (and Why Does It Matter)? Milan: Polimetrica SAS.

Harris, R. (2001). Telecentres in Rural Asia: Towards a Success Model. *Europe, 40*(23.4), 13-7.

Harris, R. W. (2007, July 10-12). *Telecentre Evaluation in the Malaysian Context.* Paper presented at the The 5th International Conference on IT in Asia, Hilton Hotel, Kuching, Sarawak, Malaysia.

Hekkert, M. P., Suurs, R. A., Negro, S. O., Kuhlmann, S., & Smits, R. (2007). Functions of innovation systems: A new approach for analysing technological change. *Technological Forecasting and Social Change, 74*(4), 413-432.

Hlungulu, B. (2010). Building a semantic web based e health component for a multipurpose communication centre (Doctoral dissertation, University of Fort Hare).

Hritonenko, N., & Yatsenko, Y. (2013). Introduction: Principles and Tools of Mathematical Modeling Mathematical Modeling in Economics, Ecology and the Environment (pp. 1-22): Springer.

Huda, I., Azman, Y., & Zulkhairi, M. D. (2010). Financial sustainability issues in Malaysia's telecentres. *Computer and Information Science, 3*(2), 235.

Huda, I., Nor Iadah, Y., Zahurin, M. A., Zulkhairi, M. D., & Mohd Khairudin, K. (2010). Lessons Learnt in the Implementation of Pusat Komuniti Pintar. Proceeding of the National Conference on Rural ICT Development (RICTD 2010): Empowering Rural Communities through Broadband Initiatives, EDC UUM Sintok, Kedah, Malaysia, 23-25 November.

Hudson, H. E. (2001). Telecentre Evaluation: Issues and Strategies. Telecentres: Case Studies and Key Issues, 169.

Jaffe, A. B., Newell, R. G., & Stavins, R. N. (2002). Environmental Policy and Technological Change. *Environmental and Resource Economics, 22*(1-2), 41-70.

Jimoyiannis, A. (2010). Designing and Implementing an Integrated Technological Pedagogical Science Knowledge Framework for Science Teachers Professional Development. *Computers & Education, 55*(3), 1259-1269.

Kremer, M., & Maskin, E. (2003). Globalization and Inequality. Harvard University, Department of Economics.

Unpublished manuscript.

Kumar, R., & Best, M. L. (2007). Social impact and diffusion of telecenter use: A study from the sustainable access in rural India project. *The Journal of Community Informatics, 2*(3).

Lashgarara, F., Karimi, A., & Mirdamadi, S. M. (2012). Effective factors on the villagers' use of rural telecentres (case study of Hamadan province, Iran). *African Journal of Agricultural Research, 7*(13), 2034-2041.

Lo, M. C., Songan, P., Cheuk, S., Atang, A., & Yeo, A. W. Communities' Attitudes towards Telecentre and Its Impact on Rural Tourism. *International Journal of Innovation, Management and Technology, 4*(6), December 2013.

Ma, T., & Nakamori, Y. (2008, October). Coping with uncertainties in endogenous technological change models. In Systems, Man and Cybernetics, 2008. SMC 2008. IEEE International Conference on (pp. 845-850). IEEE.

Makri, M., Hitt, M. A., & Lane, P. J. (2010). Complementary technologies, knowledge relatedness, and invention outcomes in high technology mergers and acquisitions. *Strategic Management Journal, 31*(6), 602-628.

Meng, C. C., Samah, B. A., & Omar, S. Z. (2013). A Review Paper: Critical Factors Affecting the Development of ICT Projects in Malaysia. *Asian Social Science, 9*(4), 42.

Mishra, G. (2013). Role of telecenters in empowering citizens: A case study of 'Mahiti Mitra'project in Kutch district of Gujarat, India. Paper presented at the Global Humanitarian Technology Conference: South Asia Satellite (GHTC-SAS), 2013 IEEE.

Misuraca, G., & Viscusi, G. (2014, October). Digital governance in the public sector: challenging the policy-maker's innovation dilemma. In *Proceedings of the 8th International Conference on Theory and Practice of Electronic Governance* (pp. 146-154). ACM.

Naik, G., Joshi, S., & Basavaraj, K. (2012). Fostering Inclusive Growth through E-Governance Embedded Rural Telecenters (EGERT) in India. *Government Information Quarterly, 29*, S82-S89.

Nor Iadah, Y., Shafiz, A. M. Y., Zahurin, M. A., Huda, H. I., Khairudin, K., Zulkhairi, Md. D. Nor Farzana, A.G., Rafidah, A. R., Syahida, H., & Abdul, R. R. (2010). The Influence of Community Characteristics towards Telecentres Success. *Computer and Information Science, 3*(2), 116-120. [ISSN 1913-8989 (Print), ISSN 1913-8997 (Online)]

Norizan, A. R. (2009). Empowering the Rural Communities via the Telecentres. *European Journal of Social Sciences, 9*(3).

Norizan, A. R., Zaharah, H., & Rosseni, D. (2010). Bridging the Digital Divide: An Analysis of the Training Program at Malaysian Telecenters.

Nusair, K. K., & Kandampully, J. (2008). The Antecedents of Customer Satisfaction with Online Travel Services: A Conceptual Model. *European Business Review, 20*(1), 4-19.

Pick, J. B., & Nishida, T. (2015). Digital Divides in The World and Its Regions: A Spatial and Multivariate Analysis of Technological Utilization. *Technological Forecasting and Social Change, 91*, 1-17.

Proenza, F. J. (2001). Telecenter sustainability: Myths and opportunities. *The Journal of Development Communication, 12*(2), 94-109.

Qureshi, S. (2013). Information and Communication Technologies in the Midst of Global Change: How do we Know When Development Takes Place? *Information Technology for Development, 19*(3), 189-192.

Qureshi, S., & Trumbly-Lamsam, T. (2008). Transcending the Digital Divide: A Framing Analysis of Information and Communication Technologies News in Native American Tribal Newspapers. Paper presented at the Hawaii International Conference on System Sciences, Proceedings of the 41st Annual.

Rajalekshmi, K. G. (2007). E-governance services through telecenters: The role of human intermediary and issues of trust. *Information Technologies & International Development, 4*(1), 19-35.

Rao, S. S. (2008). Social development in Indian rural communities: Adoption of telecentres. *International Journal of Information Management, 28*(6), 474-482.

Rao, T. R. (2004). ICT and e-Governance for Rural Development. Center for Electronic Governance, Indian Institute of Management, Ahmedabad.

Reddi, U. R. V. (2011). Primer 1: An Introduction to ICT for Development, A learning resource on ICT for development for institutions of higher education, Primer Series on ICTD for Youth, Asian and Pacific Training Centre for Information and Communication Technology for Development (APCICT), UN-APCICT/ESCAP.

Rogers, E. M. (2003). *Diffusion of Innovations* (5th ed). Free Press.

Roman, R. (2003). Diffusion of Innovations as a Theoretical Framework for Telecenters. *Information Technologies & International Development, 1*(2), 53-66.

Rothenberg-Aalami, J., & Pal, J. (2005). "Rural Telecenter Impact Assessments and the Political Economy of ICT for Development (ICT4D)", Berkeley Roundtable on the International Economy (BRIE), University of California, Berkeley, UC Berkeley. Retrieved from http://128.48.120.222/uc/item/18q2282h

Rothwell, R. (1994). Towards the Fifth-Generation Innovation Process. *International Marketing Review, 11*(1), 7-31.

Sey, A., & Fellows, M. (2009). Literature Review on the Impact of Public Access to Information and Communication Technologies, CIS Working Paper No. 6, Global Impact Study of Public Access to Information & Communication Technology, University of Washington's Center for Information & Society (CIS), www.cis.washington.edu.

Stoll, K. (2008). The Future of Telecenter Sustainability: A Multi-Sector and Multi-Stakeholder Approach.

Sun, Y., Fang, Y., Lim, K. H., & Straub, D. (2012). User satisfaction with information technology service delivery: A social capital perspective. *Information Systems Research, 23*(4), 1195-1211.

Toyama, K. (2011, February). Technology as amplifier in international development. In Proceedings of the 2011 iConference, pp. 75-82.

Wan Rozaini, S. O., Zahurin, M. A., Huda, I., Nor Iadah, Y., & Nafishah, O. (2007). Ke Arah Memperkasakan Komuniti Luar Bandar: Penilaian Situasi Semasa Pusat Internet Desa (PID). Paper presented at E-Community Research Center Coloqium, 8 February 2007, Bangi, Selangor, Malaysia.

Wang, Y. S., & Shih, Y. W. (2009). Why do People Use Information Kiosks? A Validation of the Unified Theory of Acceptance and Use of Technology. *Government Information Quarterly, 26*(1), 158-165.

Yen, C. H., & Lu, H. P. (2008). Effects of e-Service Quality on Loyalty Intention: An Empirical Study in Online Auction. *Managing Service Quality, 18*(2), 127-146.

Zahurin, M. A., Huda, I., Mohd Khairudin, K., Nor Iadah, Y., Shafiz Affendi, M. Y., & Zulkhairi, M. D. (2009). Management Practice in Sustaining Telecentres. Proceedings of National Seminar on e-Community 2009 (SKeKom2009), Hotel PNB Darby Park, Kuala Lumpur, Malaysia, 18 – 19 March, pp. 273-280.

Zahurin, M. A., Shafiz, A. M. Y., Wan, Rozaini, S. O., & Nor Iadah, Y. (2010). A Conceptual Model for Psychological Empowerment of Telecentre Users. *Computer and Information Science, 3*(3), 71-79. [ISSN 1913-8989 (Print) ISSN 1913-8997 (Online)].

Zamani-Miandashti, N., Pezeshki-Rad, G., & Pariab, J. (2014). The Influence of Telecenters on Rural Life and their Success Correlates: Lessons from a Case Study in Iran. *Technovation, 34*(5), 306-314.

A Model Driven Approach for Generating Graphical User Interface for MVC Rich Internet Application

Sarra Roubi[1], Mohammed Erramdani[1] & Samir Mbarki.[2]

[1] High School of Technology, Mohammed First University, Oujda, Morocco

[2] Computer Science Department, Ibn Tofail University, Kenitra, Morocco

Correspondence: Sarra Roubi, High School of Technology, Mohammed First University, BP 473 Complexe universitaire Al Qods, Oujda, Morocco. E-mail: s.roubi@ump.ac.ma

Abstract

Web applications have witnessed a significant improvement that exhibit advanced user interface behaviors and functionalities. Along with this evolution, Rich Internet Applications (RIAs) were proposed as a response to these necessities and have combined the richness and interactivity of desktop interfaces into the web distribution model. However, RIAs are complex applications and their development requires designing and implementation which are time-consuming and the available tools are specialized in manual design. In this paper, we present a new model driven approach in which we used well known Model-Driven Engineering (MDE) frameworks and technologies, such as Eclipse Modeling Framework (EMF), Graphical Modeling Framework (GMF), Query View Transformation (QVTo) and Acceleo to enable the design and the code automatic generation of the RIA. The method focus on simplifying the task for the designer and not necessary be aware of the implementation specification.

Keywords: model, Meta model, transformation, Graphical User Interface, Rich Internet Application, code generating

1. Introduction

Web applications concentrated all their activity around a client-server architecture where the processing is done on the server side and the client side is only used to display static content. These HTML-based Web applications are showing their limitations, especially when it comes to integrate complex activities to be performed via Graphical User Interfaces (GUI). To overcome these limitations, development in information technology has known a large evolution and several new technologies have been introduced. Among, desktop-like Web applications, called Rich Internet Applications (RIAs). We focus our work on this kind of application because it combines the benefits of the Web distribution model with the interface interactivity of desktop applications. Moreover, RIAs provide a new client-server architecture that reduces significantly network traffic using more intelligent asynchronous requests that send only small blocks of data.

In return, the design and implantation of graphical user interface for RIAs is known for its complexity and difficulty in using existing tools, on the one hand. In addition, designers need to know the computer platforms, users' characteristics, environmental interaction, etc ..., which can become tedious, time-consuming and requires additional efforts and can negatively affects the quality of the application. On the other, modeling approach is an efficient way to master complexity and ensure consistency of applications. That is to say that a model-driven approach adopted in the process of development of RIAs can significantly reduce the risk of rework and improve the overall quality of the development process for RIAs.

In this context, in this paper we present a new approach based on Model Driven Engineering paradigm that proposes a complete development process based on a set of models and transformations upon the Eclipse Modeling Project that allows obtaining the implementation of Rich Internet Applications with JavaFX platform as a target adopting a Model-View-Controller (MVC) architectural design pattern, focusing on the graphical part of the application. The proposed approach can be replicated for different design model and a different target technology platform.

The paper is organized as follows. Section II presents related work dealing with Model-Driven development approaches. In Sections III we present the Model Driven Engineering Approach. Section IV describes the proposed approach and technologies used to develop it, then we report the results of the case study of designing and generating the RIA to validate the approach. Finally we conclude.

2. Related Work

Several works dealing with GUI's automatic generation have emerged recently. (Kapitsaki et al. 2009) present a model based approach and advocates in favor of a complete separation of the web application functionality from the context adaptation at all development phases. Also, a Rich Internet Application for web based product development was presented (Ahmed & Popov 2010). Besides, (Meliá et al. 2008) proposes an approach called OOH4RIA which is a model driven development process that extends OOH methodology to generate GWT Rich Internet Application. Also, a combination of the UML based Web Engineering (UWE) method for data and business logic modeling with the RUX-Method for the user interface modeling of RIAs was proposed as model-driven approach to RIA development (Linaje et al, 2007). In addition, a research based on the plasticity of User Interface with the use of Model Driven Architecture concepts for the purpose of unifying the modeling for GUI is presented (Sottet et al, 2007). Some researches apply model based approaches for multi-device user interface development. Among them we can cite: TERESA (Transformation Environment for inteRactivE Systems representations) (Berti et al, 2003) and MARIA with (Paterno et al, 2009). Also, UsiXML (USer Interface eXtended Markup Language) (Vanderdonckt, 2005).

Another related work on applying MDA approach for RIAs is found in (Martinez-Ruiz et al, 2006). The approach is based on XML User Interface description languages using XSLT as the transformation language between the different levels of abstraction. Moreover, an MDA approach for AJAX web applications (Gharavi et al, 2008) was the subject of a study that proposes an UML scheme using profiling for modeling AJAX user interfaces; it adopts ANDROMDA tool for creating an AJAX cartridge to generate the corresponding AJAX application code with back-end integration.

These works focused on using a UML profiling to define new ways to model the RIAs application. In our case, we wanted to keep the task for designer as simple as possible and translate the user needs in terms of operations and goals to achieve. So, we proposed new meta models to simplify the task for the designer and be able to generate efficiently Rich Internet Application.

3. Model Driven Engineering

3.1 The OMG Approach and Acronyms

The OMG (The Object Management Group) initiated the Model Driven Architecture, an approach (Miller et al, 2003), to develop systems that offer more flexibility in the evolution of the system while remaining true to customer needs and satisfaction. It is based on models throughout the whole development process.

Indeed, the approach relies on the separation into three layers of abstraction and the code: Computing Independent Model (CIM), Platform Independent Model (PIM) and the Platform Specification Model (PSM). We can define the three layers as follow in figure.1:

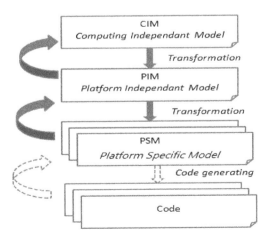

Figure 1. Levels of abstraction in Model Driven Architecture

- **CIM**: It represents a high level specification of the system's functionalities and describes what the system offers but hides all the technology specifications.
- **PIM**: It allows the extraction of the common concept of the application independently from the platform target so it enables its mapping to one or more platforms.
- **PSM**: It combines the specifications in the PIM with the details of a chosen platform. It allows having models conform to a specific platform and helps generating the appropriate code source.

3.2 Transformation Process in MDE

A transformation converts models from one level of abstraction to another, usually from a more abstract to less abstract view, by adding more detail and information supplied by the transformation rules to respect the target meta model.

There are two types of transformations in the MDA approach:

- **Model To Model**: it concerns transformation to pass from CIM to PIM or from PIM to PSM.
- **Model To Text**: it concerns the generation of the code from the entry model (the PSM) to a the programming language related to the chosen platform.

Model To Model transformation with the modeling approach allows having productive models' transformation, independently of any execution platform. The OMG has developed a standard for this transformation language which is the MOF 2.0 QVT (OMG, 2008), standing for Query View Transformation. The QVT specification has a hybrid declarative/imperative nature, with the declarative part being split into two-level architecture. For this work, we used the QVT-Operational mappings language implemented by Eclipse modeling.

For the code generation phase under the MOF Model To Text (MOFM2T) specification, there are a number of tools aimed at the automation of applications development. The principle is to parse the representation of the model in XML Metadata Interchange (XMI) form and apply templates that give the code source equivalent to each model element. Optionally, the developer will have to add or edit source code portions to complete its application code. Acceleo, among others, is an implementation of the "MOFM2T" standard, from the Object Management Group (OMG). It is used in our work for final transformation and code generation of the RIA with explicit Graphical User Interface.

4. The Model Driven Development Proposed Process

We propose a model-driven development process that adopts MDE technologies in order to enable the automatic generation of a MVC Rich Internet Application, focusing on the graphical part, starting from a simplified designed model. Indeed, we elaborated the tow meta models for the PIM and PSM as presented in the following section, then we established the transformation rules. The first transformation engine; Model To Model using QVT, generates the model respecting the MVC RIA application, while the second; Model To Text Acceleo transformations gives the source and configuration files for the JavaFX application using Acceleo.

4.1 The PIM and PSM Proposed Meta Models

While developing the meta model, that is the input to our modeling process, we focused on keeping the terms as simple as possible so the designer does not have to learn a new language or a complex design process. So, the meta model translates the user's vision of the graphical user interface in terms of actions and interactions, by describing what is expected from the application from a graphical point of view.

The major goal of the view is described through the use case that is divided into several main operations that gathers the atomic actions leading to achieve that goal. We added an enumeration of the basic actions' types that any user is familiar with (input, selection, clicks…). Finally, we assigned a property in each action (is it a password, a single choice …), to help choose the most appropriate widget while defining the transformation rules. All these elements are embraced in the UMLPackage.

Figure. 2 shows the proposed PIM meta model and the relationship between its elements described.

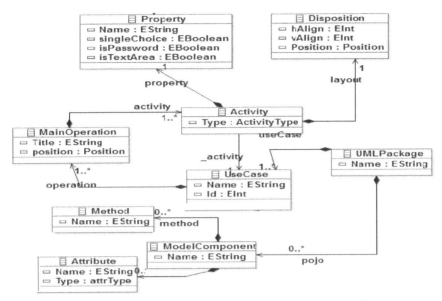

Figure 2. Platform Independent proposed Meta Model

The PSM meta model for the JavaFX was developed taking into account the relation between the different layers of the MVC architecture; which will avoid the GUI designer to worry about understanding the dynamics of appearance between the different layers of application. That is to say, as shown in figure. 3, we have the three packages: ViewPackage, ModelPackage and ControllerPackage that gather respectively the application's views, models and controllers.

Note that the View/Controller layers are responsible for describing the structure and content of views in terms of graphical elements while the navigation flow is ensure through the controller's handler that are connected to the specified services from the model layer.

In our proposed PSM meta model, we detailed the presentation layer where the composite design pattern was used to define the overlapping of graphical components in a RIA view; called the scene. The scene is composed of graphical components, named controls that could be containers as Roots.

In addition to that, we added a hierarchical relationship between graphical components base on their type, and we associate each component with its position in the grid that will divide the whole scene so we can put each component in a specific position as defined in the input model.

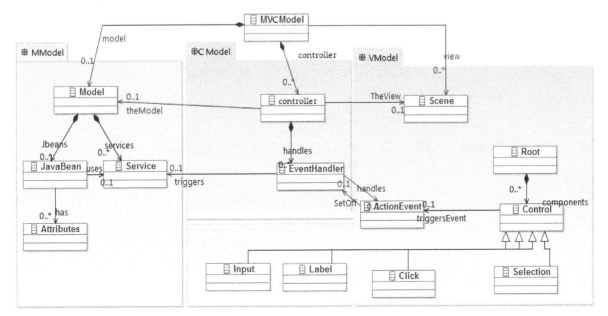

Figure 3. MVC for JavaFX RIA proposed Meta Model

4.2 The Transformation Process

Once the meta modeling phase established, comes the most important phase in the MDE approach, which is the transformation process. Figure 4 summarizes the process with adopted in our approach:

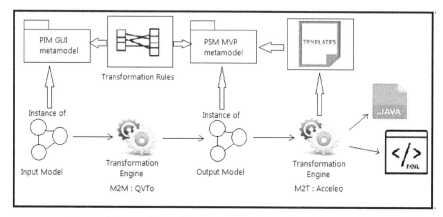

Figure 4. Transformation process in the proposed approach

Indeed, we defined the transformation rules that we developed into a transformation engine using the standard QVTo. This engine takes as input a model that is an instance of the PIM defined previously, and gives a MVC JavaFX model that could be easily used to generate the whole code of the application.

The main method is the entry point of the transformation and takes the input and output model references as arguments. It makes the correspondence between all elements under root element UmlPackage of the input model and the elements of target root element JavaFXPackage, figure 5.

```
modeltype GUI uses "http://guimm/1.0";
modeltype JAVAFX uses "http://javafxmm/1.0";

transformation umlToJavaFX(in src:GUI, out dest:JAVAFX);
main() {
        src.objectsOfType(UMLPackage)->map umlPackToMVCPack();
}
mapping UMLPackage::umlPackToMVCPack () : JavaFXPackage {
        result.Name := 'MVC ' + self.Name;
        result.VPackage := object ViewPackage {
                Name := self.Name + 'View';
                views += self.useCase->map useCaseToScene();
        };
        result.MPackage := object ModelPackage {
                Name := self.Name + 'Model';
                model += self.useCase.map useCaseToModel();
        };
        result.CPackage := object ControllerPackage {
                Name := self.Name + 'Controller';
                controller += self.useCase->map useCaseToController();
        };
}
mapping UseCase::useCaseToScene() : Scene {
        result.Name := self.Name + 'View';
        result.events+=self.operation.activity
        [not(Type=ActivityType::label)].map activityToEvents();
        ...
```

Figure 5. QVT portion of the transformation engine to JavaFX MVC

When the transformation rules defined and the engine is sufficiently working, the second step consists on generating the code from the obtained PSM model instance. The template of the target JavaFX for MVC is developed using the OMG standard Acceleo that automatically transform models obtained in the first transformation phase into Code for JavaFX. An excerpt of the template is presented in figure 6:

```
[template public createViewFiles(theRoot : Root)]

    <[theRoot.position.toString().toLowerCase()/]>
    <GridPane>
        [for (widget : Control | theRoot.hasWidgets)]
            <[if (widget.oclIsTypeOf(label))]Label text="[widget.oclAsType(label).Text/]"
            [elseif(widget.oclIsTypeOf(TextField))]TextField onAction = "#[widget.triggersEvent.Name.escapeSpecialChar()/]"
            [elseif(widget.oclIsTypeOf(PasswordField))]PassordField onAction = "#[widget.triggersEvent.Name.escapeSpecialChar()/]"
            [elseif(widget.oclIsTypeOf(Button))]Button text="[widget.oclAsType(Button).Text/]"
                            onAction = "#[widget.triggersEvent.Name.escapeSpecialChar()/]"
            [elseif(widget.oclIsTypeOf(Link))]HyperLink text="[widget.oclAsType(Link).Text/]"
                            onAction = "#[widget.triggersEvent.Name.escapeSpecialChar()/]"
            [elseif(widget.oclIsTypeOf(TextArea))]TextArea onAction = "#[widget.triggersEvent.Name.escapeSpecialChar()/]"
            [elseif(widget.oclIsTypeOf(List))]ListView
            [elseif(widget.oclIsTypeOf(ComboBox))]ComboBox
            [elseif(widget.oclIsTypeOf(CheckBox))]CheckBox
        [/for]
                [/if]

    </GridPane>
    </[theRoot.position.toString().toLowerCase()/]>
```

Figure 6. Acceleo templates for the transformation engine to JavaFX Code

The execution of these templates gives the source code of the application with Java and XML files for the views, the presenters and the models. Those generated files are loaded in an IDE as a JavaFX project respecting the MVC pattern. It gathers the three layers and specifically the graphical interface with all the components as desired with all the connections with the application's layers.

5.3 Results

We applied this approach to a running example of an online product search application. We defined the input model, respecting the proposed PIM meta model and sufficiently describing the view elements that should compose the generated view.

Figure 7. represents the result after applying the Model To Model transformation through the engine. The first element in the generated PSM model is the JavaFXPackage that includes the view Package, the model Package and the controller package standing for the MVC pattern. The controller package contains the controller for each scene to handle the user events. It is also connected to the model to call the appropriate method for the event raised.

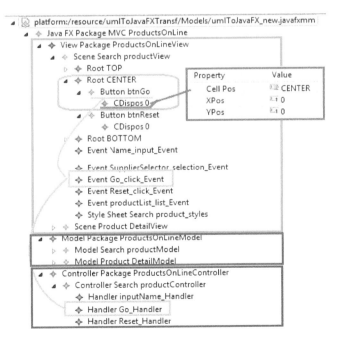

Figure 7. Generated model for MVC Rich Internet Application

The generated file has the entire description to generate the code application. Indeed, each component is typed and has its position in the scene. This file gathers all the information required to easily generate java code sources, FXML files for the views, packages and relationships between all of the layers of the MVC pattern.

After the design and generation of the application, the set of artifacts resulting from the whole process constitute a RIA ready to be deployed and can be easily loaded into an IDE. Figure 8 shows the screenshot of the generated view the application: the search product view with the form for the criteria of the research and a list that will give all the available products.

Figure 8. The research product view automatically generated

5. Conclusion

In this paper, we applied the MDE approach to generate a Rich Internet Application. The process involves first defining tow meta models as PIM and PSM respecting the MVC pattern for RIA. Second, we defined the transformation rules for both Model To Model and Model To Text transformation. A case study conducted on designing and generating a RIA for a search movie application has shown that the approach is valid and the supporting tools work properly. In the future, we aim at extending this work to allow the generation of other complex graphical components of RIAs and handling the layout management also. Furthermore, we can consider integrating other frameworks like Flex and GWT and combine the approach with existing ones.

References

Ahmed, Z., & Popov, V. (2010). Integration of Flexible Web Based GUI in I-SOAS. Retrieved from http://arxiv.org/abs/1011.3257

Berti, S., Correani, F., Mori, G., Paterno, F., & Santoro, C. (2004). Teresa: A transformation-based environment for designing and developing multidevice interfaces. *In CHI Extended Abstracts*, 793–794. http://dx.doi.org/10.1145/985921.985939

Gharavi, V., Mesbah, A., & Deursen, A. V. (2008). Modelling and Generating AJAX Applications: A Model-Driven Approach. *Proceeding of the7th International Workshop on Web- Oriented Software Technologies, New York, USA* (p. 38, Year of publication, ISBN: 978-80-227-2899-7).

Kapitsaki, G. M. et al. (2009). Model-driven development of composite context-aware web applications. *Information and Software Technology, 51*(8), 1244–1260. http://dx.doi.org/10.1016/j.infsof.2009.03.002

Linaje, M., Preciado, J. C., & Sanchez-Figueroa, F. (2007). A Method for Model Based Design of Rich Internet Application Interactive User Interfaces. *In Proceedings of International Conference on Web Engineering*, July 16-20, 2007, Como, Italy, 226–241. http://dx.doi.org/10.1007/978-3-540-73597-7_18

Martinez-Ruiz, F. J., Arteaga, J. M., Vanderdonckt, J., & Gonzalez-Calleros, J. M. (2006). A first draft of a model-driven method for designing graphical user interfaces of Rich Internet Applications. *In LA-Web 06: Proceedings of the 4th Latin American Web Congress*, p. 3238. IEEE Computer Societ.

http://dx.doi.org/10.1109/la-web.2006.1

Meliá, S. et al. (2008). A model-driven development for GWT-based rich internet applications with OOH4RIA. *Proceedings - 8th International Conference on Web Engineering, ICWE 2008,* 13–23. http://dx.doi.org/10.1109/ICWE.2008.36

Miller, J., & Mukerji, J. (2003). MDA Guide Version 1.0.1. OMG.

OMG, Q. (2008). Meta Object Facility (MOF) 2 . 0 Query / View / Transformation Specification. Transformation, (January), pp.1–230. Available at: http://www.omg.org/spec/QVT/1.0/PDF/.

Paterno, F., Santoro, C., & Spano, L. D. (2009). Maria: A universal, declarative, multiple abstraction-level language for service-oriented applications in ubiquitous environments. *ACM Trans. Comput.-Hum. Interact., 16*(4). http://dx.doi.org/10.1145/1614390.1614394

Sottet, J. S., Ganneau, V., Calvary, G., Coutaz, J., Demeure, A., Favre, J. M., & Demumieux, R. (2007). Model-driven Adaptation for Plastic User Interfaces. *Proceedings of the 11th IFIP TC 13 International Conference on Human-computer Interaction*, pp.397–410. http://dx.doi.org/10.1007/978-3-540-74796-3_38

Vanderdonckt, J. (2005). A MDA-compliant environment for developing user interfaces of information systems. *In CAiSE*, 16–31. http://dx.doi.org/10.1007/11431855_2

3

Implementing End-User Privacy through Human Computer Interaction for Improving Quality of Personalized Web

Hussain Mohammad Abu Dalbouh[1]

[1] Computer Science Department, Qassim University, Al-Qassim, Kingdom of Saudi Arabia

Correspondence: Hussain Mohammad Abu Dalbouh, Computer Sciences Department, Qassim University, Al-Qassim, Kingdom of Saudi Arabia. E-mail: hussainmdalbouh@yahoo.com

Abstract

Users are exposed to an overwhelming amount of information in several application domains. There is a remarkable increase in the usage of Internet and general technology improvements. From this, it follows that there is a demand and need to create personalized web systems. Thus, personalized web systems are a good method of handling the flood of information and information overload, by helping people to surf the net and look for what they need. Unfortunately, the privacy issues that end-users face have not been taken seriously by some of these personalized web systems, as some of them apply it partially or fail to address the privacy issues in personalization. This affects the quality of the existing personalized web. The paper aims to investigate and explain the reasons behind the end-user's fears in giving out his/her personal information on personalized websites. Then, based on the results modifying approach of personalized web through the use of Human Computer Interaction models to enhance the quality of the current personalized web. By addressing the main privacy issues in human computer interaction that helps the end-user trust the personalization web and website with his/her personal information and improve the quality of current personalized web. A survey study with 134 Internet users was conducted. The findings show that personalization plays different roles of attracting users in personalized websites. Internet users want useful personalized services, but at the same time, they are concerned with the manner in which firms use their data for personalization. If the involvement of Internet users with their current site is high, then personalized services are not attractive enough to motivate them to give their personal information.

Keywords: privacy, personalized, personal, human computer interaction, website, trust

1. Introduction

Users have access to information which loads in many application domains (e.g. the World Wide Web, electronic commerce, and digital television). Therefore, there is a necessity for creating personalized web systems based on the customer's interest and needs. According to Klusch (2001) large amounts of data and information are available on-demand, as advanced Internet solutions for the acquisition, mediation, and maintenance of information relevant to the end-user. Therefore, web personalization is a new interdisciplinary science for discovering knowledge and finding certain types of information, such as educational and even personal ones.

The Internet and the global open web allow many people worldwide to access multimedia data and knowledge. It is evident that these new technologies offer enormous opportunities to publish, find, organize and share large amounts of information. Web customization can play a key role in our information infrastructure which is constantly changing, as it has proved to be useful for individuals, organizations and businesses for intelligent information search and management. In fact, this whole process is focused on end-user support for the end-user to access, search, and find information. However, in practice, some of the web customization does not address the end-user privacy and some of it is limited to the privacy concerns of the end-user or does not address privacy. Thus, the personalization web should pay attention to both the end-user privacy and user preferences, and Internet users, whether professional or private.

Web personalization goals (1) to provide a resource, (2) to solve the impedance information to consumers and information providers, and (3) to provide information services and value-added products. According to Groot et al. (2005), custom web is supposed to address the difficulties associated with the user's information overload, preferably just in time and end-user support to find the information they need and in the way they prefer it.

The impacts of the increasing globalization of information overload have created a large amount of network resources, regardless of the end-user privacy, due to fears that the end user will not give his/her personal information at these sites. However, in practice, the personalization web is lacked concern in terms of end-user privacy. It on the web means that the site assures users that their personal information is not used and shared by anyone else using this site and keeps this data secured and protected. Indeed, as shown in some empirical studies (i) people who refuse to give information (personal) to a personalization web are estimated at 82%, (ii) those who never give personal information to a personalization web are estimated at 27%, and (iii) providing wrong or fake information to a personalization web, when they are asked to record the value, was 30%. Due to the weakness of most websites and personalization's web, existing operations with the end-user privacy and preferences should be customized. Iachello and Hong (2007) explain that privacy is becoming a critical element of the design of interactive systems in different areas, such as health services, office work, electronic commerce, and personal communications (International Labour Organization, 1993; U. S. Department of Health and Human Services, 2003; Cranor, 2003).

An important stream of Human Computer Interaction (HCI) research is Computer Supported Cooperative Work (CSCW). HCI began by examining largely single-user applications and systems. Starting in the late 1980s, CSCW began as a counter-effort to consider collaborative computer use. Although this subarea of HCI began in the consideration of cooperative or collaborative work, it quickly grew to include many different forms of coordination and social organization. It also grew to include many levels of analysis, from small groups to Internet-scale systems, and many types of activity, including work, entertainment, chat and other communication activities, and the like. Privacy is, in fact, the contrapositive of this research interest, it is what happens when many people can share data, some without their knowledge and as such has become a research interest in its own right within CSCW. Privacy can be a key aspect of the user experience with computers, online systems, and new technologies. Knowing what to consider about users and their views of computer systems can only improve privacy mechanisms.

2. Personalized Website System

2.1 Introduce the Problem

There is tremendous amount of information available on the Internet due to exponential growth of the World Wide Web. Users are now provided with more information than ever and it has become difficult for them to find the relevant or interesting information in the web page because of this information overload. The website customization leads to power and success because it affects how quickly end-user can find what they are looking for and find more relevant and interesting information easily. There is an important need to rely on the power of computers for information, data collection and web personalization to aid in classification and data management. This resulted in information flooding and created a new need: People need more help to get the right information; namely, the information that is relevant and attractive to them. A possible solution to address the described issue is by personalization, building information systems flexible to the user, assuring him that only information that is interesting to the user is retrieved and offered in a way appropriate to that user.

2.2 Problems

In recent years, this has led to the development of various personalization systems and increased their benefits, such as people surfing the Internet every day to look for a specific kind of information described (Kobsa, Koenemann, & Pohl, 2001).

In order to have a successful and effective personalized system, it is required that one should be familiar with the personal information and understand the user's need. However, people are more concerned about their privacy when they are asked to provide their personal information on the Internet, necessitating an increase in the trust from the end user in these personalization systems.

The impacts of the increasing globalization on the information overload have led to the creation of a lot of websites and personalization's web without considering the end-user privacy. This has caused fears in the end-user, resulting in not giving out his/her personal information in these websites. For example, "a meta-study of 30 surveys has shown that Internet users strongly dislike the collection and use of personal data" (Teltzrow & Kobsa, 2004). This example shows that a number of end-users do not like to share their personal information on the Internet. A major obstruction for user-adaptive e-commerce (Culnan & Milne, 2001) and a more wide-spread use of personalization (Leathern, 2002) corresponds with these privacy concerns. So far, the web privacy statements are currently being written in such a way that they do not want them to be read by the users. "Whereas 76% of respondents indicated that they find privacy policies very important" (Department for Trade and Industry, 2001), lately it has been discovered that users do not pay any attention to it. Kobsa, Koenemann and Pohl (2001) gave an example of a company that aimed at plugging the Web Search Engine gap, featured in a 60-minute segment (Excite@home) on Internet privacy. It showed that out of 20 million unique visitors, only 100 accessed the privacy pages of the company. Many site managers claimed that the users who read the privacy policies were less than 1%.

Unfortunately, the privacy issues that end-users face have not been taken seriously by some of these personalized web systems. (Wang & Kobsa, 2007) Personalized systems need to care about the privacy concerns of the user. According to Bettina and Teltzrow (2005) the existing systems are based on relatively complex syntactic methods, which skip a lot of information during the description of the references. All the existing personalization techniques select recommendations based on syntactic instruments, which lead to missing out on big amounts of information regarding the user's preferences. Wang and Kobsa (2007) indicate that the existing approaches have weaknesses, in terms of a flexible, efficient and scalable solution which respects privacy limits that may vary among users.

2.3 Purpose of the Study

End-users are very concerned about their privacy. They expect benefits in exchange for their personal data, such as free goods or services, or even non-monetary incentives, such as not having to watch ads. End-user also want companies to be transparent about what information they collect and how it will be used. Above all, end-user want to be in control of their personal information. That means having to "opt out" or turn off the flow of information from companies. To focus on this dilemma, some key factors should be considered for influencing the willingness of consumers to share personal data, including the general attitude of privacy in data collection of specific data types (Ackerman, Cranor, & Reagle, 1999; Spiekermann, Grossklags, & Berendt, 2001), reputation of the site (Earp & Baumer, 2003; Teo, Wan, & Li, 2004), the types of data collected (Ackerman, Cranor, & Reagle, 1999), intended use of the data, the recipient of the data (Cranor et al., 2002) along with the benefits, the presentation and design of personalization and privacy policy (Hui, 2004; Patrick & Kenny, 2003).

This collection of personal preferences enhances the crucial role of trust (Culnan & Armstrong, 1999; Jarvenpaa et al., 2000). Indeed, misuse of these data-mining technologies can have a major strategic impact on a company, damaging its reputation and limiting the amount of trust it can foster in relationships with customers (Bloom et al., 1994). The main problems that need to be investigated in this study: (i) people not giving out their personal information, (ii) personalized web not consideration the end-user privacy, (iii) the personalized web not consideration the user's preferences. This paper aims to explain the reasons behind the end-user's fears while giving out his/her personal information on personalization web and websites. Then, based on it modifying the approach of personalized web through the use of Human-Computer Interaction models to enhance the quality of the current personalized web. By addressing the main privacy issues in human-computer interaction that helps the end-user trust the personalization web and website with his/her personal information and improve the quality of current personalized web.

2.4 Motivations and Study Questions

There is much publicity about delivering personalized services over the web and the stakes are high for vendors selling related products. In spite of that, important questions that persist in the mind of end users are unanswered. For example, is web personalization an effective marketing strategy to attract users? What are the factors motivating users to a personalized website? How can addresses privacy concerns in human computer interaction to increase end users trust?

From understanding of the impact of web personalization is inconclusive. Thus, this study is to conduct a survey to address the above questions.

The paper is organized as follows: Section 3 provides the background and literature review. Section 4 presents the methodology and hypotheses development. Section 5 Personalized user privacy application design. Section 6 discusses the results of this study. A conclusion is presented in the last section.

3. Related Work

Customization has been associated with desktop applications. Many desktop applications have customizable menus and tool bars, with options that the user can pick from to customize their environment. In many ways, web customization achieves the same basic goals as traditional customization, making an interface better suit personal need. Yet the web's unique platform and culture bring about several differences from traditional customization. Some of the barriers to desktop customization are not as prevalent on the web; the types of changes that user make on the web are different, and the customization on the web is driven by a wider set of the motivations.

Web personalization means providing the users with their needs without asking them directly for it (Eirinaki & Vazirgiannis, 2003). Click-stream analysis, collaborative filtering, and data mining are examples of technologies that are lately applied in websites with the aim of trying to offer web personalization to users. This view has been supported in the works of Bamshad (2007) explained that the following techniques are applied to monitor the user on the website, such as, the links that have been clicked and the products that have been checked, to help the website identify the user's interests with the purpose of personalizing his/ her needs in the website.

One of the well-known techniques applied on websites known as the delivery of content, which is divided into customization and automatic personalization, the difference between them being who will be in control of the profile creation and the interface elements, was explicated by Bamshad, Robert and Jaideep (2000). Klaus, David and Andreas (1999) demonstrated the difference between Customization and Personalization. Customization is allowing the users to have full control to choose, design, and reorganize the page manually based on their preferences, and what they would like to see on the website, based on the given and built options on the website, such as MySpace (www.myspace.com). Automatic personalization is quite the opposite, because it observes the user's actions as well as the given information on the website profile to recognize his/ her needs. It then automatically creates a page, which can be easily updated from time to time to facilitate producing a page which meets the user's desire, for example, Amazon (http://www.amazon.com).

Lately, automatic personalization has become more applicable then customisation in most web browsing activities. "Web personalization can be described as any action that makes the Web experience of a user personalized to the user's taste", as stated by Bamshad, Robert and Jaideep (2000). Browsing the Internet for specific information or for example purchasing a book from Amazon.com could be the experience, where mapping the user preferences in his/ her profile depends on the methods used to create this profile or the type of chosen data. For the purpose of making predications, specific types of algorithmic approaches are used.

In a study of the WordPerfect word processor for Windows, Page et al. (1996) describe five types of customization found on the desktop. Most common was (1) setting general preferences; then (2) using or writing macros to enhance functionality of the application; (3) granting easier access to functionality, typically by customizing the toolbar with a shortcut; (4) "changing which interface tools were displayed," for example, showing or hiding the Ruler Bar; and (5) changing the visual appearance of the application. These categories are certainly relevant to web customization. In fact, the customizations encouraged by end user programming are most strongly associated with enhancing functionality and granting easier assess to existing functionality.

Wendy Mackay studied (1991) a community of customization around a shared software environment, MIT's Project Athena, and identified four classes of reasons that users customized. The top technological reason cited was that "something broke," so that the customization was actually a patch. The top individual factors cited were first that the user noticed they were doing something repetitively and second that something was "getting annoying." All of these reasons can be found in web customization as well.

3.1 Applying Human Computer Interaction to Privacy

To address the end user's privacy concerns, the study of Berendt and Teltzrow (2005) aimed at improving the web personalization proposals (the quality and performance), and gave more attention to the privacy problems of the user. Recently, many approaches have been available. (Abrams, 2003, Patrick & Kenny, 2003; Cranor, Arjula, & Guduru, 2002) applied some proposed and adoptable solutions in order to improve the privacy of the end-user in web personalization. Data type and User data are used to describe it logically. The policy can be measured and a user can be reviewed. The text of the privacy policy can sometimes be quite long (which could be too general or there may be too many technical words) and this could be a problem at times. Users are not willing to spend so much time in something they do not understand, and this is a fact that was proven by many studies, as shown in this report.

P3P Preference Exchange Language (APPEL) was recommended to overcome the abovementioned problem, the Worldwide Web Consortium (W3C, http://www.w3.org/) recommends (W3C, a P3P Preference Exchange Language 1.0 (APPEL1.0) (http://www.w3.org/TR/P3P-preferences/) and the Platform for Privacy Preferences (P3P) (W3C, The Platform for Privacy Preferences 1.0 (P3P1.0) rules P3P is a language based XML, which provides a platform for service providers (running sites of adaptation) to express their privacy policies. Appel is a similar language that allows users to express their privacy preferences.

Abrams (2003) prepossessed a non-technical approach to communication privacy. They are alternatives to the privacy statements of long and legalistic ones. Abrams (2003) suggested a layered approach which consists of a short-term brief to the standard term which highlight very important information, and which was easy to follow.

Patrick and Kenny (2003) dealt with communications privacy options on Data Protection in the European Directive. Since the start of the Directive, four guidelines were drawn by the authors for effective design, namely, HCI interface data protection, understanding, consent, awareness and control. Privacy of communication has suggested several browser-based approaches to the user. The AT & T Privacy Bird (http://www.privacybird.com; Cranor, Arjula, & Guduru, 2002) enables users to determine privacy first choice, compare privacy policy sites, P3P-encoded and was warned that this policy does not meet its standards. The latest versions of Internet browsers, such as Mozilla, enabled the users to determine specific limited P3P the privacy preferences and compare them to the visited sites. Nevertheless, these approaches suffer from the following limitations:

- They ask the users to make upfront privacy decisions, regardless of the situation in specific websites or individual pages.

- They do not improve any basic understanding of privacy settings for the users.

- They do not give any information about the benefits once the users provide them with the requested data.

Design teams have got a good help from Man-machine interaction to meet the challenges for protecting the personal information and the user's privacy. HCI can provide the power needed to help and understand many privacy concepts which the people need.

Westin (1967) describes four states of privacy: "solitude, privacy, anonymity and reserve". These standpoints can characterize differing privacy viewpoint. For instance, it was argued by some researchers that privacy is a fundamental right. On the other hand, Moor (1997) claims that "privacy is not a core value on par with life, security, and freedom", and is just an instrumental right to help people protect and secure their personal data.

It obvious that Human Computer Interaction is uniquely suited to help design teams manage the challenges brought by the need of protecting privacy and personal information as:

- HCI can help understand the many notions of privacy that people have.

- Concept of tradeoff is implicit in most discussions about privacy.

- Privacy interacts with other social concerns.

- Privacy interacts with other social concerns, such as control, authority, appropriateness, and appearance.

This study aims to help people to use the Internet and look for a specific kind of information, such as, educational information or even personal information. Besides this, it assures privacy to the end-users by applying it in a personalized web, with concern for the user preferences. It also aims to increase the trust by the end-user in personalized web through using of Human-Computer Interaction models, which reflects the performance and the quality of the personalized web.

4. Methodology and Hypotheses Development

Apart from the technology-related factors, prior Information System (IS) research also explores ethical issues related to personalization (Kramer et al., 2000; Stewart & Segars, 2002; Volokh, 2000). Users face a dilemma. Although they demand more personalized services, they are increasingly concerned about privacy infringements and how their information is being used by online firms. Users are concerned about how their purchase histories and navigation behaviours are analyzed and whether this information may be abused (Nash, 2000; Pitkow et al., 2002). Thus, we anticipate that users' concerns will affect for giving their personal information to a personalized website.

Trust, as previously discussed, refers to the consumer beliefs about certain characteristics of the supplier (The reputation of website operator, The design of a website, The presence of a privacy statement or policy, The presence of a privacy seal and Positive experience in the past) (Gefen et al., 2003). As described in the literature review, it shows that there is an effect of trust on increasing willingness of users to share personal information. Lin and Wang (2006) also proved that trust has a positive effect on increasing willingness of users to share personal information. Customers who cannot trust a personalized websites systems will not be willing to give out their personal information, even though they are satisfied with the product/services provided. In light of the above research the Hypotheses are proposed as below:

- Hypothesis 1: Privacy concerns discourage a user for giving personal information to a personalized website.

- Hypothesis 2: Website designs often rely upon the willingness of users to share personal information in order to function effectively.

- Hypothesis 3: Trust has a positive influence on users for giving personal information to a personalized website.

- Hypothesis 4: There is a significant influence of a websites design to increase willingness of users to share personal information.

- Hypothesis 5: There is a high impact and influence between factor "hours online per week" and willingness to share personal information.

These hypotheses were tested using a survey. Items used to measure the constructs were adopted from previous research. Privacy concern was operationalized as the control over the collection and usage of information.

4.1 Sampling

The sampling procedure that was adopted in this study for data collection was a random sampling method through questionnaire survey with a pre-planned sample size of 134 respondents. The total number of respondents in the study was 153. The number of valid responses was 134. The sample consisted of 71 males and 63 females and 84 were in the age group 18-29. The most of the respondents answered that their job title is student. The use of a student convenience sample was appropriate for a number of reasons. Firstly, as this study relates directly to end users, it is deemed appropriate that participants be users of the Internet. Furthermore, as "the likelihood that an adult is an Internet user decreases dramatically with age" (ABS, 2000) and as adults aged 18 to 24 hold the highest Internet usage rate (74%) consumers from within this age. students are regular users of the Internet for communication, research and the accessing of university online learning materials, this group represents a potential target. Secondly, in experimental research, the researcher is less concerned about projecting or predicting and is more concerned about testing for the existence of an effect (Kardes, 1996).

4.2 Data Analysis and Finding

4.2.1 Participants

The sample consisted of 71 males and 63 females and 84 were in the age group 18-29. Respondents consisted of 134 that were selected through a random sampling. The demographic profile of the respondents is 73 of respondents are in Malaysia, 26 of respondents are in France, 13 respondents are in USA, 9 respondents are in Philippine, 13 from other countries. Thus, the study shows mainly the views of people from Malaysia. The age of 84 of respondents are in the range from 18 to 29, in the range from 30 to 39 are 17 of respondents, less than 18 are 4 of respondents, 50 or older are 12 of respondents, in the range 40 to 49 are 15 of respondents and 2 respondents in other range.

4.2.2 Reasons for not Giving Personal Information

The main focus of the survey is to investigate that end-users would be willing to give out their personal information to personalized web systems.

Item "Would you give your personal information to a website if you know that the reason behind collecting it is to create personalized pages for you that meet your needs and interests" was formatted with simple yes (I would give my personal information to a website) vs. no (I would not give my personal information to a website) and the respondents who respond no (I would not give my personal information to a website) asked to specify the reasons why they not given their personal information to a website. Total numbers of 134 respondents were obtained from the distributed questionnaire, where it is distributed randomly. 43.0% of respondents answer "yes", 57.0% answer "no". The details are in Table 1.

Table 1. Willing to disclose personal information

Willing to disclose personal information	Frequency	Percentage
Yes	58	43%
No	76	57%
Total	134	100%

This analyses in this paper focus on the subset of respondents who are would not give their personal information to a website (i.e., the 57% would not give my personal information to a website).

76 respondents (57%) who respond "no" (I would not give my personal information to a website) are asked to specify the reasons why they not given their personal information to a website. 7 of respondents had not given any specification of the negative reasons. 27 of respondents responded that they do

not trust websites. They expressed their distrust with different words such as: *"Do not use such websites"*, *"I decide what meets my interests, not an algorithm"* and *"I want to control my own information"*. 42 of respondents who refuse to share personal information because of concerns about their privacy explanations are more specific such as: *"Privacy"*, *"Privacy concerns"*, *"To afraid of unsolicited emails"* and *"I would suspect that this would lead to attempts to sell me something"*. 34 of respondents, who refuse to share personal information because of concerns about their privacy, specify the reasons why they not given their personal information to a website responded that, they need more information about the website to make a decision whether to give out their personal information or not. They explanations such as: *"Not immediately, I would try to see if the website is trustworthy, for instance, do they have a trusted ssl certificate"*, *"It depends on how reliable it may appear to me this website"*, *"I need to know more details about the purpose"* and *"Depends"*. 5 of respondents are concerned about the security of their personal information, for example, if there is a hacker attack. Finally, 3 respondents is concerned about the *identity theft*. The details are in Table 2.

Table 2. Respondents who will not giving personal information

Respondents Comments	Frequency	Percentage
No (not given any specification of the negative reasons)	7	17%
No (do not trust websites)	27	33%
No (because of concerns about their privacy)"	42	50%
Total	76	100%

4.2.3 Time Spend on the Internet per Week

Item "How much time do you spend on the Internet per week" was formatted with simple (Less than 1 hour, 1-5 hours, 6-10 hours, 11-20 hours, 21-30 hours and more than 31 hours). Total numbers of 134 respondents were obtained from the distributed questionnaire, where it is distributed randomly. (56) 42.0% of respondent's answer more than 31 hours they spend time on the Internet per week and (31) 23% spend between the ranges 11-20 hours on the Internet per week. The details are in Table 3 and Figure 1.

Table 3. Time spend on the Internet per week

Time spend on the Internet per week	Frequency	Percentage
Less than 1 hour	8	6%
1-5 hours	16	12%
6-10 hours	14	10%
11-20 hours	31	23%
21-30 hours	9	7%
More than 31 hours	56	42%
Total	134	100%

Time spend on the Internet per week

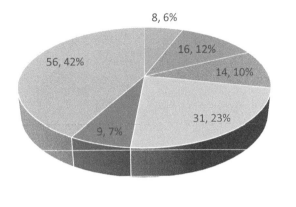

- Less than 1 hour   ▪ 1-5 hours   ▪ 6-10 hours
- 11-20 hours   ▪ 21-30 hours   ▪ More than 31 hours

Figure 1. Time spend on the Internet per week

The link between "Time spend online per week" and "Willing to give out personal information to personalized websites systems". Total numbers of 58 who willing to give out their personal information to personalized websites systems respondents were obtained from the distributed questionnaire, where it is distributed randomly. Less than 1 hour (2) 4.0% of respondent's willingness to share personal information, 1-5 hours (3) 5.0% willingness to share personal information, 6-10 hours (4) 7.0% willingness to share personal information, 11-20 hours (8) 14.0% willingness to share personal information, 21-30 hours (2) 3.0% willingness to share personal information. More than 31 hours (39) 67.0% willingness to share personal information, the details are in Table 4 and Figure 2.

Table 4. Willing to give out their personal information vs Time spend on the Internet per week

Willing to give out their personal information vs Time spend on the Internet per week	Frequency	Percentage
Less than 1 hour	2	4%
1-5 hours	3	5%
6-10 hours	4	7%
11-20 hours	8	14%
21-30 hours	2	3%
More than 31 hours	39	67%
Total	58	100%

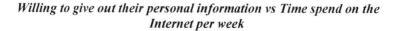

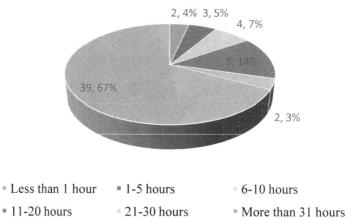

Figure 2. Link between time spend online per week and willing to give out personal information to personalized

4.2.4 The Willingness for Sharing Personal Information Depends on Website System Design

Total numbers of 134 respondents. (81) .60% of respondents answer "yes", (53) 40.0% answer "no". The details are in Table 5 and Figure 3.

Table 5. Willingness for sharing personal information depends on websites system design

Willingness for sharing personal information depends on websites system design	Frequency	Percentage
Yes	81	60%
No	53	40%
Total	134	100%

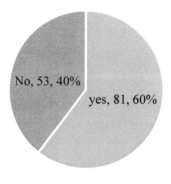

Figure 3. Willingness for sharing personal information depends on websites system design

4.2.5 Factors Increase Trust

Item "Select applicable factors that increase your trust in a website to provide personal information". The respondents had to choose and rank their five factors increasing trust from a selection list. In light of the past researches and we used regular reports from the factors that increase trust to decide which factors were included in the selection lists. Factors that increase users trust in a website to provide personal information it obvious that the factor that increase users trust in a website to provide personal information are: The reputation of website operator and The design of a website, while the factors which less increase users trust in websites are the presence of a privacy seal and positive experience in the past. The details are in Table 6.

Table 6. Factors that increase trust

Factor	Frequency (Yes)	Percentage
The reputation of website operator	116 from 134	87%
The design of a website	97 from 134	72%
The presence of a privacy statement or policy	53 from 134	40%
The presence of a privacy seal	46 from 134	34%
Positive experience in the past	45 from 134	34%

Privacy of end-user concerns is a main weakness in personalization web systems. The concerns regarding the user privacy is increasing day-by-day. In fact, personalized systems require to assure privacy to the end-user and to help the existing web personalization of protecting privacy and personal information. An alternative solution is to use Human-Computer Interaction to address privacy issues of the end-user to be better and more efficient in giving personal information and increase the trust from the end user in these personalization web systems.

5. Personalized User Privacy Application Design

End-users often do not have a correct understanding of where their personal data is stored and processed and to what entities their data is transferred. When designing and testing privacy-enhancing identity management systems, investigations are thus needed on how to evoke the correct mental models in users with regard to where, what data are transmitted and under whose control the data are stored and processed. Having a comprehensive mental model will be essential for them to estimate privacy risks correctly, to understand better how far personalized user privacy application design can protect their online privacy. The suggest approach will show to the end-user what is the required data should be entire, and by using the suggest approach can the end-user choice to add some other data or remove it from the list. It also, enable to the user where will save that data in the PC or in the server. From the respondents comments show there are a significant influence of the factor "hours online per week", the Personalized User Privacy Application Design should be designed further to include the user's needs and interests, where more information is obtained as the end-user has increase attraction by the Personalized websites. Thus, will increase hours online per week, in addition, the importance of trust in the online environment, describing some of the antecedents and consequences of trust, and provides guidelines for integrating trust into website design. The respondents comments discussed in the survey are presented under personalized user privacy application design.

As obvious from the survey results the willingness for sharing personal information depends on how users are asked for this information, as result as, the personalized user privacy application design considered that by using Add sign or Minus sign. Therefore the user will decide to share the information or not and share personal information depends on the user.

At personalized user privacy application design, we respect individuality and understand that everyone has different needs and tastes. We acknowledge that the standard look and feel of the browser, the user interface may not suit everyone, which is why we make it easy to personalize it. Based on the results discussed above, This study aims at reconciling the goals and methods of user modeling and personalization with privacy considerations, and to strive for best possible personalization within the boundaries set by privacy through including these results to design the new approach. In the following figures explain the personalized user privacy application design. Figure 6 shows all the fields that are required including the indicators and the details of indicators are mentioned in the legend, after legend box there are two main fields username and password, in front of them two indicators: Required not optional and sensitive data.

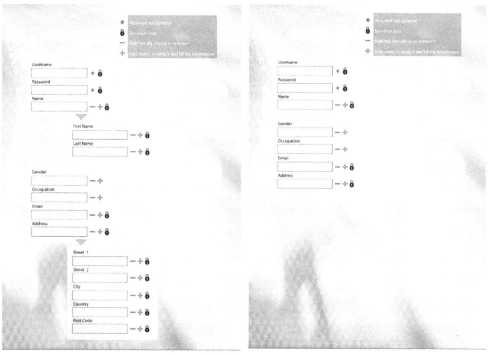

Figure 4. Main page   Figure 5. Active username and password fields

Figure 4 shows other fields as *Name*, *Gender*, *Occupation*, *Email* and *Address*. As noted the *Username* and *password* are active fields because it's required to fail it from the user. While the other fields it's optional, can the user choice to fill or remove it by using *Add* sign or *Minus* sign.

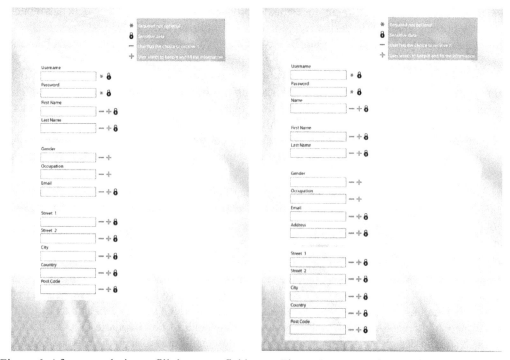

Figure 6. After user choice to fill the name field   Figure 7. User choice to fill Gender field

Figure 6 shows after pressing *Add* sign it will show two more elaborated fields asking for *First name and last name*. As noted the *First name* and *last name* are active fields after press the *Add* sign. Figure 8 shows that the user choice to fill the ***Gender.*** Figure 8 shows that the user choice to remove the ***occupation*** field.

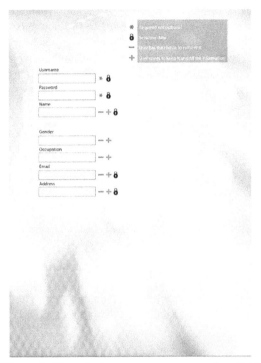

Figure 8. User choice to remove occupation field

6. Results and Discussions

HCI is a large research field in its own right. HCI's roots were in human factors and the design and evaluation of "man-machine" interfaces for airplanes and other complex and potentially dangerous mechanical systems. The first papers in what would later be known as HCI were in the 1970s and concerned the design of user interfaces in time-sharing systems. The field took off with the advent of personal computers and the single-user interface in the early 1980s. HCI's roots then were in cognitive-oriented, single-user interfaces. The so-called user interface.

HCI has since expanded to consider a variety of subareas design methodologies, usability and usability testing, intelligent interfaces, adaptive interfaces, and so on. Of particular interest here will be Computer-Supported Cooperative Work (CSCW), sometimes known as groupware. CSCW is interested in how groups of people work or interact together using computational technologies. Indeed, HCI has grown in general to consider organizational, institutional, and even societal factors affect how computer systems are put together and how users interact with systems. This has become increasingly important as systems are no longer single-user, but are also Internet-wide in their use.

Problems of trust websites and privacy concerns of web personalization are on-going. As personalized web systems it partially apply or fail to address the privacy issues in personalization. Despite of the personalized web system is incapable of providing highly relevant and meet users need and interest. In fact, a personalized websites systems should identify the exact needs of a user. The relevance of end users expectations of, and demand for, increase willingness of users to share personal information, there is a gap between system performance from the aspect of privacy issue and the online user's expectations and wants. Personalized privacy concern increases even if the personalized websites systems invests a lot in privacy.

The current research has two purposes. First, it is a first step to examining and investigating why users not willing to give out their personal information. To achieve that, this study looks at some elements for reasons for not giving personal information, Time spend on the Internet per week, websites system design and factors increase trust. Then, link between "Time spend online per week" and "Willing to give out personal information to personalized websites systems.

On the other hand, modifying the approach of personalized web through the use of Human-Computer Interaction models to enhance the quality of the current personalized web. By addressing the main privacy issues in human-computer interaction that helps the end-user trust the personalization web and website with his/her personal information and improve the quality of current personalized web.

In the improving quality of personalized web survey, discussed about "what are the main privacy issues that keep users from giving out their personal information on websites to provide personalization". The total numbers of the responders are 134. A pilot of this survey was undertaken to discover any possible problem in current personalization web, obstacles that making the End-Users not willing to give out their personal information and the factors effect on it. From the results of this survey for the main variables in revealed that:

- More than half of our study participants were not willing to disclose information regarding the privacy concerns.

- People who spend more time on Internet per week are more willing to give their personal information.

- Users responses are strongly dependent on how users were asked for personal information.

- It is much more likely to get a positive answer to indirect open question about sharing personal information, such as "how much time" or "how much information" rather than to a direct closed question.

- The most important things for a website is positive user reviews/comments. Next in importance is the design of a website, presence of privacy policy and/or privacy seal. The design is last in importance.

The results of this survey highlight ways in which instructional material should be clarified. The design of the websites it is important to increase willingness of users to share personal information, providing them with interesting content, therefore, they can spend more time on the site. The way of asking for this personal information such as simple and clear, and asking user's indirect open questions about sharing personal information.

7. Conclusion

Personalized systems need to take users privacy concerns into account. The most important issue that should be encountered in personalized web systems is privacy violation and privacy concern. Many users are reluctant to give away personal information. Privacy can be a key aspect of the user experience with computers, online systems, and new technologies. Knowing what to consider about users and their views of computer systems can only improve privacy mechanisms. Human-Computer Interaction (HCI) is the subfield of Computer Science that studies how people interact with and through computational technologies. In this paper has investigated the reasons for not giving personal information to personalized web systems. The elements effecting the end-users would be willing to give out their personal information to personalized web systems and examined how these elements influence users for giving personal information to personalized web systems. It also, investigating the concerns have a direct impact on quality of personalization that requires to collect personal data (such as the user's descriptions, preferences), and thereby makes accurate personalization based on user preferences. In order to accomplish the study objectives and improving quality of personalized web by implementing privacy through Human Computer Interaction. It helps the end-user trust the personalization web and website with his/her personal information and improve the quality of current personalized web. In general, human-computer interaction lead to a high level of competence and integrity trust. This study represents a first step toward understanding how design system using HCI affect users' trust in and their attitudes towards personalized content, and ultimately their behavioral intention to o give out their personal information.

Acknowledgments

The author wish to thank Qassim University, Kingdom of Saudi Arabia. This work was supported in part by a grant from Deanship of Scientific Research, Qassim University.

References

Abrams, M. (2003). *Making Notices Work for Real People*. 25th International Conference of Data Protection & Privacy Commissioners, Sydney, Australia.

Ackerman, M. S., Cranor, L., & Reagle, J. (1999). *Privacy in E-Commerce: Examining User Scenarios and Privacy Preferences*. In: Proceedings of the 1st ACM E-Commerce, Denver, Co, 1-8.

Australian Bureau of Statistics. (2000). *Australians just love surfing–ABS*. Retrieved October 18, 2002, from http://www.abs.gov.au/Ausstats/abs@.nsf/Lookup/NT00013716

Bamshad, M., Cooley, R., & Jaideep, S (2000). Automatic Personalization Based on Web Usage Mining. *OMMUNICATIONSOF THE ACM, 43*(8).

Berendt, B., & Teltzrow, M. (2005). *Addressing Users' Privacy Concerns for Improving Personalisation Quality: Towards an Integration of User Studies and Algorithm Evaluation.* http://dx.doi.org/10.1007/11577935_4

Bettina, B., & Teltzrow, M. (2005). *Addressing Users' Privacy Concerns for Improving Personalisation Quality: Towards an Integration Of User Studies and Algorithm Evaluation.* Intelligent Techniques in Web Personalisation. LNAI. Springer-Verlag. http://dx.doi.org/10.1007/11577935_4

Bloom, P. N., Milne G. R., & Adler, R. (1994). Avoiding misuse of new information technologies: legal and societal considerations. *Journal of Marketing, 58*(1), 98-110.

Cranor, L. (2003). *I didn't buy it for myself ': Privacy and ecommerce personalisation.* In Proceedings of Workshop on Privacy in the Electronic Society, Washington, DC, USA: ACM Press.

Cranor, L. F., Arjula, M., & Guduru, P. (2002). *Use of a P3P User Agent by Early Adopters.* In: ACM Workshop on Privacy in the Electronic Society, Washington, DC, USA, 1-10.

Culnan, M. J., & Armstrong, P. K. (1999). Information privacy concerns, procedural fairness and impersonal trust: an empirical investigation. *Organization Science, 10*(1), 104-116.

Culnan, M. J., & Milne, G. R. (2001). The Culnan-Milne Survey on Consumers & Online Privacy.

Department for Trade and Industry. (2001). *Informing Consumers about E-Commerce.* Retrieved from http://www.mori.com/polls/2001/pdf/dti-e-commerce.pdf

Earp, J. B., & Baumer, D. C. (2003). Innovative Web Use to Learn About Consumer Behaviour and Online Privacy. *Communications of the ACM, 46*(4), 81-83.

Eirinaki, M., & Vazirgiannis, M. (2003). Web Mining for Web Personalisation. *ACM Transactions on Internet Technology, 3*(1), 1–27. http://dx.doi.org/10.1145/643477.643478

Gefen, D. (2000). E-Commerce: The Role of Familiarity and Trust. *Omega, 28*(6), 725-737. http://dx.doi.org/10.1016/S0305-0483(00)00021-9

Groot, D. R. A., Boonk, M. L., Brazier, F. M. T., & Oskamp, A. (2005). An earlier version of this paper has been published in the proceedings of the 4th International Workshop on the Law and Electronic Agents 2005 (LEA '05), available on lea-online.net.

Hui, K. L. (2004). *Privacy, Information Presentation, and Question Sequence.* Retrieved from http://www.comp.nus.edu.sg/~lung/sequence.pdf

Iachello, G., & Hong, J. (2007). *End-User Privacy in Human-Computer Interaction.* http://dx.doi.org/10.1561/1100000004

International Labour Organization. (1993). Workers Privacy Part II: Monitoring and Surveillance in the Workplace Conditions of Work. *Special Series on Workers Privacy, Digest, 12*(1).

Jarvenpaa, S. L., Tractinsky, N., & Vitale, M. (2000). Consumer trust in an Internet store. *Information Technology and Management, 1*(1), 45-71. http://dx.doi.org/10.1023/A:1019104520776

Kardes, F. R. (1996). In Defence of Consumer Experimental Psychology. *Journal of Consumer Psychology, 5*(3), 279-296. http://dx.doi.org/10.1207/s15327663jcp0503_04

Klusch, M. (2001). Information agent technology for the Internet: A survey. *Data knowl. Eng., 36*(3), 337-372. http://dx.doi.org/10.1016/S0169-023X(00)00049-5

Kobsa, A., Koenemann, J., & Pohl, W. (2001). Personalised Hypermedia Presentation Techniques for Improving Customer Relationships. *The Knowledge Engineering Review, 16*(2), 111-155. http://dx.doi.org/10.1017/S0269888901000108

Kramer, J., Noronha, S., & Vergo, J. (2000). A user-centered design approach to personalization. *Communications of the ACM, 3*(8), 44-48.

Leathern, R. (2002). Online Privacy. Payments and Transactions. Jupiter Research, New York. Notices: Summary of Responses. In: Interagency Public Workshop: Get Noticed: Effective.

Lin, H., & Wang, Y. (2006). An Examination of the Determinants of Customer Loyalty in Mobile Commerce Contexts. *Information & Management, 43*(3), 271-282. http://dx.doi.org/10.1016/j.im.2005.08.001

Mackay, W. (1991). *Triggers and barriers to customizing software.* CHI '91. http://dx.doi.org/10.1145/108844.108867

Moor, J. H. (1997). Towards a Theory of Privacy in the Information Age. *Computers and Society, 2*(3), 27–32.

Nash, K. S. (2000). Personalization: clash of the killer Ps. *Computerworld, 34*(2), 66-67.

Page, S. R., Johnsgard, T. J., Albert, U., & Allen, C. D. (1996). *User customization of a word processor*. CHI '96.

Patrick, A. S., & Kenny, S. (2003). From Privacy Legislation to Interface Design: Implementing Information Privacy in Human-Computer Interfaces. In D. R. Heidelberg (Ed.), *Third International Workshop* (pp. 26-28). Germany: Springer Verlag.

Pitkow, J., Schütze, H., Cass, T., Cooley, R., Turnbull, D., Edmonds, A., ... Breuel, T. (2002). Personalized search. *Communications of the ACM, 45*(9), 50-55.

Spiekermann, S., Grossklags, J., & Berendt, B. (2001). *E-Privacy in 2nd Generation E-Commerce: Privacy Preferences versus Actual Behaviour*. In: EC'01: Third ACM Conference on Electronic Commerce, Tampa, FL, 38-47.

Stewart, K. A., & Segars, A. H. (2002). An empirical examination of the concern for information privacy instrument. *Information Systems Research, 13*(1), 36-49.

Teltzrow, M., & Kobsa, A. (2004). Impacts of User Privacy Preferences on Personalised Systems: A Comparative Study. In C. M. Karat, J. Blom, J. Karat (Eds.), *Designing Personalised User Experiences for Ecommerce* (pp. 315-332). Kluwer, Dordrecht, Netherlands. http://dx.doi.org/10.1007/1-4020-2148-8_17

Teo, H. H., Wan, W., & Li, L. (2004). *Volunteering Personal Information on the Internet: Effects of Reputation, Privacy Initiatives, and Reward on Online Consumer Behaviour*. In: 37th Hawaii International Conference on System Sciences, Big Island, Hawaii, USA.

US Department of Health and Human Services. (2003). Health Insurance Reform: Security Standards; Final Rule.

Volokh, E. (2000). Personalization and privacy. *Communications of the ACM, 43*(8), 84-85.

Wang, Y., & Kobsa, A. (2007). *Respecting Users' Individual Privacy Constraints in Web Personalisation*. In proceedings of the UM07, 11th International Conference on User Modelling. http://dx.doi.org/10.1007/978-3-540-73078-1_19

Westin, A. (1967). The origin of modern claims to privacy. In A. Westin (Ed.), *Privacy and freedom*. Association of the Bar of the City of New York. London: Bodley Head.

4

An Integrated Expert User with End User in Technology Acceptance Model for Actual Evaluation

Hussain Mohammad Abu-Dalbouh[1]

[1] Computer Science Department, Qassim University, Al-Qassim, Kingdom of Saudi Arabia

Correspondence: Hussain Mohammad Abu-Dalbouh, Computer Sciences Department, Qassim University, Al-Qassim, Kingdom of Saudi Arabia. E-mail: hussainmdalbouh@yahoo.com

Abstract

Effective evaluation is necessary in order to ensure systems adequately meet the requirements and information processing needs of the users and scope of the system. Technology acceptance model is one of the most popular and effective models for evaluation. A number of studies have proposed evaluation frameworks to aid in evaluation work. The end users for evaluation the acceptance of new technology or system have a lack of knowledge to examine and evaluate some features in the new technology/system. This will give a fake evaluation results of the new technology acceptance. This paper proposes a novel evaluation model to evaluate user acceptance of software and system technology by modifying the dimensions of the Technology Acceptance Model (TAM) and added additional success dimension for expert users. The proposed model has been validated by an empirical study based on a questionnaire. The results indicated that the expert users have a strong significant influence to help in evaluation and pay attention to some features that end users have lack of knowledge to evaluate it.

Keywords: acceptance, evaluation, expert user, end user, technology, model

1. Introduction

The expert user evaluation is usually a list of perceived problems or reservation regarding the usability of a technology, software, system and a list of recommendations for improvement. Involving a number of experts can assist in identifying whether potential problems are likely to exist, as individual expert opinion is not infallible.

(Davis, 1986; Davis 1989; Davis 1993; Davis, Bagozzi & Warshaw, 1989) introduced TAM, which is presented in Figure 1, for modeling user acceptance of information systems in 1986. TAM starts by proposing external variables as the basis for tracing the impact of external factors on two main internal beliefs, which are perceived usefulness and perceived ease of use, while perceived ease of use also affects perceived usefulness over and above external variables (Taylor & Todd, 1995). These two beliefs both influence users attitude toward using IS. Attitude toward using sequentially has influence on behavior intention to use, which is the key factor for determining actual conditions of system use, while belief of perceived usefulness also affects behavioral intention to use over attitude toward using (Taylor & Todd, 1995).

End users knowledge about evaluation factors is a very important element in continuous quality improvement of the new technology and system. Additionally, because of the increase in technology improvement and introduce new technology, the evaluation aspects and factors have changed over the time. For the reason that the Lack of knowledge to examine and evaluate some features in the system by the end users led to a fake evaluation about the acceptance of the new system or new technology that have introduced. Therefore the end users in many industries such as business, education, banking and health care face problems and difficulties to determine the strength and weaknesses of the new technology. This will affect to plan for improvement and modification that new technology have been introduced effectively and efficiency.

Expert user opinions and comments are a major source of ideas that influence to evaluate the content of the new technology and software. The rational legislator or decision-maker relies on evidence, and so is bound to be influenced by the views of the experts who present it. The expert can play a role in acceptance of new technology change, for instance by appearing as a feature in a system, software, or by being asked to investigate something that the end users cannot recognize it. This study proposes an expert users evaluation side by side with end user evaluation for actual evaluation by modifying original Technology Acceptance Model.

2. Literature Review

Our literature review indicates that TAM would be valuable and useful for explaining or predicting user acceptance of new technology or system, particularly among students and executives in a university or business organization context and health care works as we can call all of them end users. However, the validity of the model has rarely been tested with expert user side by side with end user evaluation.

This study reveal that the almost professionals in their own professional contexts such as banking and finance employees, healthcare professional including physicians and nurses, attorneys or education staff in most, if not all, they have lack of knowledge to examine and evaluate some features in the system or technology (Hartwick & Barki, 1994). Due to some features just expert in information technology and software can evaluate it.

TAM starts by proposing external variables as the basis for tracing the impact of external factors on two main internal beliefs, which are perceived usefulness and perceived ease of use, while perceived ease of use also affects perceived usefulness over and above external variables. These two beliefs both influence users attitude toward using IS. Attitude toward using IS, sequentially has influence on behavior intention to use, which is the key factor for determining actual conditions of system use as shown in Figure 1.

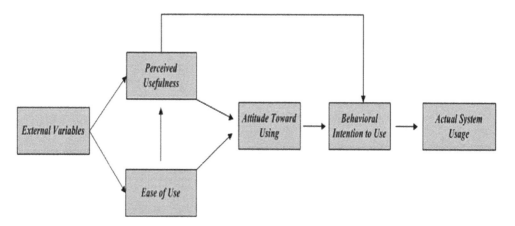

Figure 1. Original Technology Acceptance Model (TAM)

This study examined end users in a professional setting, (Physicians and Nurses, Banking workers and Education workers) for investigating the factors affecting them to evaluate acceptance of new technology that proposed to help them in their works. Choice of TAM over other IT acceptance/adoption models was made for the following reasons. First, TAM is general, parsimonious, IT-specific, and designed to provide an adequate explanation for and a prediction of a diverse user population's acceptance of a wide array of IT within various organizational contexts. Second, TAM has a well-researched and validated inventory of psychometric measurements, making its use operationally appealing. Finally, TAM is a dominant model for investigating user technology acceptance and has accumulated fairly satisfactory empirical support for its overall explanatory power, and has posited individual causal links across a considerable variety of technologies, users, and organizational contexts (Abu-Dalbouh, 2013; Chau, 1996a; Chau, 1996b; Davis, Bagozzi, & Warshaw, 1989; Mathieson, 1991; Vitalari, Venkalesh, & Cronhaug, 1985).

3. Expert Evaluation

Expert evaluation, also called heuristic evaluation, is a review of new technology or system by two or more usability specialists (Nielsen & Molich, 1990; Nielsen, 1994). Working independently, these experts use published research data, industry-accepted usability principles (heuristics) and best practices, and years of experience observing users in lab and field settings to evaluate the new technology or system and identify the strength, weaknesses and problems in that new technology or system. Expert user evaluators also can be walking through the new technology or system based on task scenarios, to assess work flow issues that the end user missed to observe and recognize it. Typical findings by expert evaluators include:

- *What features of the new technology or system are likely to cause problems and should be improved.*

- *What features are likely to be successful and should be retained.*

- ***What features should pay attention to it based on the importance of these features that the end users have some knowledge about it such as security, availability and maintainability.***

Therefore, expert users give the actual evaluation about the new technology or system more than the end users. The findings are assigned severity ratings and accompanied by actionable recommendations for improving the user experience of the new technology or system. According to the results we claimed that expert users identify a majority of the weakness and problems in the new technology and system, that behind the end users ability to discover it.

Expert users evaluators, regardless of their skill and experience, can only emulate users and not necessarily typical users of the new technology or system. Feedback from target users can add an important dimension to some expert evaluations for example, of alternative navigation approaches for an existing technology, or of a technology recently targeted to a new user audience. In these cases, list the priority of the features that the new technology or system should include based in the end users preferences. The experts may suggest solutions while end users probably do not.

In general, heuristic evaluation is difficult for a single individual to do because one person will never be able to evaluate all features in the new technology or system. Luckily, experience from many different projects has shown that different people find different usability problems. Therefore, it is possible to improve the effectiveness of the method significantly by involving multiple evaluators. As per Jakob Nielsen's study recommends, 3 to 5 expert user's evaluators.

4. Proposed Model

In this paper we seek for the possibility of creating a new model for evaluating new technology and system acceptance by involving expert user in evaluating process by applying the concepts of Technology Acceptance Model for End user to Expert users in order to get actual evaluation.

The TAM model is modified for this study to demonstrate how the proposed model can be beneficial for decision makers in organizations on evaluating the implementation of information systems and determining the strength and weaknesses of the new system/technology and plan for improvement and modification effectively and efficiency. By paying attention to expert user's opinions, comments and evaluate because it is a major source of ideas that influence to evaluate the content of the new technology and software.

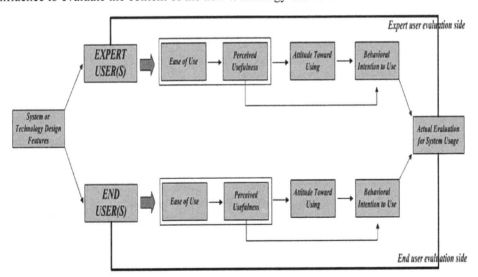

Figure 2. Proposed integrated expert user with end user in TAM model

5. Research Methodology

Regarding to the proposed model, preliminary refining of criteria has been done by the use of available literature reviews (Sureshchandar, Rajendran & Anantharaman, 2002; Yang, Jun & Peterson, 2004). The proposed model has been validated by an empirical study based on a questionnaire. Structured questionnaire was used for data collection to examine the three hypotheses in this study. The questionnaire was designed based on the proposed included expert users with end users for evaluation acceptance of new technology or system. The questionnaire consists of three dimensions.

The first dimension to examine the *Hypotheses 1: (The end users do not know some features meaning in the new technology or system, or End-user has lack of knowledge of some features meaning in the new technology or system)*.

The second dimension to examine the *Hypotheses 2: (The end users do not know how to evaluate some features in the new technology or system or End-user has lack of knowledge of how to evaluate some features in the new technology or system)*.

The third dimension to examine the *Hypotheses 3: (There is a high impact and influence to include expert users in evaluation acceptance of new technology or system in order to get actual evaluation)*.

Several professors and IS professionals were interviewed to modify the items and the construction of the questionnaire. Completed responses to the questionnaire were received from 13 organizations, in both the public and private sectors. Then, a sample of 327 participants belonging to educational, healthcare and banking end users sectors selected randomly based on the important of these three sectors.

Questionnaire distribution and returns were by Email. The participants were asked to indicate the extent of their agreement with each element on a five-point Likert-type scale with anchors from "Very bad information, bad information, neutral information, good information, very good information" for the first two dimensions and from "Strongly agree" to "Strongly disagree" for the third dimension.

A total of 186 questionnaires were returned from respondents. Table 1 shows the distribution of the received sample according to gender (Men 58% and Women 42%. Majority of the respondents are from the 35-44 years age group (39%) and Health care sector (44%).

Table 1. Sample distribution

Variable		Frequency	Percentage
Gender	Female	78	42%
	Male	108	58%
Age	< 25	13	7%
	25-34	32	17%
	35-44	73	39%
	>45	68	37%
End-user Sector	Health care	82	44%
	Education	45	24%
	Banking	59	32%

4. Result and Discussion

One of the most important aspects in evaluating a theory is developing good criteria in order to achieve reliable and valid estimate from the mentioned structure. The demand to get actual evaluation in new technology or system has grown. It follows by the need to propose model that aims to include expert user in evaluation process. The proposed model has been validated by an empirical study based on a questionnaire. The end user proved that the need of including expert in evaluation. The results of the questionnaire demonstrate that end users in the sample have a lack of knowledge in some features meaning in the new technology or system because the majority of the answers for some of these features dimension charted less than the midpoints of their respective scales. It also, demonstrate that end users in the sample have a lack of knowledge to evaluate some features in the new technology or system because the majority of the answers for some of these features dimension charted less than the midpoints of their respective scales. As shown in table 2 and 3.

Table 2. Respondents Agreements for meaning of some features

Meaning of	Respondents Agreements Very good + Good information %
Availability	62.3%
Responsiveness	54.2%
Reliability vs. Cost of execution	38.4%
Flexibility	71.3%
Portability	67.4%

Security	63.6%
Maintainability	43.7%

Table 3. Respondents Agreements for evaluating of some features

Evaluating of	Respondents Agreements Very good + Good information %
Availability	56.3%
Responsiveness	48.3%
Reliability vs. cost of execution	36.4%
Flexibility	69.3%
Portability	66.8%
Security	58.3%
Maintainability	41.8%

The descriptive statistics for the third dimension questions revealed that end user trust in expert user evaluation results and they think expert user can be determining the strength and weaknesses of the new system or technology better than end users. Therefore the expert user evaluation has a strong significant influence in order to get actual evaluation. Table 4 shows the respondents agreements about expert user evaluation and Figure 3 shows the respondents agreements for all questions.

Table 4. Respondents Agreements about expert user evaluation

Influence to include expert users in evaluation	Respondents Agreements Strongly agree + Agree %
Do you trust in expert user evaluation results about new technology or system?	92.6%
Do you believe that expert user will see behind the end user can see in new technology evaluation?	89.7%
Do you think include expert user in evaluation will give actual evaluation for the new technology?	93.4%
Do you think expert user can be determining the strength and weaknesses of the new system or Technology better than end users?	87.9%

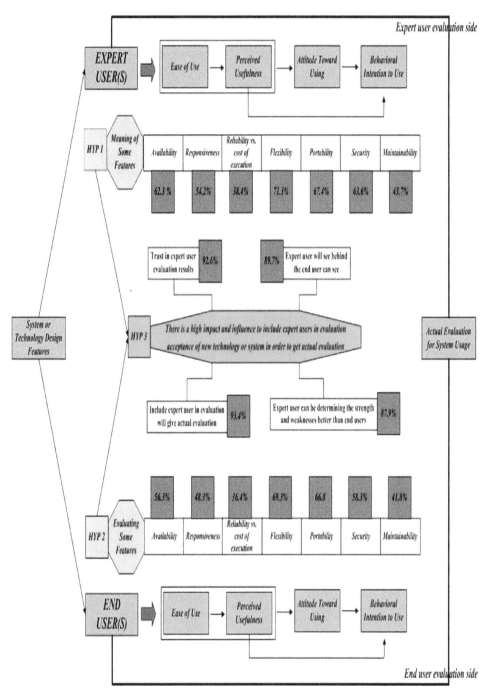

Figure 3. Respondents agreements

4. Conclusion

This paper proposed a new model for evaluating new technology and system acceptance by involving expert user in evaluating process by applying the concepts of Technology Acceptance Model for end users to expert users in order to get actual evaluation. Based on empirical findings, this study reached several conclusions. Results of the empirical analysis indicated that end users cannot evaluate all the features that included in the new technology or system and this led to give a fake evaluation results. There are high impacts and influence to include expert users in evaluation acceptance of new technology or system in order to get actual evaluation and the expert users give the actual evaluation about the new technology or system more than the end users. It also reveal the expert users identify a majority of the weakness and problems in the new technology or system, that behind the end users ability to discover it.

Acknowledgments

The author wish to thank Qassim University, Kingdom of Saudi Arabia. This work was supported in part by a grant from Deanship of Scientific Research, Qassim University.

References

Abu-Dalbouh, H. M. (2013). A questionnaire approach based on the technology acceptance model for mobile tracking on patient progress applications. *J. Comput. Sci., 9*(6), 763-770. http://dx.doi.org/10.3844/jcssp.2013.763.770

Chau, P. Y. K. (1996, September). An empirical investigation on factors affecting the acceptance of CASE by system developers. *Information and Management, 30*(6), 269-280.

Chau, P. Y. K. (Fall 1996). An empirical assessment of a modified technology acceptance model. *Journal of Management Information Systems, 13*(2), 185-204. Retrieved from http://hdl.handle.net/10722/177851

Davis, F. D. (1986). A Technology Acceptance Model for Empirically Testing New End-User Information Systems: *Theory and Results. Doctoral dissertation, Sloan School of Management., Massachusetts Institute of Technology.* Retrieved from http://hdl.handle.net/1721.1/15192

Davis, F. D. (1989). Perceived Usefulness, Perceived Ease of Use, and User Acceptance of Information Technology. *MIS Quarterly, 13*(3), 319-339. Retrieved from http://www.jstor.org/stable/249008

Davis, F. D. (1993). User Acceptance of Information Technology: System Characteristics, User Perceptions and Behavioral Impacts. *International Journal of Man Machine Studies, 38*(3), 475-487. http://dx.doi.org/10.1006/imms.1993.1022

Davis, F. D., Bagozzi, R. P., & Warshaw, P. R. (1989, August). User Acceptance of Computer Technology: A Comparison of Two Theoretical Models. *Management Science, 35*(8), 982-1003). http://dx.doi.org/10.1287/mnsc.35.8.982

Hartwick, J., & Barki, H. (1994, December). Hypothesis testing and hypothesis generating research: an example from the user participation literature. *Information Systems Research, 5*(4), 446-449). http://dx.doi.org/10.1287/isre.5.4.446

Mathieson, K. (1991, September). Predicting user intention: comparing the technology acceptance model with theory of planned behavior. *Information Systems Research, 2*(3), 173-191. http://dx.doi.org/10.1287/isre.2.3.173

Nielsen, J. (1994). Heuristic evaluation. In Nielsen, J., & Mack, R.L. (Eds.), Usability Inspection Methods. *John Wiley & Sons*, New York, NY.

Nielsen, J., & Molich, R. (1990). Heuristic evaluation of user interfaces, *Proc. ACM CHI'90 Conf.* (Seattle, WA, 1-5 April), (pp.249-256).

Sureshchandar, G. S., Rajendran, C., & Anantharaman. R. N. (2002). Determinants of customer-perceived service quality: A confirmatory factor analysis approach. *Journal of Service Mark, 16*, 9-34.

Taylor, S., & Todd, P. (1995). Understanding Information Technology Usage: A Test of Competing Models. *Information Systems Research, 6*(2), 144-176.

Vitalari, N. P., Venkalesh, A., & Cronhaug, K. (1985, May). Computing in the home: shifts in the time allocation patterns of households. *Communications of the ACM, 28*(5), 512-522.

Yang, Z., Jun, M., & Peterson, R. T. (2004). Measuring Customer Perceived Online Service Quality: Scale Development and Managerial Implication. *International Journal of Operational Production Management, 24*, 1149-69.

5

Empirical Study on How to Set Prices for Cruise Cabins Based on Improved Quantum Particle Swarm Optimization

Xi Xie[1], Wei-zhong Jiang[1], He Nie[2] & Jun-hao Chi[1]

[1] Electrical and Information School, Jinan University, Zhuhai 519070, China

[2] College of Economics, Jinan University, Guangzhou 510632, China

Correspondence: Xiao-xiang Liu, College of Electrical Engineering and Information, Jinan University, Zhuhai, China. E-mail: tlxx@jnu.edu.cn

Abstract

This essay puts forward a cruise pricing model based on improved quantum particle swarm optimization, aiming at optimizing the pricing strategy and realizing the maximum sales income expected. Firstly, we combine the two factors – actual booking records and expected booking records in the process of cruises pricing – and improve the dynamic price-setting model based on demand learning put forward earlier. Then we improve the Dynamically Changing Weight's Quantum-behaved Particle Swarm Optimization (DCWQPSO) based on multistage punish function, in order to faster the converging speed and avoid the problem of local optimum. Lastly, we use the improved DCWQPSO to find the best expected sales income in the improved pricing model. The instance analysis of cruise pricing shows that the process of constructing this model is reliable and logical. Also this model could better higher the maximum expected sales inc ome and better perform in future application.

Keyswords: cruise pricing, improved pricing model, multistage punish function, improved DCWQPSO, maximum expected sales income

1. Introduction

Regarded as *the gold industry floating on the gold waterway*, the cruise industry has now become one of the fastest developing industries in modern tourism business, and has reached 8% increment in recent years (Sun, 2011). With new cruises' being put in operation and new ports' being constructed, the cruise business is developing rapidly, showing tremendous life power and development potential (Liu, 2011). However, the China's cruise business is just setting off and immature, also lacking any theoretical studies of the cruise' profit management. In recent years, the China's cruise tourism business is in a strong developing trend and become the new form and new field of China's economy development, due to the influence of international cruise industry markets. Therefore, it has become an important issue that worth studying how to rationally increases the cruise industries' profit.

In the process of cruise business operation, the companies emphasize on three aspects mostly: demand precast, storage distribution and cabin pricing, so the pricing of the cruise directly influence the business' sales income, which could be a key problem of the study. As for the pricing of the cruise, many experts and scholars had made a great amount of studies on it. For example, Sun *et al.* (2015) made a comparison analysis on the cabin distribution of cruise profit management based on the EMS R-a and EMS R-b. Sun *et al.* (2013) put forward a dynamic pricing adjustment strategy especially for the north-American market based on demand learning, and further discusses the implementing process of this new strategy using actually statistics of American cruise companies. The study results shows that this strategy could higher cruise companies' total profit in some extent. Shen (2015) made a study on cruises' dynamic stock control and dynamic pricing of different types of cabins in different periods based mostly on profit management theory. However, he did not make transformation on the extant model, also he put in his essay that it was a difficult problem to restrictedly optimize the pricing of cruise to achieve maximum expected income.

When dealing with the optimizing problem, the Particle Swarm Optimization, PS (Kennedy J, 1995) algorithm stands out with easy understandability and access among other global optimization algorithms, which attracted scholars' attention, generated many applications (Kuok K K, 2010). But there are some aspects that remain to be improved as shown in the actual practice. For example, the easily resulted premature convergence, lack of global optimization abilities and slow convergence speed, etc.(Zhou, 2011). Sun (2004) came up with a new particle evolution model from the quantum mechanics point of view, which is based on the delta (δ) potential and the hypothesis that the particles would feature quantal behaviors. He later put forward the algorithm- Quantum Particle Swarm Optimization, QPSO based on the model. Because of the differences appeared in the particles' agglomeration state in the quantum space, the algorithm could manage to do search within the whole feasible region, since its ability at global searching is far better than the standard particle swarm algorithm. However in the actual application, the QPSO still needs to be improved to better suit the specific circumstances. At present, there are plenty of studies about improving the quantum particle swarm optimization in order to better solve the multi-object optimization problem. For example: Zhang *et al.*(2008) improved the particle swarm optimization based on multi-stage punish function; Wen *et al.*(2015) dynamically reconfigured the distribution network based on integer coded quantum particles warm optimization algorithm; Huang *et al.*(2012) studied about the quantum-behaved particle swarm algorithm with self-adapting adjustment of inertia weight; Cao *et al.*(2012) applied the Improved quantum particle swarm optimization into power network planning considering geography factor; Li *et al.*(2014) applied the adaptive parameter into adjusting the research on quantum-behaved particle swarm optimization.

This essay puts forward a cruise pricing model based on improved quantum particle swarm optimization, with improvement made in the dynamic pricing theory according to the actual circumstances, also using the multistage punish function to optimize the DCWQPSO algorithm and lastly improving the problem of optimization with the improved algorithm's restriction. We use *the eighth electrical and mathematical modeling contest* type B's statistics to prove the pricing model put forward in this essay, and the results show that this model works well with excellent precision and applicability.

2. Cruise Pricing Model

Focusing on the cruise pricing problem, this essay firstly puts the idea of improving the previously made dynamic pricing model based on demand learning by studying the actual booking records and expected booking records in cruise pricing, which would make the model more realistic. Secondly, the improving of DCWQPSO using the multistage punish function, which would help avoid local optimum and faster the convergence speed. Lastly, find the global optimized sales profit expectation, using the improved quantum particle swarm optimization.

2.1 Improved Dynamic Pricing Model

Sun et al. (2013) put forward a dynamic pricing model based on demand learning, which could not only set dynamic prices, but also dynamically dig out the information of customers' maximum reserved prices.

However, the model did not take the relations between the actual booking records and expected booking records into consideration. In reality, the expected records are in some kind of relation with the prices, which we could fit by comparing the hash maps. Also the actual records are in some kind of relation with the expected records. According to this, in this section the improvement of this dynamic pricing model based on demand learning will be discussed. With the new voyage statistics imported, the demand function will be re-evaluated, and the best prices of different future voyage could be set by using the following non-linear model.

Actual booking records (demand function) and the expected booking records function:

$$\begin{cases} D_n = f(W_n) \\ W_n = f_0(p_t) \end{cases}$$

Where, D_n stands for the actual booking records in the n-th circle, W_n stands for the expected booking records in the n-th circle.

The weekly prices p_t ($t=1,2...,n$) obey the uniform distribution between the interval of $[p_{min}, p_{max}]$.

Thus, in the demand function $D_n = f(W(p_t)) = f(p_t)$

Then, $R_n = p_n \cdot D_n$

Where, R_n stands for the total profit during the n-th circle of every cruise voyage.

From above, the improved model of maximum expected profit is presented below:

Subject function: $\max R = \sum_{t=1}^{n} p_t D(p_t)$

Restriction requirement:

$$s.t. \begin{cases} |\dfrac{p_{t+1} - p}{p_{t+1}}| < 0.2 & (t = 1, 2, ..., n) \\ \sum_{t=1}^{n} D(p_t) \le M \\ p_t > 0 & (t = 1, 2, ..., n) \\ p_{\min} \le p_t \le p_{\max} \end{cases}$$

Where, R stands for the total profit of each cruise voyage, M stands for the maximum capacity of each level's cruise cabins, p_t stands for the cabin price of the t-th circle in the same level.

By using the data of different voyages, layout the demand function $D(p_t)$, substitute the data to calculate the specific function of R, and lastly calculate the value of R then we have the profit expectation of the cruise company.

2.2 Improved QPSO Based on Multistage Punish Function

2.2.1 Dynamically Changing Weight's Quantum-Behaved Particle Swarm Optimization (DCWQPSO)

Choosing the inertia weight β of the QPSO is crucial, because it's related to the whole algorithm's convergence ability. The bigger the value of β is, the better it is the quality of global searching and the faster the convergence speed is but the less precise result is; the smaller the value of β is, the more precise result is and the slower the convergence speed is. In order to improve the convergence ability of the QPSO, Huang *et al.*(2012) came up with an algorithm DCWQPSO.

During the iterative process of the QPSO, the global optimal position value in the current iterative always excels or at least equals to that of last iterative as a result of the calculating of the particle swarm's position.

$$s_d = \frac{F(x_g(t-1))}{F(x_g(t))}$$

If the optimization object is to search for the minimal value, the define

$$s_d = \frac{F(x_g(t))}{F(x_g(t-1))}$$

Another factor that affect the QPSO's performance is the particle aggregation. Particle swarm's global optimal position value's fitness value $F(x_g(t))$ always excels that of every particle's current optimal position value. If every particle's current optimal position value's fitness value's average is

$$M_t = \frac{1}{N} \sum_{i=1}^{N} F(x_i(t))$$

During the process of optimizing the minimal value, $F(x_g(t)) \le M_t$ defines the particle aggregation degree factor:

$$j_d = \frac{F(x_g(t))}{M_t}$$

During the process of optimizing the maximal value, $F(x_g(t)) \geq M_t$, defines:

$$j_d = \frac{M_t}{F(x_g(t))}$$

This improved algorithm could dynamically adjust β according to the evolution speed factor s_d and the aggregation degree factor j_d during operation, which is

$$\beta = f(s_d, j_d) = \beta_0 - s_d\beta_1 + j_d\beta_2$$

Where, β_0 is β initial value, commonly $\beta_0 = 1$; β_1 is the weight influenced by s_d; β_2 is the weight influenced by j_d. Since $0 \leq s_d \leq 1, 0 \leq j_d \leq 1 \ 0 < j_d \leq 1$, the $\beta_0 - \beta_1 \leq \beta \leq \beta_0 + \beta_2$. Commonly in the initial state, make $s_d = 0, j_d = 0$.

2.2.2 The Punish Function

The punish function is commonly defined as (Zhang *et al.*, 2008)::

$$F(x) = f(x) + h(k)H(x), x \in S \subset R^n$$

Where, $f(x)$ is the initial object function for the constrained optimization problem, $h(x)$ is the punish function's factor, k is the iterations of the particle swarm algorithm, which means that the constrained optimization method's punish function value increases with the increase of the iteration. $H(x)$ is the multistage punish function, and is defined as:

$$H(x) = \sum_{i=1}^{m} \theta(q_i(x))q_i(x)^{\gamma(q_i(x))}$$

$$q_i(x) = \max\{0, g_i(x)\}, i = 1, ..., m$$

Where, m is the number of the constraint conditions, $q_i(x)$ is the corresponding constraint violation function, $g_i(x)$ is the constraint function, $\theta(q_i(x))$ is the multistage distribution function, $\gamma(q_i(x))$ is the series of the punish function. $q_i(x), \theta(q_i(x))$ and $\gamma(q_i(x))$ is based on the constrained optimization problem, and the value is set based on the following rules.

(1)If $q_i(x) < 1$, then the series $\gamma(q_i(x)) = 1$;

(2)If $q_i(x) \geq 1$, then the series $\gamma(q_i(x)) = 2$;

(3)If $q_i(x) < 0.001$, then $\theta(q_i(x)) = 10$;

(4)If $0.001 < q_i(x) < 0.1$, then $\theta(q_i(x)) = 20$;

(5)If $0.1 < q_i(x) < 1$, then $\theta(q_i(x)) = 100$;

(6)If $q_i(x) \geq 1$, then $\theta(q_i(x)) = 300$.

2.2.3 Improved DCWQPSO Based on Multistage Punish Function

There are many studies on expanding the QPSO in order to operate the constrained optimization, helping optimization with all kinds of constrained operation technology. Also, it's possible to transform the constrained optimization problem into non-constrained optimization problem by adding the multistage distribution punish function.

In this section, an improved algorithm DCWQPSO based on multistage punish function will be put forward, in order to further improved the DCWQPSO, and add the restrictions as a punish function form into the object function to make it a single object optimization problem. Here are the calculation steps of the DCWQPSO using the multistage punish function:

Step 1: Find the initial position of all the particles in the object space and at the same time initialize the inertial factor initial value β_0, the evolution speed factor weight β_1 and the aggregation degree factor weight β_2;

Step 2: Update the average optimal position of the particle swarm according to the particles' average optimal position;

Step 3: Calculate each particle's current adaptive value and compare it to that of the previous iteration. If the current value is smaller, then set that particles' position as the current position;

Step 4: Calculate the swarm's current global optimal position;

Step 5: Compare the current and previous global optimal position adaptive value. If the current value is smaller, then set the particle swarm's global optimal position as the current position;

Step 6: Update all the particles' position according to the position update formula;

Step 7: Update the evolution speed factor s_d and the aggregation degree factor j_d;

Step 8: Update the inertial factor value β;

Step 9: Repeat **Step 2 to 8** till the end loop condition is met.

This improved algorithm could find the global optimal solution in the fastest way and would not easily fall into local optimum.

Lastly, we use this improved DCWQPSO algorithm to calculate the solution of the improved dynamic pricing model in order to find the global optimal expected ticket sales income.

3. Instance Analysis

In this section, the cruise pricing model based on the improved particle swarm algorithm will be proved by using *the eighth electrical and mathematical modeling contest* type B's statistics (website :http://shumo.nedu.edu.cn/).

3.1 Demand Function Solving

The statistics of the first seven voyage's first class cabin picked out form the type B could be seen in the Tab.1 and 2. In the Tab.1, 4 of the first 7 circles' historic pricing data including the expected booking records, the actual booking records and the pre-set prices are shown, while in the Tab.2 different circle's pre-set prices' restriction intervals are shown. In order to make the fit result better, logic regression forecasting method was used to complete all the seven voyage's statistics. Due to the limited length of this article, we would just calculate the solution of the model using the data of the first class cabin.

Table 1. Statistics of the first 8 voyages

Expected booking records							
Circle	Voyage 1	Voyage 2	Voyage 3	Voyage 4	Voyage 5	Voyage 6	Voyage 7
12	31	136	49	96	148	39	54
13	10	40	32	35	83	24	10
14	2	9	36	25	11	7	6
15	1	0	5	4	10	5	3
Pre-set prices							
Circle	Voyage 1	Voyage 2	Voyage 3	Voyage 4	Voyage 5	Voyage 6	Voyage 7
12	1770	1900	1800	1860	1900	1760	1760
13	1730	1820	1720	1760	1810	1710	1831
14	1660	1720	1800	1810	1720	1846	1831
15	1610	1650	1680	1690	1750	1766	1720
Actual booking records							

Circle	Voyage 1	Voyage 2	Voyage 3	Voyage 4	Voyage 5	Voyage 6	Voyage 7
12	28	34	37	43	37	37	51
13	8	8	28	21	22	22	12
14	2	6	9	5	7	8	6
15	1	0	3	2	5	4	4

Table 2. Pre-set prices intervals

Circle	Prices intervals	
12	1750	1950
13	1700	1850
14	1650	1850
15	1600	1800

By observing the booking records and pricing's scatter diagram's trend, this article would talk about the exponential fitting of the 12-th circle's expected booking records and pricing, you could see the fitting graph in Figure 1. Meanwhile, and by observing the 12-th circle actual booking records and expected booking records' scatter diagram's trend, this article would talk about the linear fitting of the actual booking and expected booking records, you could see the fitting graph in Figure 2.

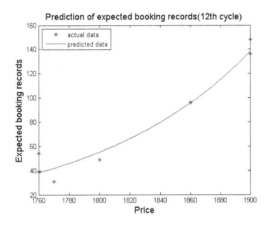

Figure 1. The fitting diagram of the expected and pricing(12th)

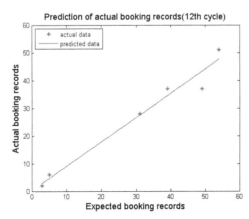

Figure 2. The fitting diagram of the actual and expected booking records(12th)

The 12th circle's expected booking records and pricing's fitting equation $W_n = e^{0.0092 p_t - 12.5}$

The 12th circle's actual and expected booking records and actual booking records' fitting equation

$$D_n = 0.8769W_n + 0.2360$$

Then the 12th circle's demand function is $D_n = 0.8769(e^{0.0092p_t - 12.5}) + 0.2360$

Thus, the 13th to 15th circles' demand function could also be calculated:

Then the 13th circle's demand function is $D_n = 0.8806(e^{0.0099p_t - 14}) + 0.5069$

Then the 14th circle's demand function is $D_n = 0.7203(e^{0.0171p_t - 27.4}) + 0.4537$

Then the 15th circle's demand function is $D_n = 0.8598(e^{0.0211p_t - 34}) + 0.3232$

3.2 Optimization Model Solving

By substituting the demand function from the 3.1 section into the maximal expected profit's optimization model then using the Matlab, we could find the solution of the improved DCWQPSO. In order to better represent the advantages of the improved algorithm, we would respectively using the DCWQPSO and the QPSO to solve the improved model, you could see the convergence comparison in Figure 3 (the red line describes the improved DCWQPSO's convergence, while the blue line describe that of the ordinary QPSO) and the solution in Tab.3.

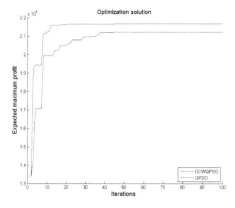

Figure 3. Convergence Comparison

Table 3. Improved model's solving result

DCWQPSO solution			QPSO solution		
Circle	Price	Booking records forecast	Circle	Price	Booking records forecast
12	1860.18	84.3	12	1799.27	48.31
13	1761.56	28.72	13	1777.49	33.55
14	1718.42	5.85	14	1650.62	2.14
15	1607.66	0.96	15	1799.41	35.98
Maximal expected income:		216599.43	Maximal expected income:		212168.02

3.3 Discussion

As shown in the Figure 3, compared with the ordinary QPSO, the improved DCWQPSO has faster convergence speed and bigger expected profit, which further proves that the improved DCWQPSO would not easily fall into local optimal problem and has better optimization and application. As for the result of the Tab.3, DCWQPSO's maximal expected profit is 216,599.43, which is a 2.09% increment compared to that of 212,168.02 of the ordinary QPSO. Also calculating the average voyage profit, which is 105,795, proves that the improved algorithm has much bigger maximal expected income than previous. Thus, the cruise-pricing model put forward in this essay is of significance and bound to make more profit to the actual cruise business.

4. Conclusion

This essay puts forward a cruise pricing model based on the improved quantum particle swarm optimization, basing on the dynamic pricing theory and the improved particle swarm algorithm, with the aim at optimizing the pricing strategy and achieving maximal sales income.

The innovation of this essay lies at two points. First, we improved Sun *et al.*(2013)'s dynamic pricing model by combining the actual situation of cruise pricing's actual and expected booking records, which proves the practicality of the improved model. Second, we put forward a improved algorithm by combining the multistage punish function and the DCWQPSO, in order to faster the finding of the global optimal solution and avoid local optimal. The examples show that, the improved algorithm has better application advantages. All in all, the model in this essay is countable and logical, and the pricing model would work well in improving the maximal expected sales income.

As for the model's application, this essay's case analysis takes relatively less statistics types, which need to be more in real cruise pricing. However, as long as there are better parameters and index for this improved model, it could work just fine.

This particle swam algorithm has a wide academic use, other than the pricing model put forward in this essay, other fields of science or business also uses this algorithm, such as the distribution network's dynamic reconstitution (Wen *et al.*, 2015) and the red wine's quality classification(Qiu *et al.*, 2015).

Acknowledgements

The authors acknowledge the financial support of this research by Natural Science Foundation of China under Grant 61201458.

References

Cao, C. D., Chang, X. R., & Liu, Y. (2012). Application of Improved Quantum Particle Swarm Optimization in Power Network Planning Considering Geography Factor. *Power System Technology, 3*, 134-139.

Han, L. Y. (2014). The Research oe the Development Strategy of Haitian Cruise Industry. University Of Hainan.

Huang, Z. X., You-Hong, Y. U., & Huang, D. C. (2012). Quantum-Behaved Particle Swarm Algorithm with Self-adapting Adjustment of Inertia Weight. *Journal of Shanghai Jiaotong University, 2*, 228-232.

Karpowicz, A., & Szajowski, K. (2007). Double optimal stopping times and dynamic pricing problem: description of the mathematical model. *Mathematical Methods of Operations Research, 66*(2), 235-253.

Kennedy, J., & Eberhart, R. (1995). *Particle swarm optimization.* Proc of IEEE International Conference on NeuralNetworks. Perth: IEEE Press, 1942-1948.

Kuok, K. K., Harun. S., & Shamsuddin, S. M. (2010). Particle swarm optimization feedforward neural network for modeling runoff.*International Journal of Environmental Science and Technology, 7*(1), 67-78.

Li, J. H. (2014). Research and Application on Adaptive Parameter Adjusting Quantum-Behaved Particle Swarm Optimization. Central South University.

Lv, J. L. (2012). Research on Quantum-behaved Particle Swarm Algorithm and Data Classificatio. Xidian University.

Qiu, J., Peng, G. Y., & Wu, R. W. et al. (2015). Application of QPSO-KM Algorithm in Wine Quality Classification. Agricultural Science & Technology, 09, 2045-2047+2059. http://dx.doi.org/10.3969/j.issn.1009-4229.2015.09.046

Shen, Y. Y. (2015). Revenue Management for Cruise. Beijing Institute of Technology.

Sun, J. (2009). Particle Swarm Optimization With Particles Having Quantum Behavior. Jiangnan University.

Sun, J., & Xu, W. B. A. (2004). *Global search strategy of quantum-behaved particle swarm optimization.* Proceedings of the IEEE Congress on Cybernetics and Intelligent System. Singapore: IEEE Press, 111-116.

Sun, X. D. (2011). Cruise Line Revenue Management: Demand Forecasting and Revenue Optimization. Shanghai Jiaotong University.

Sun, X. D., & Feng, X. (2013). Capacity Allocation for Cruise Lines Revenue Management: EMSR-a VS EMSR-b. *Tourism Tribune, 28*(11), 32-41.

Sun, X. D., & Feng, X. G. (2012). Cruise Tourism Industry in China: Present Situation of Studies and Prospect. *Tourism Tribune, 27*(2), 101-106.

Sun, X., & Feng, X. (2013). How to Set Prices for Cruise Cabins: An Empirical Study on the North America Market. *Tourism Tribune, 28*(2), 111-118.

Wen, J., Tan, Y. H., & Lei, K. J. (2015). Multi-objective optimization of distribution network dynamic reconfiguration based on integer coded quantum particles warm optimization algorithm. *Power System Protection and Control, 16*, 73-78.

Zhang, G. Y., & Wu, Y. J. (2008). Multi-constraint Optimization Algorithm Based on Multistage Punish Function and Particle Swarm Optimization. *Journal of Beijing Institute of Petro-Chemical Technology, 4*, 30-32.

Zhou, C. H. (2011). Research and Application of Quantum Particle Swarm Optimization Algorithm. Northeast Petroleum University.

6

On the Conduciveness of Random Network Graphs for Maximal Assortative or Maximal Dissortative Matching

Natarajan Meghanathan[1]

[1] Department of Computer Science, Jackson State University, USA

Correspondence: Natarajan Meghanathan, Department of Computer Science, Mailbox 18839, Jackson State University, Jackson, MS 39217, USA. E-mail: natarajan.meghanathan@jsums.edu

The research is financed by the Massie Chair Grant (#: DE-NA0000654) at Jackson State University.

Abstract

A maximal matching of a graph is the set of edges such that the addition of an edge to this set violates the property of matching (i.e., no two edges of the matching share a vertex). We use the notion of assortative index (ranges from -1 to 1) to evaluate the extent of similarity of the end vertices constituting the edges of a matching. A maximal matching of the edges whose assortative index is as close as possible to 1 is referred to as maximal assortative matching (MAM) and a maximal matching of the edges whose assortative index is as close as possible to -1 is referred to as maximal dissortative matching (MDM). We present algorithms to determine the MAM and MDM of the edges in a network graph. Through extensive simulations, we conclude that random network graphs are more conducive for maximal dissortative matching rather than maximal assortative matching. We observe the assortative index of an MDM on random network graphs to be relatively more closer to the targeted optimal value of -1 compared to the assortative index of an MAM to the targeted optimal value of 1.

Keywords: assortative index, maximal assortative matching, maximal dissortative matching, random network graphs

1. Introduction

Maximal matching is one of the classical problems of graph theory. A matching for a graph is a set of edges such that no two edges share a common vertex. A maximal matching for a graph is a set of edges such that the inclusion of an additional edge to this set violates the above property of matching. A maximum matching for a graph is the largest maximal matching for a graph. Most of the algorithms in the literature for determining a maximal matching for a graph use the notion of augmenting paths (Cormen et al., 2009) and the focus is on determining the maximal node matching (i.e., largest set of edges such that no two edges have a common end vertex). The extent of the similarity of the end vertices constituting the edges of a maximal matching has not been typically taken into consideration as part of the design of the maximal matching algorithms. In this paper, we emphasize that the similarity of the end vertices of the edges constituting a maximal matching needs to be taken into consideration in the design of matching algorithms for complex network graphs. This is because, when vertices in a complex network graph are to be paired to obtain a maximal matching, it is imperative that we pair vertices that are either very similar or very dissimilar from each other (depending on the nature of the application). For example, a maximal matching that is arbitrary with respect to the similarity of the vertices being matched need not be preferred in peer-to-peer interaction and collaborative networks: Students would prefer to be paired with students of similar characteristics when they are asked to share a dormitory, whereas faculty would prefer to collaborate with peers who have different strengths and could complement each other on a research project. Thus, we hypothesize that for complex network graphs, maximal matching of the vertices in the network graph should be conducted with the objective of maximizing either the similarity or dissimilarity of the end vertices constituting the matching and should not be arbitrary or done simply with the objective of maximizing the number of vertices paired.

We propose to use the notion of assortative index (Newman, 2010) as a measure of the similarity of the end vertices constituting a maximal matching. The assortativity index of a set of edges (with respect to any particular measure of node weight - like the node degree) is a quantitative measure of the similarity between the end vertices of the edges that are part of the set (Newman, 2010). The assortativity index values can range from -1 to 1. If the assortativity index of a set of edges calculated with respect to a particular measure of node weight is close to 1, then it implies the end vertices of the edges that form the set are very similar to each other with respect to the particular measure of node weight (for example, a high degree vertex matched to another high degree vertex, a low degree vertex matched to another low degree vertex, etc). If the assortativity index is close to 0, then the pairing of the vertices in the edge set is arbitrary with respect to the node weight. On the other hand, if the assortativity index of the set of the edges with respect to a measure of node weight is close to -1, then it implies that most of the node pairs constituting the edge set are not similar to each other with respect to the node weight (for example, if node degree is used as the node weight, then an assortativity index of -1 of a set of edges implies that most of the node pairings in this set involve a high degree vertex matched to a low degree vertex and vice-versa).

Random network graphs are a category of complex network graphs for which there exists an edge between *any* two vertices with a probability. To vindicate this characteristic, we observe the assortative index of the entire set of edges in a random network graph to be close to 0, indicating that there is no particular preference for a node to have an edge to any other node. Given the above observation, we wanted to explore whether it would be indeed possible to determine a maximal matching of the edges in a random network graph such that the assortative index of the matching is either close to 1 or -1 (depending on whether the targeted matching is an assortative matching or dissortative matching). In this paper, we show that it is possible to determine both maximal assortative matching (MAM) and maximal dissortative matching (MDM) on random network graphs. Further, we make an interesting observation that the assortative index of an MDM is relatively more closer to the targeted optimal value of -1 compared to the proximity of the assortative index of an MAM to the targeted optimal value of 1. We observe the above phenomenon for random network graphs generated with the well-known Erdos-Renyi model (for various fixed values of the probability of a link between any two nodes) with node degree as node weights and random node weights.

The rest of the paper is organized as follows: Section 2 presents the algorithms for maximal assortative matching (MAM) and maximal dissortative matching (MDM). Section 3 presents the results of the execution of the MAM and MDM algorithms on random network graphs generated according to the Erdos-Renyi model with the node degree as node weights and random node weights. Section 4 discusses related work on maximal matching and Section 5 concludes the paper. Throughout the paper, the terms 'node' and 'vertex', 'link' and 'edge' as well as 'pair' and 'match' are used interchangeably. They mean the same.

2. Algorithms for Maximal Assortative Matching and Maximal Dissortative Matching

2.1 Network Model and Assumptions

We model the input network graph $G = (V, E)$ as a set of vertices V and undirected edges E wherein each vertex $v \in V$ have a weight $w(v) \in \mathbb{R}$. We say an edge (p, q) is adjacent to an edge (r, s) if $p, q, r, s \in V$ and either $p = r$ or $p = s$ or $q = r$ or $q = s$. That is, two edges (p, q) and (r, s) are said to be adjacent to each other if they have one common end vertex. The degree of a vertex $u \in V$ is the number of edges incident on u (i.e., the number of edges that have vertex u as one of the two end vertices). Though the edges are undirected, for the sake of discussion, we refer to the first vertex (vertex u) indicated in an edge (u, v) as the upstream vertex and the second vertex (vertex v) indicated in an edge (u, v) as the downstream vertex. Also, since the edges are undirected, we conveniently adopt a convention to represent the edges: the ID of the upstream vertex of an edge (u, v) is always less than the ID of the downstream vertex of the edge (i.e., $u < v$).

For a set of edges M constituting a matching of the vertices V in the graph G, the assortativity index of M is a quantitative measure of the similarity (or equivalently the dissimilarity) of the end vertices of the edges in M (Newman, 2010). The assortativity index for a set M of edges (AI_M) with respect to the node weights $w(v)$ for every vertex $v \in V$ is calculated using the formula (1) given below, where $\overline{U}$ and $\overline{D}$ are respectively the average weight of the upstream and downstream vertices of the edges constituting the set M.

$$AI_M = \frac{\sum_{(p,q) \in M}[w(p) - \overline{U}][w(q) - \overline{D}]}{\sqrt{\sum_{(p,q) \in M}[w(p) - \overline{U}]^2}\sqrt{\sum_{(p,q) \in M}[w(q) - \overline{D}]^2}} \quad ; \quad \overline{U} = \frac{1}{|M|}\sum_{(p,q) \in M}w(p) \quad ; \quad \overline{D} = \frac{1}{|M|}\sum_{(p,q) \in M}w(q) \qquad (1)$$

We say an edge (u, v) included in a matching covers itself as well as covers the edges that are adjacent to it in the original graph. An uncovered edge is an edge in the graph that is not yet covered by an edge in the matching. We define the assortativity weight of an edge (u, v) to be the product of the number of uncovered edges that are adjacent to it and the absolute value of the difference in the weights of the end vertices u and v. The number of uncovered edges adjacent to an edge (u, v) is the sum of the number of uncovered edges incident on each of the end vertices u and v. If $w(u)$ and $w(v)$ indicate respectively the weights of the vertices u and v, and $ue(u)$ and $ue(v)$ indicate respectively the number of uncovered edges incident on vertices u and v, then: Assortativity Weight of edge $(u, v) = \{ue(u) + ue(v)\} * \{|w(u) - w(v)|\}$.

2.2 Description of the Algorithm for Maximal Assortative Matching

The MAM algorithm employs a greedy strategy; at the beginning of each iteration, the algorithm chooses the uncovered edge with the smallest assortativity weight. The pseudo code for the algorithm to determine maximal assortative matching (MAM) is outlined in Figure 1; the pseudo code for the two sub routines used in the algorithm is given in Figure 2. The algorithm maintains the set of uncovered edges (*UncoveredEdges*) that are yet to be covered by an edge in the MAM. The set *UncoveredEdges* is initialized to the set of all edges E for the input graph G.

Input: Graph $G = (V, E)$, where weight $w(v) \in \mathbb{R}$ for every $v \in V$

Output: Maximal Assortativity Matching, *MAM*

Auxiliary Variables: *UncoveredEdges*

Initialization: *UncoveredEdges* $= E$; *MAM* $= \phi$

Begin *MAM Algorithm*

1   *FindAssortativityWeights(UncoveredEdges)*

2   **while** (*UncoveredEdges* $\neq \phi$) **do**

3      $Edge(u,v) = \left\{ (p,q) \mid \underset{(p,q) \in UncoveredEdges}{Min[AssortativityWeight(p,q)]} \right\}$

4   *MAM* $=$ *MAM* $\cup \{(u, v)\}$

5   *UncoveredEdges* $=$ *UncoveredEdges* $- \{(u, v)\}$

6   *RemoveEdges*$((u, v),$ *UncoveredEdges*$)$

7   *FindAssortativityWeights(UncoveredEdges)*

8   **end while**

9   **return** *MAM*

End *MAM Algorithm*

Figure 1. Pseudo code for the maximal assortativity matching (MAM) algorithm

To start with, the assortativity weight of the edges in the set *UncoveredEdges* is determined and the edge (u, v) that has the smallest assortativity weight among the edges in *UncoveredEdges* is selected for inclusion in the MAM. An edge (u, v) selected for inclusion to the MAM is said to cover itself as well as cover its adjacent edges; accordingly, all these newly covered edges are removed from the set *UncoveredEdges*. The assortativity weight of the edges in the updated set of *UncoveredEdges* is recalculated and the edge with the smallest assortativity weight is selected for inclusion in the MAM. The above procedure is repeated as a sequence of iterations until the set of *UncoveredEdges* is empty. At this stage, we have found a maximal matching of the vertices in the graph.

The run-time complexity of the MAM algorithm depends on the time complexity to update the set of *UncoveredEdges* in each iteration. As the algorithm proceeds, with each edge added to the MAM, we expect the size of the set of *UncoveredEdges* to reduce significantly. For optimal run-time, we suggest maintaining the set of *UncoveredEdges* as a minimum heap (Cormen et al., 2009) that can be constructed in $O(|E|)$ time for the $|E|$ edges of the graph. Each update to the minimum heap (like removing an edge or updating the assortativity weight of an edge) takes $O(\log|E|)$ time. The MAM algorithm runs at most for $|V|/2$ iterations for a graph of $|V|$ vertices. During each such iteration, there would have to be at most $|E|$ updates to the heap (one update or removal for each edge, depending on the case), incurring a worst-case time complexity of $O(|E|*\log|E|)$ per iteration. Considering that there could be at most $|V|/2$ iterations, the overall run-time complexity of the MAM algorithm is $O(|E|*|V|*\log|E|)$. For sparse graphs ($|E| = O(|V|)$), the run-time complexity of the MAM algorithm would be $O(|V|^2*\log|V|)$; for dense graphs ($|E| = O(|V|^2)$), the run-time complexity of the MAM algorithm would be $O(|V|^3*\log|V|)$.

Subroutine *FindAssortativityWeights*(*UncoveredEdges*)

    for every edge $(u, v) \in UncoveredEdges$ **do**

        numUncoveredAdjacentEdges$(u, v) = 0$

        for every edge (u, p) or $(p, u) \in UncoveredEdges$ AND $p \mathrel{!=} v$ **do**

            numUncoveredAdjacentEdges$(u, v) = numUncoveredAdjacentEdges(u, v) + 1$

        end for

        for every edge (v, q) or $(q, v) \in UncoveredEdges$ AND $q \mathrel{!=} u$ **do**

            numUncoveredAdjacentEdges$(u, v) = numUncoveredAdjacentEdges(u, v) + 1$

        end for

        AssortativityWeight$(u, v) = numUncoveredAdjacentEdges(u, v) * \left| w(u) - w(v) \right|$

    end for

End Subroutine

|

Subroutine *RemoveEdges*(Edge (u, v), *UncoveredEdges*)

    for every edge $(u, v) \in UncoveredEdges$ **do**

        for every edge (u, p) or $(p, u) \in UncoveredEdges$ AND $p \mathrel{!=} v$ **do**

            UncoveredEdges = *UncoveredEdges* - $\{(u, p)$ or $(p, u)\}$

        end for

        for every edge (v, q) or $(q, v) \in UncoveredEdges$ AND $q \mathrel{!=} u$ **do**

            UncoveredEdges = *UncoveredEdges* - $\{(v, q)$ or $(q, v)\}$

        end for

    end for

End Subroutine

Figure 2. Pseudo code for the subroutines used by the maximal assortativity matching algorithm

2.3 Description of the Algorithm for Maximal Dissortative Matching

The MAM algorithm has to be only slightly modified to determine an MDM: Instead of preferring to include edges with a lower assortative weight (to maximize the assortative index of the maximal matching), we need to include the uncovered edge with the largest assortative weight (to minimize the assortative index of the maximal matching) in each iteration. The definition of the assortative weight remains the same as before: that is, the assortative weight of an uncovered edge (u, v) is the product of the number of uncovered edges adjacent to (u, v) and the absolute value of the difference in the node weights for the end vertices u and v. The pseudo code for the MDM algorithm to minimize the assortative index is shown in Figure 3. The sub routines *FindAssortativeWeights* and *RemoveEdges* remain the same as before (see Figure 2). For the MDM algorithm, the set *UncoveredEdges* will have to be maintained as a maximum heap; nevertheless, the time complexity to construct a maximum heap of $|E|$ edges would be $O(|E|)$ and the time complexity to update a maximum heap of at most $|E|$ edges during an iteration would be $O(|E|*\log|E|)$. As a result, the overall run-time complexity of the MDM algorithm would be the same as that of the MAM algorithm: $O(|V|^{2}*\log|V|)$ for sparse graphs and $O(|V|^{3}*\log|V|)$ for dense graphs.

Input: Graph $G = (V, E)$, where weight $w(v) \in \ulcorner$ for every $v \in V$

Output: Maximal Dissortativity Matching, MDM

Auxiliary Variables: *UncoveredEdges*

Initialization: *UncoveredEdges* $= E$; $MDM = \phi$

Begin *MDM Algorithm*

1   *FindAssortativityWeights*(*UncoveredEdges*)

2   **while** (*UncoveredEdges* $\neq \phi$) **do**

3    $$Edge(u,v) = \left\{ (p,q) \mid \underset{(p,q)\in Un\,cov\,eredEdges}{Max[AssortativityWeight(p,q)]} \right\}$$

4    $MDM = MDM \cup \{(u, v)\}$

5   *UncoveredEdges* = *UncoveredEdges* - $\{(u, v)\}$

6   *RemoveEdges*((u, v), *UncoveredEdges*)

7   *FindAssortativityWeights*(*UncoveredEdges*)

8   **end while**

9   **return** *MDM*

End *MDM Algorithm*

Figure 3. Pseudo code for the maximal dissortative matching (MDM) algorithm

2.4 Example for MAM and MDM

Figure 4 presents an example to illustrate the execution of the maximal assortative matching algorithm on a graph wherein the node weights are random numbers generated in the range 0 to 1. All the edges in the input graph and the initialization graph are uncovered edges. The initialization graph displays the assortative weight of the edges as a tuple. For an edge (u, v), we indicate a tuple representing (number of uncovered adjacent edges and the absolute value of the difference in the node weights of the end vertices u and v) as well as the assortativity weight of the edge, which is the product of the two entries in the tuple. In the first iteration, the algorithm encounters a tie between edges (3, 6) and (4, 7) - both of which have the lowest assortative weight of 0.6; the algorithm breaks the tie arbitrarily by including edge (3, 6) to the maximal assortative matching (MAM). As part of the inclusion of the edge (3, 6) into the MAM, all its adjacent edges are considered to be covered and are removed from the graph. We reevaluate the assortativity weight of the uncovered edges in the graph; edge (4, 7) with the currently lowest assortative weight of 0.3 is the second edge to be picked for inclusion to the MAM and all its adjacent edges are removed from the graph. At the end of the second iteration, all edges in the graph are either in the MAM or covered by an edge in the MAM. The node weights of the end vertices that are included into the MAM are (0.9, 0.8) and (0.3, 0.4) for the edges (3, 6) and (4, 7) respectively. The difference in the node weights of the end vertices for both the edges in the MAM is the bare minimum that we could get for the input graph considered (as one can notice, all the nodes in the input graph have unique weights). The % of nodes matched in the MAM is (2*2)/7 = 57% and the assortative index of the matching (based on node weights) is 1.0; the calculations are illustrated as part of Figure 4.

Figure 5 presents an example for the execution of the MDM algorithm on the same graph as in Figure 4. The initial values for the assortative weight of the edges are the same as in Figure 4. As the MDM algorithm prefers to include edges with a larger assortative weight, the first edge to get selected for inclusion to the MDM is edge (5, 6) of assortativity weight 3.5. Due to this inclusion, all the five adjacent edges of (5, 6) are considered to be covered and are removed from the graph. In the second iteration, the MDM algorithm chooses the edge (3, 4) with the currently largest assortativity weight (2.4) to be part of the matching; as a result of this inclusion, all the four adjacent edges of the edge (3, 4) are considered to be covered. At the end of the second iteration, the edges

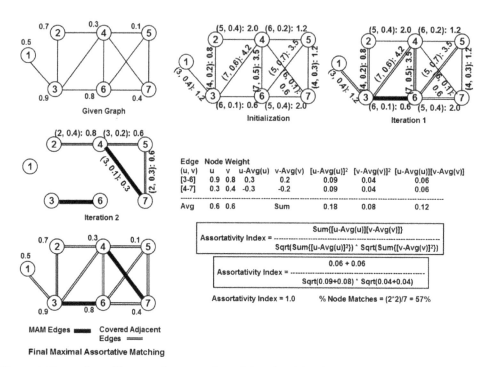

Figure 4. Example to illustrate the execution of the algorithm for maximal assortative matching

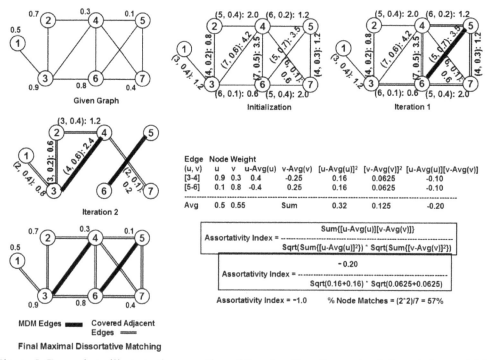

Figure 5. Example to illustrate the execution of the algorithm for maximal dissortative matching

In the graph are either covered or included to the MDM. One can notice that the weights of the pairs of vertices constituting the edges (3, 4) and (5, 6) that are part of the MDM are respectively (0.9, 0.3) and (0.1, 0.8). Given the choice of weights of the end vertices in the toy example graph, this is the best combination of edges that one could come up with even after trying all permutations and combinations. The assortativity index of the above MDM matching evaluates to -1, vindicating our assertion. Like the case of MAM, the % of node matches could not be maximized and only 2 of the 3 edges could be selected (the maximum number of edges that could be selected for a matching in the chosen toy example of 7 vertices is 3 edges).

3. Analysis of Random Network Graphs

In this section, we simulate the evolution of random network graphs generated using the well-known Erdos-Renyi model (Erdos & Renyi, 1959). The model inputs two parameters: the total number of nodes (N) and the probability of a link (p_{link}) between any two nodes in the graph. Since we simulate the evolution of an undirected random network, the links are bi-directional and we could assume that the end vertices of each link could be represented as an ordered pair (u, v) where u and v are the node IDs and $u < v$. We assume there are no self-loops and there is no more than an edge between any two nodes in the network. For an N node network, the maximum number of undirected links possible in the network is $N(N-1)/2$. We consider every such possible link in the network and generate a random number (in the range 0...1) to decide whether or not to include the link in the network. If the random number generated for a pair (u, v) is less than or equal to p_{link}, then we include the link (u, v) in the network; otherwise, not. As it is obvious, the larger the value of p_{link}, the larger the number of links in the random network graph as well as larger the chances for the network to have a degree distribution wherein the degree of each node is closer to the average node degree. The total number of nodes considered in the simulations for this section is $N = 100$ nodes. The values used for the probability of link between any two nodes in the network (p_{link}) are: 0.05, 0.07, 0.10, 0.15, 0.20, 0.30, 0.40 and 0.50. We observe that the random networks for all the 100 trials generated with $p_{link} \geq 0.05$ to be connected. Even though the number of links in the network increases with increasing p_{link} values, the assortativity of the set of all edges in a random network remains close to 0 for all the p_{link} values. This vindicates the random nature of the distribution of the edges among the vertices as per the Erdos-Renyi model.

In section 3.1, we use node degree as node weight for the assortativity calculations and in section 3.2, we use randomly generated numbers in the range (0...1) as node weight for the assortativity calculations. Accordingly, for each of the two sections, we run 100 trials of the network evolution and analyze the assortatvity of the network as well as evaluate the % of node matches and assortativity index (both the average and standard deviation) of the maximal matching obtained with the MAM and MDM algorithms for each p_{link} value. The values reported for the % of node matches and assortative index in Figures 6 and 7 are the average (the values corresponding to the markers) and standard deviation (the values corresponding to the error bars) obtained from the 100 trial runs for each p_{link} value. We observe the variation in the assortative index and % of node matches to decrease with increase in the p_{link} values.

3.1 Analysis with Node Degree as Node Weights

The values reported in Figure 6 are the average values obtained from the 100 trial runs for each p_{link} value with node degree considered as node weights. With regards to the % of node matches, the % of node matches for the MAM and MDM algorithms are respectively 85% and 84% for p_{link} value of 0.05, and reaches respectively 99% and 98% for p_{link} value of 0.5; the % of node matches for MAM crosses 95% when p_{link} is 0.15 and the % of node matches for the MDM crosses 95% when p_{link} is 0.20. However, the tradeoff is quite high with respect to the assortativity index (A.Index).

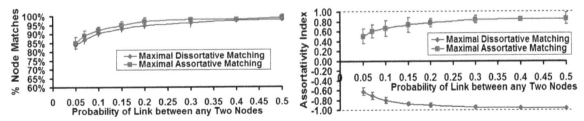

Figure 6. Random networks with node degree as node weights: Distribution of the percentage of node matches and assortativity index as a function of the probability of link between any two nodes

The A.Index values of MAM and MDM are 0.5 and -0.63 when p_{link} is 0.05 and reaches 0.85 and -0.96 when p_{link} value is 0.3. The A.Index does not increase appreciably for MAM as we further increase the p_{link} value. The average A.Index value observed for MAM is 0.90 when the p_{link} value is 0.90. On the other hand, the A.Index values for the MDM continue to vary (i.e., decrease) at a relatively faster rate and reaches -0.99 when the p_{link} value is 0.90. This is a significant observation that has been hitherto not reported in the literature for random networks. Figure 6 illustrates the nature of increase in the % of node matches and the assortativity index values as we increase the p_{link} values from 0.05 to 0.50 as explained above.

Overall, the results presented for random network graphs with node degree as node weights illustrate that the assortative index values obtained with Maximal Dissortative Matching (MDM) are more closer to the targeted optimal value (-1) compared to the closeness of the assortative index values obtained with the Maximal Assortative Matching (MAM) to the targeted optimal value (1). On the other hand, though the % of node matches obtained with Maximal Dissortative Matching appears to be less than that obtained with the Maximal Assortative Matching, the difference in the % of node matches is within 2-3% for all values of p_{link} and by observing the nature of the increase in the % of node matches with the two maximal matching strategies (MAM and MDM), we could say that the difference in the % of node matches would only further narrow down with increase in the p_{link} value. The results of Figure 6 thus illustrate that when node degree is considered for node weights, random network graphs are more conducive for a maximal dissortative matching compared to a maximal assortative matching on the basis of the proximity of the assortative index to the targeted optimal value (-1 for MDM and +1 for MAM).

3.2 Analysis with Random Node Weights

In this sub section, we present the results for the percentage of node matches and assortativity index incurred with the MAM and MDM algorithms for random networks generated under the Erdos-Renyi model wherein the node weights are random numbers generated from 0 to 1. We conducted the simulations with 100 trials for each p_{link} value and averaged the results for the network assortativity as well as the % of node matches and assortativity index for the MAM and MDM. The results presented in Figure 7 indicate the average values for these metrics from the 100 trials.

For a given p_{link} value, we observe the assortativity index of the maximal assortative matching (with random node weights) to be slightly higher (the difference is as large as 0.1 in a scale of 0 to 2) than the assortative index of the maximal assortative matching with node degree as node weights. Though the difference in the assortativity index values for maximal assortative matching with the above two categories of node weights could be observed for all p_{link} values, the difference is relatively more prominent for random networks with lower p_{link} values and reduces as the p_{link} value increases. As can be observed from Figure 7, the curve for the assortativity index for maximal assortative matching with random node weights becomes flat starting from p_{link} value of 0.40 (the assortativity index curve for the MAM with node degree as node weights became flat starting from p_{link} value of 0.30).

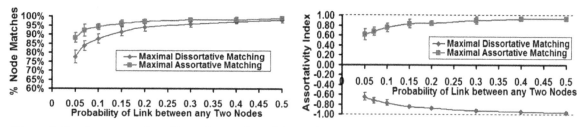

Figure 7. Random networks with random node weights: Distribution of the percentage of node matches and assortativity index as a function of the probability of link between any two nodes

An interesting observation is that (in addition to incurring a relatively larger assortativity index) the % of node matches obtained with the MAM algorithm for random network graphs with random node weights is even slightly larger than the % of node matches obtained with the MAM algorithm for random network graphs with node degree as node weights, especially for networks formed with lower p_{link} values. Overall, the maximal assortative matching algorithm could give even relatively better optimal results (with respect to both assortativity index and % of node matches) for random network graphs with random node weights and the tradeoff in the values incurred for the above two metrics is relatively less pronounced than what is observed in random network graphs with node degree as node weights. As we expect node weights in social networks to be not only a measure of the node degree, the MAM algorithm could be very useful to match vertices with any measure of node weights, especially in social network graphs that are not very dense. This vindicates the wider scope of application of the proposed maximal assortative matching (MAM) algorithm; the algorithm could give even better optimal results (with respect to assortativity) for random graphs with node weights that are independent of node degree.

With regards to the performance of the MDM algorithm on random network graphs (that evolved using the

Erdos-Renyi model) with randomly generated node weights in the range 0 to 1, we observe (from Figure 7) the assortativity index values for the maximal dissortative matching to be very close to that of the assortativity index values illustrated in Figure 6 for the maximal dissortative matching obtained on random network graphs with node degree as node weights (the difference in A.Index is within ± 0.03); the % of node matches obtained for the maximal dissortative matching with random node weights is at most 7% lower than that obtained for the maximal dissortative matching with node degree as node weights. While comparing the results obtained for the maximal assortative matching and maximal dissortative matching obtained on random network graphs with random node weights, we observe the assortativity index values of the maximal dissortative matching to be relatively more closer to the targeted optimal value of -1 compared to that of the closeness of the assortativity index values of the maximal assortative matching to its targeted optimal value of 1. Thus (like in the case of random network graphs with node degree as node weights), we could still say that for random network graphs with random node weights, it would be more apt to aim for a maximal dissortative matching compared to a maximal assortativity matching on the basis of the proximity of the assortative index to the targeted optimal value.

4. Related Work

The problem of determining a maximal matching with minimum cardinality for the set of edges constituting the matching is an NP-hard problem (Yannakakis & Gavril, 1980). It is equivalent to the problem of finding a minimum edge dominating set (Horton & Kilakos, 1993) - to find the smallest set of edges of the graph such that each edge in the set covers itself and covers one or more adjacent edges as well as satisfies the matching constraint (no two edges in the set have a common end vertex). The problem of focus in our paper is the maximal independent edge set problem (Cormen et al., 2009) wherein we want to find the largest set of independent edges such that no two edges have a common end vertex. Note that heuristics (Horton & Kilakos, 1993) for the minimum edge dominating set problem cannot be applied to determine the maximal a(di)ssortative matching. Because, heuristics for the minimum edge set problem are more likely to determine the set of edges such that each edge in the set covers a larger number of adjacent edges. The maximal matching algorithms developed in this paper take the approach of preferring to include edges that cover a smaller number of adjacent edges so that the number of independent edges determined could be as large as possible. To the best of our knowledge, we have not come across a maximal matching algorithm that is aimed at simultaneously maximizing the a(di)ssortativity of the matching as well as maximizing the cardinality of the matching for complex network graphs. In this perspective, the maximal assortative matching and maximal dissortative matching algorithms proposed in this paper are significant contributions to the literature for complex network graphs and analysis.

Wang et al (2011) showed that for networks with binomial degree distribution, the maximum and minimum assortativity vary with the density of the networks. Motivated by this observation, Winterbach et al (2012) introduced an algorithm to compute a network with maximal or minimal assortativity given a vector of valid node degrees using degree-preserving rewiring (Maslov & Sneppen, 2002) and weighted b-matching (Muller-Hannemann & Schwartz, 1999). Degree-preserving link rewiring is effective in decreasing or increasing the assortativity of a network graph without affecting the degree distribution of the vertices (Van Mieghem et al., 2010). Holme & Zhao (2007) also found that an increase in the assortativity of a graph (accomplished through degree-preserving rewiring) also contributes to an increase in the maximum modularity, average hop count, effective graph resistance as well as a decrease in the number of clusters. However, neither the work of Wang et al (2011) nor the work of Winterbach et al (2012) could be extended to determine a maximal a(di)ssortative matching of the edges of the graph. It was also shown by Wang et al (2011) that for networks whose degree distribution is binomial (like the Erdos-Renyi model-based random network graphs), the maximum assortativity and minimum assortativity are asymptotically anti-symmetric. This observation correlates well with our observation in Section 3 that the values for the assortative index for maximum assortative matching are comparable enough to the absolute values of the assortative index for maximum dissortative matching.

5. Conclusions

We explored the feasibility of determining maximal matching in random network graphs with the objective of maximizing the assortative index (targeted optimal value of 1) or minimizing the assortative index (targeted optimal value of -1). In this pursuit, we have developed two greedy strategy-based maximal matching algorithms for maximizing the assortative index (maximal assortative matching, MAM) and minimizing the assortative index (maximal dissortative matching, MDM). We showed that it is possible to determine maximal assortative matching as well as maximal dissortative matching for random network graphs, despite the observation that the assortative index of the set of all edges of a random network graph is 0. For a probability of link value of 0.30 or above, we observe that it is possible to determine maximal assortative matching as well as maximal dissortative matching with assortative index values equal to or above 0.85 and equal to or below -0.95 respectively. With regards to the relative proximity of the assortative index values to the targeted optimal values, we observe the assortative index of a maximal dissortative matching for a random network graph to be consistently more closer to the targeted optimal value of -1 (in comparison to the proximity of the assortative index values of a maximal assortative matching to the targeted optimal value of 1). We could thus conclude that random network graphs are more conducive for maximal dissortative matching. The methodology and the algorithms described in this paper could also be used to decide the conduciveness of other types of complex network graphs (like scale-free network graphs (Barabasi & Albert, 1999) as well as real-world network graphs (Krebs, 2000; Zachary, 1977) for maximal assortative or maximal dissortative matching. We intend to study this as part of future work.

Acknowledgments

The research is financed by the Massie Chair Grant (#: DE-NA0000654) at Jackson State University.

References

Barabasi, A. L., & Albert, R. (1999). Emergence of Scaling in Random Networks. *Science, 286*(5439), 509-512. http://dx.doi.org/10.1126/science.286.5439.509

Cormen, T. H., Leiserson, C. E., Rivest, R. L., & Stein, C. (2009). *Introduction to Algorithms* (3rd ed.) MIT Press.

Erdos, P., & Renyi, A. (1959). On Random Graphs I. *Publicationes Mathematicae, 6*, 290-297.

Holme, P., & Zhao, J. (2007). Exploring the Assortativity-Clustering Space of a Network's Degree Sequence. *Physics Review E, 75*(4), 1-12. http://dx.doi.org/10.1103/PhysRevE.75.046111

Horton, J. D., & Kilakos, K. (1993). Minimum Edge Dominating Sets. *SIAM Journal on Discrete Mathematics, 6*(3), 375-387. http://dx.doi.org/10.1137/0406030

Krebs, V. (2000). Working in the Connected World: Book Network. *Journal of the Institute of Health Record Information and Management, 4*(1), 87-90.

Maslov, S., & Sneppen, K. (2002). Specificity and Stability in Topology of Protein Networks. *Science, 296* (5569), 910-913. http://dx.doi.org/10.1126/science.1065103

Muller-Hannemann, M., & Schwartz, A. (1999). Implementing Weighted b-Matching Algorithms: Insights from a Computational Study. *Algorithm Engineering and Computation, Lecture Notes in Computer Science, 1619*, 18-36. http://dx.doi.org/10.1007/3-540-48518-X_2

Newman, M. E. J. (2010). *Networks: An Introduction* (1st ed.) Oxford University Press.

Van Mieghem, P., Wang, H., Ge, X., Tang, S., & Kuipers, F. (2010). Influence of Assortativity and Degree-Preserving Rewiring on the Spectra of Networks. *The European Physical Journal B, 76*(4), 643-652. http://dx.doi.org/10.1140/epjb/e2010-00219-x

Wang, H., Winterbach, W., & Van Mieghem, P. (2011). Assortativity of Complementary Graphs. *The European Physical Journal B, 83*(2), 203-214. http://dx.doi.org/10.1140/epjb/e2011-20118-x

Winterbach, W., de Ridder, D., Wang, H. J., Reinders, M., & Van Mieghem, P. (2012). Do Greedy Assortativity Optimization Algorithms Produce Good Results? *The European Physical Journal B, 5*, 151-160. http://dx.doi.org/10.1140/epjb/e2012-20899-2

Yannakakis, M., & Gavril, F. (1980). Edge Dominating Sets in Graphs. *SIAM Journal on Applied Mathematics, 38*(3), 364-372.

Zachary, W. W. (1977). An Information Flow Model for Conflict and Fission in Small Groups. *Journal of Anthropological Research, 33*(4), 452-473.

7

Anfis Based Material Flow Rate Control System for Weigh Feeder Conveyor

Dibaj Al Rosyada[1], Misbah[1] & Eliyani[1]

[1] Electrical Engineering Program, Faculty of Engineering, Universitas Muhammadiyah Gresik, Indonesia

Correspondence: Misbah, Electrical Engineering Program, Faculty of Engineering, Universitas Muhammadiyah Gresik. Jl. Sumatera 101 GKB, Gresik, 61121, Indonesia. E-mail: misbah@umg.ac.id

Abstract

Weight control system on the feeder conveyor determines the factor of the quality of products within an industry. The dynamics of the flow rate of material through the feeder conveyor weigh requires a good level of performance controllers. The base of current controllers such as FLC (Fuzzy Logic Controller) requires a certain amount of knowledge and expertise in its design that will make it difficult to achieve good system performance. These difficulties can be overcome by using systems based on ANFIS (Adaptive Neuro-Fuzzy Inference System). By doing the learning offline, using ANFIS can be obtained by fuzzy inference systems to create a controller FLC. Microcontroller have FLC controller program, its integrated with notebook can monitor and control the notebook weigh feeder conveyor system. Designing a system that has been created will give good results with an average error value of 3.86% at the set-point of 1000 grams / minute, and the average error of 5.03% on set-point 2000 grams / minute in ten times testing.

Keywords: ANFIS, weigh feeder conveyor, a microcontroller

I. Introduction

Weigh feeder conveyor control principle is to maintain the desired flow rate by adjusting the conveyor belt speed in proportion to the weigh of the material. The dynamics of the rate of material through the conveyor weigh feeder demanding good performance level controllers. Lack of optimal performance in weigh feeder conveyor controller base can cause product failure and loss.

Base controllers used in weight feeder conveyor is still using conventional technique PID (Proportional Integral Derivative). In general, conventional PID controllers have been successfully used for various processes, but there are still some limitations, its performance is highly dependent on the operational parameters of the plant (Nazarudin, 2009). To further improve the process of control may use other alternative techniques to produce better system response (Saputro, 2007).

The difficulty in designing a modern controller such as FLC (Fuzzy Logic Controller) can be overcome by using systems based on neuro fuzzy. The main advantage in neuro fuzzy systems is the learning capabilities of the data - numerical data is obtained from the measurements, so it does not require a mathematical model of the process to be controlled (Nazarudin, 2009).

Design of fuzzy inference systems on Sugeno method is designed in this study to address the dynamics of the process of controlling the conveyor weigh feeder. Learning off - line using ANFIS is done by the help of Matlab R2011b software.

2. Literature Review

2.1 Fuzzy Set Theory

Fuzzy set is a generalization of the concept of a regular set. For the universe of discourse X, fuzzy set is defined by the membership function which maps X members to membership degree $\mu(x)$ in the interval {0,1} is shown in Figure 2.1 (Widodo, 2005).

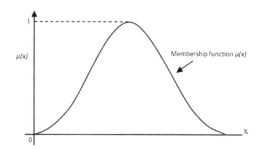

Figure 2.1. Membership Function of a Fuzzy Set

2.2 Fuzzy Inference System

Fuzzy Inference System (FIS) is a computational framework that is based on fuzzy set theory, fuzzy rules in the form of IF - THEN, and fuzzy reasoning. Broadly speaking, fuzzy inference process block diagram is shown in Figure 2.2 (Kusumadewi, 2006).

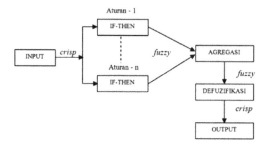

Figure 2.2. Fuzzy Inference System

2.3 Fuzzy Logic Controller (FLC)

FLC can be combined with close loop system as shown in Figure 2.3.

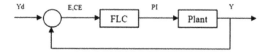

Figure 2.3. FLC Structure

Plant output desired by the reference value (Yd) compared to actual output (Y), so that there is an error (Error, E). Error (E) and the change of the error (Change of error, CE) is a variable input for FLC. FLC output is the input of plant or input process (Process Input, PI) (Widodo, 2005)..

2.4 Adaptive Neuro Fuzzy Inference System

ANFIS (Adaptive Neuro Fuzzy Inference System or Adaptive Network-based Fuzzy Inference System) is an architecture that is functionally similar to the fuzzy rule base by Sugeno models is shown in Figure 2.4. ANFIS architecture is similar to the function of the radial nerve tissue with minimal limitations. ANFIS allows rules to adapt (Kusumadewi, 2006).

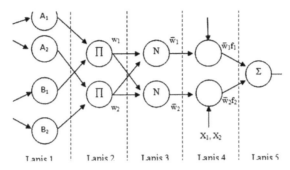

Figure 2.4. ANFIS Architecture

2.5 Weigh Feeder Conveyor

Weight feeder conveyor is used to move the material to the rotation of the motor as the main driver connected with the drum / pulley shrouded by a belt is shown in Figure 2.5. To measure the weight of the material, this object using a weight sensor load cell, whereas to measure the speed of the belt, we are using a tachometer.

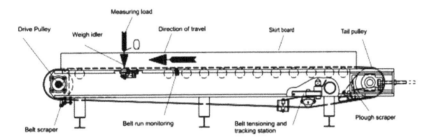

Figure 2.5. Weigh feeder conveyor

3. Designing Tools

Weight feeder conveyor system is shown in Figure 3.1.

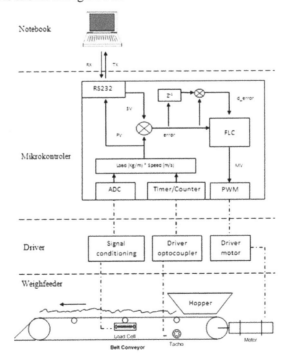

Figure 3.1. System diagram

3.1 AT Mega16 Minimum System

In this section ATmega16 microcontroller mounted with some supporting components so that the cycle of controllers can work continuously. ATMega 16 Minimum system scheme can be seen in Figure 3.2

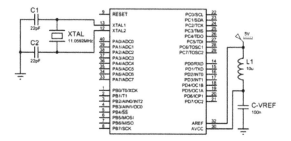

Figure 3.2. ATmega16 Minimum system

3.2 Load Cell

The maximum capacity load cell used is 10 kg with rate the characteristics of a voltage of 2mV/V. If the supply voltage of the load cell is given 20 V, then the maximum load conditions the load cell output voltage is 40 mV. In Table 3.1 it can be seen the results of calculations between the load and the load cell output voltage with an excitation voltage of 20 V.

Table 3.1. Calculation of load cell output

Load (kg)	Output (mV)
0	0
1	4
2	8
3	12
4	16
5	20
6	24
7	28
8	32
9	36
10	40

3.3 Signal Conditioning

Load cell output voltage is still too small which boosted further on signal conditioning circuit. Signal conditioning circuit serves as an amplifier output signal which is generated by loadcell.

Table 3.2. Calculation of output signal conditioners (gain = 125)

Load (kg)	Loadcell (mV)	Instrument Amplifier (V)
0	0	0
1	4	0,5
2	8	1
3	12	1,5
4	16	2
5	20	2,5
6	24	3
7	28	3,5
8	32	4
9	36	4,5
10	40	5

According to Table 3.2 above it is known that load cell output voltage in a state of maximum has a burden of 40 mV. To adjust the microcontroller ADC voltage range between 0-5 volts, then the instrument amplifier gain of the circuit is set at 125.

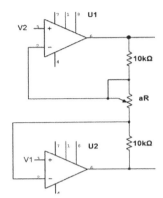

Figure 3.3. Amplifier Instrument

As shown in Figure 3.3 can be known instrument amplifier output is $V_o = (V_2 - V_1)(1+2R/aR)$. Where the

gain is $(1+2R/aR)$, aR is a potentiometer that is used to set the desired gain value. If the R value which is

selected by 10 Kohm, then: $1+2R/aR = 125$

$$aR \cong 161$$

So to get the value of a gain of 125, then the aR must be adjusted to 161 Ohm. The output signal from the instrument amplifier circuit is then entered in the differential amplifier circuit, as shown in Figure 3.4.

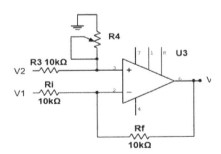

Figure 3.4. Differential amplifier

The differential amplifier circuit serves to locate the voltage difference between V1 and V2 which differenciate to the ground. Potentiometer in the Figure 3.4 that serves as a counterweight series. It can be seen that

$$Vo = \left(\left(\frac{Rf}{Ri}+1\right)\left(\frac{R2}{R1+R2}\right)V2\right) \cdot \left(\frac{Rf}{Ri}V1\right)$$ Where Rf=Ri=R2=R1=R, then the result is,

$$Vo = \left(\left(\frac{10}{10}+1\right)\left(\frac{10}{10+10}\right)V2\right) \cdot \left(\frac{10}{10}V1\right) \quad Vo = V2 = V1$$

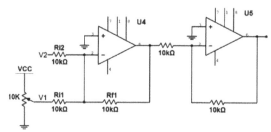

Figure 3.5. Inverting adder

Inverting adder circuit serves as input adder as shown in Figure 3.5. In this case inverting adder works as a circuit calibration (to reduce or decrease the initial load contained on conveyor belt). By changing the value of the potentiometer contained in inverting adder circuit, the load will start from zero.

3.4 Tachometer

The discs on this tachometer diameter are 2.6 cm, so can be determined the circumference by using the formula of circumference of a circle, namely:

$$\text{Circumference} = 2\pi r = \pi D$$

$$= 3{,}14 \times 2{,}6cm$$

$$= 8{,}164cm$$

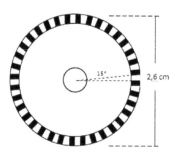

Figure 3.6. Tachometer disc

As illustrated in Figure 3.6, tachometer discs consisting of 24 holes, with a 15° angular distance between holes. Therefore, when the disc rotates one full rotation (24 holes) it is equal to move as far as 8.164 cm. By knowing the circumference of this disc, the conveyor belt speed can calculate the comparison between distance with time. This calculation is performed at the speedo coding contained in the microcontroller program.

Here is exemplified when a rotating conveyor belt can detect the rotation of the tachometer as much as half a round (12 holes = 4.082 cm) in one second, the speed of the conveyor belt are:

$$v = \frac{s}{t} \tag{1}$$

$$v = \frac{4{,}082}{1}$$

$$v = 4{,}082 \text{ cm/sec}$$

3.5 Motor Driver

The motor driver as an actuator regulates the supply voltage DC motor so that the speed can be controlled is shown in Figure 3.7. This circuit receives the PWM signal from the microcontroller via optocoupler. This optocoupler will distribute a variable voltage on the gate of MOSFET so that the current I_{DS} changes in their work area. Optocoupler also serves as an insulator to secure microcontroller.

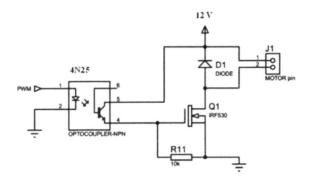

Figure 3.7. Motor Driver

3.6 Visual Basic Program 2010

Algorithm programming in Visual Basic 2010 are as follows:

a) Configuration Setting and connect to serial port.

b) Enter the value of set-point flow rate.

c) Send the "v" protocol to activate PWM.

d) Send the set-point value.

e) Activate timer.

f) Send the "x" protocol for PV data.

g) Read the PV data and display.

h) Send the "y" protocol for MV data.

i) Read MV data and display.

j) Send the "w" protocol to stop PWM.

3.7 FIS Design

By seeing to flow rate reference value in 1000 and 2000 grams / minute, it can be estimated that dynamics of the process that will occur in each of the variables; (E) and (CE) in the range of [-2000 2000]; and (U) in the range of [-20 20]. Wherein (E) is the difference between the set-point with the reading of the flow rate, and (U) is the amount of compensation for the value of PWM.

There are 81 variable compositions to be used as training data are entered on the ANFIS which are entered in the editor ANFIS Matlab toolbox in order to know the target output in Figure 3.8.

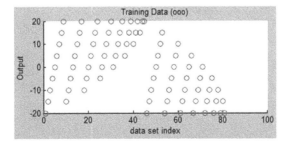

Figure 3.8. Plot training data of ANFIS

Through the configuration process of FIS generates which are entered in the editor toolbox matlab generated plots membership function of input variables E and CE as in Figure 3.9 and Figure 3.10.

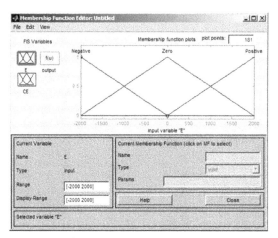

Figure 3.9. Plot membership function of E Variable

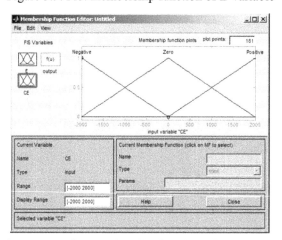

Figure 3.10. Plot membership function of CE Variable

It is known according to the Figure 3.9 and Figure 3.10 that, the type of membership function negative, zero, and positive use trimf.

From the training process based on the data input / output with error tolerance of 0.0001 and epoch in 1000 resulted in the training error of 2,4227e-06. In the form of graphs it can be seen from the plot the training error in the Figure 3.11.

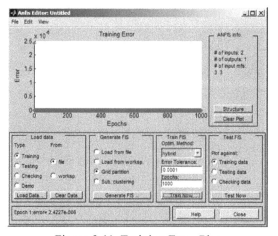

Figure 3.11. Training Error Plot

ANFIS training process based on the data input / output to produce an adaptation of the parameters of the MF and 9 fuzzy rules with the parameters in Table 3.3 and 3.4 as follows:

Table 3.3. FIS input Parameter

Variabel *Input*	Himpunan fuzzy	Parameter anteseden		
		a	b	c
E	Negative	-4000	-2000	0
	Zero	-2000	0	2000
	Positive	0	2000	4000
CE	Negative	-4000	-2000	0
	Zero	-2000	0	2000
	Positive	0	2000	4000

By choosing the constant output type then it will obtain consequent parameters as shown in Table 3.4.

Table 3.4. FIS output parameters

Rule No.	k
1	-20
2	-20
3	-20
4	-1,521e-011
5	6,471e-012
6	-5,987e-013
7	20
8	20
9	20

3.8 Microcontroller Program

In the process of data transmission between notebook and microcontrollers, communication parameters need to be adjusted to each other. Communication protocol that is sent from the notebook is received by the microcontroller on the register UDR. The structure of data transmission to the source code is as follows:

```
while(UCSRA.7) //Waiting for new data
{
 from_VB=toascii(UDR); //converse the UDR data and save
if (from_VB == 'x')
{
 printf("%ux", (unsigned int) (PVX*10)); //send PV dat
}
else if (from_VB == 'y')
{
   printf("%uy",(unsigned int)OCR0);
   //Send MV data
}
else if (from_VB == 'v')
{
   TCCR0 = 0x65; //Start PWM
}
else if (from_VB == 'w')
{
```

```
  TCCR0 = 0x00; //Stop PWM
}
else
{
  SV=from_VB*100; //Set-point value
}}
```

3.9 Source Code FLC

The parameters of input / output of FIS are applied to some function block programming. Source codes in basic language are created through software Visual Basic 2010 is as follows: Private Sub input1 () 'a representation of the membership function

If i <= a1 Then

      alpA = 0

ElseIf i >= a1 And i <= b1 Then

      alpA = (i - a1) / (b1 - a1)

ElseIf i >= b1 And i <= c1 Then

      alpA = (c1 - i) / (c1 - b1)

ElseIf i > c1 Then

        alpA = 0

End If

End Sub

4. Data Testing and Analysis

4.1 Weighing Function Tests

According to the value of ADC data it can be determined the value of x which is ADC value in the range of (25-109), and y is the weighing value in the range of (0-300), so we can get the linier equation for $y = 3,5714x - 89,2857$. This equation will later be implemented in the source code of ADC to get the weighing variable value validity such as in the Table 4.1.

Table 4.1. Weighing Variable Validity

Static Weigh (gram)	ADC	Reading of weigh(gram)	Error (%)
0	25	0,00	0,00
50	38	46,43	7,145
100	57	99,99	0,002
150	65	142,86	4,76
200	81	192,94	3,53
250	91	235,80	5,68
300	109	300,08	0,03
Average Error (%)			3,021

4.2 Belt Conveyor Speed Function Testing

Speed function testing give some variation the value of PWM in 10 times taking obtained from the data in the Table 4.2.

Table 4.2. Belt conveyor speed data testing

		PWM (10)	PWM (15)	PWM (20)	PWM (25)
Speed	of	0,34	1,02	3,4	4,76
belt		0,34	1,7	3,4	4,76

conveyor	0,34	1,36	3,4	4,42
(cm/sec)	0,68	1,7	3,74	5,1
	0,34	2,04	3,4	4,76
	0,34	1,7	3,4	4,76
	0,34	2,04	3,74	5,1
	0,34	1,7	3,4	4,76
	0,34	2,04	3,4	5,1
	0,68	1,7	3,4	4,76

4.3 Validation of Flow Rate

Validation of the flow rate is intended to determine the function of flow rate values calculated based on a constant load and speed. Flow rate value is obtained by using the formula :

$$I = Q * V \qquad (2)$$

With I : Flow rate (kg/s)

Q : Belt load (kg/m)

V : Belt speed (m/s)

By providing a static load of 200 grams and a PWM value of 20, then it will obtain logging data of flow rate for one minute as it shown in the following chart in Figure 4.1.

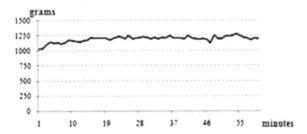

Figure 4.1. Flow rate validation

From the logging data obtained through a validation process for one minute can be calculated the flow rate value of the average - average which is 1193.4 grams / minute.

4.4 ANFIS Testing

ANFIS testing has an aim to get the training error tolerant value at the maximum of 0.0001 in 3000 times training epoch. This ANFIS testing is done based on the training data composition and FIS configuration.

By seeing to the flow rate reference value of 1000 and 2000 grams / minute, it can be estimated that dynamics of the process are will occur in each of the variables; (E) and (CE) in the range of [-2000 2000]; and U in the range of [-20 20].

From the experimental results of FIS configuration it is known the value of the smallest training error is 2,4227e-06. Training error value is derived from the type of membership function and an output triangle with the number of inputs to the first epoch of 3x3.

Antecedent parameter values obtained in the input variables E and CE as in the Table 4.3.

Table 4.3 FIS input Parameter

Input Variable	Fuzzy Set	Antecedent Parameter		
		a	b	c
E	Negative	-4000	-2000	0
	Zero	-2000	0	2000

	Positive	0	2000	4000
	Negative	-4000	-2000	0
CE	Zero	-2000	0	2000
	Positive	0	2000	4000

From the nine rules obtained we can get consequent parameter value on the output variables which are presented in Table 4.4.

Table 4.4. FIS output Parameter

Aturan ke-	k
1	-20
2	-20
3	-20
4	-1,521e-011
5	6,471e-012
6	-5,987e-013
7	20
8	20
9	20

4.5 FLC Testing

FLC testing give reference value/set-point in the amount of 1000 gr/minute and 2000 gr/minute. The first testing on the set-point of 1000 gr/ minute we can get trending flow rate and FLC output as shown in Figure 4.1.

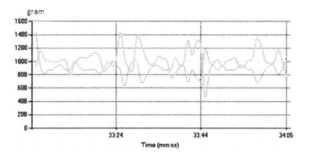

Figure 4.1. Trending on set-point of 1000 gr/mnt

By doing several times of testing on the set point of 1000 gr/min we can get the total result of weighing every one minute as in Table 4.4.

Table 4.4. Total Weighing per minute on the set point of 1000 gr/min

Test	Total Weight (gram)	*Error* (%)
1	1023	2.3
2	1055	5.5
3	1012	1.2
4	1034	3.4
5	1029	2.9
6	1072	7.2
7	1017	1.7
8	1042	4.2
9	1038	3.8
10	1064	6.4
Average *Error* (%)		3.86

Testing on the set-point of 2000 gr/min will get trending flow rate and FLC output as shown in Figure 4.2.

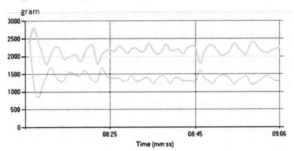

Figure 4.2. Trending on the set-point of 2000 gr/min

Tests on set-point in 2000 gr / min showed total weighing every one minute as in Table 4.5.

Table 4.5. Total weighing per minute on the set-point of 2000 gr/min

Test	Total Wight (gram)	*Error* (%)
1	2098	4.9
2	2105	5.25
3	2096	4.8
4	2101	5.05
5	2094	4.7
6	2108	5.4
7	2113	5.65
8	2087	4.35
9	2095	4.75
10	2109	5.45
Average *Error* (%)		5.03

From the FLC testing based on the given set point has total weighing error in every minute. On the set point of 1000 gr/min has average errors of 3,86% and for the set point of 2000 gr/min has an average errors of 5,03 % The existence of those errors are caused by the dynamics of fluctuate flow rate and the response if FLC.

This study is actually to support previous results focusing on Neuro-Fuzzy in renewable energies (Garcia, 2014), health monitoring (Agrawal, 2013), developing model (Bisht, 2011), information security (Altaher, 2012), edge detection technique   (Bhardwaj, 2013), temperature and humadity system (Ramesh, 2015). Other advantages of the fuzzy can also be found on automatic RNA virus classification (Dogantekin, 2013), and predicting the volumes of Chaotic Traffic (Yeh, 2012).

In sort, ANFIS (Adaptive Neuro-Fuzzy Inference System) is quiet prominant to sustain technology advancements and develop better advantages.

5. Conclusion

5.1 Conclusion

From the activities of the final of the task that has been done can be taken some conclusions as follows:

1. Validation of the flow rate can indicate a dynamic flow rate which can be used as reference data in determining the composition of the process variables to design FLC controllers using ANFIS.

2. ANFIS testing based on the data composition training has fulfilled the error tolerant limit so that we can form FIS design programmed based on the research results parameter.

3. FIS design implementation into the visual basic programming 2010 has a valid output value compared to the editor of ANFIS rule viewer. Those out values represent FLC validity which is programmed in microcontroller.

4. ANFIS can make it easier to determine the design parameters of FIS, so that the performance of the

controller can be adjusted based on the conditions of plant dynamics.

5. Overall the flow rate control system in weight feeder conveyor is working in accordance with the principle of close loop control, where the FLC controller is able to control the flow rate with total sampling results of weighing for one minute which is considered as good. Their error total weighing and oscillating flow rate is more influenced by the mechanical construction of the conveyor belt as well as friction or dynamic loads.

5.2 Suggestion

For more improvement and fixing the performance of the system that has been created it is then necessary to recommend:

Composition ANFIS training data can be augmented by sampling data from the dynamics of the process of flow rate directly to enhance the performance of the controller of FLC.

FIS configuration can be customized further by modifying the number and type of membership function and the type of output to generate value with smaller training error.

The stability of control process of flow rate in weight feeder conveyor can be increased based on the type or types of controllers which are better, for example by using artificial intelligent-based controllers or online neuro fuzzy.

References

Agrawal, A. T., & Ashtankar, P. S. (2013). Adaptive Neuro-Fuzzy Inference System for Health Monitoring at Home. *International Journal of Advanced Science and Technology, 55.*

Altaher, A., Almomani, A., & Ramadass, S. (2012). Application of Adaptive Neuro-Fuzzy Inference System for Information Secuirty. *Journal of Computer Science, 8*(6), 983-986, 2012 ISSN 1549-3636. © 2012 Science Publications.

Bhardwaj, K., & Mann, P. S. (2013). Adaptive Neuro-fuzzy Inference System (ANFIS) Based Edge Detection Technique. *International Journal for Science and Energing Technologies with Latest Trends, 8*, 7–13.

Bisht, D., & Jangid, C. S. (2011). Discharge Modelling using Adaptive Neuro - Fuzzy Inference System. *International Journal of Advanced Science and Technology, 31.*

Dogantekin, E., Avci, E., & Erkus, O. (2013). Automotic RNA Virus Classification using the Entropy-ANFIS Method. *Digital Signal Processing. Elsevier, 23*(4), 1209-1215.

Garcia, P., Garcia, C. A., Fernandez, L. M., & Llorens, F. (2014). ANFIS Based Control of a Grid-Connected Hybrid System Integrating Renewable Energies, Hydrogen and Batteries. *IEEE Transactions on Industrial Informatics, 10*(2), 1107-1117.

Kusumadewi, S. (2006). Neuro - Fuzzy Integrasi Sistem Fuzzy dan Jaringan Syaraf, Graha Ilmu, Jakarta.

Nazaruddin, Y. Y., dan Meiriansyah, A., & Pengontrol, P. I. (2009). Swatala Berbasis Neuro - Fuzzy, Skripsi, Kelompok Keahlian Instrumentasi dan Kontrol - Program Studi Teknik Fisika ITB, Bandung.

Ramesh, K. A., Kesarkar, P., Bhate, J., Ratnam, M. V., & Jayaraman, A. (2015). Adaptive neuro-fuzzy inference system for temperature and humidity profile retrieval from microwave radiometer observations. *Atmos. Meas. Tech., 8*, 369–384.

Saputro, C. A. (2007). Kendali Self Tuning Fuzzy PI Pada Pengendalian Weight Feeder Conveyor, Skripsi, Jurusan Teknik Elektro Fakultas Teknik Universitas Diponegoro, Semarang.

Widodo, S., T. (2005), Sistem, Neuro Fuzzy, Graha Ilmu, Yogyakarta.

Yeh, J. P., & Chang, Y. C. (2012). Comparison between Neural Network and Adaptive Neuro-Fuzzy Inference System for Forecasting Chaotic Traffic Volumes. *Journal of Intelligent Learning Systems and Applications, 2012*(4), 247-254

8

Iterative Soft Permutation Decoding of Product Codes

Mohamed Askali[1], Fouad Ayoub[2], Idriss Chana[1] & Mostafa Belkasmi[1]

[1] MohammedV-Souisi University, SI2M Labo, ENSIAS, Rabat, Morroco

[2] CRMEF, Kenitra, Morroco

Correspondence: Mohamed Askali, MohammedV-Souisi University SI2M Labo, ENSIAS, Rabat, Morroco. E-mail: askali11@gmail.com/ayoubfouadn@gmail.com/idrisschana@gmail.com/belkasmi@ensias.ma

Abstract

In this paper the performance of product codes based on quadratic residue codes is investigated. Our Proposed Iterative decoding SISO based on a soft permutation decoding algorithm (SPDA) as a component decoder. Numerical result for the proposed algorithm over Additive White Gaussian Noise (AWGN) channel is provided. Results show that the turbo effect of the proposed decoder algorithm is established for this family of quadratic residue codes.

Keywords: soft decoding, error correcting codes, turbo code, product codes, Iterative decoding, quadratic residue codes

1. Introduction

The turbo codes were invented in 1993 by Berrou, Glavieux and Thitimajshima, who had used the concatenation of convolutional codes, the elementary decoder BCJR (Bahl, Cocke, Jelinek and Raviv Algorithm) and SOVA (Soft output Viterbi Algorithm) as a soft output. Two years later, Pyndiah et al [4] presented an alternative for bloc codes using the product code based on BCH (Bose, Ray Chaudhurand Hocquenghem) codes, the Chase II algorithm, as a component decoder, and the Pyandiah's soft output generated according to the formula presented in. Since turbo codes have been subject of many publications for instance. The turbo codes have attracted the interest of the scientific community, especially for their high speed transmissions over the air. The word turbo is much more related to decoding than encoding. To make a turbo decoding we will need three basic elements where the first is the concatenation of several simple codes, the second is to develop or adopt an efficient elementary decoder conducted by a soft output and the third element is a decoding scheme in which the soft output is converted to extrinsic information exchanged between the components decoders in an iterative process. The implementation and the performance of an efficient turbo decoder depend on the complexity of these three elements. In addition to the computation of the extrinsic information which has to be done in a very short time, and the convergence based on the number of iterations, we will need an elementary decoder less complex. In this perspective comes our work in which we use our soft permutation decoding algorithm (SPDA) proposed in [5] as an elementary decoder given the importance of performance results obtained by our decoder SIHO, and we compute its soft output using extrinsic information according to Soleymani et al. The result obtained in terms of BER is very interesting. The rest of the paper is organized as follow: *section II* presents the quadratic residue (QR) codes, section III *describes* the construction of product codes, section IV describes the original version of Soft permutation decoding algorithm (SPDA) for QR codes, section V talks about the Soft output and the Schema of the iterative decoding of Soleymani, finally, Simulation results and analyses are given in Section VI.

2. Quadratic Residue Codes and Their Stabilizers

The n is a prime and $n \equiv \pm 1 \pmod 8$, the quadratic residue code $QR(n) = QR\left(n,(n+1)/2,d\right)$ is a cyclic code

with a generator polynomial $g(x) = \prod_{i \in Q}(x - \beta^i)$, where $Q = \{j^2 \bmod n : 1 \le j \le n-1\}$ is the set of all nonzero quadratic residue integers modulo n and β is a primitive **n**th root of unity in GF(2^m), where m is the smallest

positive integer such that n divides 2^m - 1. A $QR(n)$ code, where d is odd, can be extended to a

$EQR(n)=EQR(n+1,(n+1)/2,d+1)$ code whose codewords are obtained by adjoining a parity-check bit to a fixed

position ∞ of every codeword of the $QR(n)$ code. For all values of n, the binary $EQR(n)$ is invariant under the

projective special linear group PSL$_2$(n), which we define as follows:

For a prime $n \equiv \pm 1 (\mod 8)$, the set of permutations over {0,1,2,...,n-1,∞}, of the form

$y \rightarrow (ay+b)/cy+d$ where a, b, c and d are elements of GF(n) verifying : ad-bc=1 form a group called the

projective special linear group G=PSL$_2$(n), of order $|G| = n.(n^2 -1)/2$. PSL$_2$(n) can be generated by the

three following permutations [3]: $S:y \rightarrow y+1$; $V:y \rightarrow \rho^2 y$; $T:y \rightarrow -1/y$. where ρ is a primitive element of GF(n).

By a theorem of Gleason and Prange, the automorphism group of an extended quadratic residue code has a

subgroup which is isomorphic to either PSL$_2$(n).

3. Product Codes

The product codes are constructed by concatenation of two or more linear block codes. We consider two basic

block codes C$_1$ and C$_2$ characterized by parameters (n$_1$, k$_1$, d$_1$,R$_1$) and (n$_2$, k$_2$, d$_2$,R$_2$) where n$_i$ represent the code

length, k$_i$ the length of the message d$_i$ the minimum distance Hamming and R$_i$ the code rate . The product code

$C_p = C_1 \times C_2$ is represented in the form of matrix with n$_1$ rows and n$_2$ columns. Where the information

forms a sub-matrix M of k$_1$ lines and k$_2$ columns, each of the lines k$_1$ from M is coded by the code C$_1$ and each of

the n$_1$ columns is coded by the code C$_2$. The resultant parameters of the product code C_p are

(n_p, k_p, d_p, R_p) where $n_p = n_1 \times n_2$, $k_p = k_1 \times k_2$ and $d_p = d_1 \times d_2$, the code rate is

$R_p = R_1 \times R_2$. An important Property of these codes is that if the n1 columns are by construction the C2's

code words, and k2 lines are C1's code words, the n1-k1 remaining lines of the resultant code word are C1's

code words. In other hand the major advantage of product codes is a gain in minimum distance, and their major

disadvantage is the loss in codes rate, subsequently, we consider that codes C1 and C2 are identical.

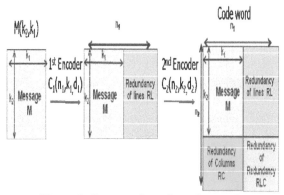

Figure 1. Construction of product code

4. Soft Permutation Decoding Algorithm (SPDA)

The SPDA algorithm proposed in [5], tries to find the closest codeword to the received word in terms of Euclidian distance. The algorithm works as shown below:

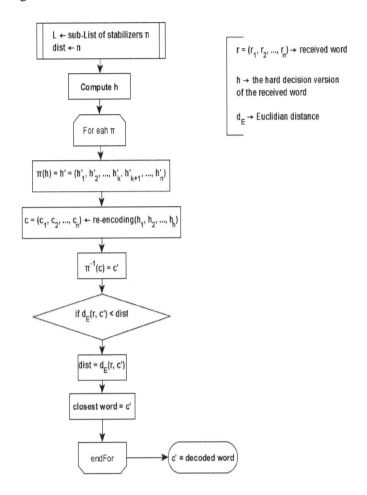

5. Soft Output and the Schema of the Iterative Decoding

5.1 Description of Confidence Value

The concept of confidence value designated by Φ is detailed in [4]. In this paragraph, we will simply give a brief description.

Let $X = \{x_0, x_1, ..., x_{n-1}\}$ be the transmitted code word, $\Phi = P\{D = X/R\}$ is the probability that the

decoder takes a correct decision $D = \{d_0, d_1, ..., d_{n-1}\}$ given the received sequence $R = \{r_0, r_1, ..., r_{n-1}\}$;

That is the assessment of the decision of the decoder. Computing Φ is impossible for a practical implementation, thus estimation has to be performed. To estimate Φ Soleymani et al are adopted a distance destructive denoted by

$Dist_{dest}$ as a metric between R and D where only the positions increasing the Euclidian distance contribute, i.e.

where the noise vector has a different polarity than the decision vector D, following.

$$Dist_{dest} = \sum_{j \in DES} (r_j - d_j)^2$$

$$where\ DES = \{ j \mid (r_j - d_j).d_j < 0 \}$$

(1)

There is a relationship between the confidence value Φ and the destructive Euclidean distance $Dist_{dest}$. Using software simulation according to [2] the influence of the variable **Eb/No** and the number of iterations may be omitted, and treat the confidence value **Φ** as a function of destructive Euclidean distance, written as:

$$\Phi = f(Dist_{dest})$$

(2)

Table 1 below resumes the function between $Dist_{dest}$ and **Φ** for some used residue codes (RQ) codes.

Table 1. Confidence Value "Φ" Versus Distance destructive

QR(23,12,7)	DEST								
		<9	9	10	11	12	13	14	15	>15
	Φ	0.99	0,97	0,95	0,91	0,72	0,5	0,36	0,33	0
QR(41,21,9)	DEST								
		<15	16	17	18	19	20	21	22	>22
	Φ	0.99	0.98	0.95	0.89	0.76	0.55	0.29	0.14	0.00
QR(47,24,11)	DEST								
		<27	27	28	29	30	31	32	33	>33
	Φ	0.99	0,95	0,93	0,84	0,71	0,53	0,21	0,12	0

5.2 Computing Soleymani's Soft Output

In this subsection we give the computation of the soft output as it's described in [2] by Soleymani et al. Recall that $X = \{x_0, x_1, ..., x_{n-1}\}$ is the transmitted Codeword, the symbol x_j $j \in \{0, ..., n-1\}$ has certain confidence value **Φ**. The probability of x_j can be expressed as:

$$P(x_j = \pm 1 \mid R) = P(x_j = \pm 1, D = X \mid R)$$
$$+ P(x_j = \pm 1, D \neq X \mid R)$$

(3)

The first term represents the probability value when the decoder gives a correct codeword. applying Bayes' rule to this term will yield

$$P(x_j = \pm 1, D = X \mid R) = P(x_j = \pm 1, D = X, R).P(D = X, R)$$
$$= P(x_j = \pm 1, D = X, R).\Phi \tag{4}$$

Since the decision bit d_j is known, then

$$P(x_j = \pm 1, D = X \mid R) = \begin{cases} \phi \; if \; d_j = x_j \\ 0 \; if \; d_j \neq x_j \end{cases} \tag{5}$$

The second term in (3) represents the probability value when the decoder decides in favor of a wrong codeword. In this case, we consider the transmitted symbol x_j is corrupted with Gaussian noise. Thus

$$P(x_j = 1, D \neq X) = \frac{\exp\left(\pm 2r_j \big/ \sigma^2\right)}{1 + \exp\left(\pm 2r_j \big/ \sigma^2\right)} \tag{6}$$

Again, we apply Bayes 'rule to the second term in (3) and get :

$$P(x_j = \pm 1, D \neq X \mid R) = P(x_j = \pm 1, D \neq X, R).P(D \neq X \mid R) = \frac{\exp\left(\pm 2r_j \big/ \sigma^2\right)}{1 + \exp\left(\pm 2r_j \big/ \sigma^2\right)}.(1 - \Phi) \tag{7}$$

Combining (3)-(7), the a posteriori probability of x_j is found as:

$$P(x_j = +1 \mid R) = \begin{cases} \phi + \dfrac{\exp\left(+2r_j \big/ \sigma^2\right)}{1 + \exp\left(+2r_j \big/ \sigma^2\right)}.(1 - \Phi) \; if \; d_j = +1 \\[4mm] \dfrac{\exp\left(+2r_j \big/ \sigma^2\right)}{1 + \exp\left(+2r_j \big/ \sigma^2\right)}.(1 - \Phi) \; if \; d_j = -1 \end{cases} \tag{8}$$

And

$$P(x_j = -1 \mid R) = \begin{cases} \dfrac{\exp\left(-2r_j \big/ \sigma^2\right)}{1 + \exp\left(-2r_j \big/ \sigma^2\right)}.(1 - \Phi) \; if \; d_j = +1 \\[4mm] \phi + \dfrac{\exp\left(-2r_j \big/ \sigma^2\right)}{1 + \exp\left(-2r_j \big/ \sigma^2\right)}.(1 - \Phi) \; if \; d_j = -1 \end{cases} \tag{9}$$

Similar to the traditional algorithm described in previous section, we can obtain the extrinsic information W_j by the following equation

$$\omega_j = \frac{\sigma^2}{2} \ln\left(\frac{P(x_j = +1 \mid R)}{P(x_j = -1 \mid R)}\right) - r_j \tag{10}$$

Substituting $P(xj = +1|R)$ and $P(xj = -1|R)$, we get

$$\omega_j = d_j \left(\frac{\sigma^2}{2} \ln\left(\frac{\Phi + \exp\left(2r_j.d_j \big/ \sigma^2\right)}{1 - \Phi}\right) - r_j d_j\right) \tag{11}$$

Unlike other list-based algorithms, soft outputs generated by (10) can be directly fed into the next decoding stage.

5.3 Iteratif Decoding Scheme

Soleymani's algorithm is intended for decoding turbo product codes; it may be considered an improvement of the chase algorithm / Pyndiah. Indeed, in their algorithm Soleymani et al. adopt the same elementary decoder that Pyndiah is that of Chase-II, by calculating the soft output based on the list of candidates provided by the elementary decoder "ie Chase-II" and the weighting factors α and β. While Soleymani base its calculation of Soft output decision on elementary decoder while rejecting the other candidates, and by evaluating the decision depending on its distance from the received word, to assign the value of trust **Φ** previously described. The latter is used to calculate the extrinsic information.

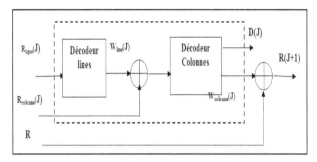

Figure 2. Iteration Jth du Turbo decodeur

Figure.2 present the **Jth** itération of Soleymani's Turbo decoder. The **R$_{line}$(J)** are the rows of the matrix **R(J)**, where **R(0)** is received at the matrix output channel. The **R$_{line}$(J)** are decoded by the first component decoder (rows decoder). And extrinsic information **W$_{line}$ (J)** of the iteration J is calculated using the formula (11). **W$_{line}$** is added to the received word **R** to form the second component of the soft input decoder for decoding **R$_{column}$(J)** which represent the columns of the matrix **R (J)** (column decoder). This allows us to get a hard decision **D (J)** and the extrinsic information **W$_{column}$(J).** For the next iteration, **W$_{column}$** is added to the original received matrix R to form a matrix R (J + 1), which in turn must be injected into the first component decoder. This operation, which injects **R(J + 1),** to be repeated, and by default, it will become **R(J).** This iterative process stops when the maximum number of iterations is reached.

6. Simulations & Results

6.1 Permutations Effect on the Elementary Decoder

The Figure 3 shows that the increase of the number of the stabilizers improves the performances.

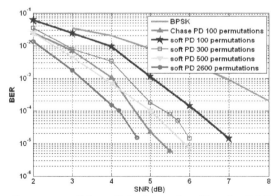

Figure 3. The performances of the soft decision algorithm for EQR(48,24,12) code

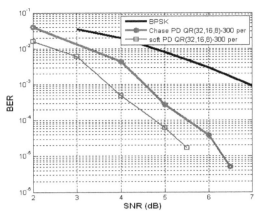

Figure 4. Comparaison between Chase PD and the soft decision algorithm for EQR (32,16,8) code

When the soft decision of permutation decoding algorithm works with 2600 stabilizers, for all values of the SNR, it is better than the Chase-2 decoding algorithm with 32 test sequences. The gain of coding is about 0.5 dB. As we see in the Figures 4, the performances of the soft decision of PD are equal or better than the Chase PD for the EQR(32,16,8).

6.2 Permutations Effect on the SISO Decoder

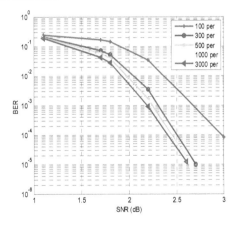

Figure 5. Effect of the number of permutations on the proposed SISO for QR (47,24,11)2 code

In Figure 5, we present the simulation results for the RQ (47, 24, 11)2 code for different numbers of stabilizers of the code. Its show that the gain depends on the number of the permutations and the improvement becomes negligible when the number of permutations is greater than 1000.

6.3 Turbo Effect

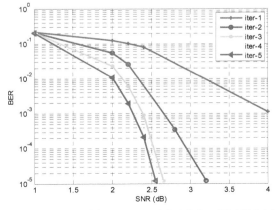

Figure 6. Turbo effect of the proposed SISO for QR(47,24,11)^2 code

The turbo effect: Figure 6 shows that the performances increase with number of iterations. According to these Figures we can see that the improvement is great after the first iterations. So, we note that the turbo effect of the proposed SISO is established for this family of codes.

7. Conclusion

In this paper, we have presented a new iterative decoding SISO of product codes based on quadratic residue codes. We have studied the effect of the number of permutations which stabilize QR codes, the number of iterations using simulations. As perspectives of this work, we will challenge other families of codes to be decoded by our iterative SISO decoder.

References

ASKALI, M., NOUH, S., & BELKASMI, M. (2012). A Soft decision version of the Permutation Decoding Algorithm", NTCCCS 12 workshop, 26-28, Oujda, Morocco.

Ayoub, F., Belkasmi, M., & Chana, I. (2010). Iterative Decoding of Generalized Parallel Concatenated OSMLD Codes. *Applied Mathematical Sciences Journal, 4*(41), 2021-2038.

Ayoub, F., Lahmer, M., Belkasmi, M., & Bouyakhf, El. H. (2010). Impact of the decoder connection schemes on iterative decoding of GPCB codes. *International Scholarly and Scientific Research & Innovation, 4*(1), 739-745.

Belkasmi, M., & Farchane, A. (2008). Iterative decoding of parallel concatenated block codes", Proceedings of ICCCE'08, Kuala Lumpur, Malaysia.

Belkasmi, M., Lahmer, M., & Benchrifa, M. (2006). Iterative Threshold Decoding of Parallel Concatenated Block Codes, Turbo Coding Conf, Munich.

C. Berrou, A., Glavieux, P., & Thitimajshima (1993). Near Shannon limit error correcting coding and decoding: Turbo Codes", IEEE Int. Conf. on Communications, ICC, 2, 1064-1070.

Chase, D. (1972). A class of algorithms for decoding block codes with channel measurement information. IEEE. Trans. *Inform. Theory, IT*(18), 170-182.

Elias, P. (1954). Error-free coding, IRE. Trans. *Inf. Theory, IT*(4), 29-37.

Fossorier, M. P. C., & Lin, S. (1995). Soft decision decoding of linear block codes based on ordered statistics, IEEE Trans. *Information Theory, 41*, 1379-1396.

Le, N., Soleymani, A. R., & Shayan, Y. R. (2005). Distance-based-decoding of block turbo codes. *IEEE Communications Letters, 9*(11).

Lucas, R., Bossert, M., & Breitbach, M. (1998). On Iterative Soft-Decision Decoding of Linear Binary Block Codes and Product Codes. *IEEE Journal on selected areas in communications, 16*(2), 276-296.

Pyndiah, R. (1998). Near optimum decoding of product codes: Block Turbo Codes. *IEEE Trans. on Communications, 46*, 1003–1010.

9

Robust Content-Based Digital Image Watermarking Scheme in Steerable Pyramid Domain

Khadija Jamali[1,2], Mohamed El Aroussi[2], Azz El Arab El Hossaini[1,2], Samir Mbarki[1] & Mohammed Wahbi[2]

[1] Departement of Computer Science, Faculty of Science, Ibn Tofail University, Kenitra, Morocco

[2] Department of Electrical Engineering, Hassania School of Public Works, Casablanca, Morocco

Correspondence: Khadija Jamali, Departement of Computer Science, Faculty of Science, Ibn Tofail University, Kenitra, Morocco. E-mail: jamalikhadija@gmail.com

Abstract

In the digital world in which we are living, the intellectual property protection becomes a concern especially with the proliferation of files transfer over networks. The ability to access data such as text, images, video, and audio has become quicker and easier for people with little to no knowledge of technology. In this paper, a robust watermarking scheme based on the original image content is proposed and simulated. Steerable pyramid transform is used as an embedding domain to its good spatial-frequency characteristics, and its wide applications in the image/video coding standards. The embedding process aims to insert some information in a digital document to identify its owner later. This process requires the original image to be protected and the watermark image related to the image's owner. It needs also a threshold value used by Sobel-Feldman operator to extract the original image features. The embedding of the watermark image is performed in high frequency components of the original image. Experimental evaluation demonstrates that the proposed watermarking scheme is able to withstand a variety of attacks and at the same time provide good visual quality of the watermarked image.

Keywords: watermarking, robustness, steerable pyramid transform, geometric attacks

1. Introduction

With the extreme development of network technology and internet, the protection of intellectual property and authentication become very important. To secure and limit the illegal distribution of digital images, many solutions are proposed in the literature. Among these solutions, only watermarking technologies can protect the digital content after been received by a user.

Digital watermarking is an advantageous solution to aforementioned issues (Cheddad, A., Condell, J., Curran, K., & Mc Kevitt, P, 2010). Image watermarking technologies consist on hiding secret information in an image called original image or host image. The inserted information is called watermark, and the image where the watermark is inserted, is called watermarked image or protected image. Thereafter, the watermark could be extracted or detected in order to use it if necessary to verify ownership and/or to distinguish product user.

According to human perception, watermarking schemes can be classified as visible or invisible watermarking. A Visible watermarking scheme means that the watermark can be seen on the protected image by human perception. For a better protection, the inserted watermark should be invisible. Indeed, a visible watermark can easily be modified or erased by another watermark. Thereby, ensuring the invisibility of the watermark returns to respect the visual quality of the proposed product. For this reason, several existing watermarking schemes as the proposed watermarking scheme in this paper tend to perform insertion into the less sensitive areas of interest to the human perception.

Digital image watermarking is performed in spatial or frequency domains. Spatial domain schemes are based on direct manipulation of pixels to embed a watermark. Such schemes are simple and fast to implement, although they are not robust against the majority of attacks. Compared to the spatial domain, transform domain schemes, for instance discrete wavelet transforms (DWT), discrete cosine transforms (DCT), and Discrete Fourier Transform (DFT), and Fourier–Mellin transform, singular value decomposition (SVD), are more robust against attacks. This is due to the fact that the image is transformed to its frequency representation to embed the watermark.

Several watermarking schemes using different concepts are proposed in the literature. Authors in (W. Lin, S. Horng, T. Kao, P. Fan, C. Lee, Y. Pan, 2008), Propose a scheme based on significant difference of wavelet coefficient quantization. DWT has also attracted interest, (B. Ma, Y. Wang, C. Li, Z. Zhang, D. Huang, 2012) designed a robust watermarking method where the watermark is distributed on the maximum positive and minimum negative coefficients. (S. Wang, Y. Lin, 2004) proposed a wavelet-tree-based watermarking scheme; the wavelet coefficients are grouped into so-called super trees. The insertion is done by quantizing super trees. (W. Lin, Y. Wang, S. Horng, T. Kao, Y. Pan, 2009) enhances the robustness of the scheme by inserting the watermark in the local maximum coefficient. (Li, C., Zhang, Z., Wang, Y., Ma, B., & Huang, D., 2015) designed a scheme that represents a dither modulation of significant amplitude difference for wavelet based robust watermarking. Differently from the above schemes, (Yahya, A. N., Jalab, H. A., Wahid, A., & Noor, R. M., 2015) use discrete wavelet and probabilistic neural network to guarantee the robustness while preserving good impeccability. By combining Fuzzy Logic and Discrete Cosine Transform, (Jagadeesh, B., Kumar, P. R., & Reddy, P. C, 2015) realize a robust digital image watermarking technique. (Agarwal, C., Mishra, A., & Sharma, A, 2015) implement a robust image watermarking scheme to embed a permuted binary watermark in gray-scale images.

Based on steerable pyramid and the original image content, this paper proposes a robust watermarking scheme. Firstly steerable pyramid transform is used to decompose the original image into several subbands to choose the low subband that will carry the watermark image. Areas to be watermarked are chosen based on the image contents that are less sensitive to the human eye. The embedding of the watermark image is performed in high frequency components of the original image that are extracted by using Sobel-Feldman operator to extract. After embedding the watermark image, the inverse steerable pyramid is performed to get the watermarked image.

The rest of this paper is organized as follows. Section 2 describes the steerable pyramid transform which is a multi-scale, multi-orientation transform. Section 3 covers the details of the watermark insertion and detection scheme. Results in Section 4 will show the high performance of our scheme in terms of robustness and impermeability. Finally, Section 5 concludes the paper.

2. Embedding Domain

In the proposed watermarking scheme, the watermark image is inserted in multiresolution domain that represents a very interesting watermarking space. In this approach, the original image is sub-sampling recursively until reaching the desire result. The original image is filtered using a low pass filter to forming a new image whose size is four times smaller. This process attempts to mimic the natural mechanism of resolution visual loss effect.

In this paper, we use the Steerable Pyramid transform introduced by (Freeman, W. T., & Adelson, E. H, 1991) as the embedding domain for our proposed watermarking scheme as we did for several watermarking schemes that are already published in the literature. Among them, we can cite the following works, In (Jamali, K., El Aroussi, M., El Hossaini, A. E. A., Mbarki, S., & Wahbi, M, 2014) we presented a robust scheme using steerable pyramide, to embed the watermark, firsty the steerable pyramid transform is applied on the both of the watermark and host image. Then deferently to others scheme we choose to insert the watermark on all levels and all orientations of the pyramid. This scheme is robust against cropping attack, for the reason that the watermark is inserted several times, the watermark is detected from the remaining part. In (Hossaini, E., El Arab, A., El Aroussi, M., Jamali, K., Mbarki, S., & Wahbi, M. (2014), we presented a new, robust digital watermarking scheme for ownership protection. In the watermarking process and after performing steerable pyramid on the original image, two independent streams representing the watermark are embedded in low and mid-frequency of DCT components. Watermark detection is based on comparison result between Pearson product moment correlations of the two independent streams with each watermarked block. In (El Hossaini, A. E. A., El Aroussi, M., Jamali, K., Mbarki, S., & Wahbi, M, 2014), we proposed a highly robust digital image watermarking scheme based on steerable pyramid transform and dual encryption technique. Before the embedding process a pretreatment on the watermark image is performed to enhance the security using Arnold transform and a proposed encryption function. The host image is decomposed into steerable pyramid coefficients and the low-subband is selected to receive the encrypted watermark. The same Keys used during the embedding process are also used during the extraction process. Unlike traditional watermarking schemes, in (El Hossaini, A. E. A., El Aroussi, M., Jamali, K., Mbarki, S., & Wahbi, M, 2016) we proposed a watermarking method that does not alter the original image by embedding the watermark image. Steerable pyramid transform is performed on the original image, and the low sub-band is selected. The watermark image is divided into two random looking images, called private and public shares using the visual secret sharing scheme and the selected low sub-band features. To reveal the watermark image, the two shares are stacked together.

In(Jamali, K., El Aroussi, M., El Hossaini, A. E. A., Mbarki, S., & Wahbi, M, 2014) we presented a robust scheme using steerable pyramide, to embed the watermark, firsty the steerable pyramid transform is applied on the both of the watermark and host image. Then deferently to others scheme we choose to insert the watermark on all levels and all orientations of the pyramid. This scheme is robust against cropping attack, for the reason that the watermark is inserted several times, the watermark is detected from the remaining portion.

The Steerable Pyramid transform is a linear multi-scale, multi-orientation image decomposition that provides a useful front-end for image-processing and computer vision applications (Freeman, W. T., & Adelson, E. H, 1991). Unlike other existing pyramid transform as laplacian pyramid and Gaussian pyramid, the number of scales and directions is variable.

The block diagrams for analysis and synthesis decomposition are shown in Figure 1 and Figure 2. The steerable pyramid transform uses three types of filters: low-pass (L0), high-pass (H0), and pass-bands (B0... BK). By using the low-pass and high-pass filters, the image is separated into low and high-pass subbands. Then, the lowpass subband is further decomposed into a set of oriented band-pass subbands and a low-pass subband. And finaly, this low-pass subband is subsampled by a factor of 2 in the X and Y directions, and a new decomposition is performed until reaching the scale fixed by the user.

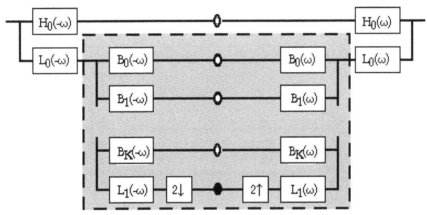

Figure 1. Tree representation of one-level 2D steerable pyramid transform

Figure 2. Tree Cameraman steerable pyramid-based image decomposition

3. The Proposed Watermarking Scheme

In general, a watermarking scheme is divided into two basic parts: the embedding and the detection of the watermark.

The embedding process aims to insert some information in a digital document to identify its owner later. This process requires the original image to be protected and the watermark image related to the digital document's owner. Another optional parameter called secret key may be used if necessary in some cases where the proposed watermarking schemes needs to scramble the watermark image to overcome some securities issues. The secret key could be used also to formatting the watermark image or to locating areas in which the embedding process should be performed (Lee, C. H., & Lee, Y. K, 1999).

The embedding process in our proposed watermarking scheme needs the original image, the watermark image and the threshold value used by Sobel-Feldman operator to extract the original image features. The embedding of the watermark image is performed in high frequency components of the original image. These components are represented by edges which give details to images and make the watermark scheme more robust to the majority of attack because these details will remain present in the watermarked image even if several degradations occur on it. Moreover, digital image pirates will not be interested in stealing an image that has being seriously distorted (because it becomes worthless).

The proposed watermarking scheme in this article is classified as non-blind watermarking schemes. To extract the watermark image previously inserted in the original image, the watermark extraction process needs the original image, the watermarked image and the secret key represented by the threshold value used by Sobel-Feldman operator.

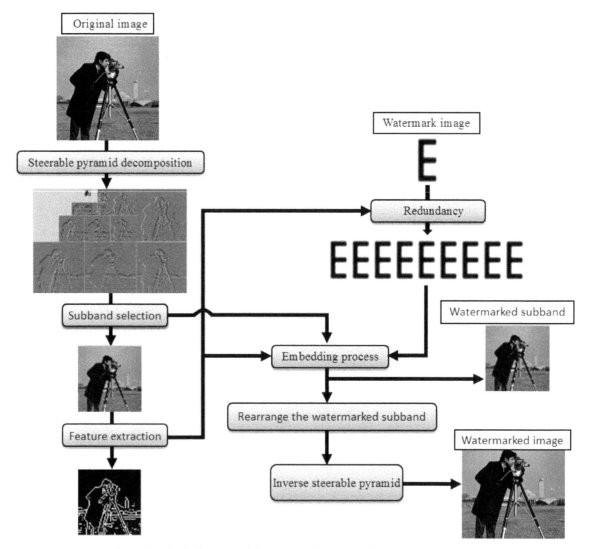

Figure 3. Block diagram of the proposed watermark embedding scheme

3.1 Watermark Embedding Process

The process of watermark embedding is shown in Figure 3, and the detailed algorithm is given as follows:

Step 1) The low subband Lsb is selected after decomposing the original image Oi into several subbands using one scale and two orientations steerable pyramid transform.

Step 2) Based on threshold value T1, the low subband features Lsf are extracted by performing Sobel-Feldman operator.

$$L_{sf} = sobel\_edge\_detection(O_i, T_1)$$ (1)

Step 3) The watermark image can be inserted several times in the original image if its size is less than the total number of extracted edge pixels. The watermark image Wo is formatted to a new Watermark image Wr using a redundancy process that duplicate the original image R times.

$$R = \frac{total\ number\ of\ extracted\ edge\ pixels}{total\ number\ of\ watermark\ image\ pixels}$$ (2)

Where **R** is the number of watermark redundancy.

Step 4) for each edge pizels location in Lsf the equation 3 is used to embed the formatted watermark's bit of value 1 and equation 4 is used to embed the formatted watermark's bit of value 0.

$$L_{sbw}(i,j) = L_{sb}(i,j) - alpha$$ (3)
$$L_{sbw}(i,j) = L_{sb}(i,j) + alpha$$ (4)

alpha   : is the watermark strength that must be adjusted to compromise between robustness and   visibility of the watermark.

L_{sbw}(i,j)   : represent a pixel value in the watermarked low subband.

L_{sb}(i,j)   : represent a pixel value in the original low subband.

i,j   : represent edge pizels location in Lsf.

Step 5) After rearranging each subband to its initial location, the watermarked image is obtained by performing the inverse steerable pyramid transform.

3.2 Watermark Extraction Process

The process of watermark extraction is shown in Figure 4, and the detailed algorithm is given as follows:

Step 1) The low subband L_{sb} is selected after decomposing the original image O_i into several subbands using one scale and two orientations steerable pyramid transform.

Step 2) The same as the step 2 in the embedding process, the low subband features L_{sf} are extracted by performing Sobel-Feldman operator.

Step 3) the same as step 3 in the embedding process, calculate the number **R** that represent the number of watermark redundancy.

Step 4) Construct an empty matrix W_{fe} of size **R** times the size of the original watermark.

Step 5) The low subband L_{wsb} is selected after decomposing the watermarked image O_w into several subbands using one scale and two orientations steerable pyramid transform.

Step 6) for each edge pixels location in L_{sf}, the formatted watermark W_{fe} is extracted as follow:

$$W_{fe} = \begin{cases} 0, & if\ (L_{wsb} - L_{sb}) < 0 \\ 1, & if\ (L_{wsb} - L_{sb}) >= 0 \end{cases}$$ (5)

Step 7) Divide the extracted W_{fe} image into **R** blocks of the same size as the original watermark. Then calculate the average of the **R** blocks and perform a threshold to make a decision of each watermark's bit.

$$W_e(a,b) = \begin{cases} 1, & if\ avg(\sum_{k=1}^{R} Block_k(a,b)) > Threshold \\ 0, & if\ avg(\sum_{k=1}^{R} Block_k(a,b)) <= Threshold \end{cases}$$ (6)

Where W_e is the extracted watermark, and *(a,b)* is the location of one pixel.

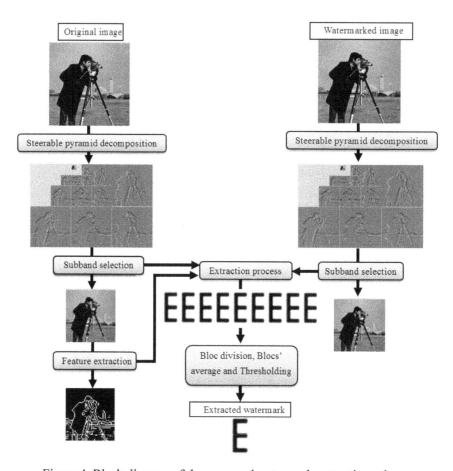

Figure 4. Block diagram of the proposed watermark extraction scheme

4. Experimental Results

In this section we present the experimental results of the proposed watermarking scheme and we compare its performance with the results reported in other existing watermarking schemes.

To get optimal results, some tests are performed to choose optimal configuration settings for the proposed watermarking scheme. Table 1 and Table 2 present various results based on the quality of the obtained watermarked images and the extracted watermarks. These results are obtained by testing different number of filters and scales using the Einstein test image for Table 1 and the Cameraman test image for Table 2. From results in Table 1 and Table 2 we can see that our algorithm obtains better performance when using: one scale / two filters, two scales / one filter and two scales / two filters.

Table 1. NC and PSNR values using different number of scales and filters for Einstein and Cameraman image.

Einstein image				Cameraman image			
Number of scales	number of filter	PSNR (dB)	NC	Number of scales	number of filter	PSNR (dB)	NC
1	1	51.2895	0.9756	1	1	46.9305	1
1	2	48.0474	1	1	2	44.8357	1
1	4	48.1691	0.9969	1	4	45.0036	1
1	6	47.2767	0.9937	1	6	44.3003	1
2	1	49.4362	1	2	1	50.0355	0.9937
2	2	46.0881	1	2	2	46.0196	1
2	4	46.0676	1	2	4	45.9653	1
2	6	44.5125	0.9969	2	6	43.2525	0.9969
3	1	51.3001	0.9969	3	1	52.9769	0.9713

3	2	45.9120	0.9969	3	2	45.0242	0.9841
3	4	45.7946	0.9969	3	4	44.7877	0.9713
3	6	43.2829	0.9969	3	6	41.0016	0.8751
4	1	54.9405	0.9727	4	1	54.5913	0.9152
4	2	45.0246	0.9557	4	2	43.5148	0.9129
4	4	44.7729	0.9464	4	4	43.0730	0.9193
4	6	41.8308	0.8599	4	6	39.8229	0.7690
5	1	57.5026	0.5396	5	1	56.4748	0.4990
5	2	39.2322	0.4593	5	2	40.0926	0.4224
5	4	39.1915	0.4593	5	4	39.7250	0.4246
5	6	38.0444	0.3899	5	6	37.0135	0.3914

Table 2. NC and PSNR values using different number of scales and filters for different images.

| Images | one scale and two filters | | two scales and one filter | | two scales and two filters | |
	PSNR	NC	PSNR	NC	PSNR	NC
Goldhill	44.4756	1	47.1695	1	43.1861	1
Lena	45.3607	1	48.3115	1	45.0064	1
Peppers	40.3727	1	47.5341	0.9876	37.9530	1
Barbara	43.7066	1	47.2353	1	42.7938	1
Baboon	39.7874	1	47.6290	0.9969	35.6088	1
Einstein	48.0474	1	49.4362	1	46.0881	1
Cameraman	44.8357	1	50.0355	0.9937	46.0196	1

To make a decision about the number of scales and filters to use by our watermarking scheme, we performed more tests using other popular images (Goldhill, Lena, Peppers, Barbara and Baboon). These tests and its results are shown in Table 3 in which we used various parameters (one scale / two filters, two scales / one filter and two scales / two filters). By considering the quality of the obtained watermarked images and the extracted watermarks, the following parameters are selected for the steerable pyramid transform: number of filters = 2 and number of scales = 1.

4.2 Imperceptibility of the wWatermark

To evaluate the impact of the embedding process on the watermarked image in terms of imperceptibility, we applied our proposed watermarking scheme on seven grayscale images (Goldhill, Lena, Peppers, Barbara, Baboon, Einstein and Cameraman) using a binary watermark image represented by the letter "E".

Table 3 displays the host image, the watermark image, the watermarked image and the extracted watermark. . In our experiments, The PSNR (Peak Signal to Noise Ratio) values obtained are above 46 dB for all test images which demonstrates a high imperceptibility of the watermark method.

$$PSNR = 10\,log_{10}\frac{255^2}{MSE} \qquad (7)$$

Where MSE (Mean Square Error) is defined as:

$$MSE = \frac{1}{N}\sum_{i=1}^{N}(I_i - ?_i)^2 \qquad (8)$$

Where N represents the number of pixels in the original (I) and watermarked ($\hat{I}$) image.

Table 3. The original image, the watermark image, the watermarked image, and the extracted watermark using our scheme

Original Image	Watermark image	Watermarked image	Extracted watermark	PSNR

Goldhill		E		E	43.1861
Lena		E		E	45.0064
Peppers		E		E	37.9530
Barbara		E		E	42.7938
Baboon		E		E	35.6088
Einstein		E		E	46.0881
Cameraman		E		E	46.0196

4.3 Robustness

The robustness of the proposed technique is validated against several attacks like JPEG compression, rotation, Gaussian noise, Speckle noise, Salt and pepper noise, Gaussian filter, Median filter, Average filter, Sharpening and Cropping. The steerable pyramid parameters used in our experiments are: number of scales = 1 and number of orientations = 2. The test images used are: Lena, Cameraman, Einstein and Zelda. In this work, we used the normalized correlation (NC) to measure the similarity between the original W and the extracted watermark $\widehat{W}$.

$$NC = \frac{\sum_{i=1}^{M} W_i \widehat{W}_i}{\sqrt{\sum_{i=1}^{M} W_i^2} \sqrt{\sum_{i=1}^{M} \widehat{W}_i^2}} \tag{9}$$

The Bit error rate (BER) is used too as the NC to evaluate the robustness of watermark.

$$BER = \frac{\sum_{i=1}^{N} \widehat{W}_i \oplus W_i}{M} \tag{10}$$

Where M is the total size of the watermark and $\oplus$ is the xor operator.

The NC values of the extracted watermarks are very close or equal to 1 for the majority of results and the BER values are close or equal to 0. These results demonstrate that our scheme is robust against all attacks used in these experiments.

Table 4. NC and BER values of the extracted watermark under different attacks

Attack	Image	NC	BER
JPEG (Q= 90)	Lena	1	0
	Cameraman	1	0
	Einstein	1	0
	Zelda	1	0
JPEG (Q= 75)	Lena	1	0
	Cameraman	1	0
	Einstein	1	0
	Zelda	1	0
JPEG (Q= 50)	Lena	1	0
	Cameraman	1	0
	Einstein	1	0
	Zelda	1	0
JPEG (Q =25)	Lena	1	
	Cameraman	0.9937	0.0091
	Einstein	1	0
	Zelda	0.9969	0.0045
JPEG (Q =10)	Lena	0.9571	0.0636
	Cameraman	0.9485	0.0773
	Einstein	1	0
	Zelda	0.9665	0.0500
Rotation (180°)	Lena	1	0
	Cameraman	1	0
	Einstein	1	0
	Zelda	1	0
1% Gaussian noise	Lena	0.9330	0.1000
	Cameraman	0.8917	0.1545
	Einstein	0.9132	0.1364
	Zelda	0.9485	0.0773
Speckle noise 0.01	Lena	0.9845	0.0227
	Cameraman	0.9845	0.0227
	Einstein	0.9937	0.0091
	Zelda	0.9235	0.1182
Salt & pepper noise (density 0.03)	Lena	0.9542	0.0682
	Cameraman	0.9534	0.0682
	Einstein	0.9538	0.0682
	Zelda	0.9401	0.0864
Gaussian filter	Lena	0.9906	0.0136
	Cameraman	0.9167	0.1273
	Einstein	0.9641	0.0545
	Zelda	0.9815	0.0273
Median filter (aperture=3.0)	Lena	1	0
	Cameraman	0.9969	0.0045
	Einstein	0.9937	0.0091

	Zelda	1	0
Median filter (aperture=5.0)	Lena	0.9906	0.0136
	Cameraman	0.9448	0.0864
	Einstein	0.9845	0.0227
	Zelda	0.9727	0.0409
Weiner filter (aperture=3.0)	Lena	1	0
	Cameraman	1	0
	Einstein	1	0
	Zelda	1	0
Average filter 3x3	Lena	1	0
	Cameraman	0.9937	0.0091
	Einstein	0.9969	0.0045
	Zelda	0.9969	0.0045
Sharpening	Lena	0.9969	0.0045
	Cameraman	0.9213	0.1091
	Einstein	0.9815	0.0273
	Zelda	1	0
Crop (quarter from the center of the watermarked image and fill the missing portion with 0's	Lena	0.9143	0.1409
	Cameraman	0.8573	0.2591
	Einstein	0.9048	0.1591
	Zelda	0.8822	0.2045
Crop (quarter from the center of the watermarked image and fill the missing portion with host image	Lena	1	0
	Cameraman	0.9678	0.0455
	Einstein	0.9969	0.0045
	Zelda	0.9873	0.0182
Crop (quarter from the top right corner of the watermarked image and fill the missing portion with 1's	Lena	0.9937	0.0091
	Cameraman	0.9937	0.0091
	Einstein	0.9815	
	Zelda	0.9242	
			0.1227
Crop (quarter from the top right corner of the watermarked image and fill the missing portion with host image	Lena	1	0
	Cameraman	1	0
	Einstein	0.9969	0.0045
	Zelda	1	0
Crop (quarter from the top left corner of the watermarked image and fill the missing portion with 1's	Lena	0.9906	0.0136
	Cameraman	0.9815	0.0273
	Einstein	0.9815	0.0273
	Zelda	0.9584	0.0636
Crop (quarter from the top left corner of the watermarked image and fill the missing portion with host image	Lena	1	0
	Cameraman	1	0
	Einstein	0.9317	0.1091
	Zelda	1	0
Crop (quarter from the bottom right corner of the watermarked image and fill the missing portion with 0's	Lena	0.9937	0.0091
	Cameraman	0.8737	0.2227
	Einstein	0.9969	0.0045
	Zelda	0.9669	0.0500
Crop (quarter from the bottom right corner of the watermarked image and fill the missing portion with host image	Lena	1	0
	Cameraman	0.9937	0.0091
	Einstein	1	0
	Zelda	0.9969	0.0045
Crop (quarter from the bottom left corner of the watermarked image and fill the missing portion with 1's	Lena	0.9119	0.1455
	Cameraman	0.8933	0.1818
	Einstein	0.9475	0.0818
	Zelda	0.9786	0.0318
Crop (quarter from the bottom left corner of the watermarked image and fill	Lena	0.9808	0.0273

the missing portion with host image	Cameraman	1	0
	Einstein	1	0
	Zelda	1	0
Crop (half from the top of the watermarked image and fill the missing portion with 0's	Lena	0.9292	0.1136
	Cameraman	0.9529	0.0727
	Einstein	0.9192	0.1318
	Zelda	0.8613	0.2500
Crop (half from the top of the watermarked image and fill the missing portion with host image	Lena	0.9776	0.0318
	Cameraman	0.9873	0.0182
	Einstein	1	0
	Zelda	0.8035	0.2545
Crop (half from the right of the watermarked image and fill the missing portion with host image	Lena	1	0
	Cameraman	0.9905	0.0136
	Einstein	0.9513	0.0682
	Zelda	1	0
Crop (half from the left of the watermarked image and fill the missing portion with host image	Lena	0.8751	0.1682
	Cameraman	1	0
	Einstein	0.9937	0.0091
	Zelda	0.9968	0.0045

4.4 Comparison Results with Other Related Schemes

In order to assess the effeciency of the proposed watermarking scheme, results reported in some related other existing schemes (W. Lin, S. Horng, T. Kao, P. Fan, C. Lee, Y. Pan, 2008), (B. Ma, Y. Wang, C. Li, Z. Zhang, D. Huang, 2012), (S. Wang, Y. Lin, 2004), (W. Lin, Y. Wang, S. Horng, T. Kao, Y. Pan, 2009), (Li, C., Zhang, Z., Wang, Y., Ma, B., & Huang, D., 2015), (Yahya, A. N., Jalab, H. A., Wahid, A., & Noor, R. M., 2015), (Jagadeesh, B., Kumar, P. R., & Reddy, P. C, 2015) and (Agarwal, C., Mishra, A., & Sharma, A, 2015) are compared with our results. The comparison includes several attacks as Median filter, Sharpening, Gaussian filter, Salt & pepper, JPEG compression, Resizing, Rotation, and Cropping.

Our proposed watermarking scheme is compared to the other schemes based on the NC values reported in their results. Higher NC values indicate higher quality of the extracted watermark. As seen in Table 5, Table 6 and Table 7, most of NC results for our proposed watermarking scheme are higher than those reported by other scheme and that demonstrates the robusteness of the proposed watermarking scheme is far better and proves superiority over the other watermarking schemes.

Table 5. NC results comparison under different attacks using Lena image

	Median filter		Resize	Crop	Rotation		Sharpening	Gauss filter
	3 x 3	5 x 5	0.5	25%	-0.25	0.25		
(S. Wang… 2004)	-	-	-	-	0.32	0.37	0.46	0.64
(W. Lin… 2008)	0.88	0.74	0.86	0.70	0.67	0.67	0.99	0.86
(W. Lin… 2009)	0.90	0.76	0.88	0.66	0.60	0.59	0.97	0.88
(B. Ma .. 2012)	0.94	0.42	**0.98**	0.87	0.38	0.35	0.21	**1**
(Li, C… 2015)	0.93	0.57	0.97	0.88	0.47	0.42	0.47	0.99
Proposed scheme	**1**	**0.9906**	0.8025	**1**	**0.8768**	**0.8768**	**0.9969**	0.9906

'-' means the attacks are not done.

The bold values indicate the best values comparing with the others.

Table 6. NC results comparison under JPEG compression attacks using Lena image

	JPEG Compression								
	10	15	20	25	30	40	50	70	90
(S. Wang… 2004)	-	-	-	-	0.15	0.23	0.26	0.57	1
(W. Lin… 2008)	0.40	0.57	0.73	0.84	0.91	0.93	0.98	1	1
(W. Lin… 2009)	0.34	0.55	0.67	0.74	0.82	0.90	0.96	0.97	0.99

(B. Ma.. 2012)	0.44	0.77	0.91	0.95	0.99	1	1	1	1
(Li, C... 2015)	0.63	0.85	0.92	0.95	0.97	0.99	0.99	1	1
Proposed scheme	**0.9571**	**0.9786**	**0.9937**	**1**	**1**	**1**	**1**	**1**	**1**

'-' means the attacks are not done.

The bold values indicate the best values comparing with the others.

Table 7. NC results comparison under different attacks using Lena image

	Rotation			JPEG Compression			Cropping 25%		Med filter	Salt & pepper
	10°	5°	45°	70	50	10	upper side	lower side	3x3	1%
(Yahya...2015)	-	0.9251	0.8965	0.8451	0.7520	0.4395	0.6660	0.9023	0.9329	-
(Jagadeesh...2015)	0.7549	-	-	0.8940	-	-	0.6456	-	0.7890	0.6450
(Agarwal... 2015)	-	-	-	1	0.9931	0.4024	0.9734	-	0.9713	-
Proposed scheme	**0.8485**	0.8573	0.8768	1	**1**	**0.9571**	1	**1**	**1**	**0.9906**

'-' means the attacks are not done.

The bold values indicate the best values comparing with the others.

5. Conclusion

In this paper, a robust watermarking scheme based on the original image content has been proposed and simulated. In this work, the steerable pyramid transform is used as an embedding domain due to its good spatial-frequency characteristics.

The experimental results of the proposed watermarking scheme have shown high perceptual quality of the watermarked image. In addition to the perceptual quality, our scheme achieves a good robustness against different intentional and non-intentional attacks.

References

Agarwal, C., Mishra, A., & Sharma, A. (2015). A novel gray-scale image watermarking using hybrid Fuzzy-BPN architecture. *Egyptian Informatics Journal, 16*(1), 83-102. http://dx.doi.org/10.1016/j.eij.2015.01.002

Cheddad, A., Condell, J., Curran, K., & Mc Kevitt, P. (2010). Digital image steganography: Survey and analysis of current methods. *Signal Processing, 90*(3), 727-752. http://dx.doi.org/10.1016/j.sigpro.2009.08.010

El Hossaini, A. E. A., El Aroussi, M., Jamali, K., Mbarki, S., & Wahbi, M. (2014). Highly Robust Digital Image Watermarking Using Steerable Pyramid and Dual Encryption Technique. *International Review on Computers and Software (IRECOS), 9*(2), 255-265.

El Hossaini, A. E. A., El Aroussi, M., Jamali, K., Mbarki, S., & Wahbi, M. (2016) A New Robust Blind Copyright Protection Scheme Based on Visual Cryptography and Steerable Pyramid. *International Journal of Network Security, 18*(2), 250-262.

Freeman, W. T., & Adelson, E. H. (1991). The design and use of steerable filters. *IEEE Transactions on Pattern Analysis & Machine Intelligence,* (9), 891-906.

Hossaini, E., El Arab, A., El Aroussi, M., Jamali, K., Mbarki, S., & Wahbi, M. (2014). A New Robust Blind Watermarking Scheme Based on Steerable pyramid and DCT using Pearson product moment correlation. *Journal of Computers, 9*(10), 2315-2327. http://dx.doi.org/10.4304/jcp.9.10.2315-2327

Jagadeesh, B., Kumar, P. R., & Reddy, P. C. (2015). Fuzzy Inference System Based Robust Digital Image Watermarking Technique Using Discrete Cosine Transform. *Procedia Computer Science, 46*, 1618-1625. http://dx.doi.org/10.1016/j.procs.2015.02.095

Jamali, K., El Aroussi, M., El Hossaini, A. E. A., Mbarki, S., & Wahbi, M. (2014). A Robust Image Watermarking Scheme Using Steerable Pyramid Transform. *International Review on Computers and Software (IRECOS), 9*(10), 1750-1759. http://dx.doi.org/10.15866/irecos.v9i10.2238

Lee, C. H., & Lee, Y. K. (1999). An adaptive digital image watermarking technique for copyright protection. Consumer Electronics. *IEEE Transactions on, 45*(4), 1005-1015. http://dx.doi.org/10.1109/30.809176

Li, C., Zhang, Z., Wang, Y., Ma, B., & Huang, D. (2015). Dither modulation of significant amplitude difference for wavelet based robust watermarking. Neurocomputing. http://dx.doi.org/10.1016/j.neucom.2015.03.039

Lin, W., Horng, S., Kao, T., Fan, P., Lee, C., & Pan, Y. (2008). An efficient watermarking method based on significant difference of wavelet coefficient quantization. *IEEE Transactions on Multimedia, 10*(5), 746–757. http://dx.doi.org/10.1109/TMM.2008.922795

Lin, W., Wang, Y., Horng, S., Kao, T., & Pan, Y. (2009). A blind watermarking method using maximum wavelet coefficient quantization. *Expert Systems with Applications, 36*(9), 11509–11516. http://dx.doi.org/10.1016/j.eswa.2009.03.060

Ma, B., Wang, Y., Li, C., Zhang, Z., & Huang, D. (2012) A robust watermarking scheme based on dual quantization of wavelet significant difference, in: Proceedings of Pacific-Rim Conference on Multimedia (PCM). http://dx.doi.org/10.1007/978-3-642-34778-8_28

Wang, S., & Lin, Y. (2004). Wavelet tree quantization for copyright protection watermarking. *IEEE Transactions on Image Processing, 13*(2), 154–165.

Yahya, A. N., Jalab, H. A., Wahid, A., & Noor, R. M. (2015). Robust watermarking algorithm for digital images using discrete wavelet and probabilistic neural network. *Journal of King Saud University-Computer and Information Sciences, 27*(4), 393-401. http://dx.doi.org/10.1016/j.jksuci.2015.02.002

10

Self-Organizing Map Learning with Momentum

Huang-Cheng Kuo[1] & Shih-Hao Chen[1]

[1] National Chiayi University, Taiwan

Correspondence: Huang-Cheng Kuo, Department of Computer Science and Information Engineering, National Chiayi University, Chia-Yi City 600, Taiwan. E-mail: hckuo@mail.ncyu.edu.tw

Abstract

Self-organizing map (SOM) is a type of artificial neural network for cluster analysis. Each neuron in the map competes with others for the input data objects in order to learn the grouping of the input space. Besides competition, neighbor neurons of a winning neuron also learn. SOM has a natural propensity to cluster data into visually distinct clusters, which show the intrinsic grouping of data.

The self-organizing map algorithm is heuristic in nature and will almost always converge. Since self-organizing map may be trapped in a local optimum, so we introduce momentum into the learning process thus the movement of a neuron may jump over local optimum. We expect this will be similar to the learning of neurons in back-propagation with momentum. Like the learning process in back-propagation, the timing for updating the amount of movement of a neuron is either batch mode or incremental mode. However, due to the neighborhood function, the movement of a non-winner neuron is relatively small as compare to when it is a winner. So when deciding the momentum, the previous movement of a neuron needs special consideration. Experiment result show that adding momentum to self-organizing map considerably contributes to the acceleration of the convergence.

Keywords: self-organizing map, clustering, learning with momentum

1. Introduction

Cluster analysis (Richard et al., 1990) groups similar data objects into clusters. Clustering algorithms differ in the data type that they can handle and the result that they produce. Some clustering algorithms handle multidimensional data and some handle any data format as long as the similarity among data objects can be derived. For example, hierarchical clustering algorithms need only the similarities among the data objects, and density-based clustering algorithms requires the distances among data objects. Only multidimensional data type can be processed by self-organizing map (SOM) clustering algorithms. K-means clustering produces exactly the specified number of clusters. Clusters produced by density-based clustering algorithms can be in arbitrary shape. Hierarchical clustering algorithms give a dendrogram without specifying the number of clusters. SOM clustering algorithms produce a map of neurons where each neuron is associated with varying number of data objects.

Self-organizing map (Kohonen, 1982) is a competitive learning based clustering neural networks. Neurons on the map compete with each other for each input data. Generally, the self-organizing map (Kohonen, 2001) requires thousands of learning iterations to converge in order to search the optimal solution. Due to the nature of learning and searching, SOM has the possibility to get stuck in a local optimum. So, we incorporate the momentum term into the learning process of SOM (Masafumi, 1996). The idea appears in some other methods, such as the back-propagation algorithm (Vogl et al., 1988). The momentum term effectively accelerates the learning of the back-propagation algorithm (Hagiwara, 1992). In this paper, we discuss the timing for updating the momentum term in the self-organizing map which is not mentioned in the work by Masafumi. Analog to the batch mode and incremental mode for updating the weight vectors in back-propagation algorithm (Mitchell, 1997), we propose a batch mode algorithm and an incremental mode algorithm for updating the momentum term. Momentum term is the product of momentum coefficient and the previous updating amount of a neuron. However, in SOM, a non-winner neuron updates its weight vector. If the non-winner neuron is not so close to the winner, the amount of update is very tiny. In order to keep a reasonable amount of momentum, the definition of momentum term is revised as the product of momentum coefficient and the momentum mass of a neuron. Momentum mass is defined on the amount of weight vector updating of a neuron. We propose a batch mode algorithm and an incremental mode algorithm to determine the momentum mass. We performed experiments and the result shows the quantization error decreases for SOM with momentum.

2. Related Work

Clustering (Kaufman, 1991) partitions a set of data objects into clusters. Objects in a cluster are similar to each another and are dissimilar to objects in other clusters. A good clustering method produces high quality clusters with high intra-class similarity and low inter-class similarity. Dissimilarity and similarity metric is expressed in terms of a distance function. The quality of clustering result depends on the similarity measure used by the method. Usually, for multidimensional data, Euclidean distance or Manhattan distance is adopted as the definition of distance function.

Major clustering methods can be classified into the following categories. The partitioning methods (Han, 2001) partition the given set of data objects into some groups. Then, the medoid of each group is computed. Each data object is re-assigned to a group whose medoid is closest to the data object. Then process iterates until there is no new re-assignment. A well-known partitioning method is k-means (Alsabti, 1988). The hierarchical methods (Carpinteiro, 2000) create a dendrogram of the given data objects. A hierarchical clustering method can be either agglomerative or divisive. Agglomerative hierarchical clustering algorithm initially treats a data object as a singleton cluster. Then, the algorithm iteratively merges two closest clusters into a cluster. There is a need to define the similarity between two clusters. The density-based method (Ankerst et al., 1999; Ester et al., 1996) is based on connectivity and density functions. A data object is called a core if there are enough neighboring data objects. Two parameters specified by the users are the minimum number of neighbors and the radius. Two data objects are called neighbors if the distance between them is within the radius. The grid-based method (Wang et al., 1997) quantizes the object space into a finite number of cells that form a gird structure. The model-based method (Dasgupta, 1998) hypothesizes a model for each cluster and finds the best fit of the data to the given model.

3. Method

3.1 Self-Organizing Map

Self-organizing map is an extensively used method. It is a common type of artificial neural network in which the neurons learn iteratively through competing for the input data, and through the cooperation with the neighboring neurons. A particular feature of self-organizing map is that it typically reduces multi-dimensional data to a low-dimensional grid of nodes, making them easy to visualize the result. In the self-organizing map, each map node has a unique coordinate. It represents a cluster of input vector. Self-organizing map algorithm matches a given input vector to its best matching unit (Lippmann, 1987). The best matching unit acts on the optimal fit ant its neighbors using a neighborhood function. Self-organizing map uses Euclidean distance as the distance between a neuron and an input vector. For an input vector, the neuron having the shortest distance from the input vector among all the neurons is called the winning neuron.

The weight vector of the wining neuron is updated toward the input vector. And its topological neighbors also move toward the input vector in the input space. The weight vectors are updated according to the following equation:

$$W_j(t+1) = W_j(t) + \alpha(t) \times \left(x(t) - W_j(t) \right) \times h_{j^*}(t) \tag{1}$$

where t is the index of the current iteration and the regression is performed for each presentation of a sample of x, denoted x(t), and $0 < \alpha(t) < 1$ is the learning rate which decreases monotonically with the regression iterations. The $h_{j^*}(t)$ is the neighborhood function which is taken as the Gaussian

$$h_{j^*}(t) = exp\left(- d^2_{j,j^*}/2R^2(t)\right) \tag{2}$$

where d^2_{j,j^*} is the distance between the map locations j and j^*, R(t) is the neighborhood radius. During an iteration, both α(t) and R(t) decrease exponentially. The decay functions for the learning rate and neighborhood radius are α(t) = α $\times$ exp(-t/T) and R(t) = R $\times$ exp(-t/T), where α, R, and T are the initial learning rate, the initial radius, and the maximum number of the iterations, respectively.

Generally, the learning process of neural networks is very slow, therefore self-organizing map requires thousands of iterations to converge.

The quantization error (QE) of a training sample is defined as the distance from the input vector to its best matching neuron in the self-organizing map. The convergence process measures the sum of quantization error. The sum of quantization error is following equation:

$$\sum_{x \in D} \left(\arg\min_j \sqrt{\sum_i (x_i - W_{ji})^2} \right), \tag{3}$$

where D is the set of input vectors, j is a neuron, i is the dimensional index of input vectors.

The momentum term effectively accelerates the learning of the back-propagation algorithm (Hagiwara, 1992). In order to effectively accelerate the reduction of quantization error, momentum term has been incorporated into the learning process of SOM (Masafumi, 1996). However, learning process was not thoroughly discussed. Analog to the batch mode and incremental mode for updating the weight vectors in back-propagation algorithm (Mitchell, 1997), we propose a batch mode algorithm and an incremental mode algorithm for updating the momentum term.

3.2 Learning with Momentum Term

Momentum term is the product of momentum coefficient and the previous movement of a neuron. The amount of movement of a neuron differs a lot, depending on whether the neuron is winner or not, and depending on the distance from the neuron to the winner. However, conventional self-organizing map with momentum term does not consider whether the previous movement is large or small. The movement of a neuron becomes previous movement immediately after the input vector is processed. We denote such conventional self-organizing map with momentum term as immediate mode momentum term algorithm. In the following subsections, we will propose a batch mode momentum term algorithm and an incremental mode momentum term algorithm.

Let D be the set of data objects. A grid size of $N_x \times N_y$ is considered as in standard self-organizing map. Let $N_x \times N_y = M$ be a set of neurons. Each neuron is associated with a weight vector which has the same dimensionality of input vectors. The elements in the weights are initialized with values between 0 and 1.

3.2.1 Momentum Term

The momentum term is used to speedup network training and to avoid local optimal. A neuron moves toward the location of an input sample that it wins. When the neuron or its neighbor wins an input sample, it moves along with its previous direction as well as toward the location of the new input sample. In other words, the previous moving direction has some effect on the movement of a neuron. The momentum term of such effect is determined by a coefficient and the previous amount of movement of the neuron. The coefficient is called momentum coefficient, which is between 0 and 1. The amount of movement of a neuron can be rewritten as the following equation:

$$\Delta W_j(t) = \alpha(t) \times \left(x(t) - W_j(t) \right) \times h_{j^*}(t) + m(t) \times \Delta W_j(t-1) \tag{4}$$

Update neuron's weight vector:

$$W_j(t+1) = W_j(t) + \Delta W_j(t) \tag{5}$$

where m(t) is the momentum coefficient at iteration t.

Typically neurons in a network use the same momentum coefficient. Momentum coefficient usually changes from iteration to iteration. In most cases, momentum coefficient decreases over time. Momentum coefficient decreases with the formula m(t) = m × exp(-t/T), where m is the initial value of the momentum coefficient. The initial momentum coefficient affects the learning process, so we use two values, i.e., 0.5 and 0.8, in the experiments to observe the effect.

SOM with momentum term was proposed by Masafumi. The algorithm always uses the previous amount of update of a neuron to compute the momentum term, no matter the neuron was a winner or not. Also, the momentum coefficient is fixed. The algorithm is as follows:

1 Initialize grid size N_x and N_y, learning rate α, neighborhood radius R, momentum coefficient m and the number of iterations T.

2 for each iteration t in T do

3     $\alpha(t) = \alpha \times exp(-t/T), R(t) = R \times exp(-t/T), m(t) = m \times exp(-t/T)$

4   for each input data x in D do

5   find the winning neuron. Let the winner neuron be j*.

6   for each neuron j

7   calculate $\Delta W_j(t)$ using equation (4)

8   update neuron's weights, using equation (5)

9   end

10   end

11 end

3.2.2 Batch Mode

When considering the momentum for the learning of a neuron, the momentum is the product of momentum coefficient and the previous movement of the neuron. In the learning of a neuron in back-propagation, the momentum is determined by the momentum coefficient and the previous movement of the neuron. The previous movement is somehow steady, so there is no special need to consider whether the previous movement is reasonable. However, in SOM, the previous movement of a neuron might be large if the neuron was the winner for the previous input vector, and might be small or even no movement due to neighborhood function if the neuron was not the winner. In average, the probability that a neuron wins two consecutive input vectors is $1/n$, where n is the number of neurons. In other words, in most of the time, if there is no special treatment on this previous movement of a neuron, it will be near none, which results in no momentum effect.

We denote this previous movement of a neuron for computing momentum as movement mass. So, the momentum is the product of momentum coefficient and movement mass.

For discussing the batch mode momentum term, we need the concept of iteration of learning. An iteration of learning process is that each input vector in the dataset is processed once. Each neuron accumulates its own movement. The movement of a neuron is accumulated only when it is the winner for the input vector. At the end of an iteration, in other words, after all the input vectors have been processed once, the accumulated movement of each neuron is averaged by the number of input vectors won by the neuron. Then, the averaged movement of each neuron becomes the new movement mass of the neuron. Therefore the amount of weight values can be rewritten as the following equation

$$\Delta W_j(t) = \alpha(t) \times \left(x(t) - W_j(t) \right) \times h_{j^*}(t) + m(t) \times \widetilde{\Delta W_j}(t-1) \qquad (6)$$

where $\widetilde{\Delta W_j}(t-1)$ is the average $\Delta W_j(t-1)$ when the neuron j won in the $(t-1)^{\text{th}}$ iteration. If a neuron did not win any input vector in previous iteration, this momentum term is 0.

Its algorithm is as follows:

1 Initialize grid size N_x and N_y, learning rate α, neighborhood radius R, momentum coefficient m and the number of iterations T.

2 for each iteration t in T do

3     $\alpha(t) = \alpha \times exp(-t/T), \text{R}(t) = R \times exp(-t/T), m(t) = m \times exp(-t/T)$

4   for each input data x in D do

5   find the winning neuron. Let the winner neuron be j*.

6   for each neuron j

7   calculate $\Delta W_j(t)$ using equation (6)

8   update neuron's weight, using equation (5)

9   if j is the winner, record $\Delta W_j(t)$ in order to compute $\widetilde{\Delta W_j}(t)$.

10   end

11   end

12   compute $\widetilde{\Delta W_j}(t)$ for each neuron

13 end

3.2.3 Incremental Mode

In this incremental mode algorithm, the amount of movement mass of a neuron is updated immediately after the neuron wins an input vector. Therefore the amount of weight values can be rewritten as the following equation:

$$\Delta W_j(t) = \alpha(t) \times \left(x(t) - W_j(t) \right) \times h_{j^*}(t) + m(t) \times \widetilde{\Delta W_j}(t-1), \qquad (7)$$

where j^* is the winning neuron, $\widetilde{\Delta W_j}(t-1)$ is the movement mass. The movement mass of the winning neuron is updated, i.e., $\widetilde{\Delta W_j}(t) = \Delta W_j(t)$.

Its algorithm is as follows:

1 Initialize grid size N_x and N_y , learning rate α, neighborhood radius R, momentum coefficient m and the number of iterations T.

2 for each iteration t in T do

3    $α(t) = α \times exp(-t/T), R(t) = R \times exp(-t/T), m(t) = m \times exp(-t/T)$

4   for each input data x in D do

5   find the winning neuron. Let the winner neuron be j*.

6   for each neuron j

7   calculate $\Delta W_j(t)$ using equation (4)

8   if j is winner, update movement_mass for neuron j, using equation (7)

9   update neuron's weights, using equation (5)

10   end

11   end

12 end

4. Results

4.1 Measurement Method

We carry out the studies on the impact of momentum term. Two convergence measures are used. The first measure is to calculate the quantization error (QE) of an input vector. QE is the Euclidean distance of the input vector and the beast matching neuron. Sum of the squared QE is minimized for given training vectors.

Another convergence measure method assumes the number of clusters is known in advance. Let *k* be the number clusters in the following discussion. The size of a neuron is defined as the number of input vectors won by the neuron after the final iteration. The method selects the largest *k* neurons, called seed neuron. Each input vector won by the small neurons is assigned to the closest seed neuron. Input vectors are now partitioned into *k* clusters. Centroid of each cluster is computed. The convergence measure is sum of the squared error (SSE). The SSE as following equation:

$$\sum_{i=1}^{k} \sum_{x \in C_i} \|x - m_i\|^2 \tag{8}$$

where *k* is the number of clustering, C_i is the i-th cluster, m_i is the clustering center, x is the data.

The SSE is to calculate all data points corresponding to the sum of its distance from the cluster center and differences. We repeat all experiments 30 times and then take the average of the 30 runs.

4.2 Data Sets

In this paper, we use two data sets, Iris and Wine, from the UCI machine learning repository (Newman et al., 1988) to carry out experiments.

4.2.1 Iris

The iris data set consists of four dimensions with small variance. The dimensions are the petal length, the petal width, the sepal length, and the sepal width. Each object belongs to one of the three classes. There are 150 training instances in the data set. Each attribute is normalized with z-score method. The evaluation of QE was carried out for self-organizing map ($15 \times 15 = 225$ model and 3000 iterations, respectively.) The neighborhood function of the self-organizing map was a two-dimensional Gaussian. Figures1- 4 show the QE and SSE which are plotted as the function of iteration, where learning rate α = 0.01, α = 0.001, and α = 0.0001, momentum m = 0.5 and m = 0.8, respectively. In each of the Figures, we compare the performance of the four methods, i.e., the original self-organizing map algorithm without momentum term, self-organizing map with immediate mode momentum term, self-organizing map with batch mode momentum term, and self-organizing map with incremental mode momentum term. In the Figures, the methods are denoted as w/o momentum, immediate mode, batch mode, and incremental mode.

4.2.2 Wine

The measurements consist of thirteen dimensions. The class attribute has 3 values. There are 178 instances in the data set. Each attribute is normalized with z-score method. The evaluation of QE was carried out for the self-organizing map ($10 \times 10 = 100$ model and 3000 iterations, respectively.) The neighborhood function is a Gaussian centered in the winner neuron. The neighborhood size, learning rate and momentum coefficient decreases exponentially during training. Experiment was conducted on original self-organizing map without momentum term, self-organizing map with immediate mode momentum term, self-organizing map with batch mode momentum term, and self-organizing map with incremental mode momentum term which were trained with 3000 iterations. After learing, Figures 5 to 8 show the QE and SSE which are plotted as the function of iteration, where learning rate $\alpha = 0.01$, $\alpha = 0.001$, and $\alpha = 0.0001$, momentum coefficient m = 0.5 and m = 0.8, respectively. In each of the Figures, we compare the performance of the four methods.

4.3 Statistics and Data Analysis

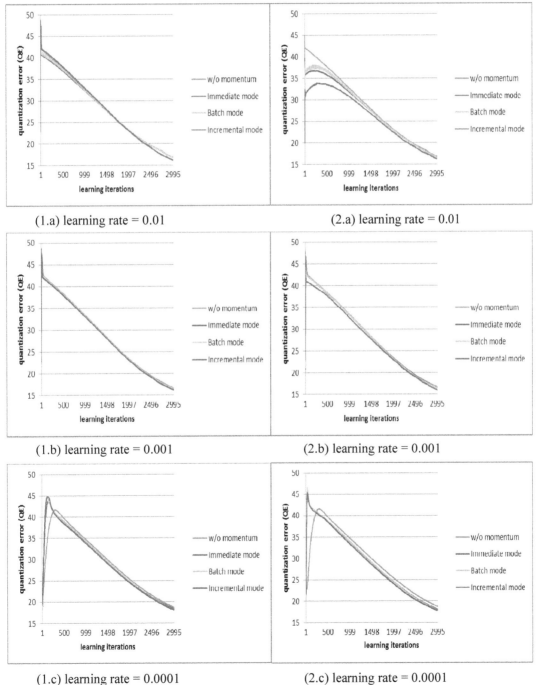

(1.a) learning rate = 0.01   (2.a) learning rate = 0.01

(1.b) learning rate = 0.001   (2.b) learning rate = 0.001

(1.c) learning rate = 0.0001   (2.c) learning rate = 0.0001

Figure 1. Quantization error of results against learning rate and momentum coefficient =0.5 in the Iris data

Figure 2. Quantization error of results against learning rate and momentum coefficient =0.8 in the Iris data

According to the experimental results shown in Figures 1 and 2, we observe that when learning rate is low, higher momentum coefficient results lower QE. From the Figure (1.a), after 250 iterations of learning, the QE value for momentum coefficient = 0.8 will be lower. For the self-organizing map method with batch mode momentum term, the QE value is less than 40. The QE value is less than 35 for the self-organizing map with incremental mode momentum term. From Figure (1.c) and (2.c), before 250 iterations of learning, the QE value of self-organizing map with batch mode momentum term and self-organizing map with incremental mode momentum term is higher. When the learning rate is small, the convergence process is slow. When momentum coefficient is larger, the QE value is higher. With the same learning rate and momentum coefficient, the incremental mode has the minimum QE value.

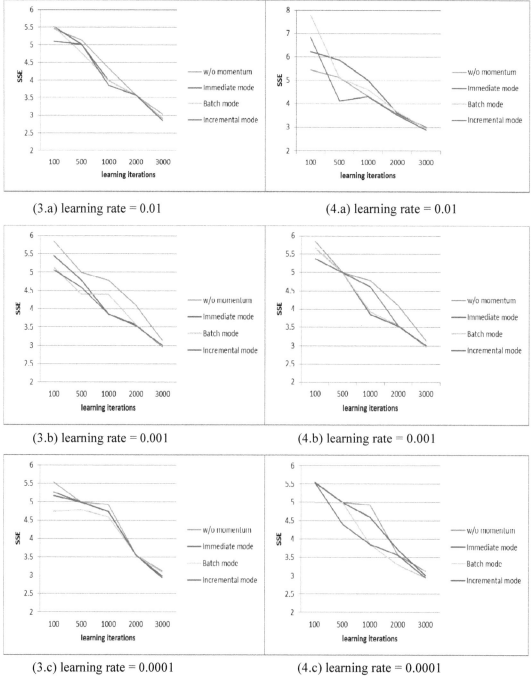

(3.a) learning rate = 0.01   (4.a) learning rate = 0.01

(3.b) learning rate = 0.001   (4.b) learning rate = 0.001

(3.c) learning rate = 0.0001   (4.c) learning rate = 0.0001

Figure 3. SSE of results against learning rate and momentum coefficient =0.5 in the Iris data

Figure 4. SSE of results against learning rate and momentum coefficient =0.8 in the Iris data

According to the experimental results shown in Figures 3 and 4, we discuss the relationship between momentum coefficient and learning rate. From Figure (3.a) and (4.a), before 250 iterations of learning, self-organizing map with any mode of momentum term has relatively high value of SSE. This is because the momentum term of such effect is determined by a coefficient and the previous amount of movement of the neuron. The higher momentum coefficient is, the higher SSE values are. After 250 iterations of learning, the SSE values for self-organizing map with any mode of momentum term are significantly lower.

From Figure (3.c) and (4.c), when learning rate = 0.0001, adding momentum term significantly accelerates convergence.

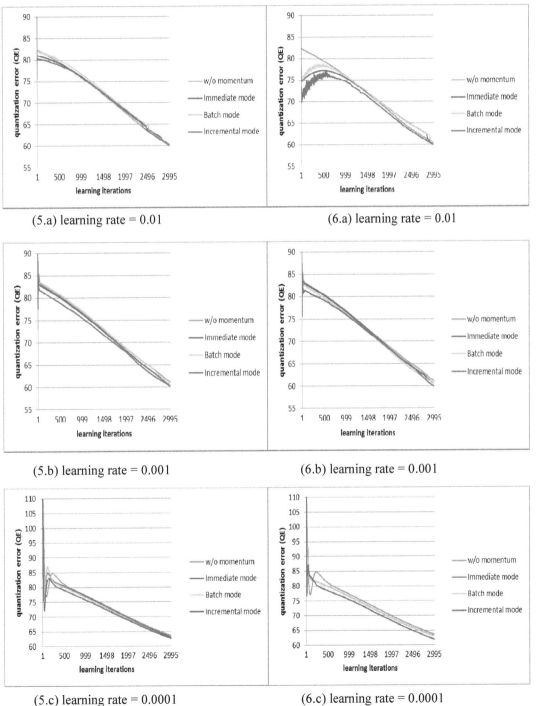

(5.a) learning rate = 0.01   (6.a) learning rate = 0.01

(5.b) learning rate = 0.001   (6.b) learning rate = 0.001

(5.c) learning rate = 0.0001   (6.c) learning rate = 0.0001

Figure 5. Quantization error of results against learning rate and momentum coefficient =0.5 in the Wine data

Figure 6. Quantization error of results against learning rate and momentum coefficient =0.8 in the Wine data

According to the experimental results shown in Figures 5 and 6, when the learning rate is low, there is slow convergence value. Whereas, when the learning rate is high, the learning process converges faster. At the same learning rate, the convergence effect with momentum coefficient =0.8 is significantly higher than that with momentum coefficient =0.5. With the same momentum and learning rate, the quantization error in incremental momentum has the lowest value.

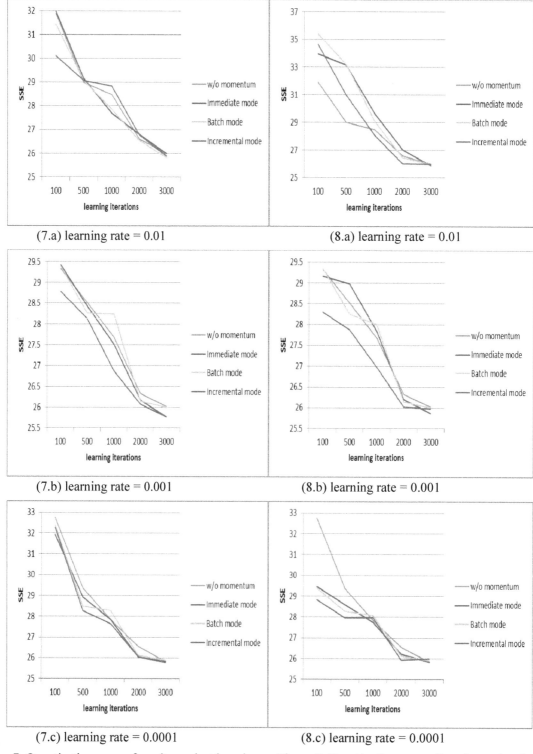

(7.a) learning rate = 0.01

(8.a) learning rate = 0.01

(7.b) learning rate = 0.001

(8.b) learning rate = 0.001

(7.c) learning rate = 0.0001

(8.c) learning rate = 0.0001

Figure 7. Quantization error of results against learning rate and momentum coefficient =0.5 in the Wine data

Figure 8. Quantization error of results against learning rate and momentum coefficient =0.8 in the Wine data

According to the experimental results shown in Figures 7 and 8, we discuss the relationship between momentum coefficient and learning rate. Since Wine contains more complex thirteen dimensions, from the Figure (a), the learning rate = 0.01, when added the momentum term, there is a higher SSE value. From Figure (8.c), the learning rate = 0.0001, the added momentum term can effectively reduce the value of SSE.

In the experiment, we compared the original self-organizing map without momentum term, self-organizing map with immediate mode momentum term, self-organizing map with batch mode momentum term, and self-organizing map with incremental mode momentum term. The results suggest that the learning process by adding the momentum term can accelerate the convergence, especially in the incremental mode.

5. Conclusion

Momentum term has been incorporated into the learning process of SOM. Momentum term of a neuron is the product of mememtum coefficient and the previous movement of the neuron. However, the previous movement of a neuron may be very small if (1) the neuron was not the winner of the previous input vector, and (2) the neuron is far away from the winning neuron of the previous input vector. Thus, the effect of momentum term in learning process will be lost. In this paper, we discuss this phenomenon and propose two modes for updating the prvious movement of a neuron when computing the momemntum term.

For discussion convenience, we temporarily coined a term, *momentum mass*, to denote the previous movement of a neuron. Thus, momentum term of a neuron is the product of mememtum coefficient and momentum mass of the neuron. The batch mode momentum term algorithm updates momentum mass of all neurons after an iteration of all input vectors. The new momentum mass of a neuron is the average movement of the neuron when it wins the input vectors in the iteration. The incremental mode momentum term algorithm updates momentum mass of a neuron after it wins an input vector.

Experimental results show that SOM with momentum term can accelerate convergence. Incremental mode momentum algorithm has the most obvious effect.

References

Alsabti, K., Ranka, S., & Singh, V. (1988). *An Efficient K-means Clustering Algorithm.* First Workshop on High Performance Data Ming.

Ankerst, M., Breunig, M., Kreigel, H. P., & Sander, J. (1999). *OPTICS: Ordering Points to Identify the Clustering Structure.* ACM SIGMOD Conference, 49-60.

Carpinteiro, O. A. S. (2000). *A Hierarchical Self-Organizing Map Model for Sequence Recognition.* International Conference on Artificial Neural Networks, 98, 815-820. http://dx.doi.org/10.1007/s100440070012

Dasgupta, A., & Raftery, A. E. (1998). Detecting Features in Spatial Point Processes with Clutter via Model-based Clustering. *Journal of the American Statistical Association, 93,* 294–302. http://dx.doi.org/10.2307/2669625

Ester, M., Kriegel, H. P., Sander, J., & Xu, X. (1996). *A Density-Based Algorithm for Discovering Clusters in Large Spatial Databases with Noise.* International Conference on Knowledge Discovery and Data Mining, 226–231.

Hagiwara, M. (1992). Theoretical Derivation of Momentum Term in Back-propagation. *Neural Networks, 1,* 692-686. http://dx.doi.org/10.1109/IJCNN.1992.287108

Han, J., & Kamber, M. (2001). *Data Mining: Concepts and Techniques.* Academic Press.

Kaufman, L., & Rousseeuw, P. J. (1991). Finding Groups in Data: an Introduction to Cluster Analysis. *Biometrics, 47*(2), 788. http://dx.doi.org/10.2307/2532178

Kohonen, T. (1982). Self-organized Formation of Topologically Correct Feature Maps. *Biological Cybernetics, 43,* 59–69. http://dx.doi.org/10.1007/BF00337288

Kohonen, T. (2001). *Self-organizing Maps, Springer Series in Information Sciences.* Springer.

Lippmann, R. (1987). Introduction to Computing with Neural Nets. *IEEE ASSP Magazine,* 4-22. http://dx.doi.org/10.1109/MASSP.1987.1165576

Masafumi, H. (1996). Self-organizing Feature Map with a Momentum Term. *International Joint Neurocomputing, 10,* 71-81. http://dx.doi.org/10.1016/0925-2312(94)00056-5

Mitchell, T. (1997). Artificial Neural Networks. Chapter 4 in *Machine Learning.* McGraw Hill.

Newman, D. J., Hettich, S., Blake, C. L., & Merz, C. J. (1988). *UCI Repository of Machine Learning Database.*

Richard C. D., & Anil K. Jain, (1990). *Algorithms for Clustering Data. Technometrics, 32*, 227. http://dx.doi.org/10.2307/1268876

Voegtlin, T. (2002). *Recursive Self-Organizing Map.* Neural Networks (Vol. 15, pp. 8-9).

Vogl, T. P., Mangis, J. K., Rigler, A. K., Zink, W. T., & Alkon, D. L. (1988). Accelerating the Convergence of the Backpropagation Method. *Biological Cybernetics, 59*, 257-263.

Wang, W., Yang, J., & Muntz, R. (1997). *STING: A Statistical Information Grid Approach to Spatial Data Mining.* International Conference on Very Large Data Bases, 186–195.

11

A Benefits Assessment Model of Information Systems for Small Organizations in Developing Countries

Amal Alshardan[1,2], Robert Goodwin[1] & Giselle Rampersad[1]

[1] School of Computer Science, Engineering and Mathematics, Flinders University, Adelaide, Australia

[2] Faculty of Computer and Information Sciences, Princess Nourah University, Riyadh, Saudi Arabia

Correspondence: Amal Alshardan, School of Computer Science, Engineering and Mathematics, Flinders University, Adelaide, Australia. E-mail: alsh0249@flinders.edu.au

Abstract

The influence of information systems (IS) on small and medium-sized enterprises (SMEs) has enjoyed much attention by managers and policy makers. Despite the hype and eagerness to commit extensive levels of investment, very little research has focuses on assessing the benefits of IS for SMEs in developing countries. Existing literature has been skewed towards developed countries and large organizations. Consequently, the purpose of this paper is to develop a model for evaluating the benefits of IS for SMEs in Saudi Arabia as a case of a developing country. In order to achieve this, the study builds on and extends past IS-impact literature. Based on quantitative results of 365 responses from SMEs, the model comprises 44 measures across five dimensions: 'Individual impact', 'Organisational impact', 'System quality', 'Information quality' and 'Vendor quality'. Applying confirmatory factor analysis and structural equation modelling, the validated model contributes to theory development of IS impact within the context of SMEs in developing countries. Additionally, it provides critical insights to policy makers and managers on assessing the benefits of IS for SMEs in developing countries.

Keywords: IS Success, IS Impact, measurement models, benefits assessment, information systems evaluation, SMEs, developing countries

1. Introduction

Information systems (IS) have been heralded as key agents for social well-being and economic prosperity in developing countries (Patel, Sooknanan, Rampersad, & Mundkur, 2012; Rampersad & Troshani, 2013). They have been recognised as critical for innovation in such economies (Lin, 1998; Rampersad, Quester, & Troshani, 2009; Rampersad, Troshani, & Plewa, 2012; Snider, da Silveira, & Balakrishnan, 2009). Additionally, small and medium sized enterprises (SMEs) have been identified for their important role in such innovation and wealth creation (Alshardan, Goodwin, & Rampersad, 2013; Lin, 1998; Snider et al., 2009). Despite this vital contribution, SMEs face significant challenges, for instance limited funding, and unfeasibly high costs of systems development and implementation (Freel, 2000). Therefore, measuring and assessing the benefits of IS in SMEs will be valuable in contributing towards the success of these systems (Mirani & Lederer, 1998).

Although many significant measurement techniques and frameworks are used to measure the benefits of IS (e.g. DeLone & McLean, 1992; DeLone & McLean, 2003; Gable, Sedera, & Chan, 2008; Shang & Seddon, 2002) these models are predominantly based on the context of large organisations. Studies have shown that SMEs are not smaller replicas of large firms as they are fundamentally different from large firms due to their special characteristics and requirements (Martin-Tapia, Aragon-Correa, & Senise-Barrio, 2008). SMEs face a digital divide from their larger counterparts, evidenced by significant differences in IS-related activities such as e-commerce and e-procurement (Lefebvre & Lefebvre, 1992; Levy & Powell, 1998). Moreover, these differences are perpetuated by the lack of agreement on what actually comprises an SME (O'Reagan & Ghobadian., 2004) as well as by the mythical concepts around SMEs (Gibb, 2000).

A digital divide exists not only between small and large organizations, but also between developed and developing countries. Developing countries have substantially different business environments compared to those of developed countries in terms of laws and regulations, governmental control, workforce characteristics, management style and customer income characteristics (Al-Mabrouk & Soar, 2006; Alghamdi, Goodwin, &

Rampersad, 2011b; Fathian, Akhavan, & Hoorali, 2008; Grazzi & Vergara, 2012). Roztocki and Weistroffer (2011) highlight the high failure rate of IS implementation in developing countries and point out that IS applications in developed countries have a "different focus as mature infrastructure is already in place, and project success is often determined by very different criteria" (p. 164). In addition, Soja (2008) emphasises the difficulties in IS implementation in developing countries that pertain primarily to the human resource constraints and high costs.

Most of the research on IS success in SMEs or in large organisations has been conducted in the developed nations' context. There is a lack of research in the developing countries' context, in general, and, in particular, on IS success in SMEs in the Saudi Arabian context (Al-Gahtani, Hubona, & Wang, 2007; AlGhamdi, Nguyen, Nguyen, & Drew, 2012; Azyabi, Fisher, Tanner, & Gao, 2014; Waverman, Coyle, & Souter, 2011; Wei, Loong, Leong, & Ooi, 2009). Saudi Arabia provides a suitable context for this study for a number of reasons. First, the ICT sector in Saudi Arabia has become the largest and fastest growing ICT marketplace in the Arab region with strong growth rates set to expand at a compound annual growth rate of 11.4% through 2015: this rapid growth is fuelled mostly by increased spending on hardware and IT services (AlGhamdi, 2012). Second, the Saudi government has made a significant commitment to growing the SME sector as exemplified by its Ninth Development Plan 2010–2014 plan for economic development focuses on smaller employers with firms encouraged through motivation and loans to increase their spending on research and development (R&D) (Alenaizan, 2014). Furthermore, the focus on software spending has improved with over 75% of manufacturing, services and trading companies in Saudi Arabia considering new deployments or upgrades of ERP solutions (Business Monitor International, 2012). Therefore, given the importance of the SME sector to Saudi Arabia, it will greatly benefit from relevant studies to ensure the success of IS implementation in SMEs in developing countries (Consoli, 2012; Manochehri, Al-Esmail, & Ashrafi, 2012).

2. Literature Review

2.1 Information Systems Success

Information Systems (IS) have become very important software applications with a significant influence on the business world, and thus have attracted high levels of investment (Petter, DeLone, & McLean, 2008). Despite the anticipated benefits, few studies actually examine the success of such systems to ensure that benefits do materialise. However, measuring such success is challenging due to the lack of consensus on contributing factors (Irani, 2008). Firstly, the impact of IS is indirect and is influenced by many factors, such as human, organisational and environmental ones. The mixture of the technical and social aspects of an IS make such measurements complex and confusing (Petter et al., 2008). Secondly, IS and work practices are very entangled thus making it difficult to identify their discrete influence on success (Agourram, 2009). The third point is related to the methodological perspectives that are used to measure IS success in which identifying dependent variables is difficult (Agourram, 2009).

Another important cause for the difficulty in evaluating results is the difference pertaining to the meaning of information systems (IS). The term 'information systems (IS)' is a broad name that can refer to many types of IS used in organisations, such as decision support systems (DSSs), computer-mediated communications, e-commerce and knowledge management systems (Petter et al., 2008). Depending on the type of system, the ways of measuring the success of IS may vary.

Moreover, the use of IS in SMEs have been underexplored. Within SMEs, the systems chosen are different to those originally used by many studies of large organizations, such as those by Gable et al. (2008) and Shang and Seddon (2002). Consequently, this may affect the measures and dimensions of the model, as many existing IS measures are related to the features of IS for large organisations.

During the past few decades, many efforts have been made to identify the factors that contribute to IS success. A number of models have been proposed for measuring IS (DeLone & McLean, 1992, 2003; Gable et al., 2008; Shang & Seddon, 2002).

To the best of the researchers' knowledge, no comprehensive benefits measurement model exists for IS success for SMEs of a developing country. The existing studies on IS success in SMEs and its evaluation remain under-developed. Many prior studies on IS in SMEs have focused on adoption (e.g. Fink, 1998; Juell-Skielse, 2006) and implementation success (e.g. Koh, Gunasekaran, & Cooper, 2009; Loh & Koh, 2004; Mabert, Soni, & Venkataramanan, 2003a, 2003b; Snider et al., 2009; Sun, Yazdani, & Overend, 2005), while few studies have attempted to measure benefits. Therefore, developing a benefits measurement framework is essential for evaluating IS in SMEs in the context of developing countries in order to justify the value and contribution of IS in relation to productivity. The following subsection firstly reviews some important IS success models, and then discusses various issues regarding these models in the context of SMEs and developing countries.

2.1.1 DeLone and McLean (1992, 2003) Models

The DeLone and McLean (1992, 2003) models are probably the most cited models in the IS community. DeLone and McLean (1992) carried out a review of the research published during the period 1981–1987. Based on this review, they created an IS success taxonomy. Thus, a full set of 119 success measures was summarised into six categories or components of IS success: 'System quality', 'Information quality', 'Use', "User satisfaction', 'Individual impact' and 'Organisational impact'. Figure 1 shows this original IS success model (DeLone & McLean, 1992).

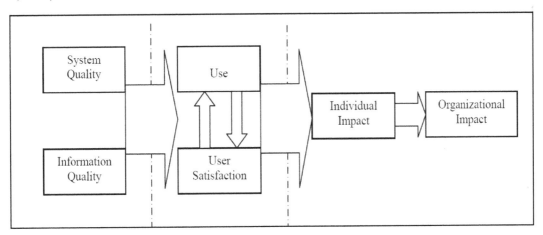

Figure 1. Delone and Mclean (1992) Is Success Model

The 1992 model was successfully tested in many empirical studies (Agourram, 2009). In addition, many researchers have suggested modifications or improvements to their model. Based on these improvements and other alternative frameworks for measuring IS effectiveness, DeLone and McLean conducted an in-depth analysis and reflection, and then updated their model and proposed the new DeLone and McLean (2003) IS success model (see Figure 2).

The D&M model opened the gate for many researchers: they either empirically tested the model in different contexts or criticised and enhanced some of its aspects.

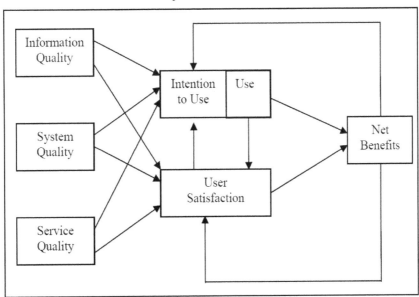

Figure 2. DeLone and McLean's (2003) IS success model

2.1.2 The IS-Impact Model

Based on DeLone and McLean's (1992) IS success model and tests of other researchers' work (Myers, Kappelman, & Prybutok, 1998; Shang & Seddon, 2002), Gable et al. (2008) developed a more advanced IS-Impact model. To obtain and validate this model, the authors employed three surveys (an identification survey, a specification survey and a confirmatory survey) with data collected from 600 respondents. The identification survey aimed to specify the salient success dimensions and measures; the specification survey was then used to identify the a priori model; while the purpose of the confirmatory survey was to validate the a priori model and instrument (Gable et al., 2008). Using a multi-method research design, Gable et al. (2008) extended the research cycle proposed by MacKenzie and House (1978) and McGrath (1964) to develop and validate a measurement model. Their research entailed two main phases: an exploratory phase to develop the hypothesised model and a confirmatory phase to test the model against the collected data.

The authors defined the IS impact of an information system (IS) as "a measure at a point in time of the stream of net benefits from the IS, to date and anticipated, as perceived by all key user groups" (Gable et al., 2008, p. 10). Thus, the IS-Impact model is represented as two halves: the 'impact' half measures the net benefits to date and the 'quality' half measures the possible future impacts (Gable et al., 2008). Three important issues addressed in their paper reconceptualise IS success, namely, the completeness, mutual exclusivity and necessity of the dimensions and measures.

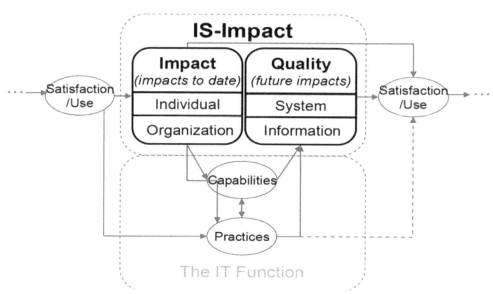

Figure 3. The IS-Impact measurement model (adopted from (Gable et al., 2008))

The IS-Impact model consists of four constructs: 'Individual impact', 'Organisational impact', 'System quality' and 'Information quality'. These represent four distinct but related dimensions of the multidimensional phenomenon, namely, enterprise systems (ES) success (otherwise termed IS success). Furthermore, it has always been debated whether the constructs of 'Use' and 'Satisfaction' are dimensions of IS success. Through a comprehensive exploratory study, Gable et al. (2008) drew the following conclusion: both 'Use' and 'Satisfaction' are antecedents or consequences of IS impact rather than being two dimensions. When evaluating an ES, measures of these dimensions represent variables that are highly comparable across time, stakeholders, various types of system and different contexts. The impact dimensions represent the benefits that have been achieved from the system. The quality dimensions reflect future potential; hence, these four dimensions reflect a complete view of the measure of ES success (Gable et al., 2008) (see Figure 3).

The IS-Impact model is differentiated from DeLone and McLean's IS success model in the following ways: (1) it illustrates a measurement model while the D&M model depicts a causal/process model of success; (2) the addition of new measures reflects a more holistic view of the context of ERP systems and organisational characteristics; (3) it includes additional measures to probe the 'Organisational impact' construct; (3) it eliminates and consolidates measures; and (4) it revisits the relevance of the 'Use' and 'Satisfaction' constructs (Gable et al., 2008). Moreover, the original 37 measures were reduced to 27 measures in this IS-Impact model, in the interests of parsimony. The 37 measures of IS impact are shown in Figure 4.

The current study focuses on the underlying theories which can explain the new phenomenon of the evaluation of IS by SMEs in developing countries. The study therefore assists in the development of a benefits measurement framework for IS in SMEs. Unlike other studies that have been based on the D&M model, the current study is based on the IS-Impact model. Justification for any update to the model is thus provided in accordance with the rationale and reasoning derived from existing theories and models. The D&M model, as stated at the outset, has been tested and used in many contexts and has proven its validity for use in other contexts (Urbach, Smolnik, & Riempp, 2009). The IS-Impact model is chosen due to its ability to measure the up-to-date impact of the system undergoing evaluation, as well as its ability to forecast the potential impact of a future system by evaluating the quality of information and the system itself. This model is concise and parsimonious which makes it practical and easy to use. Moreover, the model measures the level of impact across multiple staff perspectives in an organisation. The advantages of the IS-Impact model form a sound underlying base that can be validated in the context of SMEs.

Figure 4. IS-Impact model's 37 measures (extracted from Gable et al. [2008])

2.2 Small and Medium-Sized Enterprises (SMEs)

SMEs have a strong influence on the economic growth of all countries. They play an important role in employment and innovation (Lin, 1998; Snider et al., 2009). They differ fundamentally from large organizations in several ways, such as having limited resources, the inadequacy of employees' skills, uncertainty towards IS and a lack of vision for their prospective competitive advantages (Salmeron & Bueno, 2006).

Traditionally, IS investment has been dominated by large organisations. This phenomenon is no longer the case: SMEs are increasingly implementing IS and, in addition, many software package vendors are now considering SMEs as a focal market. Despite this trend, a feature in most SMEs is less management support for IS (Levy & Powell, 2000; Snider et al., 2009) with managers in SMEs tending to give insufficient attention to IS (Cragg & Zinatelli, 1995 ; Yap, Soh, & Raman, 1992). SMEs are also characterised by less experience with IS in comparison with large organisations: they have only become computerised relatively recently and have little experience and training in IS management (Blili & Raymond, 1993; DeLone, 1981).

With regard to the type of IS used in SMEs, IS within SMEs are not at a very advanced stage and are subordinate to the accounting function (Blili & Raymond, 1993). Moreover, most SMEs expect their IT to have a longer life than is the expectation of larger firms. What this means is that many SMEs are locked into systems developed using advanced tools that are unsupported or incompatible with current industry standards (Levy & Powell, 2000). The SME characteristics that might affect several aspects of IS and hence have the probability of changing the measures of IS success models are described in the following paragraphs. Despite the obvious effects of specific IT/IS SME characteristics, it is evident that the general characteristics of SMEs also affect many aspects of IT and information systems (IS). Many academics have remarked on some of these aspects either empirically or conceptually. For example, the centralised SME structure affects creativity, innovation, response times and the decision-making orientation of problem-solving actions (Levy & Powell, 2000; McCartan-Quinn & Carson, 2003), all of which are aspects related to IT/IS adoption and implementation.

The majority of SMEs do not have adequate financial resources and lack access to commercial lending or the ability to obtain credit. In addition, SMEs are faced with frequent raw material shortages, fluctuations in raw material price, and inadequate inventory management and stock control (Deros, Yusof, & Salleh, 2006). Consequently, in relation to IS, SMEs do not have an adequate budget for staff training and consultancy support nor for adequate hardware and software which can stifle improvement efforts and lead to difficulty in the implementation of IS projects. Therefore, SMEs may be more severely impacted by unsuccessful implementation, with these weaknesses leading to project delays or even abandonment (Snider et al., 2009). In terms of human resources, SMEs are always faced with the lack of expertise and lack of skilled employees because they are not able to offer workers better wages and working conditions (Deros et al., 2006). This, in turn, affects all phases of IS from planning and operation through to maintenance and updates. It also increases the need for external support and expertise. Snider et al. (2009) found that internal training teams often suffer from lack of time and skills to prepare and deliver effective training sessions. Moreover, the majority of SME entrepreneurs have low levels of formal education and limited training in new management principles and practices (Deros et al., 2006). General resistance to change or to the adoption of new ideas is another characteristic of SMEs (Seibert, 2004). As indicated by many researchers such as Deros et al. (2006) and Kartiwi and MacGregor (2007), the majority of SMEs rely on out-of-date technology. The reason is that some SMEs do not trust new technology, while others are unable to afford it which, in many cases, leads to inefficiency, misinformation and inadequate in-house expertise (Deros et al., 2006)

In summary, SMEs have special characteristics that differentiate them from large organisations. These characteristics play an important role in IS adoption, use and management. Having an understanding of the issues and characteristics of SMEs is crucial before making any attempt to measure IS success.

2.3 Developing Countries and the Use of Information Systems (IS)

Academic researchers have differentiated between developed and developing countries as two different contexts due to government regulations, economic laws and other social factors that could affect research findings.

This research has been undertaken in the developing countries' context. The use of IS in developing countries continues to be challenging due to several factors (Alghamdi, Goodwin, & Rampersad, 2011a; Alghamdi et al., 2011b). Information system (IS) products are not often tailored to the unique needs of developing countries as they were initially designed for the markets of developed countries (Berisha-Namani, 2009). Furthermore, limited financial resources (Berisha-Namani, 2009) and inadequate expertise and human resources in SMEs in developing countries (Berisha-Namani, 2009) and the lack of robust regulatory frameworks for IS in developing countries pose major problems. In non-English speaking contexts, the language barrier is also of consideration for developing countries as some citizens may not necessarily know other languages beyond the local language whereas IS products may, for example, be dominated by English-language content (Grazzi & Vergara, 2012).

With the growing importance of IS in SMEs in developing countries, researchers have begun to investigate the adoption and use of IS in contexts such as Malaysia (Alam & Noor, 2009), Nigeria (Irefin, Abdul-Azeez, & Tijani, 2012) and the Kingdom of Saudi Arabia (KSA) (Skoko, 2012; Skoko & Ceric, 2010). Generally, the focus of existing studies is on pre-implementation considerations surrounding IS in SMEs in developing countries rather than on post-implementation issues (e.g. Apulu & Latham, 2010; Ashrafi & Murtaza, 2008; Berisha-Namani, 2009; Manochehri, Al-Esmail, & Ashrafi, 2012; Modimogale & Kroeze, 2011). Only a limited number of studies have attempted to measure the post-implementation benefits of IS in SMEs in developing countries (Ndiege, Wayi, & Herselman, 2012). For instance, Kale, Banwait and Laroiya (2010) surveyed 130 SMEs in India to find out whether and how Indian SMEs are benefiting from IS implementation for enterprise resource planning (ERP). Their study revealed that most SMEs implemented a new IS to integrate with the existing IS and found IS implementation was mainly beneficial in reducing inventory, improving customer services and improving communications. In addition, the study found that top management support, and user involvement and participation are the major contributors to IS success (Kale et al., 2010). In Jordan, Hawari and Heeks (2010) developed a "design–reality gap" model and applied it to a case study of IS failure in a Jordanian manufacturing firm. Analysing the situation both before and during IS implementation through a combination of interviews, observations and document analyses, Hawari and Heeks (2010) found sizeable gaps between the assumptions and requirements built into the IS design and the actual realities of the client organisation. Their model was derived from different IS success measurement models which comprised seven dimensions summarised by the ITPOSMO acronym (information, technology, processes, objectives and values, staffing and skills, management system and structure and other resources) (Hawari & Heeks, 2010). Ndiege et al. (2012) focused on assessing the quality of IS used by SMEs in Kenya. They found that the low usage of IS within SMEs was attributed to the low level of IS skills of both SME management and IS users, and to poorly designed IS that did not adequately address the needs of SMEs. They also evaluated the quality of IS in SMEs in developing countries by applying the D&M model and found the quality to be barely sufficient (Ndiege et al., 2012). Similarly, in Malaysia, Wei, Loong, Leong and Ooi (2009) presented a re-specification of the D&M model. They proposed a conceptual model that resulted from a comprehensive review of the IS success literature. Their results provided an expanded understanding of the factors that measure IS success and suggested ways to improve IS usage (Wei et al., 2009). A recent study by Ghobakhloo and Tang (2015) developed an integrated IS success model based on the D&M model and the technology–organisation–environment (TOE) framework of the firm. Their model was tested using data based on 316 respondent Iranian and Malaysian manufacturing SMEs. Their model shows that the determinants of IS success for SMEs incorporate both organisational and environmental determinants in addition to the technological factors identified in the D&M model (Ghobakhloo & Tang, 2015).

Despite the value of previous studies in their examination of IS benefits in specific countries, a more comprehensive model is needed. The current study has proposed a conceptual model that stems from an extensive review of SME characteristics and IS success models. The study has also employed the highly relevant IS-Impact model as the theoretical base, extending beyond the typical D&M model.

3. The Research Model

The research model proposed in this study is the result of a synthesis process included the IS-Impact model with characteristics and studies of SMEs in developing countries. This combination was performed in order to respond to two main issues around IS success modelling, namely, the theoretical basis and validity in the SME context with these providing both rationality and generality for the measurement model (Ahlan, 2014).

Figure 5 demonstrate this model. Details of the dimensions of IS success in SMEs are shown in Table 2 and the set of measures for each dimension are shown in Table 3.

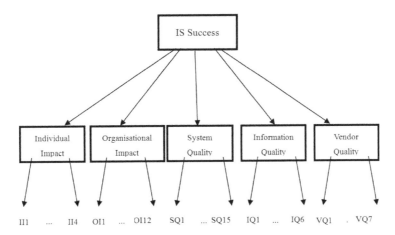

Figure 2. The a priori model of IS success measurement in SMEs in developing countries

Table 2. Dimensions of IS success in SMEs in developing countries

Dimension	# Items	Definition
Individual impact	4	The benefits received by the IS recipient due to IS applications (DeLone & McLean, 1992).
Organisational impact	12	The firm-level benefits received by an organisation due to IS applications (Gorla, Somers, & Wong, 2010).

System quality	15	The desirable characteristics of the IS applications (Petter et al., 2008).
Information quality	6	The desirable characteristics of the system's outputs (Petter et al., 2008).
Vendor quality	7	The quality of the support that system users receive from the IS vendor (Petter et al., 2008).
Total	**44**	

Table 3. Set of measures for each dimension

Individual impact	*Organisational impact*	*System quality*	*Information quality*	*Vendor quality*
II1 Learning	OI1 Organisational costs	SQ1 Ease of learning	IQ1 Importance	VQ1 Maintenance
II2 Awareness	OI2 Staff requirements	SQ2 Ease of use	IQ2 Availability	VQ2 Online service
II3 Decision effectiveness	OI3 Cost reduction	SQ3 Access	IQ3 Usability	VQ3 Reliability
II4 Individual productivity	OI4 Overall productivity	SQ4 User requirements	IQ4 Format	VQ4 Popularity
	OI5 Improved outcome	SQ5 System feature	IQ5 Content accuracy	VQ5 Expertise
	OI6 Increased capacity	SQ6 System accuracy	IQ6 Timeliness	VQ6 Locally available
	OI7 Business process change	SQ7 Flexibility		VQ7 Support empathy
	OI8 Improved planning	SQ8 Reliability		
	OI9 Improved management	SQ9 Efficiency		
	OI10 Increased competitiveness	SQ10 Sophistication		
	OI11 Business innovation	SQ11 Integration		
	OI12 Improved resource utilisation	SQ12 Multi-language		
		SQ13 Standardisation		
		SQ14 Security		
		SQ15 Scalability		
4	12	15	6	7
Total 44				

4. Model Validation

The proposed model was validated using a survey method to collect data. A total of 431 responses were received from SMEs in Saudi Arabia: 365 were complete and valid for analysis. Respondents were classified according to demographic questions which sought information about respondents and their organisation. Table 4 shows frequencies of demographic variables.

Structural equation modelling (SEM) and second-order confirmatory factor analysis (CFA) were conducted sequentially to evaluate and test statistically significant relationships between the model constructs. Based on these results, the model was further refined by removing non-significant links and then reassessed to produce the final model. The final model was assessed for goodness of fit, reliability and validity as discussed in the next subsections.

Confirmatory factor analysis (CFA) is a special form of factor analysis used to test whether the data fit a hypothesised measurement model (Schreiber, Nora, Stage, Barlow, & King, 2006). Confirmatory factor analysis (CFA) techniques were performed in this study using SPSS AMOS, Version 22 software.

The main reason for choosing CFA was that it is more theoretically driven unlike exploratory factor analysis (EFA) which has been identified as a data-driven technique (Barendse, Oort, & Timmerman, 2015). CFA allows researchers to base their hypothesised models on the required theory in order to defend the relationships between constructs and also in terms of justifying the number of factors required for each construct.

The assessment process for the model using CFA comprised scale refinement for each construct, then assessing the structural model fit. Finally, assessment of reliability and validity was undertaken.

Assessing the model at both construct and structural levels involved multiple iterations of applying goodness-of-fit indices to test statistically significant relationships between the model constructs and variables (independent and dependent variables). Based on the results of the fit indices, the model was refined by removing non-significant links and then reassessed to produce the final model. Another modification to the model that helped to achieve an acceptable fit was using correlation between errors of the variable as suggested by (Lance, 2011). Furthermore, under certain conditions of unidimensionality, parcelling can be considered for a better fit (Little, Cunningham, Shahar, & Widaman, 2002; Yang, Nay, & Hoyle, 2009).

First, in line with the suggestions of many scholars (e.g. Rampersad, Quester, & Troshani, 2010; Schumacker & Lomax, 2004), the model was tested at the construct level using CFA, prior to combining the constructs structurally (the structural model). This was important for diagnosing and reducing problems that could amalgamate at later stages (Rampersad, 2008). Therefore, a test was performed for each construct in isolation and some modification was undertaken to achieve the required fit. The structural model fit was then assessed as a second stage with the third stage being the assessment of reliability and validity. Slight modifications were performed in order to achieve a perfect fit for the structural model, with validity and reliability addressed.

The following subsections detail the procedure for the three stages: assessment of constructs' fit; assessment of structural model fit; and assessment of reliability and validity.

Table 4. Frequencies of demographic variables

Class	Group	Frequency	Percentage
Gender	Male	244	66.8%
	Female	112	30.7%
Age	Less than 20	17	4.7%
	Between 20 and 29	121	33.2%
	Between 30 and 39	158	43.3%
	Between 40 and 49	55	15.1%
	50 or over	8	2.2%
Position	Owner	175	47.9%
	Management staff	94	25.8%
	Operational staff	31	8.5%
	IT staff	51	14.0%
Qualifications	Less than high school	27	7.4%
	High school	94	25.8%
	Bachelor degree	194	53.2%
	Postgraduate degree	45	12.3%
Organisation's main sector	Manufacturing	77	21.1%
	Trade	145	39.7%
	Services	137	37.5%
Size of the organisation	Small	173	47.4%
	Medium-sized	178	48.8%
	Large	12	3.3%
Number of employees	< 10	134	36.7%
	10 to < 50	126	34.5%
	50 to < 100	69	18.9%
	> or = 100	32	8.8%
	Total in each group	365	100.0%

4.1 Assessment of Constructs' Fit

As a first step in using CFA as the analysis technique, each construct was assessed by applying various measures of model fit, seeking a good fit that could be justified according to previous theories and studies. Checking for model fit at the construct level prior to combining the constructs structurally was important as a scale refinement step to help identify and tackle model fit problems that could otherwise emerge later (Rampersad, 2008).

The sequential evaluation and tests indicated the final representation of each construct with the factor loading of the items on their expected latent constructs being greater than 0.70 and significant at $p < 0.001$. All constructs showed a perfect to acceptable fit as shown in Table 5.

Table 5. Model fit at the construct level

Construct	Chi-sq	df	p-value > 0.05	GFI > 0.90	AGFI	CFI > 0.95	TLI > 0.95	RMSEA < 0.08	SRMR < 0.05
Individual impact	3.34	1	0.68	0.99	0.95	0.99	0.99	0.80	0.0059
Organisational impact	65.6	19	0	0.95	0.915	0.98	0.97	0.82	0.0246
System quality	87.42	26	0	0.95	0.912	0.98	0.97	0.061	0.0259
Information quality	14.32	8	0.074	0.99	0.97	0.99	0.99	0.47	0.0123
Vendor quality	7.515	5	0.185	0.99	0.98	0.99	0.99	0.037	0.0126

4.2 Assessment of Structural Model Fit

Structural equation modelling (SEM) was sequentially conducted to evaluate and test the statistically significant relationships between the model constructs.

Some adjustments to the scales were required, such as the removal of items and parcelling. In the initial phase, five constructs with 44 items in a second-order CFA (the original model) were used to test the structural model. Based on the results, the model was further refined sequentially by removing non-significant links and then reassessed for reliability and validity. Another suggested refinement based on the result was also applied by constructing an upper-level construct, with this process called 'parcelling' (Little et al., 2002). Figure 6 shows this refinement where the impact constructs are combined into another latent variable called 'Impacts' which refers to both 'Individual impact' and 'Organisational impact'. Similarly, 'System quality', 'Information quality' and 'Vendor quality' are combined into the latent construct 'Quality'. This refinement fulfils Gable et al.'s (2008) IS impact definition and the IS-Impact conceptual model. This result was also supported by Rabaa'i (2012) study in which the original IS-Impact model was combined with the IS support model in a structural model that related to satisfaction. This refinement shows good fit, convergent validity and discriminant validity. Therefore, this model was chosen as the final model for the study. Table 6 shows the goodness-of-fit indices for the final model.

Table 6. Goodness-of-fit indices for the final model

Model	Chi-sq.	df	p-value > 0.05	X^2	GFI > 0.90	AGFI	CFI > 0.95	TLI > 0.95	RMSEA < 0.08	SRMR < 0.05
Final model	485.8	262	0	1.9	0.90	0.88	0.97	0.97	0.048	0.036

4.3 Assessment of Reliability and Validity

All scales were evaluated for reliability and validity. Owing to the importance of this validation, Straub, Boudreau, and Gefen (2004) suggested the use of more than one method to test validity and reliability arguing that "establishing construct validity should be a mandatory research practice" (p. 398). In this study, each construct was assessed against the following aspects: indicator reliability, internal consistency reliability, convergent validity and discriminant validity.

4.3.1 Reliability

Reliability is a crucial analysis to be performed on the scale refers to its consistency, given the same conditions (Pallant, 2013). In this study, the analysis of scale reliability was performed through an assessment of indicator reliability and internal consistency reliability (Bannigan & Watson, 2009; Hinkin, 1995).

Internal consistency refers to the homogeneity of the items in the measure or the extent to which item responses correlate with the total test score. Internal consistency can be measured using different methods, for instance, split halves, Kuder–Richardson approaches (KR-21) and Cronbach's alpha (Fraenkel & Wallen, 2009). The current study evaluated internal consistency using Cronbach's alpha value as it is the most frequently employed method for determining internal consistency (Cooper & Schindler, 2006; Fraenkel & Wallen, 2009; Gliem & Gliem, 2003; Kimberlin & Winterstein, 2008). The values of Cronbach's alpha range between zero (0) and one (1), with a value between 0.8 and 0.95 referring to very good reliability. (Gliem & Gliem, 2003). Five independent scales were used in the survey questionnaire that constructed the proposed model, namely, 'Individual impact', 'Organisational impact', 'System quality', 'Information quality' and 'Vendor quality'. Table 7 summarises the results of Cronbach's alpha for all constructs, showing that the internal reliability for all the variables/dimensions was very good as their values are greater than 0.92. Based on these scores, the internal consistency (or the homogeneity) of the measures was confirmed.

Indicator reliability refers to how much of the indicator's variance is explained by the corresponding factor that it measures (Bannigan & Watson, 2009; Gliem & Gliem, 2003; Kimberlin & Winterstein, 2008). Some researchers have proposed that at least 50% of the indicator's variance should be explained by the latent variable that it measures (Gliem & Gliem, 2003; Kimberlin & Winterstein, 2008). However, others have suggested that construct reliability scores should exceed 0.7 (Bagozzi & Yi, 2011; Gefen, Straub, & Boudreau, 2000; Gliem & Gliem, 2003). In the current study, the indicator reliability for each construct is shown on Table 7. All constructs demonstrated indicator reliability.

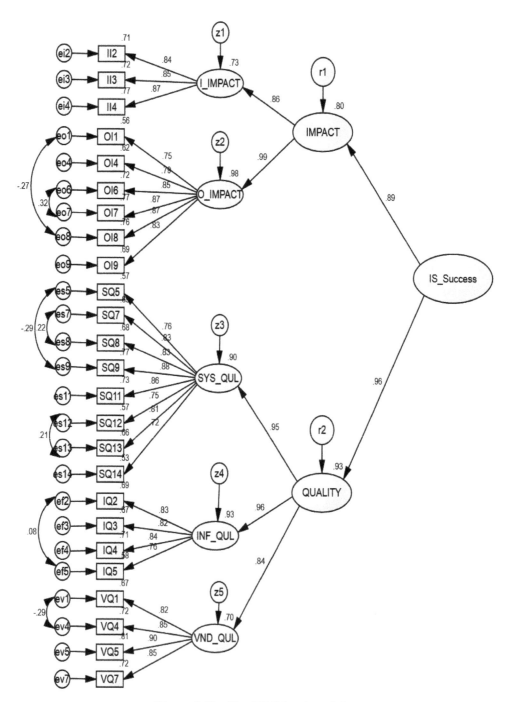

Figure 6. The Final Validated model

Table 7. Reliability results for the final model

Construct	Cronbach's alpha	Indicator reliability*
Individual impact	.925	.716
Organisational impact	.962	.888
System quality	.963	.955
Information quality	.928	.949
Vendor quality	.938	.846

*Indicator reliability = standardised regression weights = factor loadings

4.3.2 Validity

Validity is the measure of the accuracy of an instrument used in a study: checking the validity is essential to ensure that the scale measures what it is intended to measure (Bannigan & Watson, 2009; Hair, Black, Babin, Anderson, & Tatham, 2006; Said, Badru, & Shahid, 2011). This study has examined for convergent validity and discriminant validity which are usually termed 'construct validity' (Doll, Xia, & Torkzadeh, 1994; Hurley et al., 1997).

Convergent validity is intended to assess the extent to which the indicators are related to the same construct (Davis, 1989). To demonstrate convergent validity, the magnitude of the direct structural relationship between the indicator and latent construct should be statistically different from zero (0); that is, the final items should be loaded highly on one construct (Anderson & Gerbing, 1988) with a factor loading of 0.50 or greater (Hair et al., 2006). In addition to the standardised factor loadings, convergent validity in this study was examined by observing the value of composite or construct reliability (CR) and variance extracted (VE) for each construct (Fornell & Larcker, 1981; Hair et al., 2006). According to Hair et al. (2006), composite or construct reliability (CR) values should be greater than 0.6 while variance extracted (VE) should be above 0.5. Values outside these limits indicate that the items have a convergent validity issue and might not consistently measure the hypothesised model. The values of composite or construct reliability (CR) and AVE were computed as shown in Table 8. The results confirmed the convergent validity of all constructs.

Discriminant validity determines that each measurement item does not correlate too highly with all other constructs except the one to which it is theoretically associated. Average variance extracted (AVE) is also used to substantiate the evidence of the discriminant validity of the latent construct (Fornell & Larcker, 1981). The values of average variance extracted (AVE) between the constructs are compared to their squared multiple correlations (SMCs) (Hair et al., 2006). Thus, the AVE for a latent construct should be greater than the variance shared between the construct and other latent constructs in the model (Fornell & Larcker, 1981; Hair et al., 2006). As shown in Table 9, all constructs in this study exhibited discriminant validity as their values for variance extracted (AVE) were all above 0.500, thus exceeding the square of the highest shared variance between factors.

Table 8. Validity results for the final model

Construct	CR*	AVE*	MSV*	ASV*
Impact	0.92	0.85	0.74	0.74
Quality	0.94	0.84	0.74	0.74

*CR = composite reliability; AVE = average variance extracted; MSV = maximum shared variance; and ASV = average shared variance.

Table 9. Assessment criteria for reliability and validity

Assessment	Criterion/ Criteria	Accepted values or conditions	Related references
Indicator reliability	Factor loading	Factor loading should be > 0.60, or ideally > 0.7, and statistically significant	(Bagozzi & Yi, 2011; Gefen et al., 2000; Gliem & Gliem, 2003)
Internal consistency reliability	Cronbach's alpha	For confirmatory research, value should be > 0.8	(Cronbach, 1951)
Convergent validity	AVE	AVE > 0.5	(Fornell & Larcker, 1981; Hair et al., 2006)
	CR	CR > 0.7	(Hair et al., 2006)
	Factor loading	Factor loading ≥ 0.50	(Anderson & Gerbing, 1988; Hair et al., 2006)
Discriminant validity	Fornell and Larcker's (1981) criterion using AVE	Latent variable's AVE is greater than the squared bivariate correlations between it and other latent variables in the model	(Fornell & Larcker, 1981; Hair et al., 2006)

5. Conclusion

This research proposed and evaluated a measurement model for SMEs in developing countries. The focus of the study is on Saudi Arabian SMEs. The findings of the model test have suggested that a significant relationship exists between the five dimensions and IS success, and that the developed scale for each factor was rational and supported by other studies. The contexts of SMEs and developing countries were found to affect many parts of the model.

This research contributes to both theory and practice. In terms of the contribution to academic theory, this research contributes to the body of knowledge around research on SMEs and the measurement of IS success. First and foremost, this research has introduced a theoretical model to measure the success of IS in SMEs in Saudi Arabia as a case in the developing countries' context. The focus of previous studies in measuring IS success were on developed countries whereas the developing country context is still under-researched (Alghamdi et al., 2011a; Alshardan et al., 2013; Grazzi & Vergara, 2012; Roztocki & Weistroffer, 2011; Vrgovic, Glassman, Walton, & Vidicki, 2012).

In addition, this study has contributed to the theory by extending and further empirically testing the IS-Impact model developed by Gable et al. (2008) in a different setting than was used in previous studies. In developing the current study's model, it was argued that the previously implemented IS-Impact model was deficient in the 'Vendor (service) quality' dimension in the context of SMEs in developing countries, whereas the other four dimensions of the IS-Impact model were confirmed. The study thus incorporated the 'Vendor quality' dimension into the existing dimensions of the IS-Impact model which was found to be relevant in this discourse on IS system success. Moreover, the operationalised set of measures offers comprehensive items that can be used as a basis for research in other contexts in order to establish standardised scales.

Last but not least, this research has contributed to the literature in the Saudi Arabian SME context on which there was a paucity of research, in general, and, in particular, on the IS aspects. Although this research was conducted in the Saudi context, the findings could be applicable to similar business contexts in developing countries, particularly in countries of the Gulf Cooperation Council (GCC) (i.e. Kuwait, United Arab Emirates [UAE], Qatar, Bahrain and Oman).

In addition, the study offers important implications for policy makers and managers in developing countries. At the government level, for example, this research could help policy makers in determining interventions to optimise the monitoring of IS initiatives to ensure the effective allocation of scarce public funding. Consequently, development goals pertaining to redressing digital divide concerns in relation to IS success could be achieved. SMEs could also find this research valuable in offering insights into the development of processes to manage IS implementation to ensure that organisations could reap the anticipated benefits. Useful guidelines could be provided for the senior management of SMEs that suggest the particular factors which SME management should use in assessing the success of IS in their companies. In addition, by assessing the benefits of IS, this research could help IS vendors to identify key growth opportunities for achieving desirable benefits and a way by which to evaluate IS applications, thus being able to address any shortfall in promised benefits. Hence, this study could provide valuable insights for both government and businesses in developing strategies to realise the anticipated benefits of IS for SMEs in developing countries. Indeed, this study is instrumental as a necessary first step in equipping SMEs in developing countries with a useful framework by which to assess the benefits of information systems (IS).

6. Future Work

The limitations of this research provide a natural guide to future research. As is typical, the investigation of more SMEs could result in more accurate findings. This could include SMEs in the Saudi Arabian context, or in the context of other developing countries.

Future research could examine the use of other types of IS such as customer relationship management (CRM), supply chain management (SCM) and the content management system (CMS). In addition, more advanced technical systems could be involved by using the implementation of cloud computing, such as software as a service (SaaS) that provides users with complete software applications on the internet (Tate, Sedera, McLean, & Burton-Jones, 2014). Therefore, studies on major differences in the success factors of different IS projects in the organisation could form a key direction for future research.

In summary, this study has made an important contribution in paving the way for such future research by providing a more holistic framework for the measurement of IS benefits in the context of SMEs and developing countries. It is anticipated that the findings of this research, along with the areas identified for guiding future

A Benefits Assessment Model of Information Systems for Small Organizations...

119

research, will motivate researchers to pursue this exciting research stream.

References

Agourram, H. (2009). Defining information system success in Germany. *International Journal of Information Management, 29*(2), 129-137. http://dx.doi.org/10.1016/j.ijinfomgt.2008.05.007

Ahlan, A. R. (2014). Implementation of Input-Process-Output Model for Measuring Information System Project Success. *TELKOMNIKA Indonesian Journal of Electrical Engineering, 12*(7). http://dx.doi.org/10.11591/telkomnika.v12i7.5699

Alam, S. S., & Noor, M. K. M. (2009). ICT adoption in small and medium enterprises: an empirical evidence of service sectors in Malaysia. *International Journal of Business and Management, 4*(2), P112. http://dx.doi.org/10.5539/ijbm.v4n2p112

Al-Gahtani, S. S., Hubona, G. S., & Wang, J. (2007). Information technology (IT) in Saudi Arabia: Culture and the acceptance and use of IT. *Information & Management, 44*(8), 681-691. http://dx.doi.org/10.1016/j.im.2007.09.002

Alghamdi, I. A., Goodwin, R., & Rampersad, G. (2011b). E-Government Readiness Assessment for Government Organizations in Developing Countries. *Computer and Information Science, 4*(3), 1913-1938. http://dx.doi.org/10.5539/cis.v4n3p3

Alghamdi, I., Goodwin, R., & Rampersad, G. (2011a). A Suggested E-Government Framework for Assessing Organizational E-Readiness in Developing Countries *Informatics Engineering and Information Science* (pp. 479-498). http://dx.doi.org/10.1007/978-3-642-25453-6_41

AlGhamdi, R., Nguyen, A., Nguyen, J., & Drew, S. (2012). Factors Influencing e-commerce Adoption by Retailers in Saudi Arabia: A quantitative analysis. *International Journal of Electronic Commerce Studies.*

Al-Mabrouk, K., & Soar, J. (2006, 19-21 Nov). *Identification of Major Issues for Successful IT Transfer in the Arab World: The Preliminary Results.* Paper presented at the Innovations in Information Technology, Dubai. http://dx.doi.org/10.1109/innovations.2006.301885

Alshardan, A., Goodwin, R., & Rampersad, G. (2013). Measuring the benefits of IS in small organizations in developing countries. *International Journal of Conceptions on Computing and Information Technology, 1*(2), 12-17.

Anderson, J. C., & Gerbing, D. W. (1988). Structural equation modeling in practice: A review and recommended two-step approach. *Psychological bulletin, 103*(3), 411. http://dx.doi.org/10.1037/0033-2909.103.3.411

Apulu, I., & Latham, A. (2010). Benefits of information and communication technology in small and medium sized enterprises: a case study of a Nigerian SME. *UK Academy for Information Systems Conference Proceedings 2010,* 7.

Ashrafi, R., & Murtaza, M. (2008). Use and Impact of ICT on SMEs in Oman. *The Electronic Journal of Information Systems Evaluation, 11*(3), 125-138.

Azyabi, N., Fisher, J., Tanner, K., & Gao, S. (2014, 06-09 January). *The Relationship between KM Strategies and IT Applications in SMEs.* Paper presented at the 47th Hawaii International Conference on System Sciences (HICSS), Big Island, Hawaii. http://dx.doi.org/10.1109/hicss.2014.453

Bagozzi, R. P., & Yi, Y. (2011). Specification, evaluation, and interpretation of structural equation models. *Journal of the Academy of Marketing Science, 40*(1), 8-34. http://dx.doi.org/10.1007/s11747-011-0278-x

Bannigan, K., & Watson, R. (2009). Reliability and validity in a nutshell. *Journal of clinical nursing, 18*(23), 3237-3243. http://dx.doi.org/10.1111/j.1365-2702.2009.02939.x

Barendse, M., Oort, F., & Timmerman, M. (2015). Using exploratory factor analysis to determine the dimensionality of discrete responses. *Structural Equation Modeling: A Multidisciplinary Journal, 22*(1), 87-101. http://dx.doi.org/10.1080/10705511.2014.934850

Berisha-Namani, M. (2009, 24-27 March). *The role of information technology in small and medium sized enterprises in Kosova.* Paper presented at the Fulbright Academy 2009 Conference Small Places Can Change the World. , Skopje, Macedonia.

Blili, S., & Raymond, L. (1993). Information technology: Threats and opportunities for small and medium-sized enterprises. *International Journal of Information Management, 13*(6), 439-448. http://dx.doi.org/10.1016/0268-4012(93)90060-H

Cooper, D. R., & Schindler, P. S. (2006). *Business research methods* (Eleventh ed.): The McGraw-Hill/Irwin series (Operations and decision sciences).

Cragg, P. B., & Zinatelli, N. (1995). The evolution of information systems in small firms. *Information & Management, 29*(1), 1-8. http://dx.doi.org/10.1016/0378-7206(95)00012-L

Cronbach, L. J. (1951). Coefficient alpha and the internal structure of tests. *psychometrika, 16*(3), 297-334. http://dx.doi.org/10.1007/bf02310555

Davis, F. D. (1989). Perceived Usefulness, Perceived Ease of Use, and User Acceptance of Information Technology. *MIS Quarterly, 13*(3), 319-340. http://dx.doi.org/10.2307/249008

DeLone, W. H. (1981). Firm Size and the Characteristics of Computer Use. *MIS Quarterly, 5*(4), 65-77. http://dx.doi.org/10.2307/249328

DeLone, W. H., & McLean, E. R. (1992). Information Systems Success: The Quest for the Dependent Variable. *Information Systems Research, 3*(1), 60-95. http://dx.doi.org/10.1287/isre.3.1.60

DeLone, W. H., & McLean, E. R. (2003). The DeLone and McLean model of information systems success: a ten-year update. *Journal of Management Information Systems, 19*(4), 9-30.

DelVecchio, M. (1994). Retooling the staff along with the system. *Bests Review, 94*(11), 82-83.

Deros, B. M., Yusof, S. M., & Salleh, A. M. (2006). A benchmarking implementation framework for automotive manufacturing SMEs. *Benchmarking, 13*(4), 396-430. http://dx.doi.org/10.1108/14635770610676272

Doll, W. J., Xia, W., & Torkzadeh, G. (1994). A confirmatory factor analysis of the end-user computing satisfaction instrument. *MIS Quarterly*, 453-461. http://dx.doi.org/10.2307/249524

Fathian, M., Akhavan, P., & Hoorali, M. (2008). E-readiness assessment of non-profit ICT SMEs in a developing country: The case of Iran. *Technovation, 28*(9), 578-590. http://dx.doi.org/10.1016/j.technovation.2008.02.002

Fink, D. (1998). Guidelines for the Successful Adoption of Information Technology in Small and Medium Enterprises. *International Journal of Information Management, 18*(4), 243-253. http://dx.doi.org/10.1016/S0268-4012(98)00013-9

Fornell, C., & Larcker, D. F. (1981). Structural equation models with unobservable variables and measurement error: Algebra and statistics. *Journal of marketing research*, 382-388. http://dx.doi.org/10.2307/3150980

Fraenkel, J. R., & Wallen, N. E. (2009). *How to design and evaluate research in education* (7th ed.). New York, NY: McGraw-Hill.

Freel, M. S. (2000). Barriers to product innovation in small manufacturing firms. *International Small Business Journal, 18*(2), 60-80. http://dx.doi.org/10.1177/0266242600182003

Gable, G. G., Sedera, D., & Chan, T. Z. (2008). Re-conceptualizing information system success: The IS-Impact measurement model. *Journal of the Association for Information Systems, 9*(7), 377-408.

Gefen, D., Straub, D., & Boudreau, M. C. (2000). Structural equation modeling and regression: Guidelines for research practice. *Communications of the Association for Information Systems, 4*(1), 7.

Ghobakhloo, M., & Tang, S. H. (2015). Information system success among manufacturing SMEs: case of developing countries. *Information Technology for Development*, 1-28. http://dx.doi.org/10.1080/02681102.2014.996201

Gibb, A. A. (2000). SME Policy, Academic Research and the Growth of Ignorance, Mythical Concepts, Myths, Assumptions, Rituals and Confusions. *International Small Business Journal, 18*(3), 13. http://dx.doi.org/10.1177/0266242600183001

Gliem, J. A., & Gliem, R. R. (2003, 8-10 October). *Calculating, interpreting, and reporting Cronbach's alpha reliability coefficient for Likert-type scales.* Paper presented at the Midwest Research-to-Practice Conference in Adult, Continuing, and Community Education, The Ohio State University, Columbus, OH.

Gorla, N., Somers, T. M., & Wong, B. (2010). Organizational impact of system quality, information quality, and service quality. *The Journal of Strategic Information Systems, 19*(3), 207-228. http://dx.doi.org/10.1016/j.jsis.2010.05.001

Grazzi, M., & Vergara, S. (2012). ICT in developing countries: Are language barriers relevant? Evidence from Paraguay. *Information Economics and Policy, 24*(2), 161-171.

http://dx.doi.org/10.1016/j.infoecopol.2011.11.001

Hair, J. F., Black, W. C., Babin, B. J., Anderson, R. E., & Tatham, R. L. (2006). *Multivariate data analysis* (Vol. 6): Pearson Prentice Hall Upper Saddle River, NJ.

Hawari, A. a., & Heeks, R. (2010). Explaining ERP failure in a developing country: a Jordanian case study. *Journal of Enterprise Information Management, 23*(2), 135-160. http://dx.doi.org/10.1108/17410391011019741

Hinkin, T. R. (1995). A review of scale development practices in the study of organizations. *Journal of management, 21*(5), 967-988. http://dx.doi.org/10.1177/014920639502100509

Hurley, A. E., Scandura, T. A., Schriesheim, C. A., Brannick, M. T., Seers, A., Vandenberg, R. J., & Williams, L. J. (1997). Exploratory and confirmatory factor analysis: Guidelines, issues, and alternatives. *Journal of organizational behavior, 18*(6), 667-683. http://dx.doi.org/10.1002/(SICI)1099-1379(199711)18:6<667::AID-JOB874>3.0.CO;2-T

Irani, Z. (2008). Information systems evaluation: what does it mean? *Construction Innovation, Vol. 8* (No. 2, 2008), pp. 88-91. http://dx.doi.org/10.1108/14714170810867014

Irefin, I., Abdul-Azeez, I., & Tijani, A. (2012). An Investigative Study of The Factors Affecting The Adoption of Information and Communication Technology in Small and Medium Scale Enterprises in Nigeria. *Australian Journal of Business and Management Research Vol, 2*(02), 01-09.

Juell-Skielse, G. (2006). *ERP adoption in small and medium sized enterprises.* Thesis, Data- och systemvetenskap University, Kista. Retrieved from http://urn.kb.se/resolve?urn=urn:nbn:se:kth:diva-3982

Kale, P., Banwait, S., & Laroiya, S. (2010). Performance evaluation of ERP implementation in Indian SMEs. *Journal of Manufacturing Technology Management, 21*(6), 758-780. http://dx.doi.org/10.1108/17410381011064030

Kartiwi, M., & MacGregor, R. (2007). Electronic Commerce Adoption Barriers in Small to Medium-Sized Enterprises (SMEs) in Developed and Developing Countries: A Cross-Country Comparison. *Journal of Electronic Commerce in Organizations,, 5*(3), 35-51. http://dx.doi.org/10.4018/jeco.2007070103

Kimberlin, C. L., & Winterstein, A. G. (2008). Validity and reliability of measurement instruments used in research. *American Journal of Health-System Pharmacy, 65*(23). http://dx.doi.org/10.2146/ajhp070364

Koh, S. C. L., Gunasekaran, A., & Cooper, J. R. (2009). The demand for training and consultancy investment in SME-specific ERP systems implementation and operation. *International Journal of Production Economics, 122(1),* 241–254. http://dx.doi.org/10.1016/j.ijpe.2009.05.017

Lance, C. E. (2011). More statistical and methodological myths and urban legends. *Organizational Research Methods, 14*(2), 279-286. http://dx.doi.org/10.1177/1094428110391814

Lefebvre, E., & Lefebvre, L. A. (1992). Firm innovativeness and CEO characteristics in small manufacturing firms. *Journal of Engineering and Technology Management, 9*(3), 243-277. http://dx.doi.org/10.1016/0923-4748(92)90018-Z

Levy, M., & Powell, P. (1998). SME flexibility and the role of information systems. *Small Business Economics, 11*(2), 183-196. http://dx.doi.org/10.1023/A:1007912714741

Levy, M., & Powell, P. (2000). Information systems strategy for small and medium sized enterprises: an organisational perspective. *The Journal of Strategic Information Systems, 9*(1), 63-84. http://dx.doi.org/10.1016/S0963-8687(00)00028-7

Lin, C. Y.-Y. (1998). Success Factors of Small- and Medium-Sized Enterprises in Taiwan: An Analysis of Cases. *Journal of Small Business Management, 36*(4), 43-56.

Little, T. D., Cunningham, W. A., Shahar, G., & Widaman, K. F. (2002). To parcel or not to parcel: Exploring the question, weighing the merits. *Structural Equation Modeling, 9*(2), 151-173. http://dx.doi.org/10.1207/S15328007SEM0902_1

Loh, T. C., & Koh, S. C. L. (2004). Critical elements for a successful enterprise resource planning implementation in small-and medium-sized enterprises. *International Journal of Production Research, 42*(17), 3433-3455. http://dx.doi.org/10.1080/00207540410001671679

Mabert, V. A., Soni, A., & Venkataramanan, M. A. (2003a). Enterprise resource planning: Managing the implementation process. *European Journal of Operational Research, 146*(2), 302-314.

http://dx.doi.org/10.1016/S0377-2217(02)00551-9

Mabert, V. A., Soni, A., & Venkataramanan, M. A. (2003b). The impact of organization size on enterprise resource planning (ERP) implementations in the US manufacturing sector. *Omega, 31*(3), 235-246. http://dx.doi.org/10.1016/S0305-0483(03)00022-7

MacKenzie, K. D., & House, R. (1978). Paradigm Development in the Social Sciences: A Proposed Research Strategy. *Academy of Management Review*, 7-23. http://dx.doi.org/10.5465/AMR.1978.4296297

Manochehri, N., Al-Esmail, R., & Ashrafi, R. (2012). Examining the Impact of Information and Communication Technologies (ICT) on Enterprise Practices: A Preliminary Perspective from Qatar. *The Electronic Journal of Information Systems in Developing Countries, 51*.

Martin-Tapia, I., Aragon-Correa, J. A., & Senise-Barrio, M. E. (2008). Being green and export intensity of SMEs: The moderating influence of perceived uncertainty. *Ecological Economics, 68*(1-2), 56-67. http://dx.doi.org/10.1016/j.ecolecon.2008.01.032

McCartan-Quinn, D., & Carson, D. (2003). Issues which Impact upon Marketing in the Small Firm. *Small Business Economics, 21*(2), 201-213. http://dx.doi.org/10.1023/A:1025070107609

McGrath, J. E. (1964). Toward a "theory of method" for research on organizations. *New perspectives in organization research, 533*, 533-547.

Mirani, R., & Lederer, A. L. (1998). An Instrument for Assessing the Organizational Benefits of IS Projects. *Decision Sciences, 29*(4), 803-838. http://dx.doi.org/10.1111/j.1540-5915.1998.tb00878.x

Modimogale, L., & Kroeze, J. H. (2011). The Role of ICT within Small and Medium Enterprises in Gauteng. *Communications 2011*. http://dx.doi.org/10.5171/2011.369288

Myers, B. L., Kappelman, L. A., & Prybutok, V. R. (1998). A comprehensive model for assessing the quality and productivity of the information systems function: toward a theory for information systems assessment. *Information systems success measurement* (pp. 94-121). North Texas University, Information Systems Research: IGI Publishing.

Ndiege, J. R. A., Wayi, N., & Herselman, M. E. (2012). Quality Assessment of Information Systems in SMEs: A Study of Eldoret Town in Kenya. *The Electronic Journal of Information Systems in Developing Countries, 51*.

O'Reagan, N., & Ghobadian., A. (2004). Testing the homogeneity of SMEs: The impact of size on managerial and organisational processes. *European Business Review, 16*(1), 64-79. http://dx.doi.org/10.1108/09555340410512411

Pallant, J. (2013). *SPSS survival manual*: McGraw-Hill International.

Patel, F., Sooknanan, P., Rampersad, G., & Mundkur, A. (2012). *Information Technology, Development, and Social Change* (Vol. 32). New York: Routledge.

Petter, S., DeLone, W., & McLean, E. (2008). Measuring information systems success: models, dimensions, measures, and interrelationships. *European Journal of Information Systems, 17*(3), 236-263. http://dx.doi.org/10.1057/ejis.2008.15

Rabaa'i, A. A. (2012). *Evaluating the success of large-scale, integrated information systems through the lens of IS-impact and IS-support.* (PhD thesis), Queensland University of Technology.

Rampersad, G. (2008). *Management of Innovation Networks in Technology Transfer.* (PhD thesis), Business School, The University of Adelaide,.

Rampersad, G., & Troshani, I. (2013). High-speed broadband: assessing its social impact. *Industrial Management & Data Systems, 113*(4), 541-557. http://dx.doi.org/10.1108/02635571311322784

Rampersad, G., Quester, P., & Troshani, I. (2009). Developing and evaluating scales to assess innovation networks. *International Journal of Technology Intelligence and Planning, 5*(4), 402-420. http://dx.doi.org/10.1504/IJTIP.2009.029378

Rampersad, G., Quester, P., & Troshani, I. (2010). Managing innovation networks: Exploratory evidence from ICT, biotechnology and nanotechnology networks. *Industrial Marketing Management, 39*(5), 793-805. http://dx.doi.org/10.1016/j.indmarman.2009.07.002

Rampersad, G., Troshani, I., & Plewa, C. (2012). IOS adoption in innovation networks: a case study. *Industrial Management & Data Systems, 112*(9), 1366-1382. http://dx.doi.org/10.1108/02635571211278974

Roztocki, N., & Weistroffer, H. R. (2011). Information technology success factors and models in developing and emerging economies. *Information Technology for Development, 17*(3), 163-167. http://dx.doi.org/10.1080/02681102.2011.568220

Said, H., Badru, B. B., & Shahid, M. (2011). Confirmatory Factor Analysis (Cfa) for Testing Validity And Reliability Instrument in the Study of Education. *Australian Journal of Basic & Applied Sciences, 5*(12).

Salmeron, J. L., & Bueno, S. (2006). An information technologies and information systems industry-based classification in small and medium-sized enterprises: An institutional view. *European Journal of Operational Research, 173*(3), 1012-1025. http://dx.doi.org/10.1016/j.ejor.2005.07.002

Schreiber, J. B., Nora, A., Stage, F. K., Barlow, E. A., & King, J. (2006). Reporting structural equation modeling and confirmatory factor analysis results: A review. *The Journal of Educational Research, 99*(6), 323-338. http://dx.doi.org/10.3200/JOER.99.6.323-338

Schumacker, R. E., & Lomax, R. G. (2004). *A beginner's guide to structural equation modeling*: Psychology Press. http://dx.doi.org/10.4324/9781410610904

Seddon, P. B. (1997). A Respecification and Extension of the DeLone and McLean Model of IS Success. *Information Systems Research, 8*(3), 240-253. http://dx.doi.org/10.1287/isre.8.3.240

Seddon, P., & Kiew, M. Y. (1996). A Partial Test and Development of Delone and Mclean's Model of IS Success. *Australasian Journal of Information Systems, 4*(1). http://dx.doi.org/10.3127/ajis.v4i1.379

Seibert, M. J., III. (2004). *The identification of strategic management counseling competencies essential for the Small Business and Technology Development Center: A modified Delphi study.* (Doctor of Philosophy Thesis), North Carolina State University, United States - North Carolina.

Shang, S., & Seddon, P. B. (2002). Assessing And Managing The Benefits Of Enterprise Systems: The Business Manager's Perspective. *Information Systems Journal, 12(4),* 271-299. http://dx.doi.org/10.1046/j.1365-2575.2002.00132.x

Skoko, H. (2012). Influencing Factors Model of Information and Communication Technology (ICT) in Saudi Arabian Small and Medium Enterprises (SMEs). *The GCC Economies,* 229-234. http://dx.doi.org/10.1007/978-1-4614-1611-1_19

Skoko, H., & Ceric, A. (2010, 29 June- 2 July). *Study on Information and Communication Technology (ICT) Models of Adoption and Use in the Kingdom of Saudi Arabian SMEs.* Paper presented at the The 6th International Conference on Social and Organizational Informatics and Cybernetics: SOIC 2010 in the context of The 4th International Multi-Conference on Society, Cybernetics and Informatics: IMSCI 2010, Orlando, FL USA.

Snider, B., da Silveira, G. J. C., & Balakrishnan, J. (2009). ERP implementation at SMEs: analysis of five Canadian cases. *International Journal of Operations & Production Management, 29*(1/2), 4-29. http://dx.doi.org/10.1108/01443570910925343

Soja, P. (2008). Difficulties in enterprise system implementation in emerging economies: Insights from an exploratory study in Poland. *Information Technology for Development, 14*(1), 31-51. http://dx.doi.org/10.1002/itdj.20086

Straub, D., Boudreau, M. C., & Gefen, D. (2004). Validation guidelines for IS positivist research. *The Communications of the Association for Information Systems, 13*(1), 63. http://dx.doi.org/10.4018/978-1-59140-144-5.ch002

Sun, A. Y. T., Yazdani, A., & Overend, J. D. (2005). Achievement assessment for enterprise resource planning (ERP) system implementations based on critical success factors (CSFs). *International Journal of Production Economics, 98*(2), 189-203. http://dx.doi.org/10.1016/j.ijpe.2004.05.013

Tate, M., Sedera, D., McLean, E., & Burton-Jones, A. (2014). Information Systems Success Research: The "20-Year Update?" Panel Report from PACIS, 2011. *Communications of the Association for Information Systems, 34*(1), 63.

Urbach, N., Smolnik, S., & Riempp, G. (2009). The state of research on information systems success. *Business & Information Systems Engineering, 1*(4), 315-325. http://dx.doi.org/10.1007/s12599-009-0059-y

Vrgovic, P., Glassman, B., Walton, A., & Vidicki, P. (2012). Open innovation for SMEs in developing countries-an intermediated communication network model for collaboration beyond obstacles (revision). *INNOVATION: Management, Policy & Practice*(0), 587-614. http://dx.doi.org/10.5172/impp.2012.587

Waverman, L., Coyle, D., & Souter, D. (2011). ICT in Saudi Arabia: A Socio-Economic Impact Review. Kingdom of Saudi Arabia: Produced by STC in collaboration with VHM-Beirut, Regulatory Affairs.

Wei, K. S., Loong, A. C., Leong, Y. M., & Ooi, K. B. (2009, 7-8 December). *Measuring ERP system success: a respecification of the Delone and McLean's IS success model.* Paper presented at the Symposium on Progress in Information and Communication Technology (SPICT'09), Kuala Lumpur, Malaysia

Yang, C., Nay, S., & Hoyle, R. H. (2009). Three approaches to using lengthy ordinal scales in structural equation models: Parceling, latent scoring, and shortening scales. *Applied Psychological Measurement.* http://dx.doi.org/10.1177/0146621609338592

Yap, C., Soh, C., & Raman, K. (1992). Information systems success factors in small business. *Omega, 20*(5-6), 597-609. http://dx.doi.org/10.1016/0305-0483(92)90005-R

12

A Synthetic Player for Ayò Board Game Using Alpha-Beta Search and Learning Vector Quantization

Oluwatobi, A. Ayilara[1], Anuoluwapo, O. Ajayi[1] & Kudirat, O. Jimoh[1]

[1] Computer Science and Engineering, Obafemi Awolowo University, Nigeria

Correspondence: Anuoluwapo Ajayi, Computer Science & Engineering, Obafemi Awolowo University, Nigeria.
E-mail: anuajayi@yahoo.com

Abstract

Game playing especially, Ayò game has been an important topic of research in artificial intelligence and several machine learning approaches have been used, but the need to optimize computing resources is important to encourage significant interest of users. This study presents a synthetic player (Ayò) implemented using Alpha-beta search and Learning Vector Quantization network. The program for the board game was written in Java and MATLAB. Evaluation of the synthetic player was carried out in terms of the win percentage and game length. The synthetic player had a better efficiency compared to the traditional Alpha-beta search algorithm.

Keywords: intelligence, board game, win ratio, computing resources

1. Introduction

Developers are utilizing various computing techniques to create efficient games that will run in reasonable time to encourage interest from users. Ayò is an African game board made of a wooden substance. It is a rectangular board with twelve circular carved out pits (pockets) arranged in two rows of six pits, and each pit containing four seeds. The game belongs to the class of two-person, zero-sum game (Van den Herik, Uiterwijk, &Van Rijswijck, 2002). In playing the game, a player selects one of the non-empty pits and starts sowing in a counter clockwise direction and whenever the sowing reaches the originated pit, it is ignored. Seeds are captured when the last seed falls in an enemy's pit containing 1 or 2 seeds. Additional seeds are captured in pits immediately preceding the captured pit if they contain 2 or 3 seeds. Capturing occurs only in the enemy's pits. The game ends when any player has obtained 25 or more seeds. Mancala is the general name for the many variations (Awale, Oware,Awari, et al.) of the game played throughout Africa, as well as in other parts of the world. Refer to (Allis, Van Der Meulen, & Vanden Herik, 1991; Allis, 1994; Romein & Bal, 2002) for further information. However, one limiting feature of strategically played board games like Ayò is that they consume computational resources (Romein & Bal, 2002), due to their huge game states. Awale for instance, has a game tree complexity of 10^{31}(Allis, 1994; Van den Herik et al., 2002). This feature makes playing the game on most low-cost devices computationally challenging.

There is no doubt that numerous literature on computer games (Gomboc, Buro,& Marsland, 2005; Guid et al., 2006; Al-Mahmuda, Mubin, Shahid, & Martens, 2010) exist, and the need to design more storage efficient algorithms for games has encouraged the proposition of several techniques. However, only few exist in terms of design and architecture for resource optimization.Allis (1994) proposed a Minimax Search Algorithm (MSA), which employed the backward induction to predict game in Awale. However, the main difficulty posed by minimax search is how to develop and apply an evaluation function to a game tree. A database containing all board positions with 35 or less seeds to improve the playing strength of Awale was constructed in (Lincke & Marzetta, 2000). The retrograde analysis was proposed to find the optimal play for all the possible board positions of Awari (Romein & Bal, 2002; Romein & Bal, 2003). However, both endgame databases and retrograde analysis techniques are expensive to implement as the game requires more storage space. Meta-heuristic based hybrid technique was proposed to mine endgame databases for relevant features that are useful in the construction of a static evaluation function (Davis & Kendall, 2002; Daoud, 2004). Akinyemi, Adebiyi, and Longe (2009) proposed a refinement based heuristic technique for human-like decision making for playing *Ayò* game. The performance of Minimax search and aggregate Mahalanobis distance function in Evolving an Ayo Player was investigated by (Randle, Olugbara & Lall, 2012).

The Learning Vector Quantization (LVQ) network is an algorithm widely used in the classification of high-dimensional data (Biehl, Ghosh,& Hammer, 2007). Successful applications of LVQ include medical image analysis, fault detection, or classification of satellite spectral data (Bojer, Hammer, & Koers, 2003; Kuncheva, 2004; Schleif, 2006). Its popularity can be attributed to the modest implementation of its procedures and the fact that its complexity can be controlled during training according to specific needs. Both, the training algorithm and the resulting classification scheme are fairly easy to implement. In practice, the computational effort of LVQ training usually scales linearly with the training set size, and its classification depends on the (fixed) number of learning techniques (prototypes) andinput dimensionality (Biehl et al., 2007). This study therefore, proposes a synthetic player (called Ayò) that combined the Alpha-beta search algorithm with LVQ to enhancethe efficiency of Alpha-beta search.

2. The Synthetic Player Framework

The section describes the techniques and tools used in the design and implementation of the synthetic player for the game.

2.1 Alpha-Beta Pruning

Alpha-beta pruning is an algorithm that minimizes the game-tree search for some wrong moves. It simply identifies moves that are not beneficial and eliminate them from the game tree (Jones, 2008). The algorithm simply calculates and maintains two variables (alpha and beta) during the depth-first search of the game tree. The alpha variable defines the best move that maximizes the Alpha-beta search's best move while the beta variable defines the best move that minimizes the opposing player's best move.Although, Alpha-beta pruning method provides its best performance when the game tree is arranged such that the best choice at each level is the first one to be examined by the algorithm. That is, it only removes only one leaf node from the tree, but in larger game trees, this can result in fairly valuable reductions in tree size. In most cases, it will not necessarily remove large portions of the game tree. While simulating the playing of Ayò boardgame between Alpha-beta search and Random player (a computer program that uses stochastic algorithm to select any non empty pit to play), it was discovered after a careful analysis of the game data (playing patterns) generated by both players that Alpha-beta search made few wrong moves (though infrequent) by not distributing seeds from pits with heavily loaded seeds (called Odù in Yorubálanguage) as appropriate.Figure1illustrates an example of this problem, assuming the transition from state n to state n+1. For a given state n in the game, where it is the Alpha-beta's turn to make a move. Unfortunately, Alpha-beta search distributed the four seeds in pit E (Figure 1a) instead of distributing the 17 seeds in pit C (see Figure1b)which could have fetched additional 5 seeds (two seeds in pit c and 3 seeds in pit d as gains(see Figure1c). Unfortunately, Alpha-beta search had missed the opportunity to gain additional five seeds in that given state (state n).Not playing heavily loaded pits at the appropriate time may unnecessarily elongates the game length, which implicitly may affect computing resources.We intend to avoid this problem by combining LVQ with Alpha-beta to minimize this effect. The introduction of LVQ is to help in determining the appropriateness at which heavily loaded pits (Odù)are played.

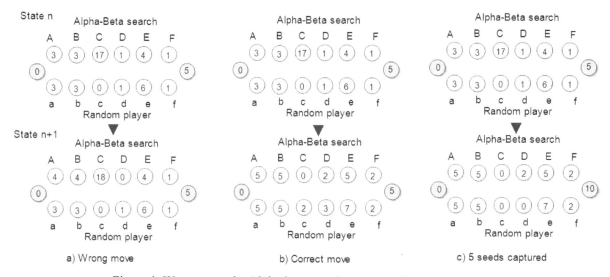

Figure 1. Wrong move by Alpha-beta search (a) versus the right move (b)

2.2 Learning Vector Quantization Network

To minimize the Alpha-beta limitation, the key states (locations of heaped seeds that when played will shorten playing length) were determined experimentally using simulated games between Alpha-beta search and Random player. The key states were then used to train the LVQ in order to optimally select and play seeds in the heavily loaded pits appropriately, to reduce game length. The LVQ network architecture adapted from (Demuth & Beale, 2001) and depicted in Figure2, has R number of elements in the input vector, S^1 number of competitive neurons, and S^2 number of linear neurons. The network has two layers, the competitive and the linear layer. The neurons in a competitive layer distribute themselves to recognize frequently presented input vectors while the linear layer transforms the competitive layer's classes into target classifications defined by the user. The LVQ for the Ayò player has eight (8) neurons in the hidden layer and one neuron in the output layer. The training data (derived experimentally)for the network is the vector [33.2, 27.2], which represents the class percentages or frequencies at which seeds are heaped in the pits (indices D, C, B, and A) of the Ayò player. In practice, these pits have large number of seeds as observed from the several simulated games played by the Alpha-beta search against the Random player. The network learning rate was 0.01 and its learning function was Learning Vector Quantization 1 weight learning function (learn 1v1). The LVQ network was trained for a maximum of 500 epochs. The following equations were used as the LVQ input.

$$c = argmax_{i:i\in\{7,8...,12\}} pit_i \tag{1}$$

$$d = \frac{\sum_{i=7}^{12} pit_i}{6} \tag{2}$$

$$v = \begin{bmatrix} c \\ \lfloor d \rfloor \end{bmatrix} \tag{3}$$

where c is the pit (belonging to Ayò player) which contains the largest number of seeds, variable d is the averagenumber of seeds in the pits belonging to the syntheticplayer, and $\lfloor d \rfloor$ is the largest integer less than or equal to d. The input v is passed to the competitive layer which used the winner takes all Hebbian learning approach to determine the network's output, that is, the particular heavily loaded pit (Odù) to play.

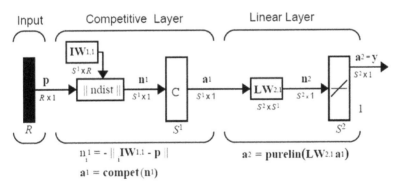

Figure 2. LVQ network architecture

2.3 Performance Evaluation

The Ayò board game was simulated in both Java and MATLAB R2012a environment. Java language was used to implement the Alpha-beta search algorithm due to its recursive nature. Moreover, creating recursive algorithms in Java can be easily accomplished. The MATLAB software includes Java Virtual Machine (JVM) software, that enables Java interpreter to be used via MATLAB commands, purposely to assist in the creation and running of programs that access Java objects. This feature enables MATLAB users to take advantage of the special capabilities of the Java programming language. The Java class implementing the Alpha-beta search algorithm was made available in the MATLAB workspace by placing it on the static Java class path and then invoked within the MATLAB environment. The Alpha-beta search algorithm implemented in this study used a 4-level depth minimax search together with the LVQ described above to evolve the Ayò player. The simulation was run on an Intel (R) Pentium 2.20 GHz machine. Figure 3 depicts sample simulation result. To compare the performance of Alpha-beta search with the synthetic player (LVQ_Alpha-beta), several games between Alpha-beta search versus Random player (a program having its playing patterns or moves unpredictable) andLVQ_Alphabeta versus Random player were simulated. Four simulation experiments were conducted as follows. The first experiment consisted of 1000 simulated games between Alpha-beta search versus Random player; and LVQ_Alphabeta against Random player. In the second experiment, 4000 simulated games between Alpha-beta versus Random and LVQ_Alphabeta against Random player were simulated. Similarly, the third and forth experiments consisted of 7000 and 10000 simulated games between the opposing players as configured for experiments 1 and 2 above. All experiments were repeated x times and the average game length for games played between LVQ_Alphabeta and Random player; and the average game length for games between Alpha-beta search against Random player were recorded and compared. Also recorded were the number of games won and loss by both LVQ_Alphabeta and Alpha-beta search against the Random player. The average game length (avl) is as defined as follows.

$$avl = \frac{1}{n}\left(\sum_{i=1}^{n} t_i\right) \qquad (4)$$

Where $t_i$isthe average turns made by eitherLVQ_Alphabeta or Alpha-beta search against the Random playerin game i, and n is the total number of games played. The notation for the Win percentage is given as:

$$winPercentage = (games\ won)/(total\ games\ played\ excluding\ draws) \times 100 \qquad (5)$$

The average number of turns used by all the three players- Random, Alpha-beta search and *Ayò* were noted. The Win percentage of games (excluding draws) played between the Random player and the Alpha-beta search, and the Random player versus the *Ayò* (LVQ-Alpha-beta) player were also recorded.

Figure3. Sample screenshot of the board game

3. Results

The average game lengths recorded for both LVQ_Alpha-beta and Alpha-beta search against the Random playerare shown in Table 1. The overall average game lengths for the two players were 36.48 and 51.93 respectively, resulting in approximately 30% reduction in game length usingLVQ-Alphabeta. Also shown in Table 1, is the percentage number of games (excluding draws) won by both Alpha-beta search and LVQ-Alphabeta players. The percentage numbers of games won by both players against the Random player were approximately70% and 83%, respectively.The results obtained in this study showed that the LVQ has enhanced the Alpha-beta search performance with shorter game length and with a higher win ratio. Thus, the addition of LVQ to Alpha-beta search has brought significant improvement in efficiency. The implication of this result is that Ayo will reduce computing processing time and also run conveniently on low cost handheld devices.

Table 1.Results of Random player versus LVQ_Aphabeta and Alpha-beta

Experiment	Win Percentage		Average game length (95%CI)	
	LVQ_Alphabeta	Alpha-beta search	LVQ_Alphabeta	Alpha-beta search
#1	82.7(0.51)	70.5(0.55)	35.6(3.26)	47.9(8.21)
#2	83.5(0.82)	70.6(0.59)	35.9(2.78)	47.6(7.01)
#3	83.3(0.68)	70.4(0.27)	37.6(3.32)	54.4(6.35)
#4	82.6(0.55)	70.3(0.18)	36.8(2.51)	57.8(9.85)

4. Conclusion and Future Direction

In this study, a synthetic player utilizing Alpha-beta search and LVQ network is presented. The synthetic player (Ayò) was simulated in MATLAB environment and evaluated in terms of the game length and win percentage.The result of performance evaluation has indicated that LVQ was able enhance Alpha-beta search by producing improved synthetic player for the Ayo board game that will optimize computing resources most importantly, the low-cost devices with limited capabilities.

References

Akinyemi, I. O., Adebiyi, E. F., & Longe, H. O. D. (2009). Critical analysis of decision making experience with a machine learning approach in playing Ayo game. *Engineering and Technology, 56*, 49-54.

Al-Mahmuda, A., Mubin, O., Shahid, S., & Martens, J. (2010). Designing social games for children and older adults: Two related case studies. *Entertainment Computing, 1*,147–156.http://dx.doi.org/10.1016/j.entcom.2010.09.001

Allis, L. V., Van der Meulen, M., & Van den Herik, H. J. (1991). Databases in Awale. In: Levy,D.N.L. &Beal,D.F. (Eds.).*Heuristic Programming in Artificial Intelligence, 2*, 73–86. Ellis Horwood, Chichester.

Allis, L. V. (1994). *Searching for solutions in games and artificial intelligence* (Unpublished Ph.D. thesis). University ofLimburg, Maastricht.

Biehl, M., Ghosh, A., & Hammer, B. (2007). Dynamics and generalization ability of LVQ algorithms. *Journal of Machine Learning Research, 8*, 323-360.

Bojer, T., Hammer, B., & Koers, C. (2003). Monitoring technical systems with prototype based clustering. In Verleysen,M. (Eds.). *European Symposium on Artificial Neural Networks*, 433–439. Evere, Belgium.http://dx.doi.org/10.1.1.13.5198/citeseerx.ist.psu.edu/viewdoc/summary?

Daoud, M., Kharma, N., Haidar, A., & Popoola, J. (2004). Ayo, the Awale player, or how better representation trumps deeper search. *Proceeding of the IEEE Congress on Evolutionary Computation*, 1001-1006.

Davis, J. E., & Kendall, G. (2002). An Investigation, using co-evolution, to evolve an Awale player. *Proceedings of Congress on Evolutionary Computation*, 1408-1413.

Demuth, H., & Beale, M. (2001). *Neural Network Toolbox for Use with MATLAB*. Massachusetts, MA: The MathWorks, Inc.

Gomboc, D., Buro, M., & Marsland, T. A. (2005). Tuning evaluation functions by maximizing concordance.*Theoretical Computer Science, 349*, 202–229.http://dx.doi.org/*10.1016/j.tcs.2005.09.047*

Guid, M., & Bratko, I. (2006). Computer analysis of world chess champions.*International Computer Games Association Journal, 29*, 65–73.

Jones, M. T. (2008). *Artificial intelligence a systems approach*. Massachusetts, MA: Infinity Science Press.

Kuncheva, L. I.(2004). In Roli, F., Kittler, J. &Windeatt,T. (Eds.), *Multiple Classifier Systems*, 1–15.Berlin: Springer.

Lincke, T. R., & Marzetta, A. (2000). Large endgame databases with limited memory space. *International Computer Games Association Journal, 23*, 131-138.

Randle, O. A., Olugbara, O. O., & Lall, M. (2012). Investigating the performance of Minimax search and aggregate Mahalanobis distance function in evolving an Ayo/Awale player. *International Journal of*

Computer, Electrical, Automation, Control and Information Engineering, 6, 953-956.

Romein, J. W., & Bal, H. C. (2002). Awale is solved. *International Computer Games Association Journal, 25*, 162-165.

Romein, J. W., & Bal, H. C. (2003). Solving the game of Awale using parallel retrograde analysis.*IEEE Computer, 36*, 23-33.http://dx.doi.org/10.1.1.57.7918/citeseerx.ist.psu.edu/viewdoc/summary?

Schleif, F. M., Villmann, T., & Hammer, B. (2006). Local metric adaptation for soft nearest prototype classification to classify proteomic data. In Bloch, I.,Petrosino, A.,&Tettamanzi, A.G.B. (Eds.).*International Workshop on Fuzzy Logic and Applications*, 290–296. Berlin.

Van den Herik, H. J., Uiterwijk, W. H. M., & Van Rijswijck, J. (2002). Games solved: Now and in the future. *Artificial Intelligence, 134*, 277–311.http://dx.doi.org/10.1016/S0004-3702 (01)00152-7

13

Ten Heuristics from Applying Agile Practices across Different Distribution Scenarios

Raoul Vallon[1] & Thomas Grechenig[1]

[1] Research Group for Industrial Software, Vienna University of Technology, Vienna, Austria

Correspondence: Raoul Vallon, Research Group for Industrial Software, Vienna University of Technology, Vienna, Austria. E-mail: raoul.vallon@inso.tuwien.ac.at

Abstract

Distributed software development (DSD) has become increasingly popular due to benefits such as cost savings, access to large multi-skilled workforces and a reduced time to market. Agile practices can potentially help increase transparency and mitigate communication and coordination issues in these complex environments. While empirical studies in the field exist, most are single-case studies that miss out on the chance to compare different distribution scenarios, which calls for further investigation. We report on results of a four-year exploratory multiple-case study investigating the agile process implementation in three different distribution scenarios: within-city, within-country and within-continent. We purposefully selected the three different cases and found ten common heuristics emerge which are based on empirical evidence in at least two cases as well as four further candidate heuristics that lack evidence in more than one case. In particular, the understanding of and adaptation to each development site's inherent challenges, travelling ambassadors/proxies between sites, and a balanced distribution of decision makers proved to be important heuristics for a successful process implementation.

Keywords: distributed software development, distributed teams, agile, scrum, multiple-case study

1. Introduction

Agile software development is built around empowered and self-organizing teams with a strong focus on collaboration and communication supported by various agile practices including pairing, customer collaboration, stand-ups, reviews, retrospectives and the planning game (Šmite et al., 2010). Developing software globally is a daily reality for many organizations. The benefits of global software development include cost savings, access to large multi-skilled workforces and reduced time to market, among others (Ó Conchúir et al., 2009). Agile software development may potentially improve collaboration in distributed environments as it relies strongly on frequent communication (Hossain et al., 2011a). However neither the leading agile process scrum (Schwaber & Beedle, 2002) nor eXtreme Programming (XP) (Beck, 2000) was designed for distributed teams working in distributed environments. Hence adaptations to the original process are necessary (Batra, 2009). The goal of these process adaptations is to transfer agile values, which produced excellent results in the last decade for collocated teams (Dingsøyr et al., 2012), to distributed software development (DSD) environments.

This study provides the following contributions to the evolving research field of applying agile process in DSD environments:

1. Empirical evidence from a long-term four-year multiple-case study

2. Cross-case analysis of agile practices among these three different distribution scenarios (within-city, within-country and within-continent distribution)

3. Addressing the need for robust primary empirical studies researching DSD (Marques et al., 2012) and agile practices in DSD in particular (Hanssen et al., 2011)

The remainder of the paper is organized as follows. Section 2 discusses our research objective with regard to previously reported work. The detailed multiple-case research design is explained in Section 3. Section 4 presents each case individually. Section 5 analyzes cross-case results and describes limitations of the study. Section 6 offers conclusions and an outlook to future work.

2. Research Objective in Light of Previous Work

There are various systematic literature reviews covering (globally) distributed software development (Verner et al., 2012; Marques et al., 2012). Most relevant to our line of research are the ones focusing on agile practices in DSD environments (Hossain et al., 2009; Jalali & Wohlin, 2011; Hanssen et al., 2011). We were especially interested in the multiple-case studies conducted in the field and looked at all relevant studies in the systematic review of Jalali and Wohlin (2011) (who cover years 1999-2009) and extended the analysis to years 2010-2014. We found seven multiple-case studies for the years of 2010-2014 as compared to three multiple-case studies for 1999-2009 (Jalali & Wohlin, 2011) which indicates an increasing research focus and interest on agile practices in DSD. Jalali and Wohlin (2011) showed that context is not richly described in empirical studies in the area of agile DSD. We further investigated how context has been described in past studies and built a conceptual framework (cf. Figure 1) to use for our multiple-case study and address the identified shortcoming. Moreover, in previous multiple-case studies we found methodological triangulation to be scarce. The most often used approach was semi-structured/open-ended interviews (Ramesh et al., 2006; Sison & Yang, 2007; Paasivaara et al., 2009; Srinivasan & Lundqvist, 2010; Paasivaara, 2011; Hossain et al., 2011a; Bass, 2012; Paasivaara et al., 2012; Ramesh et al., 2012; Badampudi et al., 2013), followed by document analysis (Sison & Yang, 2007; Hossain et al., 2011b; Ramesh et al., 2012) and observation (Hossain et al., 2011b). This finding supports the claim (Marques et al., 2012) that there is a need for robust primary empirical studies researching DSD and agile practices in DSD in particular (Hanssen et al., 2011).

We identified the following research gap: *As context information in past empirical studies is often not richly provided, it is hard to generalize from past studies in the field. This study aims to investigate three cases implementing agile practices in DSD in significantly different distribution scenarios and presents rich contextual information for each case respectively. The nature of our multiple-case study is exploratory in the way that is has no clear, single set of outcomes* (Yin, 2003) *and that it is to the best of our knowledge unprecedented in the approach of analyzing the emergence of common heuristics* (Heeager & Rose, 2014) *in several distribution scenarios (within-city, within-country and within-continent).*

Based on that objective, our main research question (RQ) is: Which heuristics, if any, can we see emerge when applying agile practices in different distribution scenarios? Within this research question, we define the following sub-questions to guide our research:

RQ1. *How have agile practices been applied in the different distribution scenarios?*

RQ2. *Which DSD practices have been used to complement agile practices?*

3. Research Context and Study Design

This multi-case study is a major step in a several-year research project aimed at empirically investigating the application of agile practices in DSD. As such it adds to the empirical basis of the research field and represents an important link between our initial systematic mapping (Vallon et al., forthcoming) and a comprehensive process framework for agile DSD yet to be developed in a future step.

Our research design follows the guidelines of Yin (2003) for general case study design and Verner et al. (2009) for conducting multiple-case studies in software engineering in particular. Furthermore we based our case study protocol on the template by Brereton et al. (2008) and the decisions along the way are embedded in this section.

3.1 Multiple-Case Study Design

We chose a case study design as a natural fit to our research problem as it "investigates a contemporary phenomenon within its real-life context, especially when the boundaries between phenomenon and context are not clearly evident" (Yin, 2003, p.13). Moreover, we want to focus on covering contextual background for which the case study is especially well-suited (Yin, 2003). Evidence from multiple cases is generally considered more compelling (Herriott & Firestone, 1983). Our unit of analysis is a project within an organization for which agile processes are applied in a distributed development environment, i.e. the development itself has to take place on at least two sites. Hence, our multiple-case study is an embedded case study focusing on the output of individual projects as compared to a holistic one (Yin, 2003). For selecting information-rich cases we used purposeful maximum variation (heterogeneity) sampling (Patton, 2002), i.e. we chose heterogeneous cases based on the characteristics developed in our conceptual framework (cf. Figure 1). Since scrum is the most widely used agile process also in DSD (Jalali & Wohlin, 2011) we decided to limit our case selection to scrum and choose the distribution scenario of the project as the primary dimension for selecting heterogeneous cases. The final selection involved three cases applying scrum practices in greatly different distribution scenarios: city-wide, country-wide and continent-wide. The assumed problem that individual cases are too different can be intentionally turned into strength: "Any common patterns that emerge from great variation are of particular interest and value in capturing the core experiences and central, shared dimensions of a setting or phenomenon" (Patton, 2002, p.235). First, each case is treated individually with an individual case report before the cross-case analysis (Yin, 2003).

3.2 Conceptual Framework

Based on our review of previous work in Section 2, we defined a conceptual framework with the key factors that we will focus on for our data collection (Verner et al., 2009). We base our conceptual framework on three main factors relevant to the context of our empirical study: DSD inspired by (Šmite et al., 2012; Jalali & Wohlin, 2011), scrum practices extraction inspired by (Paasivaara et al., 2009; Hossain et al., 2011b) and general information with regard to our unit of analysis (project) inspired by (Jalali & Wohlin, 2011; Hossain et al., 2011b). Figure 1 drafts our conceptual framework with all identified relevant empirical factors.

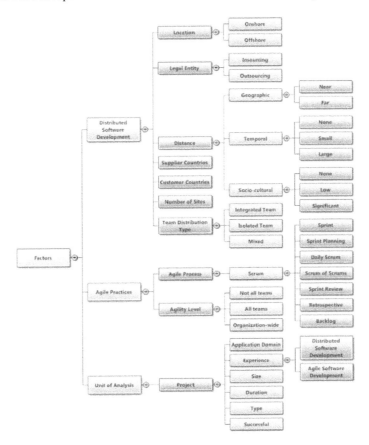

Figure 1. Conceptual framework developed from literature

3.3 Case Organizations

We purposefully selected three heterogeneous cases with regard to their varying distribution scenarios. Identities are withheld to preserve privacy and the three projects receive pseudonyms which will be used throughout the paper: *WithinCity* (sites within the same city), *WithinCountry* (sites within the same country) and *WithinContinent* (sites within the same continent).Table 1 shows an overview of the contextual factors *DSD* and *unit of analysis (project)*. The remaining contextual factor *agile (scrum)* is discussed during case analysis.

3.4 Data Collection

The data collection strategy is aimed at finding out which scrum practices organizations have applied to distributed projects in what way (RQ1), and which DSD practices have been used to complement the agile process (RQ2).

Our multiple-case study is qualitative and triangulation was a major concern because each method reveals different aspects of empirical reality (Denzin, 1978). Denzin (1978) has identified four types of triangulation:

Table 1. Contextual information on the selected cases

Factors	Sub-factors	Case WithinCity	Case WithinCountry	Case WithinContinent
DSD	Location	Onshore	Onshore	Offshore
	Legal Entity	Insourcing	Outsourcing	Insourcing
	Geographic Distance	Close	Near	Close
	Temporal Distance	None	None	-
	Socio-cultural Distance	None	None	Low
	Supplier Country	Austria	Austria	Austria and two other European Countries
	Customer Country	Austria	Germany	Austria
	Number of sites	2	2	3
	Team Distribution Type	Integrated Teams	Integrated Teams	Isolated Teams
Project	Application Domain	Web & Hardware	Enterprise Software	Web
	Experience with Agile	7+ years	3 years	3+ years
	Experience with DSD	10 years	2 years	15+ years
	Project Size	19	30	39
	Team Size	Site A (13), Site B (6)	Site A (20), Site B (10)	Site A (14), Site B (19), Site C (6)
	Project Duration	15 months	6 months	9 months
	Project Type	Industry	Industry	Industry
	Successful	Yes	Yes	Yes

Table 2. Different types of triangulation in the three cases

Cases	Method and Data Triangulation	Investigator and Theory Triangulation
WithinCity	Participant-Observation (1 Action researcher) Documentation (160 documents) Archival Records (3863 tickets in issue tracking system, 274 wiki pages) Physical Artifacts (thousands of sticky notes and dozens of paper boards)	Vallon (Primary Investigator) +1 Senior Researcher +2 Supporting Investigators
WithinCountry	Interviews (N=7) Direct Observation (5 meetings across several sprints) Documents (15 documents) Archival Records (579 tickets, 37 wiki pages) Physical Artifacts (thousands of sticky notes and dozens of paper boards)	Vallon (Primary Investigator) +1 Senior Researcher +3 Supporting Investigators
WithinContinent	Interviews (N=11) Documents (273 documents) Archival Records (only limited view)	Vallon (Primary Investigator) +1 Senior Researcher +4 Supporting Investigators

Data triangulation (variety of data sources), investigator triangulation (use of different researchers), theory triangulation (multiple perspectives to interpret a single set of data achieved by using multiple investigators (Stake, 1995)) and methodological triangulation (multiple methods to study a single problem). Table 2 shows how triangulation was achieved for each of the respective cases. Since triangulation is expensive, we employed it reasonably and practically (Patton, 2002) within the possibilities and limitations of each case. The triangulation sources are used as described by Yin (2003). With one exception, all supporting investigators were only involved in one case of the multiple-case study in an effort to minimize bias. The authors served as investigators in all three cases.

3.5 Data Analysis

Figure 2 illustrates our data analysis process. In case WithinCity we used Action Research (AR) as the primary research approach. AR uses "a spiral of steps, each of which is composed of a circle of planning, action, and fact-finding about the result of the action" (Lewin, 1946, p.38). Researchers and participants collaborate to meet respective goals. We had one researcher participate in the action research assuming the role of a scrum master. The supporting investigators and senior researcher (who were not participating in the action research on site) analyzed new data, discussed findings in regular research meetings each sprint with the action researcher and corroborated findings with documents and archival records. Overall the action researcher engaged in the following activities: explore data in ticket management tool, write notes in project diary, discuss impediments with practitioners and record actions and track their results, discuss and analyze the data collected with the off-site supporting investigators and senior researcher (each sprint).

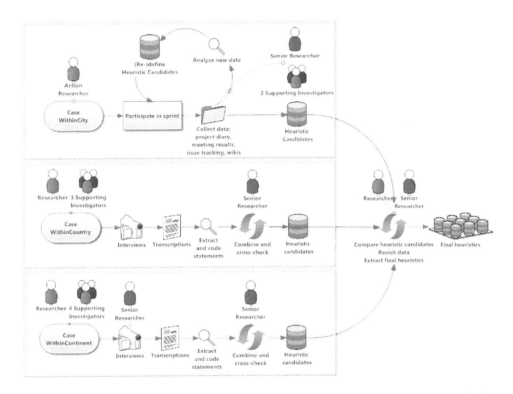

Figure 2. Research methodology of the three individual cases and the cross-case analysis

For cases WithinCountry and WithinContinent we used semi-structured interviews (Patton, 2002) which allow a conversational manner but still follow an interview protocol (Yin, 2003). The interviews were recorded and later transcribed and lasted from 0.5-3 hours (on average 100.5 minutes). We interviewed all different roles at least once for each case and also involved stakeholders. For analysis we applied grounded theory to start with empirical specifics and move towards general statements (Denzin & Lincoln, 2011). To extract findings we applied open coding (Strauss & Corbin, 1998), where the researcher generates categories fitting the data in relation to a general issue of concern (Bryman & Burgess, 1994). The process has been facilitated by using the ATLAS.ti qualitative data analysis software. In case WithinContinent the interview transcripts were additionally formally approved by the case organization before they were used for analysis. In case WithinCountry we also employed direct observation and observed the following meetings: several daily scrums, scrum of scrums, planning, review and retrospective.

For cases WithinCity and WithinCountry we were also able to collect physical artifacts in form of sticky notes and paper boards and extensively collected documents and archival records to triangulate findings. For WithinContintent we also collected documents but were only allowed limited access to archival records. We also held feedback sessions in each case with the participating organization to validate our theory.

4. Individual Case Results

This section presents results of the individual cases by reporting the background (context), challenges and agile practices specific to the case and the identified *heuristic candidates* for the cross-case analysis.

4.1 Case within City

4.1.1 Background

This case covers software development within an organization spread across two sites in Vienna, Austria. Before the beginning of the case study, the development of the product had started as a research and development (R&D) effort on one site for two years aiming at establishing a set of technologies covering both hardware and software. In the herein analyzed 15-month case study time frame, the goal was to turn the R&D prototype into a deliverable product. With the beginning of full-scale product development, the team size doubled and project personnel were distributed across two sites. The team members were split into a development and a test site forming fully distributed cross-functional teams (Sutherland et al., 2007), i.e. teams integrated across both sites. We analyzed 27 two-week sprints over the case study period.

4.1.2 Challenges

The initial process implementation suffered from a strong focus on the former R&D site, the development site, since the testing site was a new addition to the process after the initial two-year R&D phase. The development site used isolated sprints without involving the test site to the end that developed stories in one sprint had to be tested in the next one by the test site. Furthermore, the teams had to deal with technically complex implementations regarding communication between hardware and software and decided to split in closely collaborating on-site micro teams with 3-4 team members. The process implementation exhibited massive problems: Stories were accepted at the end of the sprint without having been tested, which was done in the next sprint. This behavior led to a great number of features with low quality and resulted in a failed shipment to the customer in sprint 7, which was an eye-opener and the test site was then included properly as part of the same sprint. The micro teams were extended to 2-3 developers and one (remote) tester. The amount of contact visits to the other site improved, especially towards the end of each sprint, making sure to deliver high quality stories. Greater effort was put into realistic planning and commitment with the customer shipment always in mind. The retrospective turned out to be a great means to drive continuous improvement and manage frustration with the current process implementation by allowing everybody to voice their opinion.

4.1.3 Agile Practices

Sprint: Two-week iterations were used which were on few occasions prolonged to cope with holidays and customer's deadlines. Sprint planning: A joint sprint planning was held in person at the development site with all developers and one or two testers (ambassadors) to represent the testing site. The ambassador(s) then travelled back to the test site to discuss the planning results. Daily Scrum: This project environment worked with very closely collaborating micro teams and the practice of daily scrums, although practiced in the beginning, was eventually dropped. The testers contacted the developers directly for information and updates when needed. Vice versa the developers tried to give a heads-up to the testers when possible. Both formal (ticket management system and emails) and informal (instant messaging, chats and phone calls) were extensively used between the two sites to compensate the lack of face-to-face communication. Scrum of Scrums: Although there were several micro teams, no scrum of scrums has been used as it was regarded as an overhead and the communication mechanisms in-place sufficed. Sprint review and retrospective: These meetings were held in a similar fashion as the sprint planning, at the developer's site with one or more ambassadors from the testing site present. For the retrospective, the ambassador(s) made sure to collect positive and negative comments from all members of the testing site in advance and presented them at the retrospective. Backlog: As the customer preferred to work with milestones, there was a rough set of user stories planned for each milestone, a generally two-month time frame. The backlog planning relates to the process described by Hong et al. (2010): The roadmap planning was done for milestones and the detailed planning was done for sprints. Naturally with agile development, the roadmap was subject to change as stories were implemented by priority sprint after sprint.

4.1.4 Heuristic Candidates

HC1.1: Fully distributed cross-functional teams need to synchronize and work towards the same goal in a sprint. Synchronization can be achieved with contact visits, emails, phone calls, chats, instant messaging and an up-to-date ticket management system. HC1.2: Informal face-to-face communication needs substitution in DSD. Tool support can help keep track of changes in requirements. Instant messaging was particularly capable to substitute some of the informal face-to-face coordination unavailable in DSD. HC1.3: Frequent deployments to the customer set a common goal across all sites and thus enable more accuracy for planning and commitment and better quality of delivered stories. HC1.4: Documentation needs to be updated timely as team members need to rely on it more than in collocated settings. Still it cannot be used to substitute frequent interaction. HC1.5: Results from informal on-site enquiries or meetings need to be accessible to other distant team members. Contact visits can further be used to review test cases for critical stories. HC1.6: Keeping the retrospective as a constant in an ever-changing process environment proved to be a powerful means. The retrospective meeting gathers members from all sites to reflect on the process and discuss improvements. It further functions as an important mood barometer across all sites. HC1.7: Process adaptation in DSD is slower and more difficult to achieve than in regular collocated scrum.

4.2 Case within Country

4.2.1 Background

This case covers two unaffiliated organizations, a main supplier (MainSupp) and an additional supplier (AddSupp), co-developing three product variations of the same code base, resulting in three product owners. Both suppliers have successfully applied regular scrum before and chose to implement an adapted version of scrum to better suit the needs of a DSD environment. The two organizations develop at their own sites in two different cities in Austria, separated by about a four-hour car ride. MainSupp is a large organization whose IT department is involved in the development of the three software products. It acts as point of contact to customers and provides the bigger part of the development staff. AddSupp is a medium-sized core software development company and a subcontractor to MainSupp for the software development. It complements the MainSupp's development with additional staff and know-how. The teams are all integrated (cross-site) distributed ones (Sutherland et al., 2007).

4.2.2 Challenges

Although both companies had previous experience with applying regular scrum successfully, both lacked experience in DSD. Transparency was a big issue between the two suppliers and low quality video conferences and little available documentation for AddSup handicapped communication and coordination in the first months. There was no high level overview of the progress of all three teams available to everyone since paper scrum boards and burndown charts were used. All three scrum teams were staffed by members of both suppliers, yet all product owners and scrum masters were based on the MainSupp's site. The resulting coordination issues are best described in the words of one of the AddSupp's developers: "I would love to break down tasks to a decent level, but if we do not know what should be developed exactly, that is hard to achieve". The situation eventually improved with heavy use of video conferencing to complement the scrum process meetings.

4.2.3 Agile Practices

Sprint: Two-week sprint iterations were used with reviews every sprint and planning and retrospective meetings only every other sprint. Sprint planning is a two-tiered process and covers two sprints. The first tier involved planning at the MainSupp's site with one ambassador from AddSupp present. The second-tier planning continued at the AddSupp's site. The ambassador returned with pre-estimated user stories which were then broken down into tasks by AddSupp's developers. When a developer accepted a task, he adjusted the original estimation of the MainSupp to his own. An updated planning spreadsheets was then returned to MainSupp. Daily Scrum: Each scrum team held a daily video conference meeting, where respective team members of the MainSupp and AddSupp participated. Scrum of Scrums: One of the AddSupp's developers travelled to the MainSupp's site once a week for face to face updates and discussions. Both sites also engaged in their own intra-site coordination scrum of scrum right after the daily scrum. The testers of each team also felt the need to coordinate across all teams in their own scrum of scrums. The sprint review was held jointly for all the distributed teams. It was primarily held at the MainSupp's site with one or two "proxies" from AddSupp on site. In contrast to the sprint planning, for the review and retrospective, AddSupp joined directly via video conference. The review consisted of story demonstrations and discussions about different areas of the current product increment. The retrospective followed the review in the same setup, but only every other sprint. Backlog: Each product owner maintained a product backlog on the MainSupp' site for his product. AddSupp worked only with the sprint backlog which was a planning spreadsheet created during the two-tiered planning process.

4.2.4 Heuristic Candidates

HC2.1: Establish several means of both formal and informal communication as a substitute for missing face-to-face communication. HC2.2: A travelling ambassador/proxy can help to build trust, exchange information and discuss critical issues or impediments face to face. HC2.3: Beware of a superficial adoption of agile values, even more so in distributed settings where several sites rely on a working flow of information/communication and transparency. HC2.4: In agile processes all sites should be as equal as possible under the given constraints (such as a subcontractor relationship) as the process does not scale well with hierarchical sites and the withholding of information. HC2.5: Tool choices are secondary as long as everybody is committed to using the same tool. Organizational impediments regarding electronic tool usage may be circumvented with paper boards.

4.3 Case within Continent

4.3.1 Background

This case covers a customer based in Austria and a supplier based in both Austria and two further European countries, which are withheld for privacy reasons. The project had a rushed start because of a tight schedule and deadline. Moreover it was one of the first projects to be done in this setup and there were organizational restrictions on the supplier's side to use the V-model (Boehm, 1979) also in this distributed development. Still, agile practices were eventually used in an effort to improve collaboration among the three development sites. The project spanned 9 months. There were no time zone issues and cultural issues can be regarded as minor between Austria and European countries due to their proximity. Since the overall process was the V-model, there was no scrum master in place, yet several PMO roles such as project manager, test manager, solution architect and change manager.

4.3.2 Challenges

We identified three problem categories in this case, the inflexibility of the V-model, weak feedback loops and collaboration with the customer and further intra-supplier issues. The V-model was implemented because the supplier had many years experience with it, but the project had been under a very tight schedule from the very beginning and the V-model did not allow enough flexibility to cope with unforeseen problems (both technical and organizational in nature). The supplier's internal problems, being distributed across three sites, were in the end successfully mitigated by employing several agile meetings such as daily scrum and daily scrum of scrums that helped bring the project back on track. The customer collaboration could only be improved up to a certain point, because it is not an integral part of the V-model. The customer felt left out of feedback loops and was not fully content with the final product. A mitigation strategy was to make a dashboard available to the customer for live test reports, but it only came late in the project's timeline. This project also served as a ramp-up for future collaborations and as such was a great learning experience for all parties. The customer and the supplier decided to alter the process for future projects in favor of the implementation of more agile practices.

4.3.3 Agile Practices

There was no sprint, sprint planning or backlogs in use as the V-model worked with milestones and formal reviews and a fixed set of requirements with little flexibility other than change requests. Still, a few agile practices were implemented as a crucial improvement to the development collaboration: there was a 15 minutes daily scrum within teams and another daily scrum of scrums including development lead, PMO, solution architect and test manager. Furthermore there were also weekly meetings between development lead of European country #1 and specialists from Austria and European country #2 and two-weekly meetings of all teams and stakeholders to spread knowledge on project's status. In short, communication was very important for the supplier internally but not towards the customer. There was no retrospective meeting, only a one-time lessons-learned workshop after the completion of the project.

4.3.4 Heuristic Candidates

HC3.1: Also in traditionally structured environments agile practices can help establish more frequent communication and thus have a positive output on the quality of software delivery. HC3.2: Understand each other's (customer's and supplier's) internal processes and find a compromise that works for both sides. HC3.3: Define roles clearly, make them known and act on them. This regards both the customer-supplier communication and the supplier's internal communication (among different sites). HC3.4: Shutting the customer out does not build quality in as different understanding of requirements is inevitable that will be spotted very late in the project. HC3.5: Provide environments for both formal and informal means of communication and try to break language barriers by offering language courses and keep documentation in a language acceptable to all parties. HC3.6: Promote contact visits for team building and face-to-face information sharing. Occasional team events to bring together teams on one site may also be beneficial for establishing trust. HC3.7: Try to equally distribute decision makers among different sites to facilitate the flow of information.

Table 3. Cross-case summary of the implemented scrum practices with highlighted cells indicating a modified usage for DSD

Agility Level	WithinCity All teams	WithinCountry All teams	WithinContinent Not all teams
Sprint	Used (two-week)	Used (two-week)	Not Used
Sprint Planning	Used modified (joint sprint planning held at the development site with all developers and one or two ambassadors to represent the other site)	Used modified (two-tiered process, held at main site with all developers and an ambassador from other site, followed by a continued planning effort on the other site with returning ambassador)	Not Used
Daily Scrum	Not used (due to highly collaborative micro teams, successfully substituted with several other formal and informal means of communication)	Used modified (daily scrum in video conference)	Used (daily scrum within teams)
Scrum of Scrums	Not used	Used modified (ambassador travels to main site for scrum of scrums, both sites engage in their own cross-team meetings; also a separate cross-site tester's scrum of scrums was held)	Used modified (daily with development lead, PMO, solution architect and test manager; on top of that also a weekly cross-site specialist meeting and two-weekly global all-site meetings)
Sprint Review	Used modified (same setup as sprint planning)	Used modified (joint sprint review held at the main site with all developers and one or two proxies to represent the other site	Not Used
Retrospective	Used modified (same setup as sprint planning)	Used modified (same setup as sprint review, but only every other sprints)	Not Used (only lessons learned workshop after project's end)
Backlog	Used (coarse-grained product backlog with "milestones" in accordance with customer and a detailed sprint backlog)	Used modified (the main site groomed the product backlog, the other site only worked with the sprint backlog)	Not Used

5. Results of Cross-Case Analysis

With our multiple-case study research approach we are looking for two kinds of findings (Patton, 2002, p.235):

- High quality, detailed descriptions of each case, useful for documenting uniqueness (Section 4)
- Important shared patterns that cut across cases and derive their significance from having emerged out of heterogeneity (Section 5)

Figure 2 presented our analysis process including the cross-case analysis. Table 3 shows how scrum practices have been applied in three different cases (RQ1) and what DSD practices have been used to enhance the collocated practices (RQ2).

5.1 Agile Practices

5.1.1 Sprint

Cases WithinCity and WithinCountry used two-week sprints, while WithinContinent worked with a V-model and thus did not use iterations. No DSD methods were applied in any of the cases to alter the sprint practice.

5.1.2 Sprint Planning

Cases WithinCity and WithinCountry applied a similar approach using an ambassador and focused the planning physically on one site only. In case WithinCountry the other site also held another (second-level) planning following the return of the ambassador. Case WithinContinent worked with a V-model and up-front heavy-weight requirements and planning. The DSD enhancement of adding a travelling ambassador worked well in both cases and was a substantial improvement for a working scrum process.

5.1.3 Daily Scrum

WithinCity worked in micro teams and dropped the practice in favor of using several other means of formal and informal communication (ticket management system, phone calls, emails, chat, instant messaging and a wiki). WithinCountry and WithinContinent both implemented the practice of a daily scrum, for case WithinCountry with the help of video conferences (integrated distributed teams) and on-site for case WithinContinent (isolated distributed teams).

5.1.4 Scrum of Scrums

WithinCity also did not use scrum of scrums due to the same rationale as not using daily scrums. WithinCountry used scrum of scrums for on-site inter-team coordination. WithinContinent applied several scrum of scrums for cross-team and cross-site coordination by means of video conferencing and screen sharing sessions.

5.1.5 Sprint Review and Retrospective

These two practices have been applied in the same setup within the respective case of WithinCity and WithinCountry with the introduction of a travelling proxy/ambassador similar to the sprint planning acting on behalf of the colleagues not present in case WithinCity and serving as a proxy (with the team joining in video conference) in case WithinCountry. WithinContinent used a V-model with its respective phases and reviews.

5.1.6 Backlog

Case WithinCity used a product backlog with coarse-grained low-priority stories and fine-grained high-priority ones, planned for the next "milestone", usually a time span of about 4-5 sprints, which would then each have a regular sprint backlog. Case WithinCountry had the product backlog handled by the main site (as consequence of all the product owners residing there) and handed only the sprint backlog to the additional site for co-development by both sites. No DSD practices have been used to facilitate this practice other than ticket management systems. WithinContinent used a V-model with a pre-defined release plan and no backlog practices.

5.1.7 Summary of DSD Enhancements

In our multiple-case study the following DSD practices supported the application of a scrum practices in a distributed environment: Contact visits by a travelling proxy/ambassador (sprint planning, review and retrospective), different types of formal and informal means of communication such as video conferences, phone calls, chat, emails, screen sharing sessions, ticket management systems and wikis (sprint planning, review, retrospective, daily scrum, scrum of scrums, backlog) in order to mitigate the lack of face-to-face communication in DSD environments.

5.2 Final Theory: Ten Heuristics and Four Candidates

Table 4 shows a summary of all agile heuristic candidates as identified during the cases. The table also notes the source (case) for each heuristic and thus describes how the final heuristics have been derived from the heuristic candidates. Heuristic candidates that did not gain empirical support in more than one case retain candidate status but are listed for the sake of completeness.

We can see that ten heuristics H1, H3, H4, H5, H6, H7, H8, H9, H10 and H12 emerged from the heterogeneous cases with empirical evidence in at least two cases. The themes of these ten heuristics can be summarized as frequent formal and informal communication (H1), necessity of up-to-date documentation (H3), informal information sharing across sites (H4), retrospective as driver for continuous improvement (H5), slower process adaptation (H6), travelling ambassador/proxy (H7), risk of a superficial scrum adoption (H8), equal sites with a balanced distribution of decision makers (H9), tools not dictating a sub-par process implementation (H10) and understanding each other's internal processes (H12).

5.3 Limitations

Like any empirical study our study exhibits certain threats to validity (Yin, 2003). The generalizability of the results of our multiple-case study is limited in light of its limitations. We addressed *construct validity* by using multiple sources of evidence, a chain of evidence and had respective informants validate our results for each of the three cases in separate feedback sessions. To achieve *internal validity* we employed method, data, investigator and theory triangulation. For *external validity* we provided a theoretical framework deducted from previous work as a basis for the analysis of the three cases. We established *reliability* by following a case study protocol, as described in this report, a case study data drive, and the data analysis software ATLAS.ti for consistent handling. The great difference in the cases' context was purposefully introduced via maximum variation (heterogeneity) sampling with the objective of finding that "a theme song emerged from all the scattered noise" (Patton, 2002, p.235). While multiple-case studies provide more value for generalization than single-case studies, empirical evidence from other related studies needs to be systematically analyzed, which we aim to address in the next step of our research. Until then, the heuristics should be regarded as specific to the individual case's context and thus generalized with caution.

Table 4. Agile DSD heuristics emerging from the multiple-case study: the dot (●) indicates that empirical support was found after revisiting data but that there was no initial heuristic candidate and heuristics with an asterisk (*) are candidates

ID	Heuristics from Applying Agile Practices in DSD Environments	Within City	Within Country	Within Continent
H1	Fully distributed cross-functional teams need to synchronize and work towards the same goal in a sprint. Both formal and informal face-to-face communication needs substitution in DSD by means of tool support, contact visits, video conferences, phone calls, instant messaging, emails, chat, wiki, an up-to-date ticket management system and test case or code review. Try to break language barriers by offering language courses and keep documentation in a language acceptable to all parties.	HC1.1 HC1.2	HC2.1	HC3.5
H2*	Continuous customer deployments can help establish focus in DSD and lead to more realistic sprint planning and commitments. Continuous flow means more reliable estimations and higher software quality.	HC1.3		
H3	While up-to-date documentation does not substitute direct interaction, it plays a bigger part in agile DSD than in on-site scrum since direct communication is harder to achieve.	HC1.4	●	●
H4	Results from informal on-site enquiries or meetings need to be made available to other sites, either in terms of updated documentation or updated tickets in the electronic ticket management system.	HC1.5	●	
H5	Keeping the retrospective as a constant in an ever-changing process environment proved to be a powerful means. The retrospective meeting gathers members from all sites to reflect on the process and discuss improvements. It further functions as an important mood barometer across all sites.	HC1.6	●	
H6	Process adaptation in DSD is slower and more difficult to achieve than in regular collocated scrum.	HC1.7	●	●
H7	A travelling Ambassador/Proxy can help to build trust, exchange information and discuss critical issues or impediments face to face. Promote contact visits for team building and face-to-face information sharing. Occasional team events to bring together teams on one site may also be beneficial to establishing trust.	●	HC2.2	HC3.6
H8	Beware of a superficial adoption of agile values, even more so in distributed settings where several sites rely on a working flow of information/communication and transparency.		HC2.3	●
H9	In agile processes all sites should be as equal as possible under the given constraints (such as a subcontractor relationship) as the process does not scale well with hierarchical sites and the withholding of information. Try to equally distribute decision makers among different sites.	●	HC2.4	HC3.7

ID	Heuristics from Applying Agile Practices in DSD Environments	Within City	Within Country	Within Continent
H10	Tool choices are secondary as long as everybody is committed to using the same tool. Organizational impediments regarding electronic tool usage may be circumvented with paper boards.	•	HC2.5	
H11*	Also in traditionally structured environments agile practices can help establish more frequent communication and thus have a positive output on the quality of software delivery.			HC3.1
H12	Understand each other's (customer's and supplier's) internal processes and find a compromise that works for both parties.	•	•	HC3.2
H13*	Define roles clearly, make them known and act on them. This regards both the customer-supplier communication and the supplier's internal communication (among different sites).			HC3.3
H14*	Shutting customer out does not build quality in as different understanding of requirements is inevitable that will be spotted very late in the project.			HC3.4

6. Conclusion

In this paper we presented the results of our multiple-case study spanning an overall timeframe of four years. Through careful analysis we identified ten heuristics with empirical evidence in at least two cases and four heuristic candidates with support in only one case. The heuristics concern the application of agile practices in distributed development environments which evolved from three different distribution scenarios:

- Case WithinCity: sites distributed within one city, spanning two districts
- Case WithinCountry: sites distributed within one country, spanning two cities
- Case WithinContinent: sites distributed within one continent, spanning three countries

Although agile methods are increasingly being adapted to distributed software development, they are no panacea for success and need to be carefully tailored to each individual distributed environment. With our research we strive provide empirical evidence for other researchers to build upon and to help the practitioner find advice on tailoring agile methods to distributed environments. To this end, our future work will include the improvement and enhancement of the heuristics, supported by a full-scale systematic literature review, with the goal of accumulating empirical evidence for designing a process framework to improve the chances of a successful implementation of agile practices in today's complex distributed software development environments.

Acknowledgments

This research was partly funded by the Austrian Marshall Plan Foundation (http://www.marshallplan.at) by providing a scholarship to the first author. The research report has been finalized during a research visit at the Center for Design Research at Stanford University. The first author thanks Professor Larry Leifer for hosting the research visit. The authors thank the participating organizations as well as the supporting investigators/researchers throughout the multiple-case study for their assistance in conducting the study and fruitful discussions.

References

Badampudi, D., Fricker, S. A., & Moreno, A. M. (2013). Perspectives on Productivity and Delays in Large-Scale Agile Projects. *Agile Processes in Software Engineering and Extreme Programming*, 180–194. http://dx.doi.org/10.1007/978-3-642-38314-4_13

Bass, J. M. (2012). Influences on Agile Practice Tailoring in Enterprise Software Development. *Proceedings of the 2012 Agile India Conference*. http://dx.doi.org/10.1109/agileindia.2012.15

Batra, D. (2009). Modified agile practices for outsourced software projects. *Commun. ACM, 52*(9), 143. http://dx.doi.org/10.1145/1562164.1562200

Beck, K. (2000). *Extreme programming eXplained*. Reading, MA: Addison-Wesley.

Boehm, B. (1979). *Guidelines for Verifying and Validating Software Requirements and Design Specifications* (Technical Report). University of Southern California, Redondo Beach, California.

Brereton, P., Kitchenham, B., Budgen, D., & Li, Z. (2008, June). Using a protocol template for case study planning. *Proceedings of the 12th International Conference on Evaluation and Assessment in Software Engineering.* University of Bari, Italy.

Bryman, A., & Burgess, R. (1994). *Analyzing qualitative data.* London; UK: Routledge.

Denzin, N. (1978). *The Research Act: A Theoretical Introduction to Sociological Methods* (2nd ed.). New York: McGraw-Hill.

Denzin, N., & Lincoln, Y. (2011). *The Sage handbook of qualitative research.* Thousand Oaks, Calif.: Sage Publications.

Dingsøyr, T., Nerur, S., Balijepally, V., & Moe, N. B. (2012). A decade of agile methodologies: Towards explaining agile software development. *Journal of Systems and Software, 85*(6), 1213–1221. http://dx.doi.org/10.1016/j.jss.2012.02.033

Hanssen, G. K., ŠŠmite, D., & Moe, N. B. (2011). Signs of Agile Trends in Global Software Engineering Research: A Tertiary Study. *Proceedings of the 2011 IEEE Sixth International Conference on Global Software Engineering Workshop.* http://dx.doi.org/10.1109/icgse-w.2011.12

Heeager, L. T., & Rose, J. (2014). Optimising agile development practices for the maintenance operation: nine heuristics. *Empir Software Eng, 20*(6), 1762–1784. http://dx.doi.org/10.1007/s10664-014-9335-7

Herriott, R. E., & Firestone, W. A. (1983). Multisite Qualitative Policy Research: Optimizing Description and Generalizability. *Educational Researcher, 12*(2), 14–19. http://dx.doi.org/10.3102/0013189x012002014

Hong, N., Yoo, J., & Cha, S. (2010). Customization of Scrum Methodology for Outsourced E-Commerce Projects. *Proceedings of the 2010 Asia Pacific Software Engineering Conference.* http://dx.doi.org/10.1109/apsec.2010.43

Hossain, E., Babar, M. A., & Paik, H. (2009). Using Scrum in Global Software Development: A Systematic Literature Review. *Proceedings of the 2009 Fourth IEEE International Conference on Global Software Engineering.* http://dx.doi.org/10.1109/icgse.2009.25

Hossain, E., Bannerman, P. L., & Jeffery, D. R. (2011b). Scrum Practices in Global Software Development: A Research Framework. *Lecture Notes in Computer Science,* 88–102. http://dx.doi.org/10.1007/978-3-642-21843-9_9

Hossain, E., Bannerman, P. L., & Jeffery, R. (2011a, May). Towards an understanding of tailoring scrum in global software development: a multi-case study. *Proceedings of the 2011 International Conference on Software and Systems Process.* http://dx.doi.org/10.1145/1987875.1987894

Jalali, S., & Wohlin, C. (2011). Global software engineering and agile practices: a systematic review. *J. Softw. Evol. and Proc., 24*(6), 643–659. http://dx.doi.org/10.1002/smr.561

Lewin, K. (1946). Action Research and Minority Problems. *Journal of Social Issues, 2*(4), 34–46. http://dx.doi.org/10.1111/j.1540-4560.1946.tb02295.x

Marques, A. B., Rodrigues, R., & Conte, T. (2012). Systematic Literature Reviews in Distributed Software Development: A Tertiary Study. *Proceedings of the 2012 IEEE Seventh International Conference on Global Software Engineering.* http://dx.doi.org/10.1109/icgse.2012.29

Ó Conchúir, E., Holmström Olsson, H., Ågerfalk, P. J., & Fitzgerald, B. (2009). Benefits of global software development: exploring the unexplored. *Software Process: Improvement and Practice, 14*(4), 201–212. http://dx.doi.org/10.1002/spip.417

Paasivaara, M. (2011). Coaching Global Software Development Projects. *Proceedings of the 2011 IEEE Sixth International Conference on Global Software Engineering.* http://dx.doi.org/10.1109/icgse.2011.33

Paasivaara, M., Durasiewicz, S., & Lassenius, C. (2009). Using Scrum in Distributed Agile Development: A Multiple Case Study. *Proceedings of the 2009 Fourth IEEE International Conference on Global Software Engineering.* http://dx.doi.org/10.1109/icgse.2009.27

Paasivaara, M., Heikkila, V. T., & Lassenius, C. (2012). Experiences in Scaling the Product Owner Role in Large-Scale Globally Distributed Scrum. *Proceedings of the 2012 IEEE Seventh International Conference on Global Software Engineering.* http://dx.doi.org/10.1109/icgse.2012.41

Patton, M. (2002). *Qualitative research and evaluation methods.* Thousand Oaks, Calif.: Sage Publications.

Ramesh, B., Cao, L., Mohan, K., & Xu, P. (2006). Can distributed software development be agile? *Commun. ACM, 49*(10), 41. http://dx.doi.org/10.1145/1164394.1164418

Ramesh, B., Mohan, K., & Cao, L. (2012). Ambidexterity in Agile Distributed Development: An Empirical Investigation. *Information Systems Research, 23*(2), 323–339. http://dx.doi.org/10.1287/isre.1110.0351

Schwaber, K. & Beedle, M. (2002). *Agile software development with Scrum.* Upper Saddle River, NJ: Prentice Hall.

Sison, R., & Yang, T. (2007). Use of Agile Methods and Practices in the Philippines. *Proceedings of the 14th Asia-Pacific Software Engineering Conference.* http://dx.doi.org/10.1109/aspec.2007.35

Šmite, D., Moe, N. B., & Ågerfalk, P. J. (2010). *Fundamentals of Agile Distributed Software Development. Agility Across Time and Space,* 3–7. http://dx.doi.org/10.1007/978-3-642-12442-6_1

Šmite, D., Wohlin, C., Galviņa, Z., & Prikladnicki, R. (2012). An empirically based terminology and taxonomy for global software engineering. *Empirical Software Engineering, 19*(1), 105–153. http://dx.doi.org/10.1007/s10664-012-9217-9

Srinivasan, J., & Lundqvist, K. (2010). Agile in India. *Proceedings of the 3rd India Software Engineering Conference on India Software Engineering Conference.* http://dx.doi.org/10.1145/1730874.1730898

Stake, R. (1995). *The art of case study research.* Thousand Oaks, Calif.: Sage Publications.

Strauss, A. & Corbin, J. (1998). *Basics of qualitative research.* Thousand Oaks, Calif.: Sage Publications.

Sutherland, J., Viktorov, A., Blount, J., & Puntikov, N. (2007). *Distributed Scrum: Agile Project Management with Outsourced Development Teams.* Proceedings of the 2007 40th Annual Hawaii International Conference on System Sciences. http://dx.doi.org/10.1109/hicss.2007.180

Vallon, R., Estácio, B., Prikladnicki, R., & Grechenig, T. (forthcoming). *Trends and Directions of Applying Agile Practices in Global Software Development: A Systematic Mapping* (Working paper in revision).

Verner, J. M., Brereton, O. P., Kitchenham, B. A., Turner, M., & Niazi, M. (2012). *Systematic literature reviews in global software development: a tertiary study.* Proceedings of the 16th International Conference on Evaluation & Assessment in Software Engineering. http://dx.doi.org/10.1049/ic.2012.0001

Verner, J. M., Sampson, J., Tosic, V., Bakar, N. A. A., & Kitchenham, B. A. (2009). *Guidelines for industrially-based multiple case studies in software engineering.* Proceedings of the 2009 Third International Conference on Research Challenges in Information Science. http://dx.doi.org/10.1109/rcis.2009.5089295

Yin, R. (2003). *Case study research.* Thousand Oaks, Calif.: Sage Publications.

14

Improving Analysis and Visualizing of JVM Profiling Logs Using Process Mining

M. M. MohieEl Din[1], Neveen I. Ghali[1], Mohamed S. Farag[1] & O. M. Hassan[1]

[1] Department of Mathematics, Facility of Science Al-Azhar University Cairo, Egypt

Correspondence: Mohamed S. Farag, Department of Mathematics, Facility of Science Al-Azhar University, Nasr city, 11884, Cairo, Egypt. E-mail: mohamed.s.farag@azhar.edu.eg

Abstract

Growing size and complexity of modern software applications increase the demand to make the information systems self-configuring, self-optimizing and with flexible architecture. Although managed languages have eliminated or minimized many low-level software errors there are many other sources of errors that persist. Java Virtual Machine (JVM), as managed language has many adaptive optimization techniques, which needs tools to analysis program behavior determines where the application spends most of its time. In this paper, new approached has been introduced to use process-mining techniques to represent the analysis and visualize phases of JVM profilers. They are flexible enough to cover so many perspectives in several ways. That can form a unified layer for analysis and visualize across profiling.

Keywords: JVM profiling, process mining, heuristics miner

1. Introduction

The modern software applications are complicated enough that leads to increasing the demand for automating the process of managing the software environments that allows developers to identify performance bottlenecks with minimum effort.

Likewise for the Java Virtual Machine (JVM), as managed language based on interpreter it requires more processing for execution, and there are several approaches to enhance JVM performance like Just-In-Time Compilation (JIT), interpretation directly in hardware by specialized architecture and improving JVM performance by understanding of the behavior of Java-based applications (Bowers & Kaeli, 1998). Optimizing the compilers and software applications by understanding the dynamic behavior of it; it is an effective approach (Driesen et al., 2003).

The process of automatic collection and presentation of data that is representing the dynamic behavior of the program is called profiling (Dmitriev, 2004). After profilers collect and analyze the data, it can be either automatically feedback to the compiler or present it for the developers. Each case has different requirements in designing the profiler (Liang & Viswanathan, 1999). For example the feedback profilers should avoid the "observer effect" program that may affect the program's behavior (Snyder et al., 2011), while this problem not critical if profile will just present the result for developers.

From Another Perspective, Process Mining techniques aim to extract non-trivial information from event logs recorded by information systems. According to their abilities to assist in understanding and (re)design the complex process by extracting the workflow model that represent the information system behavior, the process mining techniques have received notable attention and promising vision (Van Der Aalst & Weijters, 2004). ProM framework is a pluggable environment for process mining. This framework is flexible with respect to the input and output format, and is also open enough to allow for the easy reuse of code during the implementation of new process mining ideas (De Medeiros et al., 2005).

This paper is mainly concerned with profilers that provide information about java program or JVM (HotSpotTM); these profilers mainly have three phases: collecting data, analyzing data and visualizing results. In this paper, the process mining techniques and ProM tool implemented to represent the analysis and visualize phases. They are flexible enough to cover so many perspectives in several ways. That can form a unified layer for analysis and visualize across profiling perspectives. Process mining applied on two different profiling data for java programs/VM, and the result compared with the original profiling tools. The profiling data mapped to process-based, and with each different mapping new analysis perspective obtained. The DaCapo (Garner et al., 2006) benchmark suite has been used to apply profiling perspectives on some of its component. In this context, the java-event-logs tool has been provided to mapping Java profiling data to process mining event logs.

This paper organized as follows. Section 2 provides background information about the profiling data and process mining. Section 3 describes related work. Section 4 describes the architecture of java-event-logs tool. Section 5 provides a detailed description on how to use process mining during profiling and presenting the experimental results. Finally, Section 6 concludes and suggests directions for future work.

2. Literature Review

In this section, the profiling data will be dissected and study the existence tool for analysis and visualizing, then an overview about process mining perspectives and event log format will be discussed.

2.1 JVM Profilers

There are two different profiling data with different perspectives selected to study. The following is a breakdown of them:

2.1.1 Dependence Graph

The Java HotSpotTM server compiler uses a program dependence graph as the intermediate data structure when compiling Java bytecodes to machine code. When using the compiler in debug mode, it is providing a textual output of the graph (Ottenstein et al., 1987; Vick et al., 2001; Wimmer et al., 2008). The Ideal Graph Visualizer (IGV) tool used to analyze the compiler by providing a graphical representation of the program dependence graph. During the compilation process, the IGV tool captures snapshots of the graph then use it to create visual presentation to reconstruct the transformations applied to the graph by compiler optimizations. Figure 1 shows the interaction between the visualization tool and the server compiler (Würthinger, 2007; Wimmer et al., 2008). In IGV the data transferred from the server compiler to the visualization tool is represented in XML. Figure 2 shows the XML elements and their relations (Würthinger, 2007).

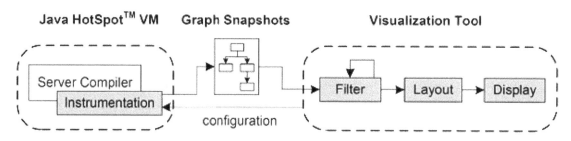

Figure 1. Interaction between the compiler and the visualization tool

Table 1. Description of the main elements in IGV XML

Element	Level	Description
graphDocument	1st	top-level element and can contain group child elements
group	2nd	server compiler creates a group element for every traced method
method	3rd	describes the bytecodes and inlining of the method
graph	3rd	describe the traced states of the graph during compilation of the method, it include the state title and starting time.
nodes	4th	contain definitions of nodes as node elements or removeNode elements, which state that a certain node of the previous graph is no longer present
edges	4th	contain definitions of edges as edge elements or removeEdge elements, which state that a certain edge of the previous graph is no longer present
controlFlow	4th	contains the information necessary to cluster the nodes into blocks

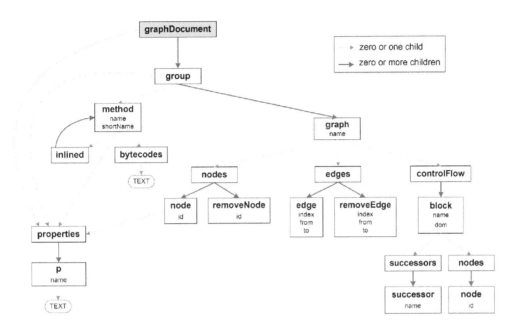

Figure 2. IGV XML elements and their relations

Figure 3 shows the output of the IGV tool, which represents the dependency graph; also, IGV tool supports some options like filtering the graph component manually or using JavaScript function and display the difference between snapshots graphically.

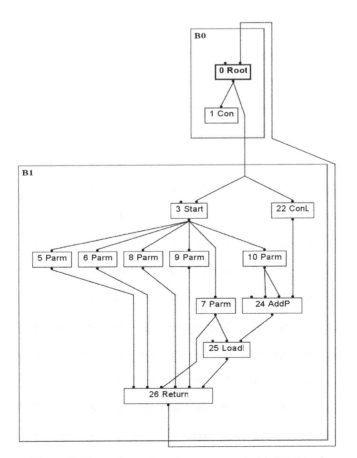

Figure 3. Dependence Graph as represented in IGV tool

2.1.2 Compilation Logs

The JVM HotSpotTM developers create internal diagnostic option in the JVM itself. The diagnostic options "-XX: +LogCompilation" emits a structured XML log of compilation related activity during a run of the virtual machine. By default it ends up in the standard "hotspot.log" file, though this can be changed using the -XX: LogFile= option. Note that both of these are considered diagnostic options and have to be enabled using -XX: +UnlockDiagnosticVMOptions (Snyder et al., 2011).

Figure 4 shows very rough overview of the LogCompilation output XML, and Table 2 describes the main elements in this XML.

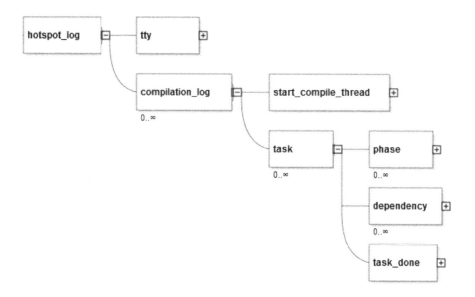

Figure 4. Very rough overview of the LogCompilation XML

Table 2. Description of the main elements in LogCompilation XML

Element	Level	Description
hotspot_log	1st	The main element in the XML.
tty	2nd	Output from normal Java threads and contains events for methods being enqueued for compilation, uncommon traps that invalidate a method and other events.
compilation_log	2nd	Comes from the compiler threads themselves. The output from the compiler is basically a log of the stages of the compile along with the high level decisions made during the compile such as inlining.
start_compile_thread	3rd	Mainly gives a timestamp for the start time of the compiler thread.
task	3rd	Methods to be compiled are placed into the compile queue and the compiler threads dequeue them and compile them as long as there are elements in the queue. Each individual compile is shown as a 'task' element.
phase	4th	Each phase of the compilation is wrapped by a 'phase' element which records the name of the phase, the maximum number of nodes in the IR at that point and the timestamp. Phases may nest and may be repeated.
dependency	4th	A "dependency" element indicates that class hierarchy analysis has indicated some interesting property of the classes that allows the compiler to optimistically assume things like there are no subclasses of a particular class or there is only one implementor of a particular method.
task_done	4th	indicates completion of the compile and includes a 'success' element to indicate whether the compile succeeded.

The LogCompilation tool created to parse the related XML file. This tool is part of the JVM HotSpotTM and provides textual output. This output provides information about compilation statistics (Number of compilation tasks, Number of bytes of the compiled method, Compilation type, …) and list the compilation events ordered by start time or elapsed time. Figure 5 shows sample for the output of this tool.

```
@ 12 java.util.HashMap::get (29 bytes)
  @ 11 java.util.HashMap::getEntry (77 bytes)
    @ 10 java.util.HashMap::hash (59 bytes)
      @ 31 java.lang.Integer::hashCode (5 bytes)
    @ 24 java.util.HashMap::indexFor (6 bytes)
    @ 59 java.lang.Integer::equals (29 bytes)
      @ 15 java.lang.Integer::intValue (5 bytes)
  @ 25 java.util.HashMap$Entry::getValue (5 bytes)
```

Figure 5. Sample for the output of the LogCompilation tool

2.1.3 Other Profilers

In (Sewe et al., 2012) the JP2 tool designed to extract the valuable calling context tree without exposure to analysis or visualize. In each of (Krinke, 2004; Balmas, 2001; Lee & Sim, 2015) specially programmed tools have been provided to display the program dependence graph. In (Driesen et al., 2003; Hendren et al., 2003) a new tool has been developed to use the internal JVM profiling APIs for gathering the information about the program then computing and presenting the results from the standpoint of the dynamic metrics. The NetBeans/JFluid Profiler (Dmitriev, 2004; Schulz et al., 2015) depends on dynamic bytecode instrumentation and code hotswapping to turn profiling on and off dynamically. However, this tool needs a customized JVM and is therefore only available for a limited set of environments. The Spy framework (Banados et al., 2012) builds profilers and visualizes profiling information for the Pharo-Smalltalk programming language. However, the limitations of the language reflect on the profiler. There is a wide range of related work in the area of profiling perspectives and tools; but the common thing across all that there is no unified data model and each tool designs its analysis and visualize technique which make it hard to integrate.

2.2 Process Mining

The main goal of process mining is to extract the information from the logs of the systems and representing it in workflow model to reconstruct the order of activities in the form of a graphical model. The basic idea of process mining is to learn from observed executions of a process (Van der Aalst & Weijters, 2004; Van Dongen et al., 2007); this used to: Discover new models (e.g., constructing a Petri Net that is able to reproduce the observed behavior), Check the conformance of a model by checking whether the modeled behavior matches the observed behavior and Extend an existing model by projecting.

The basic perspective of process mining is the so-called control-flow (process) perspective, which focuses on the control-flow, i.e., the ordering of activities. However, in addition to that could also consider: the organization perspective which focuses on which performers are involved and how they are related, and the case perspective that focuses on properties of cases (Van der Aalst & Weijters, 2004).

Event logs can be very different in nature, i.e. an event log could show the events that occur in a specific machine that produces computer chips, or it could show the different departments visited by a patient in a hospital. However, all event logs have one thing in common: they show occurrences of events at specific moments in time, where each event refers to a specific process and an instance thereof, i.e. a case (Van Der Aalst & De Medeiros, 2005).

ProM framework (De Medeiros et al., 2005) is a pluggable environment for process mining. Since each system has its own format for output log files, ProM framework works with a generic XML formats like MXML and XES (Van Der Aalst & Van Der Aalst, 2011). Regardless the elements name in file formats; there are main elements for each process that should be represented in any format, these elements listed in Table 3.

Plug-ins in ProM framework can be divided to mining plug-in which implements algorithms that mine models from event logs, analysis plug-in which typically implement some property analysis on some mining result and others plug-ins related to file formats input/output. Moreover, ProM has enormous potential in filtration and general statistics about the input event logs.

Table 3. The main elements in the event log

Element	Required	Description
Case	Mandatory	Each case has unique ID and includes related actions.
Activity	Mandatory	The name of the action.
Timestamp	Optional	The time of the action.
Originator	Optional	The name of the action performer.

3. Proposed Tool Architecture

In this section, the architecture of java-event-logs tool and the usage of it described in details. XML format is the common thing between the types of input files and the output files too. So, the XMLBeans library for accessing XML by binding it to Java types, XMLBeans provides a way to get at the XML through XML schema that has been compiled to generate Java types that represent schema types, the XML schemas that descript the three types of input data has been have been included in the tool.

Figure 6 shows the class diagram for the java-event-logs tool. The "MainMiner" is the main class which receives the user options and delegates it to the right miner. The "LogMiner" is the abstract parent class for the three miners which applies the factory method pattern, the "IGVLogMiner","LogCompilationLogMiner" are the miners that responsible for extract the event logs patterns from dependence graph and compilation logs and finally the "MXMLLogBuilder" class which is responsible about the event logs output format.

The java-event-logs tool has two execution options "-igv" and "-logc" for dependence graph and compilation logs respectively. As shown in Figure 7 and Figure 8, the tool apply certain algorithm based on each log input.

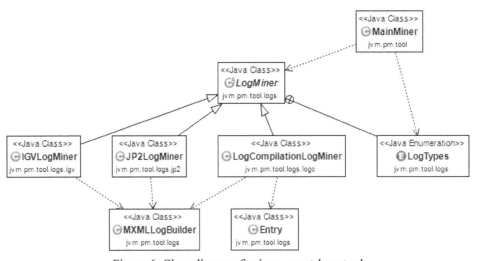

Figure 6. Class diagram for java-event-logs tool

4. Process-Based Profiling in Action

In this section, the process mining techniques applied on the profiling data that previously mentioned by mapping the data using java-event-logs tool and present the faces of various analysis perspectives supported by ProM. Data extracted by profiling the fop application in the DaCapo benchmark suite. As in Table 3, time of the action is one of elements that process mining uses during analysis, although it is optional, some important analysis techniques rely on it. So, the time attribute added to profiling data by modifying the profiler agent.

The Heuristics Miner (HM) algorithm (Weijters & Van Der Aalst, 2003; Van Der Aalst et al., 2006; Burattin, 2015) focuses on the control flow perspective and generates a process model in form of a Heuristics Net for the underlying event log. Also HM is a practical applicable mining algorithm that can deal with noise, and can be used to express the main behavior of the event log. So, for the control flow perspective of the next cases, the HM algorithm selected. The HM provides list of parameters to control the level of details in the extracted model by it.

The following parameter values have been used: (1, 1, 0.01, 0.01, 0.01, 0.01, 1, 0.1, false, true, false) for ("Relative-to-best threshold", "Positive observations", "Dependency threshold", "Length-one-loops threshold", "Length-two-loops threshold", "Long distance threshold", "Dependency divisor", "AND threshold", "Extra information", "Use-all-events-connected heuristic", "Long distance threshold dependency heuristics") respectively.

```
Input: graph Document GD.
Output: even log L
Method: Perform the following steps:

1.      Initialize L as empty log // this log will contain all processes extracted from graph document
2.      Initialize G as list of all graphs in GD // each graph g in G is representing code execution state
3.      For each graph g in G do
3.1.        Let N := list of nodes in g;
3.2.        Let E := list of edges in g;
3.3.        Filter list of nodes N to discard nodes marked as removed in graph g
3.4.        Filter list of edges E to discard edges marked as removed in graph g
3.5.        For each edge e in E do
3.5.1.          Add new Process Instant P to event log L
3.5.2.          Let ns := search list of nodes N and get the one is linked to start of edge e
3.5.3.          Let ne := search list of nodes N and get the one is linked to end of edge e
3.5.4.          Add new Entity ws to process instance P where Activity and Time is node ns title and time.
3.5.5.          Add new Entity we to process instance P where Activity and Time is node ne title and time.
3.6.        End for
4.      End for
```

Figure 7. The algorithm steps to convert dependency graph to event log

```
Input: Compilation logs CL.
Output: even log L
Method: Perform the following steps:

1.      Initialize L as empty log // this log will contain all processes extracted from graph document
2.      Initialize E as empty list of task entities
3.      For each log cl in CL do // flat line all entities in all tasks in compilation logs to be single list
3.1.        Let T := list of tasks in cl;
3.2.        For each task t in T do
3.2.1.          Let e := new task entity
3.2.2.          Set title of e := method name in task t
3.2.3.          Set time of e := time of task t
3.2.4.          Set origin of e := class name in task t
3.2.5.          Add e to E
3.3.        End for
4.      End for
5.      Sort the list of entities E // sort the list after adding all entities from all tasks in compilation log
6.      For each entity e in E do
6.1.        Let P := empty process instance of event log L
6.2.        Let fe := new process entry
6.3.        Let te := new process entry
6.4.        Add fe to process instance P
6.5.        Add te to process instance P
7.      End for
```

Figure 8. The algorithm steps to convert Compilation logs to event log

The timestamp of an activity used to calculate these ordering. Therefore, HM introduce the following notations and defines an event log as follows:

Let T be a set of activities, $\sigma \in T^*$ is an event trace and $W \subseteq T^*$ is an event log. And let a, b $\in$ T, a >W b iff there is a trace σ =t1,t2,t3 …tn and i$\in$ {1, …, n-1} such that $\sigma\in$ W and ti = a and ti+1=b, a →W b iff a >W b and b $\not>$W a, a#W b iff a $\not>$W b and b $\not>$W a, a‖W b iff a $>$W b and b $>$W a, a $>>$W b iff there is a trace σ =t1t2t3 …tn and i∈{1, …, n-2} such that σ∈ W and ti = a and ti+1=b and ti+2 = a, a $>>>$W b iff there is a trace σ =t1t2t3 …tn and i<j and i,j ∈{1, …, n} such that σ∈ W and ti = a and tj=b.

HM Algorithm Steps: The HM algorithm is a three-step algorithm: Construct a dependency graph on the basis of the event log. For each task in the event log establish the input-output expressions in form of type of dependencies between activities. Discover the long distance dependency relations.

Mining of the dependency graph: The starting point of the Heuristics Miner is the construction of a so-called dependency graph. A frequency based metric is used to indicate how certain that there is truly a dependency relation between two events a and b (notation a $\Rightarrow$W b).

Let W be an event log over T, and a, b ∈ T. Then |a $>$W b| is the number of times a $>$W b occurs in W, and

$$a \Rightarrow_W b = \left(\frac{|a >_W b| - |b >_W a|}{|a >_W b| + |b >_W a| + 1} \right)$$

Equation 1. Dependency measure between a and b

4.1 JVM Dependence Graph Implementation

For each different data mapping from dependence graph to event log, different analysis perspective obtained. The timestamp attribute added for each graph element. Two different mapping listed below:

4.1.1 Method Snapshots

This pattern provides a graphical representation of each method snapshot of the program dependence graph. This represent an equivalent for what provided by the IGV tool. Each process will represent states of single method; each case will represent two nodes attached with one edge, any case constructed in two actions, first one is the source node and second action is the destination node. The filtration functionality used to select the specific state to work on. The profiling data mapped to event log as in Table 4.

Table 4. Data mapping to extract the method snapshot

Event Log	Profiling Data	Description
Case	Graph: state title	Each case represents graph stat of the method
Activity	node & edge	Each activity represents connection between nodes

Figure 9 shows the control flow graph represent method state extracted using HM algorithm after filtering it using instance name filter with regular expression value "^(?!After|Parsing).*$" to model "After Parsing" state only. Also there are different analysis techniques are available for direct applying like LTL and SCIFF checkers (Lamma et al., 2009) which uses a logic-based approach to mining declarative models and DWS clustering algorithm (Guzzo et al., 2008) which provides solution for over-fitting problem that appear with complex methods and which is not handled in IGV tool.

4.1.2 Compilation Workflow

This pattern provides very detailed information about compiler behavior during the process of compilation of the monitored code, the compilation process changes based on method structure and complexity. The event log will have only one process; ach case will represent one method compilation steps and each action will include the step title, event time is the time of starting this step and the originator will be the full name of the method itself. The profiling data mapped to event log as in Table 5.

Table 5. Data mapping to extract compilation workflow from dependency graph

Event Log	Profiling Data	Description
Case	method	Each case represents single method compilation states.
Activity	Graph: state title	Each activity represents one state.
Timestamp	Graph: state time	The starting time of this state.
Originator	method	Putting originator as method full name to use in analysis.

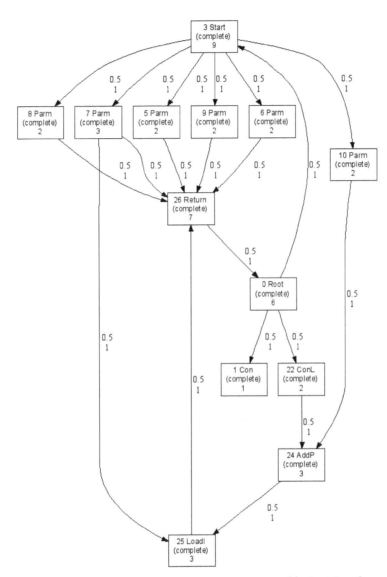

Figure 9. Dependence Graph state as represented in ProM tool

Starting with the control flow model for compilation process, Figure 10 shows part of the HM model that explains which compiler state has triggered and in which sequence and frequency, that allows understanding the code complexity and the corresponding compiler behavior. For example, how many "Phase Ideal Loop" states compiler has to call, did the compiler call the "eliminating allocations and locks" state or not and for how many times and so on. The applying of LTL and SCIFF checkers allows defining which compilation pattern to check, also clustering over-fit patterns and simplify then using DWS.

Some different analysis perspectives can be extracted directly; like basic statistics about the occurrences of the compilation states as in Figure 11, using the basic performance analysis we can easily identify the time that each state takes in average as in Figure 12 to identify the costly states or the time that each method takes in general while compilation, by using the "Originator by Task Matrix" we can identify which method trigger specific state in high frequency as in Figure 13.

To study the compilation patterns we can use "Sequence Diagram Analysis" to list the paths that the control flow constructed from them with identification for the most frequent path that was happened during compilation as in Figure 14, in this case the total unique compilation paths is 9 paths represent 38 cases and the most frequent path happened 21 times. For studying the changes in compiler behavior from method to another, we can use the "Trace Diff Analysis" to compare compilation steps for two methods, Figure 15 shows the common steps in order between two method and when changes start and end.

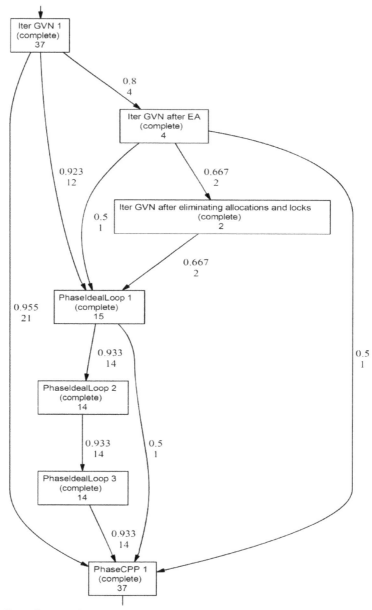

Figure 10. Workflow diagram that represent some methods compilation processes in JVM according to dependency graph

Model element	Occurrences (absolute)	Occurrences (relative)
After Parsing	38	10.243%
Iter GVN 1	37	9.973%
PhaseCPP 1	37	9.973%
Iter GVN 2	37	9.973%
Optimize finished	37	9.973%
Before Matching	37	9.973%

Figure 11. Compilation states basic statistics

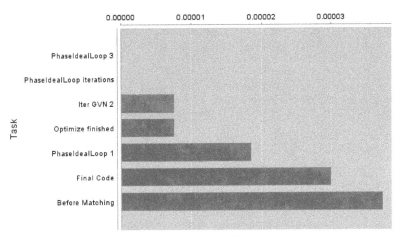

Figure 12. Bar chart for compilation states time

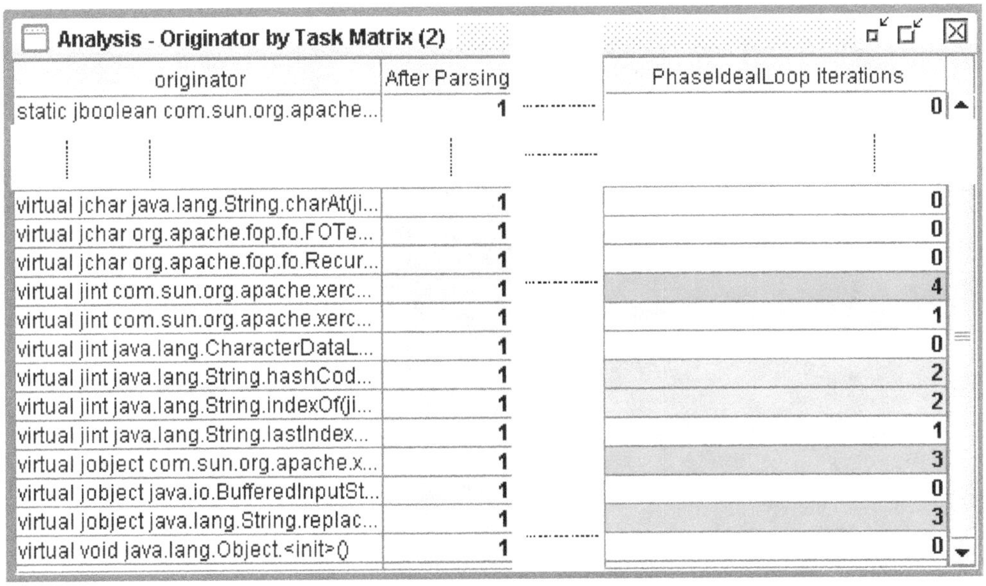

Analysis - Originator by Task Matrix (2)		
originator	After Parsing	PhaseIdealLoop iterations
static jboolean com.sun.org.apache...	1	0
virtual jchar java.lang.String.charAt(ji...	1	0
virtual jchar org.apache.fop.fo.FOTe...	1	0
virtual jchar org.apache.fop.fo.Recur...	1	0
virtual jint com.sun.org.apache.xerc...	1	4
virtual jint com.sun.org.apache.xerc...	1	1
virtual jint java.lang.CharacterDataL...	1	0
virtual jint java.lang.String.hashCod...	1	2
virtual jint java.lang.String.indexOf(ji...	1	2
virtual jint java.lang.String.lastIndex...	1	1
virtual jobject com.sun.org.apache.x...	1	3
virtual jobject java.io.BufferedInputSt...	1	0
virtual jobject java.lang.String.replac...	1	3
virtual void java.lang.Object.<init>()	1	0

Figure 13. States' frequency for each individual method

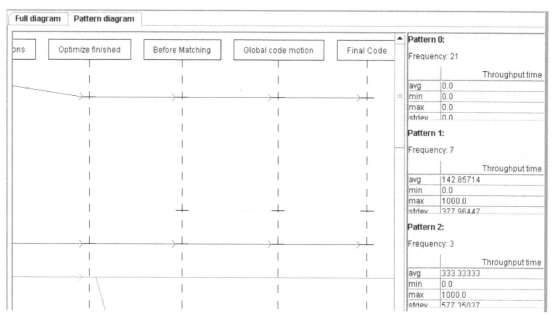

Figure 14. Sequence Diagram for the compilation paths

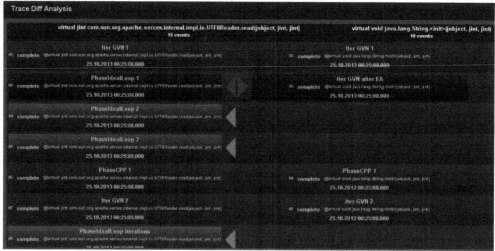

Figure 15. Compare two compilation paths by comparing the process activities

4.2 Compilation Logs Implementation

Compilation logs provided by JVM HotSpot developers inspects the compilation process. Compilation logs focuses on the compilation of method without describing the method architecture. Two patterns listed below, first is about classes relationship according to compilation, and the other pattern is compilation workflow to describe compiler behavior during the process of compilation.

4.2.1 Classes Relationship Based on Compilation

In JVM HotSpot method compilation happens under some optimization conditions, for this pattern, and to extract a valid classes relationship based on compilation, the compilation should happens for all method. So, the "-Xcomp" option has been used in this pattern to force compilation for all methods. Each process will represent single classes sequence; each case will represent two classes relationship according to the order of compilation methods in both of them as in Table 6.

Figure 16 shows part of the HM workflow model that describes the classes' relationship based on compilation process. The dependency between classes is so clear in such a model, by filtering this model to cover specific classes with predefine relation, we can make sure that what we designed actually applied. Obviously there are some basic statistic can be extracted from this pattern directly. Like the time has been consumed with each method, frequencies of method compilations in each class and which class has more compilation frequency. Listing the methods based on their compilation order as in the LogCompilation tool extracted directly from the log inspector as in Figure 17.

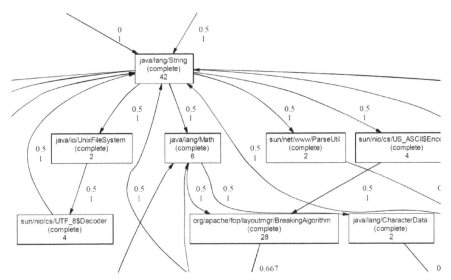

Figure 16. HM workflow model that represent classes relationship based on compilation

Table 6. Data mapping to extract classes' relationship based on compilation

Event Log	Profiling Data	Description
Case	Two Tasks	Each case represents one sequence of compilation
Activity	Task: Class Name	Each activity represents connection between two classes

Figure 17. Methods compilation order as shows in log inspector

4.2.2 Compilation Workflow

This pattern describes compiler behavior during the process of compilation as organized in JVM compilation logs. The event log will have only one process; ach case will represent one method compilation process and each action will include the compilation phase, event time is the time of starting this phase and the originator will be the full name of the class that contains this method. The profiling data mapped to event log as in Table 7. Figure 18 shows the HM model, and all the analysis patterns that mentioned with dependency graph can be extract as well from JVM compilation logs.

Table 7. Data mapping to extract compilation workflow from JVM compilation logs

Event Log	Profiling Data	Description
Case	Task	Each case represents one method compilation process.
Activity	Phase	Each activity represents one phase of compilation process.
Timestamp	Phase time	The starting time of this phase.
Originator	Task: Class Name	Putting originator as method full name to analysis.

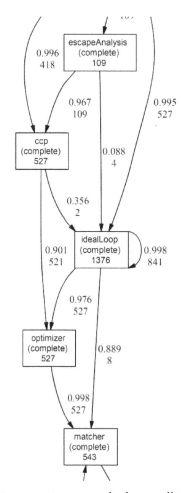

Figure 18. Workflow diagram that represent some methods compilation processes in JVM according to compilation logs

5. Conclusions

In this paper, new approach has introduced to use process-mining techniques to represent the analysis and visualize phases of JVM profilers. They are flexible enough to cover so many perspectives in several ways. That can form a unified layer for analysis and visualize across profiling perspectives.

To do so, new tool java-event-logs has introduced to implement this approach. The java-event-logs tool has two execution options "-igv" and "-logc" for dependence graph and compilation logs respectively, and the outputs provide new perspectives for profiling data analysis.

Applying this new approach on the JVM profilers provides information about java program or JVM (HotSpotTM) and helps JVM developers with new aspect of analysis with each process mining perspective. On the other hand, we will work on how to use process mining to provide interactive approached that can help to analysis the Java Byte code program and provide feedback to JVM to enhance execution time and memory management.

References

Ahmad, S. et al. (2014). Dependence flow graph for analysis of aspect-oriented programs. *International Journal of Software Engineering & Applications, 5*(6), 125.

Balmas, F. (2001). *Displaying dependence graphs: A hierarchical approach.* Reverse Engineering, 2001. Proceedings. Eighth Working Conference on, IEEE.

Bergel, A. et al. (2012). Spy: A flexible code profiling framework. *Computer Languages, Systems & Structures 38*(1), 16-28.

Blackburn, S. M. et al. (2006). *The DaCapo benchmarks: Java benchmarking development and analysis.* ACM SIGPLAN Notices, ACM.

Bowers, K. R., & Kaeli, D. (1998). *Characterizing the SPEC JVM98 benchmarks on the Java virtual machine.* Te hnical Report ECE-CEG-98-026, Northeastern University, Department of Electrical and Computer Engineering.

Burattin, A. (2015). *Heuristics Miner for Time Interval.* Process Mining Techniques in Business Environments, Springer: 85-95.

Chesani, F. et al. (2009). *Exploiting inductive logic programming techniques for declarative process mining.* Transactions on Petri Nets and Other Models of Concurrency II, Springer: 278-295.

De Medeiros, A. K. A. et al. (2008). *Process mining based on clustering: A quest for precision.* Business Process Management Workshops, Springer.

Dmitriev, M. (2004). *Profiling Java applications using code hotswapping and dynamic call graph revelation.* ACM SIGSOFT Software Engineering Notes, ACM.

Dufour, B. et al. (2003). *Dynamic metrics for Java.* ACM SIGPLAN Notices, ACM.

Dufour, B. et al. (2003). *J: a tool for dynamic analysis of Java programs.* Companion of the 18th annual ACM SIGPLAN conference on Object-oriented programming, systems, languages, and applications, ACM.

Ferrante, J. et al. (1987). The program dependence graph and its use in optimization. *ACM Transactions on Programming Languages and Systems (TOPLAS), 9*(3), 319-349.

Krinke, J. (2004). *Visualization of program dependence and slices.* Software Maintenance, 2004. Proceedings. 20th IEEE International Conference on, IEEE.

Lee, S. H., & Sim, S. (2015). Aspect Refactoring Techniques for System Optimization. *Indian Journal of Science and Technology, 8*, 412.

Liang, S., & Viswanathan, D. (1999). *Comprehensive Profiling Support in the Java Virtual Machine.* COOTS.

Paleczny, M. et al. (2001). *The java hotspot TM server compiler.* Proceedings of the 2001 Symposium on Java TM Virtual Machine Research and Technology Symposium-Volume 1, USENIX Association.

Sarimbekov, A. et al. (2012). *JP2: Call-site aware calling context profiling for the Java Virtual Machine.* Science of Computer Programming.

Sjoblom, I. et al. (2011). *Can You Trust Your JVM Diagnostic Tools?* MICS.

Van Der Aalst, W. M. et al. (2007). *ProM 4.0: comprehensive support for real process analysis.* Petri Nets and Other Models of Concurrency–ICATPN 2007, Springer, 484-494.

Van Der Aalst, W. M., & De Medeiros, A. K. A. (2005). Process mining and security: Detecting anomalous process executions and checking process conformance. *Electronic Notes in Theoretical Computer Science 121*, 3-21.

Van Der Aalst, W. M., & Van Der Aalst, W. (2011). *Process mining: discovery, conformance and enhancement of business processes.* Springer.

Van Der Aalst, W. M., & Weijters, A. (2004). Process mining: a research agenda. *Computers in Industry, 53*(3), 231-244.

Van Dongen, B. F. et al. (2005). *The ProM framework: A new era in process mining tool support.* Applications and Theory of Petri Nets 2005, Springer, 444-454.

Weijters, A. et al. (2006). *Process mining with the heuristics miner-algorithm.* Technische Universiteit Eindhoven, Tech. Rep. WP 166.

Weijters, A. J., & Van Der Aalst, W. M. (2003). Rediscovering workflow models from event-based data using little thumb. *Integrated Computer-Aided Engineering, 10*(2), 151-162.

Wert, A. et al. (2015). *AIM: Adaptable Instrumentation and Monitoring for automated software performance analysis.* Automation of Software Test (AST), 2015 IEEE/ACM 10th International Workshop on, IEEE.

Würthinger, T. (2007). *Visualization of program dependence graphs.* Johannes Kepler University Linz. Master.

Würthinger, T. et al. (2008). *Visualization of program dependence graphs.* Compiler Construction, Springer.

15

Correlation Analysis between Maximal Clique Size and Centrality Metrics for Random Networks and Scale-Free Networks

Natarajan Meghanathan[1]

[1] Department of Computer Science, Jackson State University, USA

Correspondence: Natarajan Meghanathan, Department of Computer Science, Mailbox 18839, Jackson State University, Jackson, MS 39217, USA. E-mail: natarajan.meghanathan@jsums.edu

The research is financed by the NASA EPSCoR sub award (#: NNX14AN38A) from University of Mississippi.

Abstract

The high-level contribution of this paper is a comprehensive analysis of the correlation levels between node centrality (a computationally light-weight metric) and maximal clique size (a computationally hard metric) in random network and scale-free network graphs generated respectively from the well-known Erdos-Renyi (ER) and Barabasi-Albert (BA) models. We use three well-known measures for evaluating the level of correlation: Product-moment based Pearson's correlation coefficient, Rank-based Spearman's correlation coefficient and Concordance-based Kendall's correlation coefficient. For each of the several variants of the theoretical graphs generated from the ER and BA models, we compute the above three correlation coefficient values between the maximal clique size for a node (maximum size of the clique the node is part of) and each of the four prominent node centrality metrics (degree, eigenvector, betweenness and closeness). We also explore the impact of the operating parameters of the theoretical models for generating random networks and scale-free networks on the correlation between maximal clique size and the centrality metrics.

Keywords: complex network graphs, correlation coefficient, centrality metrics, maximal clique size, scale-free networks, random networks

1. Introduction

Network Science (a.k.a. Complex Network Analysis) is an emerging area of interest in the big data paradigm and corresponds to analyzing complex real-world networks and theoretical model-based networks from a graph theory point of view. Among the various measures used for complex network analysis, node centrality is a prominently used measure of immense theoretical interest and practical value. The centrality of a node is a link statistics-based quantitative measure of the topological importance of the node with respect to the other nodes in the network (Newman, 2010). Applications for node centrality metrics could be for example to identify the most influential persons in a social network, the key infrastructure nodes in an internet, the super-spreaders of a disease, etc. The existing centrality metrics could be broadly classified into two categories (Newman, 2010): neighbor-based and shortest path-based. Degree centrality (DegC) and Eigenvector centrality (EVC; Bonacich, 1987) are well-known measures for neighbor-based centrality, while Betweenness centrality (BWC; Freeman, 1977) and Closeness centrality (ClC; Freeman, 1979) are well-known measures for shortest path-based centrality. Various time-efficient and space-efficient algorithms (e.g., Brandes, 2001; Kang et al., 2011) have been proposed in the literature to determine each of the above centrality metrics. Hence, we refer to node centrality as a computationally light-weight measure.

In addition to node centrality, there exists several other informative measures for quantitatively assessing the importance of a node in a complex network - some of which are too time consuming to determine. We consider one such measure in this paper - the maximal clique size for a node. The maximal clique size for a node is defined as the largest size clique the node is part of (Cormen et al., 2009). A "clique" in a graph is a subset of the vertices such that there exists an edge between any two vertices in the subset (Cormen et al., 2009). The size of a clique is the number of vertices that are part of the clique. Each node in a graph could be part of one or more cliques of different sizes. The largest size clique that a node is part of is of interest for community detection in complex networks (in order to identify nodes that are highly modular). A community of vertices is a subset of the vertices in a graph such that there are more links among vertices within this subset and relatively fewer links to vertices outside this subset (Newman, 2010). The effectiveness of the partitioning of a network into communities is evaluated using a metric called the modularity score (Newman, 2006). The larger the number of vertices within a community and larger the number of links between these vertices, the larger the modularity score for the community. Hence, it is of logical interest to identify vertices that are highly modular and design algorithms for community detection involving such vertices.

Unfortunately, the problem of determining the maximal clique size for a vertex is NP-hard (Cormen et al., 2009) and we refer to it as a computationally hard measure. One would have to rely on either time consuming exact algorithms or sub optimal (but relatively less time consuming) approximation heuristics to determine the maximal clique size for a vertex. Also, the focus of the research community has been mostly on developing exact algorithms and approximation heuristics (e.g., Carraghan & Pardalos, 1990; Ostergard, 2002; Pattabiraman et al., 2013) for a related problem called the maximum clique size, which is the largest clique size for the entire graph. The maximal clique size for one or more vertices could correspond to the maximum clique size for the graph; but not all vertices are likely to be part of the maximum clique. There could be several vertices in a graph for which the maximal clique size would be less than the maximum clique size.

Our contributions in this paper are as follows: We identify one or more computationally light-weight centrality metrics that have a high correlation with that of the maximal clique size (a computationally hard measure). In this pursuit, we run the most time-efficient algorithms for each of the four centrality metrics (DegC, EVC, BWC and ClC) and an adapted version of the exact algorithm originally proposed for maximum clique size (Pattabiraman et al., 2013) to determine the maximal clique size of the vertices in complex networks. We run these algorithms on random networks and scale-free networks generated respectively from the well-known Erdos-Renyi (Erdos & Reny, 1959) and Barabasi-Albert (Barabasi & Albert, 1999) theoretical models. We evaluate the correlation between maximal clique size for a node and each of the four centrality metrics using three well-known correlation measures (Triola, 2012): (i) Pearson's product-moment based correlation coefficient, (ii) Spearman's rank based correlation coefficient and (iii) Kendall's concordance based correlation coefficient. We identify the centrality metrics that have the highest correlation as well as the lowest correlation with the maximal clique size with respect to each of the above three correlation measures for random networks and scale-free networks. We also identify the correlation measures for which we incur the largest and smallest values for the correlation coefficient for different combinations of the centrality metrics and the theoretical networks. In addition, we evaluate the impact of the operating parameters of the theoretical models on the nature of the correlation observed between each of the four centrality metrics and maximal clique size.

The rest of the paper is organized as follows: Section 2 introduces the maximal clique size of a graph and describes an exact algorithm to determine the same. Section 3 reviews the two neighbor-based centrality metrics (DegC and EVC) and the two shortest path-based centrality metrics (BWC and ClC) and briefly describes an efficient algorithm to determine each of them. Section 4 introduces the three measures for evaluating the correlation coefficient between node centrality and maximal clique size per node. Sections 5 and 6 respectively present the results for correlation coefficient analysis on random network graphs (generated from the Erdos-Renyi model) and scale-free network graphs (generated from the Barabasi-Albert model). Section 7 reviews related work on correlation studies involving centrality metrics and maximal/maximum clique size. Section 8 concludes the paper. Throughout the paper, the terms 'node' and 'vertex' as well as 'link' and 'edge' are used interchangeably. Likewise, a vertex might be referred to either as i or v_i. They mean the same. We model all the theoretical-model generated graphs as undirected graphs.

2. Maximal Clique Size

The maximal clique size of a node is the largest size clique that the node is part of. The maximal clique size of a node is a measure of the level of modularity of the node and could be used to identify seed nodes (for a community detection algorithm) around which communities could evolve. In spite of its importance for identifying highly modular nodes in complex networks, most of the research focus in the literature has been on a related measure called the maximum clique size - the size of the largest clique in a graph. As the problems of determining both the maximum clique size and maximal clique size are NP-hard (Cormen et al., 2009), we decided to adapt an exact algorithm for determining maximum clique size in a graph to determine the maximal clique size for the vertices in the graph. We choose the recently proposed exact algorithm by Pattabiraman et al (Pattabiraman et al., 2013) for maximum clique size of a graph and slightly modify it to determine the maximal clique size of the individual vertices in a graph.

2.1 Original Exact Algorithm to Determine Maximum Clique Size for a Graph

The original exact algorithm by Pattabiraman et al (2013) follows a branch and bound approach of searching through all possible cliques and limiting the exploration only to vertices whose agglomeration has scope of being larger than the size of the largest clique known until then. Figure 1 illustrates the pseudo code of the exact algorithm for maximum clique size. As one can notice, the algorithm uses a variable *max* to keep track of the largest size clique determined during the search process. The procedure MAXCLIQUE proceeds in iterations, and in the ith iteration, the algorithm explores whether a clique of size greater than the current value of *max* could be determined involving vertex v_i (the vertices are considered in the increasing order of their IDs) and its neighbors. For each such vertex v_i, a candidate set of vertices U is constructed involving v_i's neighbors (each of whose degree is at least the value of *max*) and is passed to the sub routine CLIQUE along with a variable *size* whose value at any time during the execution of the sub routine represents the size of the largest clique known until then involving vertex v_i and its neighbors.

Subroutine CLIQUE($G = (V, E)$, U, *size*)
    // *size* is the size of clique found so far
    if $U = \phi$ **then**
        if *size* > *max* **then**
            max ← *size*
        return
    while $|U| > 0$ **do**
        if *size* + $|U| \leq$ *max* **then**
            return

Procedure MAXIMUMCLIQUE ($G = (V, E)$)
    max ← 0
    for i : 1 to $|V|$ **do**
        if degree(v_i) ≥ *max* **then**
            $U \leftarrow \phi$
            for each $v_j \in$ Neighbor(v_i) **do**
                if degree(v_j) ≥ *max* **then**
                    $U \leftarrow U \cup \{v_j\}$
            CLIQUE(G, U, 1)

        select any vertex u from U
        $U \leftarrow U \setminus \{u\}$
        $N'(u) := \{w | w \in$ Neighbor(u) $\wedge$ degree(u) ≥ *max*$\}$
        Clique(G, $U \cap N'(u)$, *size* + 1)

Figure 1. Exact Algorithm to Determine Maximum Clique Size for a Graph (adapted from Pattabiraman et al., 2013)

The sub routine CLIQUE expands the size of the clique involving v_i with one vertex at a time (starting with v_i itself) through a combination of iterations and recursions. In each such iteration, a random node u is removed from the set U passed to the sub routine and the set U is filtered to retain only those vertices that are also neighbors of the node u; the value of *size* is incremented by 1 to account for the inclusion of node u to the clique and a recursive call to CLIQUE is made with the updated U and value of *size*. A recursive call to the sub routine CLIQUE runs as long as the current value of *max* is less than the sum of the size of the set U passed to the sub routine and the *size* of the current clique found until then. During the sequence of returns from the recursive calls, it is also possible that a different neighbor node u of v_i gets selected and the size of the clique involving the new node u and its neighbors along with v_i could be larger the current value of *max*. Also, during any such recursive call to CLIQUE, if the size of the set U reaches zero, the algorithm terminates the sequence of recursions and updates the value of *max* if it is less than the *size* of the clique found until then involving vertex v_i and its neighbors.

The efficiency of the algorithm is severely impacted by the order the vertices are considered for the iterations. A labeling of the vertices in the decreasing order of their degree increases the chances of finding the maximum size clique much earlier than a random labeling of the vertices (Pattabiraman et al., 2013). If the maximum size clique is found in the earlier iterations itself, the subsequent iterations could end up to be mere pruning operations if the vertices involved in these iterations have a degree smaller than the maximum size clique determined until then.

2.2 Modified Exact Algorithm to Determine Maximal Clique Size for a Vertex

Figure 2 illustrates the pseudo code that we propose for a modified exact algorithm to determine the maximal clique size for any vertex in a given graph. Unlike the procedure MAXIMUMCLIQUE (discussed in Section 2.1), we can no longer discard vertices with degree lower than the maximum clique size found until then for the entire graph. We need to run the procedure for every vertex to determine the maximal clique size involving the vertex.

For each vertex v_i, to start with, the maximal clique size known until then is 0; so, we construct the candidate set of vertices (U) involving all the neighbors of v_i and pass them to the sub routine CLIQUE. We could retain all the pruning strategies (discussed in Section 2.1) in the sub routine CLIQUE: we need not explore node u (chosen from the set U) and its neighbors if their degree is smaller than the value of *size* (the maximal clique size involving vertex v_i) known until then. For speedup, we list the neighbors of a vertex v_i in the initial set U passed from the procedure MAXIMAL CLIQUE to the sub routine CLIQUE in the decreasing order of their degree.

Procedure MAXIMALCLIQUE ($G = (V, E)$)
     for i : 1 to $|V|$ **do**
         $maximalCliqueSize[v_i] \leftarrow 0$
         $U \leftarrow \phi$
         for each $v_j \in$ Neighbor(v_i) **do**
            $U \leftarrow U \cup \{v_j\}$
         CLIQUE($G, v_i, U, 1$)

Subroutine CLIQUE($G = (V, E), v_i, U, size$)   // *size* is the size of clique found so far for vertex v_i
     if $U = \phi$ **then**
         if $size > maximalCliqueSize[v_i]$ **then**
            $maximalCliqueSize[v_i] \leftarrow size$
         return
     while $|U| > 0$ **do**
         if $size + |U| \leq maximalCliqueSize[v_i]$ **then**
     return
         select any vertex u from U
         $U \leftarrow U \setminus \{u\}$
         $N'(u) := \{w \mid w \in$ Neighbor(u) $\wedge$ degree(u) $\geq maximalCliqueSize[v_i]\}$
         Clique($G, v_i, U \cap N'(u), size + 1$)

Figure 2. Exact Algorithm to Determine Maximal Clique Size for a Vertex (adapted from Pattabiraman et al., 2013)

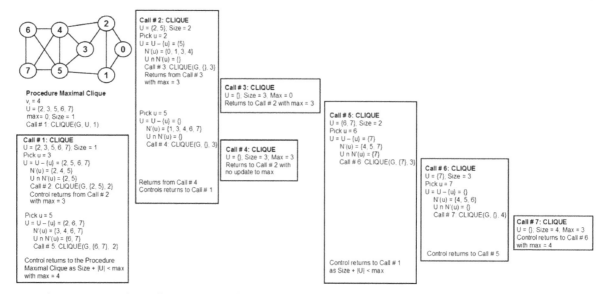

Figure 3. Example to Illustrate Execution of the Exact to Determine Maximal Clique Size for a Vertex

Figure 3 presents an example to illustrate the execution of the modified exact algorithm to determine the maximal clique size for a vertex. We consider vertex $v_i = 4$ as the vertex for which we want to find the maximal clique size. We identify each recursive call to the sub routine CLIQUE with a unique identification number (Call # 1, 2, etc) so that it is easy trace the execution of the algorithm. The first few recursive calls (Call #s 1 - 2 - 3 - 4) lead to the identification of clique {4, 2, 3} of size 3. However, the next set of recursive calls (Call #s: 1 - 5 - 6 - 7) lead to the identification of the maximal size clique {4, 5, 6, 7} involving vertex 4. Figure 4 illustrates the maximal clique size of all the vertices in the sample graph used in Figure 3.

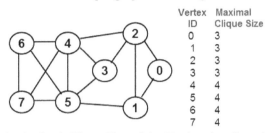

Vertex ID	Maximal Clique Size
0	3
1	3
2	3
3	3
4	4
5	4
6	4
7	4

Figure 4. Maximal Clique Size of the Vertices in a Sample Graph

3. Maximal Clique Size

We now review the centrality metrics that are used for the correlation coefficient analysis studies in this paper. These are the neighbor-based degree centrality (DegC) and eigenvector centrality (EVC) metrics and the shortest path-based betweenness centrality (BWC) and closeness centrality (ClC) metrics.

3.1 Degree Centrality

The degree centrality of a vertex is the number of neighbors for the vertex in the graph and can be easily computed by counting the number of edges incident on the vertex. If A is the n x n adjacency matrix for a graph such that $A[i, j] = 1$ if there is an edge connecting v_i to v_j (for undirected graphs) and $A[i, j] = 0$ if there is no edge connecting v_i and v_j. The degree centrality of a vertex v_i is defined quantitatively as follows:

$$\text{DegC}(v_i) = \sum_{j=1}^{n} A[i, j] \tag{1}$$

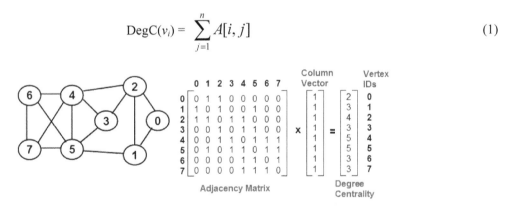

Figure 5. Example to Illustrate the Computation of Degree Centrality

Figure 5 illustrates an example for computing the degree centrality of all the vertices in a graph as the product of the adjacency matrix of the graph and a unit column vector of 1s corresponding to the number of vertices in the graph.

3.2 Eigenvector Centrality

The eigenvector centrality (EVC) of a vertex is a quantitative measure of the degree of the vertex as well as the degree of its neighbors. A vertex that has a high degree for itself as well as located in the neighborhood of high-degree vertices is likely to have a larger EVC. The EVC values of the vertices in a graph correspond to the entries for the vertices in the principal eigenvector of the adjacency matrix of the graph. An n x n adjacency matrix has n eigenvalues and the corresponding eigenvectors. The principal eigenvector is the eigenvector corresponding to the largest eigenvalue (principal eigenvalue) of the adjacency matrix, A. Moreover, if all the entries in a square matrix are positive (i.e., greater than or equal to zero), the principal eigenvalue as well as the entries in the principal eigenvector are also positive (Lay, 2011).

We determine the EVC of the vertices using the Power-iteration method (Lay, 2011). According to this method, we start with a unit vector $X_0 = [1\ 1\ 1\ 1\ \ldots\ 1\ 1]$ of all 1s corresponding to the number of vertices in the graph and go through a sequence of iterations. The tentative eigenvector computed during the $(i+1)^{th}$ iteration is given as: $\mathbf{A}X_i/\|\mathbf{A}X_i\|$, where $\|\mathbf{A}X_i\|$ is the normalized value of the vector resulting from the product of the adjacency matrix and the tentative eigenvector computed during the ith iteration. We continue the iterations until the normalized value $\|\mathbf{A}X_i\|$ does not change significantly and converges to a constant value (when rounded to the second decimal). The normalized value at this juncture also corresponds to the principal eigenvalue of the adjacency matrix and the tentative eigenvector computed with this normalized value corresponds to the principal eigenvector of the adjacency matrix. We illustrate the execution of the Power-iteration method with the example shown in Figure 6. As can be noticed from Figure 6, even though both vertices 4 and 5 have the same larger degree (five) - the EVC of vertex 4 is larger than the EVC of vertex 5 - this could be attributed to the degree distribution {3, 3, 3, 4, 5} of the neighbors of vertex 4 vis-a-vis the degree distribution {3, 3, 3, 2, 5} of the neighbors of vertex 5.

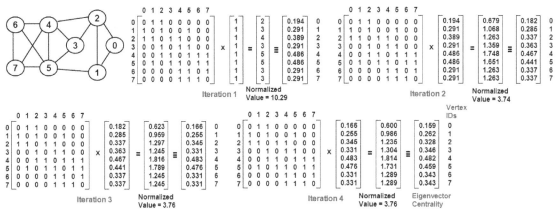

Figure 6. Example to Illustrate the Calculation of Eigenvector Centrality using Power Iteration Method

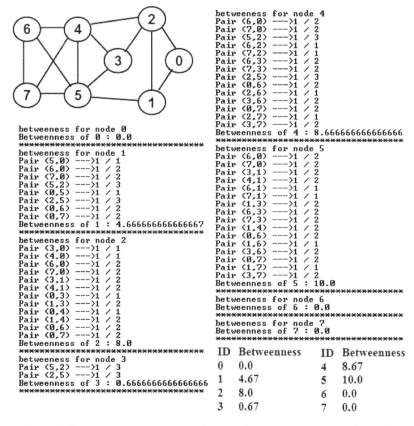

Figure 7. Example to Illustrate the Calculation of Betweenness Centrality

3.3 Betweenness Centrality

The betweenness centrality (BWC) of a vertex is the sum of the fraction of shortest paths going through the vertex between any two vertices, considered over all pairs of vertices. In this paper, we determine the BWC of the vertices using the Breadth First Search (BFS)-variant of the well-known Brandes algorithm (Brandes, 2001). We run the BFS algorithm on each vertex in the graph and determine the level of each vertex (the number of hops/edges from the root) in each of these BFS trees. The root of a BFS tree is said to be at level 0 and the number of shortest paths from the root to itself is 1. On a BFS tree rooted at vertex r, the number of shortest paths for a vertex i at level l ($l > 0$) from the root r is the sum of the number of shortest paths from the root r to each the neighbors of vertex i (in the original graph) that are at level l-1 in the BFS tree.

Since we are working on undirected graphs, the total number of shortest paths from vertex i to vertex j (denoted sp_{ij}) is simply the number of shortest paths from vertex i to vertex j in the shortest path tree rooted at vertex i or vice-versa. The number of shortest paths from a vertex i to a vertex j that go through a vertex k (denoted $sp_{ij}(k)$) is the maximum of the number of shortest paths from vertex i to vertex k in the shortest path tree rooted at i and the number of shortest paths from vertex j to vertex k in the shortest path tree rooted at vertex j.

$$BWC(k) = \sum_{\substack{k \neq i \\ k \neq j}} \frac{sp_{ij}(k)}{sp_{ij}} \qquad (2)$$

Figure 7 illustrates an example to calculate the BWC of vertices in the same graph used in Figures 3-6. We can observe the betweenness values for vertices 0, 6 and 7 are zero each, because no shortest path between any two vertices go through them. We observe that even though vertices 4 and 5 have the same larger degree, the average degree of the neighbors of vertex 5 is slightly lower than the average degree of the neighbors of vertex. As a result, vertex 5 is more likely to occupy a relatively larger fraction of the shortest path between any two vertices and incur a relatively larger BWC value compared to vertex 4 (even though vertex 4 has a larger EVC value). Also, even though vertex 3 has a larger degree than vertex 1, the BWC of vertex 1 is significantly larger than that of vertex 3. This could be attributed to vertex 1 lying on the shortest path from vertices 0 and 2 to vertices 4, 5, 6 and 7; on the other hand, vertex 3 lies only on the shortest path between 2 and 5.

3.4 Closeness Centrality

The closeness centrality (ClC) of a vertex is the inverse of the sum of the number of shortest paths from the vertex to every other vertex in the graph. We determine the ClC of the vertices by running the BFS algorithm on each vertex and summing the number of shortest paths from the root vertex to every other vertex in these BFS trees. Figure 8 illustrates an example to compute the ClC of the vertices. We observe vertices with a larger degree are more likely to have shortest paths of lower hop count to the rest of the vertices, leading to a larger ClC value.

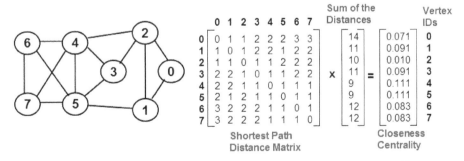

Figure 8. Example to Illustrate the Calculation of Closeness Centrality

4. Correlation Coefficient Measures

We now discuss the three well-known correlation coefficient measures that are used to evaluate the correlation between maximal clique size and the four centrality metrics presented in Section 3. These are the Product-moment based Pearson's correlation coefficient, Rank based Spearman's correlation coefficient and Concordance based Kendall's correlation coefficient. All the three measures evaluate the extent of the degree of linear dependence (Triola, 2012) between two datasets or performance metrics (in our case, the maximal clique size and each of the four centrality metrics).

The correlation coefficient values obtained for all the three measures range from -1 to 1. Correlation coefficient values closer to 1 indicate a stronger positive correlation between the two metrics considered (i.e., a vertex having a larger value for one of the two metrics is more likely to have a larger value for the other metric too), while values closer to -1 indicate a stronger negative correlation (i.e., a vertex having a larger value for one of the two metrics is more likely to have a smaller value for the other metric). Correlation coefficient values closer to 0 indicate no correlation (i.e., the values incurred by a vertex for the two metrics are independent of each other). We will adopt the ranges (rounded to two decimals) proposed by Evans (1995) to indicate the various levels of correlation, shown in Table 1. For simplicity, we refer to the two datasets as *M* and *C* respectively corresponding to the maximal clique size and centrality. We will use the results from Figures 4-8 to illustrate examples for the computation of the correlation coefficient under each of the three measures.

Table 1. Range of Correlation Coefficient Values and the Corresponding Levels of Correlation

Range of Correlation Coefficient Values	Level of Correlation	Range of Correlation Coefficient Values	Level of Correlation
0.80 to 1.00	Very Strong Positive	-1.00 to -0.80	Very Strong Negative
0.60 to 0.79	Strong Positive	-0.79 to -0.60	Strong Negative
0.40 to 0.59	Moderate Positive	-0.59 to -0.40	Moderate Negative
0.20 to 0.39	Weak Positive	-0.39 to -0.20	Weak Negative
0.00 to 0.19	Very Weak Positive	-0.19 to -0.01	Very Weak Negative

4.1 Pearson's Product-Moment Correlation Coefficient

The Pearson's product moment-based correlation coefficient for two datasets is defined as the covariance of the two datasets divided by the product of their standard deviation (Triola, 2012). Let M_{avg} and C_{avg} denote the average values for the maximal clique size and a centrality metric for a graph of *n* vertices and let M_i and C_i denote respectively the values for the maximal clique size and the centrality metric of interest incurred for vertex *i*. The Pearson's correlation coefficient (indicated PCC) is quantitatively defined as shown in equation (3). The term product moment is associated with the product of the mean (first moment) adjusted values for the two metrics in the numerator of the formulation. Figure 9 presents the calculation of the PCC for the maximal clique size (*M*) and degree centrality (*C*) values obtained for the example graph used in Figures 3-8. We obtain a Correlation Coefficient value of 0.5 (see Figure 9) indicating a moderately positive correlation between the two metrics for the example graph.

$$PCC(M,C) = \frac{\sum_{i=1}^{n}(M_i - M_{avg})(C_i - C_{avg})}{\sqrt{\sum_{i=1}^{n}(M_i - M_{avg})^2 \sum_{i=1}^{n}(C_i - C_{avg})^2}} \tag{3}$$

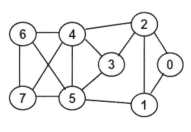

Vertex	M	C (DegC)	M - M_{avg}	C - C_{avg}	(M - M_{avg}) * (C - C_{avg})	(M - M_{avg})^2	(C - C_{avg})^2
0	3	2	-0.5	-1.5	0.75	0.25	2.25
1	3	3	-0.5	-0.5	0.25	0.25	0.25
2	3	4	-0.5	0.5	-0.25	0.25	0.25
3	3	3	-0.5	-0.5	0.25	0.25	0.25
4	4	5	0.5	1.5	0.75	0.25	2.25
5	4	5	0.5	1.5	0.75	0.25	2.25
6	4	3	0.5	-0.5	-0.25	0.25	0.25
7	4	3	0.5	-0.5	-0.25	0.25	0.25
Avg	3.5	3.5			Sum	2	2	8

Correlation Coefficient = 2 / √(2*8) = 0.5

Figure 9. Example to Illustrate the Computation of Pearson's Correlation Coefficient (between Maximal Clique Size: *M* and Degree Centrality: *C*)

4.2 Spearman's Rank-Based Correlation Coefficient

Spearman's rank correlation coefficient (SCC) is a measure of how well the relationship between two datasets (variables) can be assessed using a monotonic function (Triola, 2012). To compute the SCC of two datasets M and C, we convert the raw scores M_i and C_i for a vertex i to ranks m_i and c_i and use formula (2) shown below, where $d_i = m_i - c_i$ is the difference between the ranks of vertex i in the two datasets. We follow the convention of assigning the rank values from 1 to n for a graph of n vertices, even though the vertex IDs range from 0 to n-1. To obtain the rank for a vertex based on the list of values for a performance metric, we first sort the values (in ascending order). If there is any tie, we break the tie in favor of the vertex with a lower ID; we will thus be able to arrive at a tentative, but unique, rank value for each vertex with respect to the performance metric. We determine a final ranking of the vertices as follows: For vertices with unique value of the performance metric, the final ranking is the same as the tentative ranking. For vertices with an identical value for the performance metric, the final ranking is assigned to be the average of their tentative rankings. Figure 10 illustrates the computation of the tentative and final ranking of the vertices based on their maximal clique size and degree centrality values in the example graph used in Figures 3-9 as well as illustrates the computation of the Spearman's rank-based correlation coefficient.

$$SCC(M,C) = 1 - \frac{6\sum_{i=1}^{n} d_i^2}{n(n^2 - 1)} \qquad (4)$$

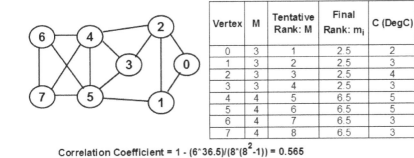

Vertex	M	Tentative Rank: M	Final Rank: m_i	C (DegC)	Tentative Rank: C	Final Rank: c_i	Rank Difference (d_i): $m_i - c_i$	d_i^2
0	3	1	2.5	2	1	1	1.5	2.25
1	3	2	2.5	3	2	3.5	-1	1
2	3	3	2.5	4	6	6	-3.5	12.25
3	3	4	2.5	3	3	3.5	-1	1
4	4	5	6.5	5	7	7.5	-1	1
5	4	6	6.5	5	8	7.5	-1	1
6	4	7	6.5	3	4	3.5	3	9
7	4	8	6.5	3	5	3.5	3	9
							Sum	36.5

Correlation Coefficient = 1 - (6*36.5)/(8*(8²-1)) = 0.565

Figure 10. Example to Illustrate the Computation of Spearman's Correlation Coefficient (between Maximal Clique Size: M and Degree Centrality: C)

In Figure 10, we observe ties among vertices with respect to both the maximal clique size and degree centrality. The tentative ranking is obtained by breaking the ties in favor of vertices with lower IDs. In the case of maximal clique size (M), we observe the four vertices 0-3 have an identical M value of 3 each and their tentative rankings are 1-4; the final ranking (2.5) of each of these four vertices is thus the average of 1, 2, 3 and 4. Likewise, the four vertices 4-7 have an identical M value of 4 each and their tentative rankings are 5-8; the final ranking (6.5) of each of these four vertices is thus the average of 5, 6, 7 and 8. In the case of degree centrality (D), we observe ties among vertices with degree 3 (tentative rankings of 2, 4 and 5; final ranking: 3.5 - average of 2, 4 and 5) and among vertices with degree 5 (tentative rankings of 7 and 8; final ranking: 7.5 - average of 7 and 8). The Spearman's rank-based correlation coefficient (SCC) computed for maximal clique size and degree centrality for the example graph used from Figures 3-9 is 0.565. We observe the SCC value to be slightly larger than the PCC value obtained in Figure 9 for the same graph; but, the level of correlation for both the measures still falls in the range of moderately positive correlation.

4.3 Kendall's Concordance-Based Correlation Coefficient

Kendall's concordance-based correlation coefficient (KCC) for any two performance metrics (say, M and C) is a measure of the similarity (a.k.a. concordance) in the ordering of the values for the metrics incurred by the vertices in the graph (Triola, 2012). We define a pair of distinct vertices v_i and v_j as concordant if $\{M_i > M_j$ and $C_i > C_j\}$ or $\{M_i < M_j$ and $C_i < C_j\}$. In other words, a pair of vertices v_i and v_j are concordant if either one of these two vertices strictly have a larger value for the two metrics M and C compared to the other vertex. We define a pair of distinct vertices v_i and v_j as discordant if $\{M_i > M_j$ and $C_i < C_j\}$ or $\{M_i < M_j$ and $C_i > C_j\}$. In other words, a pair of vertices v_i and v_j are discordant if a vertex has a larger value for only one of the two performance metrics. A pair of distinct vertices v_i and v_j are neither concordant nor discordant if either $\{M_i = M_j\}$ or $\{C_i = C_j\}$ or $\{M_i = M_j$ and $C_i = C_j\}$. The Kendall's concordance-based correlation coefficient is simply the difference between the number of concordant pairs (denoted #*conc.pairs*) and the number of discordant pairs (#*disc.pairs*) divided by the total number of pairs considered. For a graph of n vertices, KCC is calculated as shown in formulation (5).

$$KCC(M,C) = \frac{\#conc.pairs - \#disc.pairs}{\frac{1}{2}n(n-1)} \qquad (5)$$

Figure 11 illustrates the calculation of the Kendall's correlation coefficient between maximal clique size and degree centrality for the example graph used in Figures 3-9. For a graph of 8 vertices, the total number of distinct pairs that could be considered is 8(8-1)/2 = 28 and out of these, 10 pairs are classified to be concordant and 2 pairs as discordant. The remaining 16 pairs are neither concordant nor discordant (denoted as N/A) in the figure. We get a correlation coefficient of 0.286, falling in the range of weakly positive correlation, and it is lower than the correlation coefficient values (falling in the range of moderately positive correlation) obtained with the Pearson's and Spearman's measures. The KCC is also observed to return the lowest correlation coefficient values for all our experiments with the random networks and scale-free networks (Section 5-6). Thus, the KCC could be construed to provide a lower bound for the correlation coefficient values and the level of correlation between maximal clique size and the centrality metric considered.

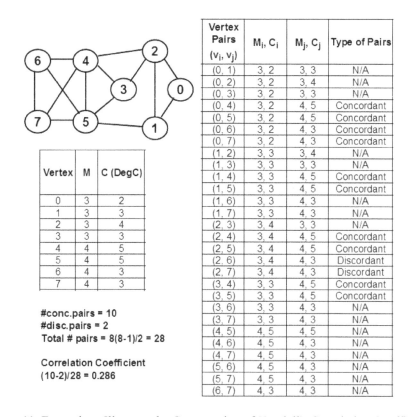

Figure 11. Example to Illustrate the Computation of Kendall's Correlation Coefficient
(between Maximal Clique Size: M and Degree Centrality: C)

5. Random Network Graphs

In this section, we discuss the results of our correlation analysis studies for maximal clique size vs. centrality metrics on the random network graphs generated from the well-known Erdos-Renyi (ER) model (Erdos & Renyi, 1959). Under the ER model, there could exist a link between any two nodes in the network with a probability p_{link}. We conduct the simulations for a network of 100 nodes and vary the p_{link} values from 0.01 to 0.50. For each p_{link} value, we run 100 runs of the simulations and average the results for the correlation coefficient with maximal clique size for each centrality metric under each of the three correlation measures. For a given p_{link} value, we consider all pairs of nodes in the network and set up a link between any two nodes if the random number (in the range 0...1) generated for the pair of nodes is less than or equal to p_{link}.

The larger the p_{link} value, the larger the number of links generated in a random network and lower the variation in node degree, measured in terms of the spectral radius ratio for node degree, denoted λ_{sp} (Meghanathan, 2014). The spectral radius ratio for node degree for a graph is the ratio of the principal eigenvalue of the adjacency matrix of the graph to that of the average node degree. The λ_{sp} values are always greater than or equal to 1.0. The larger the value, the larger the variation in node degree. Random networks exhibit a Poisson-style degree distribution and have a lower variation in node degree; their λ_{sp} values are typically closer to 1.0. Scale-free networks have a larger variation in node degree (especially those with a few hubs - high degree nodes, and the rest of the nodes are of relatively much lower degree) - incurring a larger λ_{sp} value. With a larger number of links for a fixed number of nodes, the robustness of the network (with regards to disconnection due to link failures) also increases (as is measured in terms of the algebraic connectivity of the network). The algebraic connectivity (Maia de Abreu, 2007) of a connected network is the second smallest eigenvalue of the Laplacian matrix (Triola, 2012) of a graph. If **A** and **D** are respectively the adjacency matrix and degree matrix of a graph, the Laplacian matrix **L** is simply **A** - **D**. The degree matrix is also a square matrix whose non-diagonal entries are all zeros and the diagonal entries correspond to the degree of the vertices. From Figure 12, we observe the spectral radius ratio for node degree to show a sharp decrease (a power-law style decrease) with increase in p_{link}, where as the algebraic connectivity exhibits a moderate rate of increase with increase in p_{link}.

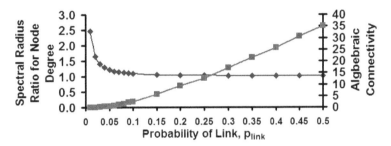

Figure 12. Spectral Radius and Algebraic Connectivity of Random Networks under the ER Model

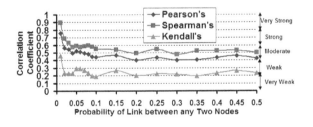
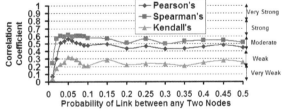

Maximal Clique Size vs. Degree Centrality   Maximal Clique Size vs. Eigenvector Centrality

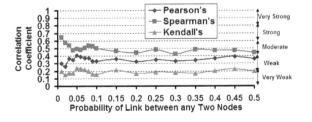
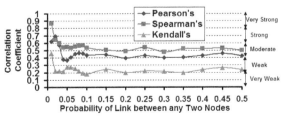

Maximal Clique Size vs. Betweenness Centrality   Maximal Clique Size vs. Closeness Centrality

Figure 13. Distribution of the Correlation Coefficient Values for the ER Model based-Random Networks (from the Correlation Measures Viewpoint)

With respect to the correlation measures used, from Figure 13, we observe the Spearman's rank-based correlation and Kendall's concordance-based correlation measures to respectively serve as an upper bound and lower bound for the level of correlation. All the four centrality metrics incur relatively closer values for the correlation coefficient under the Pearson's and Spearman's correlation measures to an extent that the level of correlation between a centrality metric and maximal clique size is the same under both the measures for a majority of the p_{link} values. The betweenness centrality incurs the lowest correlation coefficient values with maximal clique size under all the three correlation measures. Hence, when we just plot the correlation coefficient values of the three centrality metrics under a particular correlation measure (Figure 14), for p_{link} values greater than or equal to 0.05 (referred to as the fully connected regime: see the discussion below), we observe a negligible difference in the level of correlation for DegC, EVC and ClC with maximal clique size, with the EVC incurring slightly larger correlation coefficient values (the maximum difference is within 0.05 for $p_{link} \geq 0.1$).

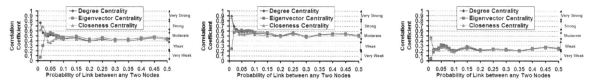

Pearson's Correlation Measure   Spearman's Correlation Measure   Kendall's Correlation Measure

Figure 14. Distribution of the Correlation Coefficient Values for Random Networks (from the Centrality Metrics Viewpoint)

From Figure 13, we observe that for random networks with p_{link} values starting from 0.05, the level of correlation (for any centrality metric with the maximal clique size under any of the three correlation measures) is at best moderately positive. The degree centrality and closeness centrality metrics exhibit strong-very strong positive correlation (a decrease in the level of correlation as p_{link} increases) for p_{link} values ranging from 0.01 to 0.04 (scenarios when the variation in node degree is larger, and the connectivity of the network is low). The eigenvector centrality metric exhibits weak-moderate positive correlation (an increase in the level of correlation as p_{link} increases) for p_{link} values ranging from 0.01 to 0.04 and the level of correlation remains the same for p_{link} values greater than or equal to 0.05. The betweenness centrality metric exhibits a relatively higher level of correlation for p_{link} values 0.01 to 0.09, compared to the level of correlation observed for p_{link} values greater than or equal to 0.1. Thus, for at least three of the four centrality metrics, the transition from a relatively higher or lower level of positive correlation to at best a moderately positive level of correlation (that remains the same henceforth) occurs at p_{link} value of 0.05 (for a network of $n = 100$ nodes, $p_{link} = 0.05 \approx \ln(n)/n$) and this could be termed as the critical probability at which the random network is considered to be in the fully connected regime (Christensen et al., 1998) and have a single giant component with no isolated nodes or clusters. For $p_{link} \geq 1/n$ (i.e., $p_{link} \geq 0.01$ for $n = 100$ nodes) and $p_{link} < \ln(n)/n$, we could refer to the random network to be in the supercritical regime (Christensen et al., 1998) with a single giant component, but with one or more isolated nodes or clusters. Hence, for a random network under evolution according to the ER model, we could conclude that the centrality metrics exhibit at best a moderately positive correlation with the maximal clique size in the fully connected regime; whereas the degree centrality and closeness centrality metrics exhibit a strong-very strong positive correlation with the maximal clique size in the supercritical regime.

6. Scale-Free Network Graphs

In this section, we discuss the results of correlation analysis obtained for scale-free network graphs generated from the well-known Barabasi Albert (BA) model (Barabasi & Albert, 1999). The BA model for network evolution is based on the notion of preferential attachment: i.e., a newly introduced node prefers to attach itself to nodes with relatively larger degree. In addition to the total number of nodes (n) in the network, the BA model works based on two parameters: the initial number of nodes (n_0) and the initial number of links added per node introduction (m_0). We start with a network of n_0 nodes (identified with ids 1, ..., n_0) such that there exists at least one link incident on each node. We then start introducing new nodes to the network, one node at a time, and these nodes are identified based on the time of their introduction. The first node is considered to be introduced at time n_0+1, the second node at time n_0+2, ..., and the last node is considered to be introduced at time n. Let $k_i(t)$ denoted the degree of node i (introduced at time i) at some time instant t (such that $t \geq i$). When a new node is to be introduced at time $t+1$, the probability for node i to be considered for a link to the newly introduced node is:

$$\frac{k_i(t)}{\sum_{\substack{j=1 \\ A[j,t+1]=0}}^{t} k_j(t)} \tag{6}$$

All the existing nodes (to which the newly introduced node at time instant $t+1$ does not have a link yet; i.e. $\mathbf{A}[j, t+1] = 0$ for $j = 1, ..., t$, where $\mathbf{A}$ is the adjacency matrix of the network graph) are considered while computing the above probability formulation for adding each of the m_0 links to the newly introduced node.

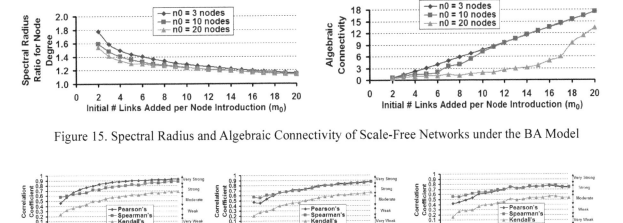

Figure 15. Spectral Radius and Algebraic Connectivity of Scale-Free Networks under the BA Model

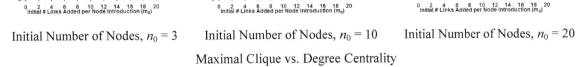

Initial Number of Nodes, $n_0 = 3$　　　Initial Number of Nodes, $n_0 = 10$　　　Initial Number of Nodes, $n_0 = 20$

Maximal Clique vs. Degree Centrality

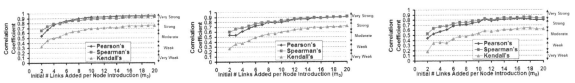

Initial Number of Nodes, $n_0 = 3$　　　Initial Number of Nodes, $n_0 = 10$　　　Initial Number of Nodes, $n_0 = 20$

Maximal Clique vs. Eigenvector Centrality

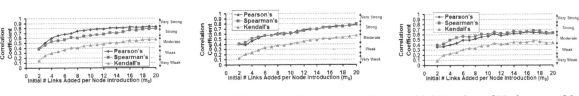

Initial Number of Nodes, $n_0 = 3$　　　Initial Number of Nodes, $n_0 = 10$　　　Initial Number of Nodes, $n_0 = 20$

Maximal Clique vs. Betweenness Centrality

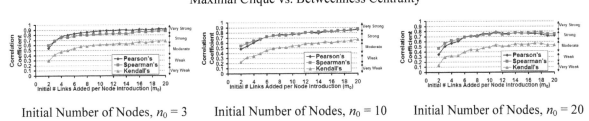

Initial Number of Nodes, $n_0 = 3$　　　Initial Number of Nodes, $n_0 = 10$　　　Initial Number of Nodes, $n_0 = 20$

Maximal Clique vs. Closeness Centrality

Figure 16. Distribution of the Correlation Coefficient Values for the BA Model based Scale-Free Networks (from the Correlation Measures Viewpoint)

For the simulations, we generated scale-free networks comprising of $n = 100$ nodes and varied the initial number of nodes and links respectively with values of $n_0 = 3$, 10 and 20, and $m_0 = 2$, 3, ..., 20 (in increments of 1). For a fixed n_0 and m_0, we ran the simulations 100 times and averaged the results for the correlation coefficient values obtained for maximal clique size with each of the four centrality metrics under each of the three correlation measures. Figure 15 displays the impact of n_0 and m_0 on spectral radius ratio for node degree and algebraic connectivity for a scale-free network of 100 nodes (the results are the average of the 100 simulation runs for each combination n_0 and m_0). We observe the networks to be relatively more scale-free for lower values of n_0 and m_0, and as either of them or both increases, we observe the variation in node degree to decrease. For a fixed m_0, we observe both the spectral radius ratio for node degree and algebraic connectivity to decrease with increase in n_0; the decrease in the algebraic connectivity is more prominent for larger values of n_0 (especially, with increase in m_0). For a fixed n_0, we observe the spectral radius ratio for node degree (λ_{sp}) to decrease at a much faster rate and the algebraic connectivity to increase (sub linearly for $m_0 < n_0$ and linearly for $m_0 \geq n_0$) with increase in m_0. We could thus characterize the scale-free networks (under evolution with the BA model) to fall into two regimes: the sub-linear connectivity regime (where $m_0 < n_0$) and the linear connectivity regime (where $m_0 \geq n_0$).

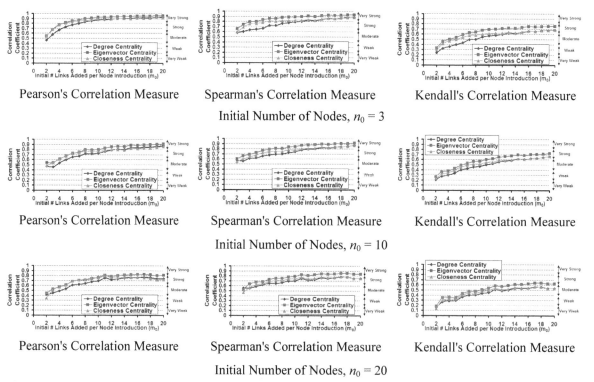

Figure 17. Distribution of the Correlation Coefficient Values for the BA Model-based Scale-Free Networks (from the Centrality Metrics Viewpoint)

The overall trend of the results (see Figure 16) with respect to the correlation measures is that when operated in the linear connectivity regime ($m_0 \geq n_0$), the Pearson's product moment-based correlation measure is likely to determine higher level of correlation compared to that of the Spearman's rank-based correlation measure; on the other hand, when operated in the sub-linear connectivity regime ($m_0 < n_0$), both the Pearson's and Spearman's correlation measures return almost the same level of correlation (the Spearman's correlation coefficient values are just marginally larger and the difference is almost negligible for most of the scenarios). The Kendall's correlation measure returns the lowest levels of correlation for both the linear and sub-linear connectivity regimes for all the centrality metrics.

For any given centrality metric, we observe the level of correlation with the maximal clique size to increase as we transition from a sub-linear connectivity regime to a linear connectivity regime (especially when the number of new links added per node introduction gets significantly larger than the initial number of nodes in the network). For a given value of n_0 and m_0, we observe the neighbor-based centrality metrics to exhibit a relatively higher level of correlation compared to the shortest path-based centrality metrics, with the betweenness centrality exhibiting the lowest level of correlation in all the cases. For a given m_0, as we increase the initial number of nodes, the level of correlation for each centrality metric is likely to drop by one level (from very strong to strong or from strong to moderate, etc).

From Figure 17, it is evident that given a particular value of m_0 and n_0, for both the linear and sub- linear connected regimes, the eigenvector centrality (EVC) is more likely to exhibit the largest value for the correlation coefficient (under all the three correlation measures), followed by the closeness centrality (ClC) and degree centrality (DegC) metrics. Under the Pearson's and Spearman's correlation measures, the three centrality metrics (EVC, ClC and DegC) are likely to exhibit a moderate-strong positive correlation in the sub-linear connectivity regime and strong-very strong correlation in the linear connectivity regime; on the other hand, the betweenness centrality metric is likely to exhibit a weak-moderate positive correlation in the sub-linear connectivity regime and moderate-strong correlation in the linear connectivity regime. Under the Kendall's correlation measure, for any given n_0 and m_0, the level of correlation appears to drop by one or two levels (the drop is just by one-level for most of the scenarios) for any centrality metric compared to that incurred with the Pearson's and Spearman's measures.

7. Related Work

Recently, we published two articles (Meghanathan, 2015a; Meghanathan, 2016) analyzing the correlation between the maximal clique size and the centrality metrics for complex real-world network graphs (DuBois & Smyth, 2008; Newman, 2013; Leskovec & Krevl, 2014). The two articles are restricted to just using the Pearson's product moment-based correlation measure and analyzed only the real-world network graphs. In this paper, in addition to the Pearson's measure, we have also used two other correlation measures (Spearman's rank-based and Kendall's concordance-based measures) so that we are able to identify the best-case and worst-case levels of correlation between maximal clique size and the centrality metrics. Instead of analyzing the real-world network graphs, we have analyzed theoretical networks generated from the Erdos-Renyi (ER) model (for random networks) and the Barabasi-Albert (BA) model (for scale-free networks). We observe that it is possible to directly associate the correlation levels with the state of the random networks in the supercritical and fully connected regimes of evolution under the ER model as well as with the state of the scale-free networks in the sub-linear and linear connectivity regimes of evolution under the BA model. To the best of our knowledge, there is no other work that has reported the correlation between maximal clique size and the centrality metrics for random networks and scale-free networks.

Prior to (Meghanathan, 2015a; Meghanathan, 2016) and this paper, researchers have analyzed the centrality metrics and maximal clique size only in isolation. Li et al (2015) and Meghanathan (2015b) conducted correlation analysis study among the centrality metrics for real-world network graphs using the Pearson's product moment-based correlation measure. In addition, centrality metrics have also been widely studied for the analysis and visualization of complex networks in several domains, ranging from biological networks to social networks (Koschutzki, 2008; Opsahl et al., 2010). With regards to the maximal clique size of the individual vertices (the largest size clique that a vertex is part of), Meghanathan (2015c) observed the distribution of the maximal clique size values for the vertices in several real-world network graphs as well as those of the small-world networks under the evolution of the Watts-Strogatz model (Watts & Strogatz, 1998) to follow a Poisson-style distribution. Most of the other works in the literature focused on developing efficient approximation heuristics as well as exact algorithms to determine the maximum clique size (an NP-hard problem) for the entire network graphs. Though branch-and-bound has been the common theme among the exact algorithms to determine the maximum clique size, the difference lies in the approach used to prune the search space: node degree (Pattabiraman et al., 2013), vertex coloring (Ostergard, 2002) and vertex ordering (Carraghan & Pardalos, 1990). As is observed in this paper, the savings in time (due to pruning) incurred by the branch-and-bound based exact algorithms for maximum clique size of an entire graph is lost to a certain extent when these algorithms are adapted to determine the maximal clique size of the individual vertices of the graph. Owing to the time-consuming nature of the exact algorithms to determine maximal clique size of the vertices in a graph, it becomes imperative to identify one or more computationally light-weight metrics (like the degree centrality) that can be used to rank the vertices in a complex network graph in almost the same order (if not exact) that would be obtained using the maximal clique size.

8. Conclusions

Overall, the work presented in this paper could serve as a framework for evaluating the various levels of correlation (inclusive of identifying the best-case and worst-case scenarios) between any two metrics for complex network graphs. We qualitatively categorize the levels of correlation based on the quantitative values of the correlation coefficient observed. We also show that the computationally light-weight centrality metrics (especially the neighbor-based degree and eigenvector centrality metrics) could serve as alternate metrics to rank the vertices of a network graph in lieu of the maximal clique size, a computationally hard metric. The above assertion holds very much true for scale-free networks and random networks in the supercritical regime; but, only to a certain extent for random network graphs in the fully connected regime (for which we observe only a moderately positive correlation).

The more specific results are as follows: For random networks generated under the ER model, the degree centrality and closeness centrality metrics exhibit strong-very strong positive correlation when the network is under the supercritical regime of evolution; whereas we observe all the centrality metrics to at best exhibit a moderately positive correlation when the network is under the fully connected regime of evolution (with a single giant component encompassing all the nodes). For scale-free networks generated under the BA model, we observe the eigenvector centrality to exhibit the largest levels of correlation (under all the three correlation measures) in both the sub-linear and linear connectivity regimes of the network. For all the four centrality metrics, we observe the correlation level to increase as we transition from the sub-linear connectivity regime to the linear connectivity regime of a scale-free network under evolution. The betweenness centrality metric incurs the lowest levels of correlation with the maximal clique size for both the theoretical networks. With respect to the correlation measures used, we observe the following: There is negligible difference in the correlation levels identified with the Spearman's and Pearson's correlation measures for both the random and scale-free networks generated from the theoretical models. The Kendall's concordance-based correlation measure provides the lowest possible levels of correlation that could be observed between a centrality metric and the maximal clique size.

Acknowledgments

The research is financed by the NASA EPSCoR sub award (#: NNX14AN38A) from University of Mississippi.

References

Barabasi, A. L., & Albert, R. (1999). Emergence of Scaling in Random Networks. *Science, 286*(5439), 509-512. http://dx.doi.org/10.1126/science.286.5439.509

Bonacich, P. (1987). Power and Centrality: A Family of Measures. *American Journal of Sociology, 92*(5), 1170-1182. http://dx.doi.org/10.1086/228631

Brandes, U. (2001). A Faster Algorithm for Betweenness Centrality. *The Journal of Mathematical Sociology, 25*(2), 163-177. http://dx.doi.org/10.1080/0022250X.2001.9990249.

Carraghan, R., & Pardalos, P. M. (1990). An Exact Algorithm for the Maximum Clique Problem. *Operations Research Letters, 9*(6), 375-382. http://dx.doi.org/10.1016/0167-6377(90)90057-C

Christensen, K., Donangelo, R., Koiller, B., & Sneppen, K. (1998). Evolution of Random Networks. *Physical Review Letters, 81*(11), 2380-2383. http://dx.doi.org/10.1103/PhysRevLett.81.2380

Cormen, T. H., Leiserson, C. E., Rivest, R. L., & Stein, C. (2009). *Introduction to Algorithms*. (3rd Ed.) MIT Press.

DuBois, C. L., & Smyth, P. (2008). *UCI Network Data Repository*. Retrieved from http://networkdata.ics.uci.edu/

Erdos, P., & Renyi, A. (1959). On Random Graphs I. *Publicationes Mathematicae, 6*, 290-297. http://dx.doi.org/10.1016/0167-6377(90)90057-C

Evans, J. D. (1995). *Straightforward Statistics for the Behavioral Sciences*. (1st ed.) Brooks Cole Publishing Co.

Freeman, L. (1977). A Set of Measures of Centrality based on Betweenness. *Sociometry, 40*(1), 35-41. http://dx.doi.org/10.2307/3033543

Freeman, L. (1979). Centrality in Social Networks Conceptual Clarification. *Social Networks, 1*(3), 215-239. http://dx.doi.org/10.1016/0378-8733(78)90021-7

Kang, U., Papadimitriou, S., Sun, J., & Tong, H. (2011). *Centralities in Large Networks: Algorithms and Observations*. Paper presented at the 2011 SIAM International Conference on Data Mining, Mesa, AZ, USA. http://dx.doi.org/10.1137/1.9781611972818.11

Koschutzki, D., & Schreiber, F. (2008). Centrality Analysis Methods for Biological Networks and their Application to Gene Regulatory Networks. *Gene Regulation and Systems Biology, 2*(1), 193-201.

Lay, D. C. (2011). *Linear Algebra and its Applications* (4th ed.) Pearson.

Leskovec, J., & Krevl, A. (2014). *Stanford Large Network Dataset Collection, SNAP Datasets*. Retrieved from https://snap.stanford.edu/data/

Li, C., Li, Q., Van Mieghem, P., Stanley, H. E., & Wang, H. (2015). Correlation between Centrality Metrics and their Application to the Opinion Model. *The European Physical Journal B, 88*(65), 1-13. http://dx.doi.org/10.1140/epjb/e2015-50671-y

Maia de Abreu, N. M. (2007). Old and New Results on Algebraic Connectivity. *Linear Algebra and its Applications, 423*(1), 53-73. http://dx.doi.org/10.1016/j.laa.2006.08.017

Meghanathan, N. (2014, December). *Spectral Radius as a Measure of Variation in Node Degree for Complex Network Graphs*. Paper presented at the 7th International Conference on u- and e- Service, Science and Technology, Haikou, China. http://dx.doi.org/10.1109/UNESST.2014.8

Meghanathan, N. (2015a). *Maximal Clique Size vs. Centrality: A Correlation Analysis for Complex Real-World Network Graphs*. Paper presented at the 3rd International Conference on Advanced Computing, Networking, and Informatics, Rourkela, India. http://dx.doi.org/10.1007/978-81-322-2529-4_9

Meghanathan, N. (2015b). *Correlation Coefficient Analysis of Centrality Metrics for Complex Network Analysis*. Paper presented at the 4th Computer Science Online Conference. http://dx.doi.org/10.1007/978-3-319-18503-3_2

Meghanathan, N. (2015c). Distribution of Maximal Clique Size of the Vertices for Theoretical Small-World Networks and Real-World Networks. *International Journal of Computer Networks and Communications, 7*(4), 21-41. http://dx.doi.org/10.5121/ijcnc.2015.7402

Meghanathan, N. (2016). Correlation Coefficient Analysis: Centrality vs. Maximal Clique Size for Complex Real-World Network Graphs. *International Journal of Network Science, 1*(1), 3-27. http://dx.doi.org/10.1504/IJNS.2016.073560

Newman, M. (2006). Modularity and Community Structure in Networks. *Proceedings of the National Academy of Sciences USA, 103*(23), 8557-8582. http://dx.doi.org/10.1073/pnas.0601602103

Newman, M. (2010). *Networks: An Introduction* (1st ed.) Oxford University Press.

Newman, M. (2013). *University of Michigan, Network Datasets*. Retrieved from http://www-personal.umich.edu/~mejn/netdata/

Opsahl, T., Agneessens, F., & Skvoretz, J. (2010). Node Centrality in Weighted Networks: Generalizing Degree and Shortest Paths. *Social Networks, 32*(3), 245-251. http://dx.doi.org/10.1016/j.socnet.2010.03.006

Ostergard, P. R. J. (2002). A Faster Algorithm for the Maximum Clique Problem. *Discrete Applied Mathematics, 120*(1-3), 197-207. http://dx.doi.org/10.1016/S0166-218X(01)00290-6.

Pattabiraman, B., Patwary, M. A., Gebremedhin, A. H., Liao, W. K., & Choudhury, A. (2013, December). *Fast Algorithms for the Maximum Clique Problem on Massive Sparse Graphs*. Paper presented at the 10th International Workshop on Algorithms and Models for the Web Graph, Cambridge, MA, USA. http://dx.doi.org/10.1007/978-3-319-03536-9_13

Triola, M. F. (2012). *Elementary Statistics* (12th ed.) Pearson.

Watts, D. J., & Strogatz, S. H. (1998). Collective Dynamics of Small-World Networks. *Nature, 393*, 440-442. http://dx.doi.org/10.1038/30918

16

A Simplified Model of Bit Error Rate Calculation

Saed Thuneibat[1], Huthaifa Al Issa[1] & Abdallah Ijjeh[1]

[1] Department of Electrical Engineering, Al-Balqa Applied University, Jordan

Correspondence: Saed Thuneibat, Department of Electrical Engineering, Al-Balqa Applied University, Jordan. E-mail: Thuneibat@hotmail.com/alissahu@yahoo.com/dr.a.ijjeh@gmail.com

Abstract

The Bit Error Rate (BER) is a key parameter of the Quality of Service (QoS) for engineers and designers of digital communication systems and networks. At the present time, a set of models and methods are exist for calculating the BER. But these methods are complex and require large computing cost.

In this paper, we provide a new model for calculating the BER. This model simplifies the procedures in the existing models and reduces the computing time. In the same time, the proposed model save the accuracy and the state consideration of existing models.

Keywords: Bit Error Rate, Quality of Service, Modeling, Communication System

1. Introduction

Many countries have built or developed their local and national telecommunication networks. Nowadays, the issue is in providing the adequate QoS parameters of the data transmission and delivery to the end user.

Real-world communication channels experience noise and distortions. If we represent noise and Intersymbol Interference (ISI) on Euclidian space with power and time axis, then the noise internal and external, impulsive and induced, cross talk and attenuation are represented by power axis. Distortion, fading channel, phase distortion, delays, jitters and ISI are reflected by time axis.

Noise and ISI cause errors in a digital communication channels. Error, in a digital communication system is a condition when the transmitted bit is 1, while the received is 0, and vice versa.

In digital transmission, BER is the percentage of bits that have errors relative to the total number of bits received in one connection or session of communication. Usually, an electrical transmission of data might have a BER of 10^{-6}, meaning that, out of 1,000,000 bits transmitted, one bit was in error. While an optical system might achieve 10^{-12}. The BER is an indication of how often data has to be retransmitted because of an error, using one of the Automatic Repeat request (ARQ) methods (Jahangir, 2011). Alternatively, errors might be corrected without retransmission by applying channel coding schemes and redundant forward error correction codes such as Hamming codes (Thuneibat, 2012).

Digital communication channel encounters the errors in a bursty fashion. This means that in the transmitted frame of data, a group of bits, not single bit, had changed. The reason of such behaviour is found in the serial transmission mode and in the nature of random noise. The error control techniques are function of the data link layer of the Open System Interaction (OSI) reference model.

In order to design effective communication systems for such channels, it is critical to fully understand their behaviour and define an estimation equation for there calculation. This is achieved via system modelling, where the primary objective is to provide a model whose properties are both complex enough to closely, as possible, match the real system statistical characteristics, and simple enough to allow software simulation system analysis.

Providing guaranteed BER, data rates, delays and other indicators of subscriber loyalty requires the search for new solutions to make full use of the bandwidth. To compare the effectiveness of the decisions, simulation is implemented effectively. Modeling involves the selecting of a channel model; development of models linking qualitative indicators with the internal parameters of systems and channels; development of techniques to optimize the internal parameters to achieve the required transmission quality indicators.

The BER is the key of QoS parameter for the engineers and designers of digital communication systems and networks. At the present time, a set of models and methods are exist for calculating BER, but these methods are complex and require large computing cost.

In this paper, we discuss the calculation methods of $P(m,n)$, where $P(m,n)$ is the probability of m errors in the received n frames of data elements (bits) for the channels described by Gilbert and Gilbert-Elliot models (Elliott, 1963). Definition of $P(m,n)$ is necessary for the analysis and optimization of data transmission system. Therefore, our research is become more significant.

A new model for calculating the BER is proposed in this paper, where this model simplifies the existing procedures and reduces the computing time. In the same time, the proposed model save the accuracy and the state consideration of existing models.

2. Exploring the Existing Models

Gilbert-Elliott channel model is a two-state Markov channel, each state satisfies a communication channel quality, one state for noiseless, while the other is very noisy. The crossover probabilities for each state are 0 and 0.5, respectively.

According to the existing models under considerations, implementing the Gilbert–Elliott model, which is a simple channel model introduced by Edgar Gilbert and E. O. Elliott (Elliott, 1963). These models are widely used for mapping burst error patterns in a digital transmission channels, that enables simulations of the digital error performance of communication links (Hong, 1995). It is based on a Markov chain with two states G (for good or gap) and B (for bad or burst), where in state G, the probability of transmitting a bit correctly is k, and in state B the probability is h. Usually, it is assumed that $k=1$ and Gilbert also assumed that $h=0.5$ (Gilbert, 1960) .

The BER in states G and B is different, so before we calculate $P(m,n)$, we determine the probability of i bits where transferred in the bad state of channel from n frames $B(i,n)$. Then the probability of the m errors in n frames of bits can be determined using the following expression

$$P(m,n) = \sum_{i=0}^{n} B(i,n)P(m/i), \tag{1}$$

where

$$P(m/i) = C_i^m \, p_{error}^m (1 - p_{error})^{i-m} . \tag{2}$$

According to Gilbert model, $P(m/i)$ is the conditional probability of m errors in i bits transmitted in the B state, while p_{error} is the probability of errors in the B state and C_i^m is number of combinations of i from m.

Major accounted cost when calculating $B(i,n)$ is spent on determining the probability $B(i,n)$.

Covariance matrix method is proposed for the exact solution of this issue, which reduces the requirements to computing resources in the calculation of $B(i,n)$ (Holzlöhner, 2003) .

The modeling of communication system as two-state Gilbert-Elliott channel is not adequate when the channel quality varies dramatically. The solution is to design a model with more than two states.

In this paper, we add a new state for reflecting a combination of the physical condition of the channel s_j and the

combination state denoted as $s_j(k,l)$, as shown in figure 1.

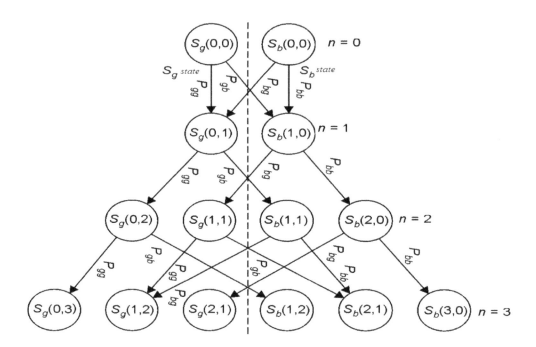

Figure 1. State graph of a system with combined states

In the figure, n is the number of hops of existence in the introduced state, k is the number of hops of existence in S_b state, and l is the number of hops of existence in S_g state, where $k + l = n$.

The initial states when $n = 0$ are represented by $S_b(0,0)$ and $S_g(0,0)$ respectively. Let the initial probabilities to be p_b and p_g, the initial probability vector through $\|p_b \quad p_g\|$ while $p_b + p_g = 1$.

The developed structure increases the number of states at each hop. Thus, at each hop we increase the transition matrix dimension and the system state vector.

In the first transition hop, the probability matrix satisfies the original matrix of Gilbert models. The transition probability matrix of the n-th step has a dimension of $2(n-1) \times 2n$; as follow:

$$\mathbf{A}(n) = \begin{Vmatrix} A_{bb} \mid \dot{0} & A_{bg} \mid \dot{0} \\ \dot{0} \mid A_{gb} & \dot{0} \mid A_{gg} \end{Vmatrix} \tag{3}$$

where $A_{bb} \mid \dot{0}$ is a diagonal matrix, extended from the right side by one zero column; $\dot{0} \mid A_{gb}$ is diagonal matrix, extended from the left side by one zero column; A_{bb}, A_{bg}, A_{gb}, A_{gg} are diagonal matrixes of (n-1) order, the non-zero elements are equal to $P_{bb}, P_{bg}, P_{gb}, P_{gg}$; $\dot{0}$ is a column of zeros, expanding the matrix to the right or left.

The above explained approach provides a distribution vector of the probabilities for the combined state at any hop $\bar{b}(n)$. For the calculation of $B(i,n)$ values, the summation probability of states $b_j(k,l)$ is taken having the same first index. Thus, the scheme of forming probabilities $B(i,3)$ as example has the form as shown in figure 2.

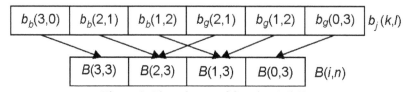

Figure 2. The scheme of forming B(i,3)

As will these probabilities may be written in the form of:

$B(3,3) = b_b(3,0)$;

$B(2,3) = b_b(2,1) + b_g(2,1)$;

$B(1,3) = b_b(1,2) + b_g(1,2)$;

$B(0,3) = b_g(0,3)$.

In general we write:

$B(n,n) = b_b(n,0);$

$B(0,n) = b_g(0,n);$

$B(i,n) = b_b(i,n-i) + b_g(i,n-i)$

When the packet of data has the length of hundreds of bits, which is the situation faced in the Internet, the packet size may reach 65336 bytes of data, then the required computing time increase notably. This situation may reduce the effectiveness of the application of technique in adaptive data transmission systems. For significant time saving, we show in the next section, the proposed simplified method of calculation.

3. The Proposed Model

We introduce the concept of the channel state vector as an array of binary numbers, where zero corresponds to the transfer of the current bit to good state, and one - the transfer of the current bit to bad state of channel. We notify the number of bad state sections of the channel on the length of the frame as the number of returned bad state.

The required value $B(i,n)$ is the sum of the probabilities of all state vectors of the channel with length n and weight i.

Unlike channels with independent errors, in channels with dominant burst errors, the probability of vectors of the same weight will depend on the number of returns to the bad states of the length of the vector. Probability vectors with frequent alternation between 0 and 1 (i.e., multiple transitions from good to bad states) may have smaller probabilities than the vectors of the same weight, but with a small number of returns to bad states.

By excluding from the calculation the vectors, reflecting the multiple return of B-state, as show in figure 3, we can significantly reduce the time of calculation, while maintaining an acceptable accuracy level.

Naturally, such an approach would give some uncertainty of the result, depending on the number of accounted returns, the length of the frame and the probability of changing the states of channel. The criterion for the estimation of the uncertainty introduced by discarding terms that take into account multiple returns, can be written as

$$\delta = 1 - \sum_{i=0}^{n} B(i,n) \tag{4}$$

The expressions that take into account the contribution of vectors with one, two and v returns to the probability of $B(i,n)$ are written below

$$C_{i-1}^{v-1} \cdot P_b \cdot P_{bb}^{i-v} \cdot P_{bg}^{v-1} \cdot P_{gg}^{n-i-v-1} \cdot P_{gb}^{v-1}[C_{n-i-1}^{v-2} \cdot P_{gg}^2 + 2C_{n-i-1}^{v-1} \cdot P_{bg} \cdot P_{gg} + C_{n-i-1}^{v} \cdot P_{bg}^2]$$

for $v \le i \le n - v - 1$;

$$C_{i-1}^{v-1} \cdot P_b \cdot P_{bb}^{i-v} \cdot P_{bg}^{v-1} \cdot P_{gg}^{n-i-v} \cdot P_{gb}^{v-1}[C_{n-i-1}^{v-2} \cdot P_{gg}^2 + 2C_{n-i-1}^{v-1} \cdot P_{bg}]$$

for $i = n - v$;

$$C_{i-1}^{v-1} \cdot P_b \cdot P_{bb}^{i-v} \cdot P_{bg}^{v-1} \cdot P_{gg}^{n-i-v+1} \cdot P_{gb}^{v-1} \cdot C_{n-i-1}^{v-2}$$

for $i = n - v + 1$.

These expressions are valid for the number of returns from the $v=3$ and higher.

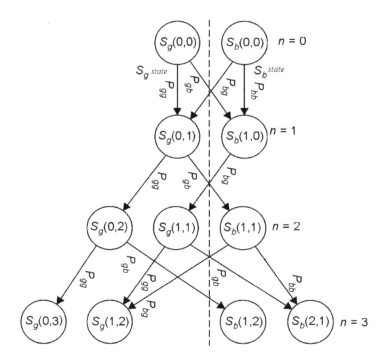

Figure 3. Simplified state graph of model

4. Evaluation of the Simplified Model

Further, we evaluate the uncertainty of results in simplified methodology relative to the values obtained by the exact algorithm, using the following expression

$$\Delta_b = \frac{P_E - P_S}{P_E} \cdot 100 \qquad (5)$$

where P_E, P_S the values obtained by exact algorithm and simplified methodology, respectively.

The dependence of the relative difference Δ_b of calculation results $B(i,n)$, obtained by the use of accurate and simplified methods when the number of returns v equals 2, 3, 4 and 5 are shown in figure 4.

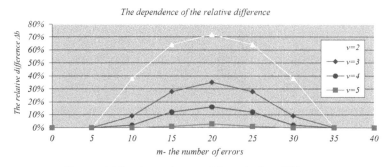

Figure 4. The dependence of the relative difference

From the figure, we see that the maximum error observed near the middle of the frame and noticeably reduced by increasing the number of returns. Practically, we are interested in the error probability, which is much less than half the length of the data packet, and in this area the uncertainty is much less than the maximum, which also justifies the use of the simplified model.

For the comparison of calculation costs of different models, we select the parameters that quantifiably characterizing these costs and not dependent on the speed of the processor or the algorithm.

We choose parameters such as the number of additions and multiplications required to compute the value of probability $P(m,n)$ and perform the calculation.

Figure 5 shows the dependence of the number of operations of and multiplication in the computation of $P(5,n)$ for n, ranges from 5 to 100 in the calculations by the Elliott method, and a simplified methodology if the number of returns equals 7.

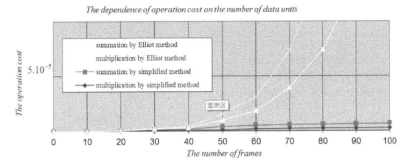

Figure 5. The dependence of the operations cost in calculating P(5,n)

The curves in figure 5 clearly show the advantage of the simplified method. The operation cost increases exponentially for data length greater than 40 frames for both summation and multiplication operations by Elliot method. While the operation cost remains approximately constant using the proposed simplified method.

5. Conclusion

The matrix method of calculating the exact probabilities of burst error in data packet of fixed length for communication channel described by Gilbert model is explained. The new simplified model, which proposed in this paper, provides a significant reduction in the computing cost while maintaining acceptable accuracy level.

References

Elliott E. N. (1963). Estimates of error rates for codes on burst-noise channels (pp. 1977-1997). *Bell Syst. Tech. J., 42.*

Gilbert, E. N. (1960). Capacity of a burst-noise channel, burst-noise channel. *Bell Syst. Tech. J., 39.*

Holzlöhner, R., Menyuk, C. R., Kath, W. L., & Grigoryan, V. S. (2003). A covariance matrix method to compute bit error rates in a highly nonlinear dispersion managed solution system (pp. 688-690). IEEE Photon. Technol. Lett., 15.

Hong, S. W., & Nader, M. (1995). Finite-State Markovf Channel-A Useful Model for Radio Communication Channels (pp. 1253-1265). *IEEE Transaction On Vehicular Technology, 44*(1).

Jahangir, A., Alam, M. R., Hu, G. Q., & Mehrab, M. Z. (2011). Bit Error Rate Optimization in Fiber Optic Communications (pp. 435-440). *International Journal of Machine Learning and Computing, 1*(5).

Thuneibat S. A. (2012). 3-D Hamming Code for Burst Error Correction Over Wireless Communication Channel (pp. 80-85). *International Journal on Communications Antenna & Propagation, 2*(1).

17

Assortativity Analysis of Real-World Network Graphs Based on Centrality Metrics

Natarajan Meghanathan[1]

[1] Department of Computer Science, Jackson State University, USA

Correspondence: Natarajan Meghanathan, Department of Computer Science, Mailbox 18839, Jackson State University, Jackson, MS 39217, USA. E-mail: natarajan.meghanathan@jsums.edu

The research is financed by the NASA EPSCoR sub award (#: NNX14AN38A) from University of Mississippi.

Abstract

Assortativity index (*A. Index*) of real-world network graphs has been traditionally computed based on the degree centrality metric and the networks were classified as assortative, dissortative or neutral if the *A. Index* values are respectively greater than 0, less than 0 or closer to 0. In this paper, we evaluate the *A. Index* of real-world network graphs based on some of the commonly used centrality metrics (betweenness, eigenvector and closeness) in addition to degree centrality and observe that the assortativity classification of real-world network graphs depends on the node-level centrality metric used. We also propose five different levels of assortativity (strongly assortative, weakly assortative, neutral, weakly dissortative and strongly dissortative) for real-world networks and the corresponding range of *A. Index* value for the classification. We analyze a collection of 50 real-world network graphs with respect to each of the above four centrality metrics and estimate the empirical probability of observing a real-world network graph to exhibit a particular level of assortativity. We claim that a real-world network graph is more likely to be neutral with respect to the betweenness and degree centrality metrics and more likely to be assortative with respect to the eigenvector and closeness centrality metrics.

Keywords: Assortativity Index, Centrality, Correlation, Real-World Network Graph

1. Introduction

The assortativity index (*A. Index*) of a network is a measure of the similarity of the end vertices of the edges in the network with respect to a particular node-level metric (Newman, 2010). That is, the *A. Index* of a network is a measure of the extent to which a vertex with a higher value for a particular node-level metric is connected to another vertex that also has a higher value for the node-level metric. Since the *A. Index* is nothing but a correlation coefficient (Pearson's product-moment correlation coefficient) (Newman, 1999) quantifying the extent of similarity of the end vertices of the edges, its value ranges from -1 to 1 (Strang, 2006). Traditionally, in the literature (Newman, 1999), networks with positive values of *A. Index* (closer to 1) are referred to as assortative networks; networks with negative values of *A. Index* (closer to -1) are referred to as dissortative networks and networks with *A. Index* values closer to 0 are classified as neutral. The similarity has been typically evaluated with respect to the degree centrality metric of the vertices, and the classification of networks (as either as assortative, dissortative or neutral) has been so far only based on the degree centrality metric (Newman & Girvan, 2003; Noldus & Van Mieghem, 2015).

Our hypothesis in this paper is that the assortativity classification of a real-world network could depend on the centrality metric used to compute the *A. Index* value of the network. In other words, a network could be classified as assortative with respect to one centrality metric and it could end up being classified as dissortative or neutral with respect to another centrality metric. Also, just having three different levels (assortative, neutral and dissortative) would not be sufficient to accurately assess the extent of assortativity of real-world network graphs whose *A. Index* values are neither close to 0, but nor close to 1 or -1. Until now, a formal range of *A. Index* values has not been defined to assess the level of assortativity of real-world networks. In this paper, we propose to divide the range of values (-1.0 to 1.0) for the *A. Index* fairly even to five levels and setup the following rule: strongly assortative (0.6 ≤ *A. Index* ≤ 1.0), weakly assortative (0.2 ≤ *A. Index* < 0.6), neutral (-0.2

< *A. Index* < 0.2), weakly dissortative (-0.6 < *A. Index* ≤ -0.2) and strongly dissortative (-0.2 < *A. Index* ≤ -1.0).

We investigate the validity of our hypothesis by analyzing a broader collection of 50 real-world networks whose spectral radius ratio for node degree (a measure of the variation in node degree) ranges from 1.01 to 3.48 (Meghanathan, 2014). We compute the *A. Index* values for these 50 real-world networks with respect to each of the four commonly used centrality metrics: degree centrality (DegC), eigenvector centrality (EVC; Bonacich, 1987), betweenness centrality (BWC; Freeman, 1977) and closeness centrality (ClC; Freeman, 1979), and apply the above proposed range of values to assess the assortativity levels of the real-world networks with respect to each of these four centrality metrics. For 40 of the 50 real-world networks analyzed, we observe that the level of classification of the network (strongly or weakly assortative, neutral, strongly or weakly dissortative) depends on the centrality metric under consideration.

Since we have analyzed a vast collection of networks with varying levels of complexity, we use the results of our assortativity analysis to empirically propose the likelihood of a real-world network being classified neutral or assortative (strongly assortative or weakly assortative) with respect to a particular centrality metric. Based on the results of our assortativity analysis on 50 real-world networks, we claim that any chosen real-world network is more likely (i.e., with a probability of 0.72) to be classified as neutral (neither assortative nor dissortative) with respect to the betweenness centrality metric, and more likely (i.e., with a probability of 0.66) to be classified as assortative (strongly or weakly) with respect to the ClC and EVC metrics. More specifically, we expect a chosen real-world network to be somewhat strongly assortative (with a probability of 0.38) with respect to the ClC metric and somewhat weakly assortative (also with a probability of 0.38) with respect to the EVC metric.

To the best of our knowledge, we have not come across a paper that has conducted a comprehensive assortativity analysis of complex real-world networks with respect to the four commonly used centrality metrics as well as empirically proposed the likelihood of observing a real-world network to be neutral, strongly assortative or weakly assortative with respect to a particular centrality metric. The rest of the paper is organized as follows: Section 2 reviews the four centrality metrics along with an example to illustrate their computation on a sample graph. Section 3 introduces the formulation for Assortativity Index (*A. Index*) and the proposed range of *A. Index* values to classify the assortativity level of a real-world network as well as presents a motivating example to illustrate that the *A. Index* of a network and its classification (as neutral, strongly/weakly assortative or dissortative) could depend on the centrality metric under consideration. Section 4 introduces the 50 complex real-world networks that are analyzed in this paper. Section 5 presents the results of assortativity analysis conducted on the real-world networks with respect to the four centrality metrics. Section 6 discusses related work and highlights the novel contribution of the work done in this paper. Section 7 concludes the paper. Throughout the paper, we use the terms 'node' and 'vertex', 'link' and 'edge', 'network' and 'graph' interchangeably. They mean the same. All the real-world networks analyzed in this paper are modeled as undirected graphs.

2. Centrality Metrics

The four commonly used centrality metrics in complex network analysis are: degree centrality (DegC), eigenvector centrality (EVC; Bonacich, 1987), betweenness centrality (BWC; Freeman, 1977) and closeness centrality (ClC; Freeman, 1979). DegC and EVC are degree-based centrality metrics; whereas BWC and ClC are shortest path-based centrality metrics. Until now, the DegC metric has been typically used for assortativity analysis of real-world networks (Newman & Girvan, 2003; Noldus & Van Mieghem, 2015). In this paper, we are interested in conducting assortativity analysis of real-world networks with respect to all the above four centrality metrics. In this section, we briefly review these four centrality metrics and the procedure to compute them, along with an example for each.

2.1 Degree Centrality

The degree centrality (DegC) of a vertex is the number of edges incident on the vertex. The DegC of the vertices is computed by multiplying the adjacency matrix of the graph with a unit vector of 1s (the number of 1s in the unit vector corresponds to the number of vertices in the graph). Figure 1 illustrates an example to compute the degree centrality of the vertices. As can be noticed from this example, the DegC metric is vulnerable to incurring several ties among the vertices (as the metric values are integers and not real numbers).

2.2 Eigenvector Centrality

The eigenvector centrality (EVC) of a vertex is a measure of the degree of the vertex as well as the degree of its neighbors. The EVC values of the vertices in a graph correspond to the entries in the principal eigenvector of the adjacency matrix of the graph. We use the JAMA: A Java Matrix package (http://math.nist.gov/javanumerics/jama/) to compute the principal eigenvector of the adjacency matrix of a real-world network graph. The entries in the principal eigenvector can also be computed using the Power-Iteration method (Strang, 2006) that is illustrated in Figure 2. The tentative eigenvector X_{i+1} of a network graph at the end of the $(i+1)^{th}$ iteration is given by: $X_{i+1} = \dfrac{AX_i}{\|AX_i\|}$, where $\|AX_i\|$ is the normalized value of the product of the adjacency matrix and the tentative eigenvector X_i at the end of the ith iteration. We continue the iterations until the normalized value of the product vector converges and the tentative eigenvector at that juncture corresponds to the principal eigenvector of the adjacency matrix of the graph. As the EVC values of the vertices are likely to be real numbers and are dependent on the degree of a vertex as well as the degrees of its neighbors, the EVC values of the vertices are more likely to be unique and relatively fewer ties are incurred (compared to degree centrality).

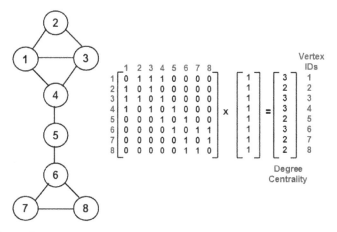

Figure 1. Example to Illustrate the Computation of the Degree Centrality of the Vertices in a Graph

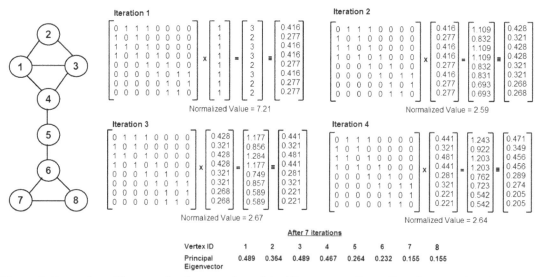

Figure 2. Example to Illustrate the Computation of the Eigenvector Centrality of the Vertices in a Graph

2.3 Betweenness Centrality

The betweenness centrality (BWC) of a vertex is a measure of the fraction of shortest paths going through the vertex when considered across all pairs of vertices in the graph (Freeman, 1977). If $sp_{jk}(i)$ is the number of shortest paths between vertices j and k that go through vertex i and sp_{jk} is the total number of shortest paths between vertices j and k, then $BWC(i) = \sum_{j \neq k \neq i} \dfrac{sp_{jk}(i)}{sp_{jk}}$. The BWC of vertices is computed using a Breadth First Search (BFS; Cormen et al., 2009)-based implementation of the Brandes' algorithm (Brandes, 2001). We use the BFS algorithm to determine the shortest path trees rooted at each vertex and thereby deduce the level numbers of the vertices in the shortest path trees rooted at every vertex in the graph. The level number of a vertex i in the shortest path tree rooted at vertex j is the minimum number of hops from vertex j to i. The root vertex of a shortest path tree is said to be at level 0. The number of shortest paths from a vertex j to itself is 1. The number of shortest paths from a vertex j to a vertex k (at level l in the shortest path tree rooted at vertex j) is the sum of the number of shortest paths from vertex j to each of the vertices that are neighbors of vertex k in the graph and located at level l-1 in the shortest path tree rooted at j. The number of shortest paths between vertices j and k that go through vertex i is the maximum of the number of shortest paths from vertex j to vertex i and the number of shortest paths from vertex k to vertex i. Figure 3 illustrates an example for the computation of the BWC of the vertices in the same sample graph used in Figures 1-2. We notice that vertices with a high degree and/or EVC need not have a high BWC and vice-versa. For example, vertices 0 and 2 that had the largest value for the EVC metric have relatively low BWC value; whereas, vertex 4 (with a low degree and low EVC) has the largest value for the BWC.

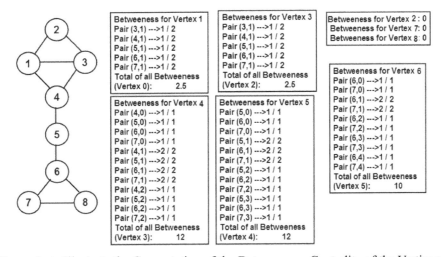

Figure 3. Example to Illustrate the Computation of the Betweenness Centrality of the Vertices in a Graph

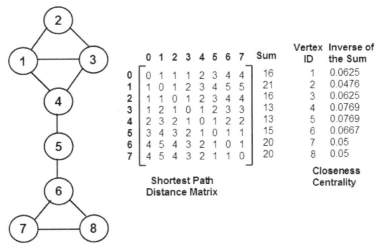

Figure 4. Example to Illustrate the Computation of the Closeness Centrality of the Vertices in a Graph

2.4 Closeness Centrality

The closeness centrality (ClC) of a vertex (Freeman, 1979) is a measure of the relative closeness of the vertex with the rest of the vertices in the graph. The ClC of a vertex is measured by running the BFS algorithm on the vertex and determining the minimum number of hops to each vertex on the shortest path tree rooted at the vertex. The ClC of a vertex is the inverse of the sum of the shortest path lengths (hop counts) to the rest of the vertices in the graph. Figure 4 illustrates an example for the calculation of ClC of the vertices on the same sample graph used in Figures 1-3.

3. Assortativity Analysis

3.1 Network Model

Let $G = (V, E)$ be the set of vertices and edges constituting a real-world network and let $C(i)$ be the value of a centrality metric (C) for any node i in the network. We refer to the first vertex (vertex u) in an edge (u, v) as the upstream vertex and the second vertex (vertex v) in an edge (u, v) as the downstream vertex. As the focus of this research is on undirected graphs, we conveniently adopt the following convention to represent the edges: the ID of the upstream vertex of an edge (u, v) is always less than the ID of the downstream vertex of the edge (i.e., $u < v$). Let U and D be respectively the set of upstream and downstream vertices constituting the edges of a graph. Let $C_{\bar{U}}$ and $C_{\bar{V}}$ (calculated as in formulation-1 below) be respectively the average values for the centrality metric of interest among the vertices constituting the sets U and V.

$$C_{\bar{U}} = \frac{1}{|U|} \sum_{(u,v)\in E} C(u) \qquad\qquad C_{\bar{V}} = \frac{1}{|V|} \sum_{(u,v)\in E} C(v) \qquad (1)$$

3.2 Assortativity Index

The Assortativity Index (*A. Index*) of a network (Newman, 1999) with respect to a particular node-level centrality metric is a quantitative measure of the extent of similarity of the end vertices of the edges with respect to the chosen centrality metric. The extent of similarity is calculated as the Pearson's Product-Moment Correlation Coefficient (Strang, 2006) between the set of upstream vertices (*U*) and set of downstream vertices (*D*) constituting the end vertices of the edges in a real-world network graph. Accordingly, the *A. Index* of a network with respect to a centrality metric *C* could be formulated as below.

$$A.Index_C = \frac{\sum_{(u,v)\in E} \left[C(u) - C_{\bar{U}}\right]\left[C(v) - C_{\bar{V}}\right]}{\sqrt{\sum_{(u,v)\in E} \left[C(u) - C_{\bar{U}}\right]^2}\sqrt{\sum_{(u,v)\in E} \left[C(v) - C_{\bar{V}}\right]^2}} \qquad (2)$$

3.3 Range of Values for Assortativity Classification

As Assortativity Index is a measure of the level of correlation between the sets of upstream and downstream vertices constituting the edges in a network graph, the values for *A. Index$_C$* with respect to any centrality metric (C) would range from -1 to 1. Until now in the literature, a network is considered to be assortative (dissortative) with respect to the chosen node-level metric (C) if the *A. Index$_C$* value is closer to 1 (-1). If the *A. Index$_C$* value is closer to 0, the network is considered to be neutral with respect to the metric C. However, we do not have a formally defined range of values that clearly indicate how the network should be classified if the *A. Index$_C$* values are neither close to 1 or -1 and nor to 0.

Table 1. Range of Correlation Coefficient Values and the Corresponding Levels of Correlation

Range of Correlation Coefficient Values	Level of Correlation	Range of Correlation Coefficient Values	Level of Correlation
0.80 to 1.00	Very Strong Positive	-1.00 to -0.80	Very Strong Negative
0.60 to 0.79	Strong Positive	-0.79 to -0.60	Strong Negative
0.40 to 0.59	Moderate Positive	-0.59 to -0.40	Moderate Negative
0.20 to 0.39	Weak Positive	-0.39 to -0.20	Weak Negative
0.00 to 0.19	Very Weak Positive	-0.19 to -0.01	Very Weak Negative

We seek to address this concern as follows: Since *A. Index$_C$* is evaluated as a measure of correlation, we will adapt the range of correlation coefficient values (rounded to two decimals) proposed in the literature (Evans, 1995) for the level of correlation (shown in Table 1) and propose the range of assortativity index values (shown in Table 2) for classifying a network with respect to the level of assortativity. We propose only two levels of assortativity and two levels of dissortativity (rather than 5 levels for each) to give enough space for the range of *A. Index* values to classify a network at a particular level, including neutral (i.e., neither assortative nor dissortative), but still be able to differentiate a strongly assortative (dissortative) network from a weakly assortative (dissortative) network or neutral network with respect to a node-level metric. The color code to be used for the various levels of assortativity are also shown in Table 2.

Table 2. Range of Assortativity Index Values and the Corresponding Levels of Assortativity

Range of Assortativity Index Values	Level of Assortativity	Range of Assortativity Index Values	Level of Assortativity
0.60 to 1.00	Strongly Assortative	-1.00 to -0.60	Strongly Dissortative
0.20 to 0.59	Weakly Assortative	-0.59 to -0.20	Weakly Dissortative
0.00 to 0.19	Neutral	-0.19 to -0.01	Neutral

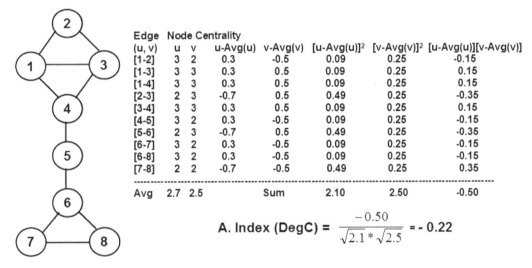

Figure 5. Example to Illustrate the Calculation of the Assortativity Index based on Degree Centrality

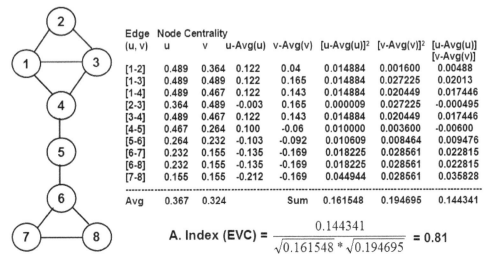

Figure 6. Example to Illustrate the Calculation of the Assortativity Index based on Eigenvector Centrality

3.4 Motivating Example

In this sub section, we illustrate the computation of the assortativity index of the sample graph used in Figures 1-4 with respect to the degree centrality (Figure 5) and eigenvector centrality (Figure 6) metrics. Adopting the proposed range of classification for the level of assortativity, we notice that the sample graph of Figures 1-4 could be classified as "weakly dissortative" (*A. Index* value of -0.22; see Figure 5) with respect to the degree centrality metric and "strongly assortative" (*A. Index* value of 0.81; see Figure 6) with respect to the eigenvector centrality metric. This is a motivating example to vindicate our hypothesis that the assortativity level classification for a network could vary depending on the centrality metric used to compute the *A. Index* values.

4. Real-World Network Graphs

We now present a brief overview of the 50 real-world network graphs analyzed in this paper. We model each network as an undirected graph of nodes and edges. The networks are identified with a unique ID (1, ..., 50) and a three character acronym. We use the spectral radius ratio for node degree (Meghanathan, 2014) to capture the extent of variation in the degree of the nodes: the spectral radius ratio for node degree is the ratio of the principal eigenvalue (Strang, 2006) of the adjacency matrix of the network graph to that of the average node degree. The values for the spectral radius ratio for node degree are 1 or above; the farther is the value from 1, the larger is the variation in node degree. We analyze real-world networks ranging from random networks to scale-free networks as the spectral radius ratio for node degree of the real-world networks analyzed in this graph ranges from 1.01 to 3.48. Table 3 lists the 50 networks along with the values for the number of nodes and edges, the spectral radius ratio for node degree (λ_{sp}) and average degree (k_{avg}). A brief description of the networks is as follows:

1) Word Adjacency Network (ADJ; Newman, 2006): This is a network of 112 words (adjectives and nouns, represented as vertices) in the novel *David Copperfield* by Charles Dickens; there exists an edge between two vertices if the corresponding words appeared adjacent to each other at least once in the novel.

2) Anna Karnenina Network (AKN; Knuth, 1993): This a network of 140 characters (vertices) in the novel *Anna Karnenina*; there exists an edge between two vertices if the corresponding characters have appeared together in at least one scene in the novel.

3) Jazz Band Network (JBN; Geiser & Danon, 2003): This is a network of 198 Jazz bands (vertices) that recorded between the years 1912 and 1940; there exists an edge between two bands if they shared at least one musician in any of their recordings during this period.

4) C. Elegans Neural Network (CEN; White et al., 1986): This is a network of 297 neurons (vertices) in the neural network of the hermaphrodite Caenorhabditis Elegans; there is an edge between two vertices if the corresponding neurons interact with each other (in the form of chemical synapses, gap junctions and neuromuscular junctions).

5) Centrality Literature Network (CLN; Hummon et al., 1990): This is a network of 118 papers (vertices) published on the topic of centrality in complex networks from 1948 to 1979. There is an edge between two vertices v_i and v_j if one of the corresponding papers has cited the other paper as a reference.

6) Citation Graph Drawing Network (CGD; Biedl & Franz, 2001): This is a network of 259 papers (vertices) that were published in the Proceedings of the Graph Drawing (GD) conferences from 1994 to 2000 and cited in the papers published in the GD'2001 conference. There is an edge between two vertices v_i and v_j if one of the corresponding papers has cited the other paper as a reference.

7) Copperfield Network (CFN; Knuth, 1993): This is a network of 89 characters in the novel *David Copperfield* by Charles Dickens; there exists an edge between two vertices if the corresponding characters appeared together in at least one scene in the novel.

8) Dolphin Network (DON; Lusseau et al., 2003): This is a network of 62 dolphins (vertices) that lived in the Doubtful Sound fiord of New Zealand; there is an edge between two vertices if the corresponding dolphins were seen moving with each other during the observation period.

9) Drug Network (DRN; Lee, 2004): This is a network of 212 drug agents (vertices) of different ethnicities. There is a link between two vertices if the corresponding agents know each other.

10) Dutch Literature 1976 Network (DLN; Nooy, 1999): This is a network of 37 Dutch literary authors and critics (vertices) in 1976; there exists an edge between two vertices v_i and v_j if the person corresponding to one of them is a critic who made a judgment (through a review or interview) on the literature work of the author corresponding to the other vertex.

Table 3. Fundamental Properties of the Real-World Network Graphs used for Assortativity Analysis

#	Net.	λ_{sp}	#nodes	#edges	k_{avg}	#	Net.	λ_{sp}	#nodes	#edges	k_{avg}
1	ADJ	1.73	112	425	7.589	26	LMN	1.82	77	254	6.597
2	AKN	2.48	140	494	7.057	27	MDN	1.04	62	1167	37.645
3	JBN	1.45	198	2742	27.697	28	MTB	1.95	64	295	9.219
4	CEN	1.68	297	2148	14.465	29	MCE	1.12	77	1549	40.23
5	CLN	2.03	118	613	10.39	30	MSJ	3.48	475	625	2.632
6	CGD	2.24	259	640	4.942	31	AFB	2.29	171	940	10.994
7	CFN	1.83	89	407	9.146	32	MPN	1.23	35	117	6.686
8	DON	1.40	62	159	5.129	33	MMN	1.59	30	61	4.067
9	DRN	2.76	212	284	2.679	34	PBN	1.42	105	441	8.4
10	DLN	1.49	37	81	4.378	35	PSN	1.22	238	5539	46.546
11	ERD	3.00	433	1314	6.069	36	PFN	1.32	67	142	4.239
12	FMH	2.81	147	202	2.748	37	SJN	1.29	75	155	4.133
13	FHT	1.57	33	91	5.515	38	SDI	1.94	230	359	3.122
14	FTC	1.21	48	170	7.083	39	SPR	1.57	92	477	10.37
15	FON	1.01	115	613	10.661	40	SMN	1.05	126	5973	94.81
16	CDF	1.11	58	967	33.345	41	SWC	1.45	35	118	6.743
17	GD96	2.38	180	228	2.533	42	SSM	1.22	24	38	3.167
18	MUN	2.54	167	301	3.605	43	TEN	1.06	22	39	3.545
19	GLN	2.01	67	118	3.522	44	TWF	1.49	47	77	3.277
20	GD01	1.80	101	190	3.762	45	UKF	1.35	83	578	13.928
21	HTN	1.21	115	2164	37.635	46	APN	3.22	332	2126	12.807
22	HCN	1.66	76	302	7.947	47	USS	1.25	49	107	4.367
23	ISP	1.69	309	1924	12.453	48	RHF	1.27	217	1839	16.949
24	KCN	1.47	34	78	4.588	49	WSB	1.22	43	336	15.628
25	KFP	1.70	37	85	4.595	50	WTN	1.38	80	875	21.875

11) Erdos Collaboration Network (ERD; Batagelj & Mrvar, 2006): This is a network of 433 authors (nodes) who have either directly published an article with Paul Erdos or through a chain of collaborators leading to Paul Erdos. There is an edge between two nodes if the corresponding authors have co-authored at least one publication.

12) Faux Mesa High School Friendship Network (FMH; Resnick et al., 1997): This is a network of 147 students (vertices) at a high school community in the rural western part of US; there exists an edge between two vertices if the corresponding students are friends of each other.

13) Friendship Ties in a Hi-Tech Firm (FHT; Krackhardt, 1999): This is a network of 33 employees (vertices) of a small hi-tech computer firm that sells, installs and maintains computer systems; there exists an edge between two vertices v_i and v_j if the employee corresponding to at least one of them considers the employee corresponding to the other vertex as a personal friend.

14) Flying Teams Cadet Network (FTC; Moreno, 1960): This is a network of 48 cadet pilots (vertices) at an US Army Air Forces flying school in 1943 and the cadets were trained in a two-seated aircraft; there exists an edge between two vertices v_i and v_j if the pilot corresponding to at least one of them has indicated the pilot corresponding to the other vertex as a preferred partner with whom s/he likes to fly during the training schedules.

15) US Football Network (FON; Girvan & Newman, 2002): This is a network of 115 football teams (nodes) of US universities that played in the Fall 2000 season; there is an edge between two nodes if the corresponding teams have played against each other in the league games.

16) College Dorm Fraternity Network (CDF; Bernard et al., 1980): This is a network of 58 residents (vertices) in a fraternity college at a West Virginia college; there exists an edge between two vertices if the corresponding residents were see in a conversation at least once during a five day observation period.

17) GD'96 Network (GD96; Batagelj & Mrvar, 2006): This is a network of 180 AT&T and other WWW websites (vertices) that were cited in the proceedings of the Graph Drawing (GD) conference in 1996; there exists an edge between two vertices if the website corresponding to one of them has a link to the website corresponding to the other vertex.

18) Marvel Universe Network (MUN; Gleiser, 2007): This is a collaborative network of 167 characters (vertices) in the comic books published by the Marvel Universe publishing company; there exists an edge between two vertices if the corresponding characters had appeared together in at least one publication.

19) Graph and Digraph Glossary Network (GLN; Batagelj & Mrvar, 2006): This is a network of 67 terms (vertices) that appeared in the glossary prepared by Bill Cherowitzo on Graph and Digraph; there appeared an edge between two vertices if the term corresponding to one of them is used to describe the meaning of the term corresponding to the other vertex.

20) Graph Drawing 2001 (GD01) Network (Batagelj & Mrvar, 2006): This is a network of 101 papers (vertices) that were cited as references in the papers published in the proceedings of the 2001 Graph Drawing (GD'01) conference; there exists an edge between two vertices if the corresponding papers have been co-cited in at least one paper published in the GD'01 conference.

21) Hypertext 2009 Network (HTN; Isella et al., 2011): This is a network of the face-to-face contacts of 115 attendees (vertices) of the ACM Hypertext 2009 conference held in Turin, Italy from June 29 to July 1, 2009. There exists an edge between two vertices if the corresponding conference visitors had face-to-face contact that was active for at least 20 seconds.

22) Huckleberry Coappearance Network (HCN; Knuth, 1993): This is a network of 76 characters (vertices) that appeared in the novel Huckleberry Finn by Mark Twain; there is an edge between two vertices if the corresponding characters had a common appearance in at least one scene.

23) Infectious Socio-patterns Network (ISP; Isella et al., 2011): This is a network of 309 visitors (vertices) who visited the Science Gallery in Dublin, Ireland during Spring 2009. There existed an edge between two vertices if the corresponding visitors had a continuous face-to-face contact for at least 20 seconds when they participated in the *Infectious Socio-patterns* event (an electronic simulation of the spreading of an epidemic through individuals who are in close proximity) as part of an art science exhibition.

24) Karate Club Network (KCN; Zachary, 1977): This is a network of 34 members (nodes) of a Karate Club at a US university in the 1970s; there is an edge between two nodes if the corresponding members were seen interacting with each other during the observation period.

25) Korea Family Planning Network (KFP; Rogers & Kincaid, 1980): This is a network of 37 women (vertices) at a Mothers' Club in Korea; there existed an edge between two vertices if the corresponding women were seen discussing family planning methods during an observation period.

26) Les Miserables Network (LMN; Knuth, 1993): This is a network of 77 characters (nodes) in the novel *Les Miserables*; there exists an edge between two nodes if the corresponding characters appeared together in at least one of the chapters in the novel.

27) Macaque Dominance Network (MDN; Takahata, 1991): This is a network of 62 adult female Japanese macaques (monkeys; vertices) in a colony, known as the "Arashiyama B Group", recorded during the non-mating season from April to early October, 1976. There existed an edge between two vertices if a macaque corresponding to one of them was recorded to have exhibited dominance over the macaque corresponding to the other vertex.

28) Madrid Train Bombing Network (MTB; Hayes, 2006): This is a network of 64 suspected individuals and their relatives (vertices) reconstructed by Rodriguez using press accounts in the two major Spanish daily newspapers (El Pais and El Mundo) regarding the bombing of commuter trains in Madrid on March 11, 2004. There existed an edge between two vertices if the corresponding individuals were observed to have a link in the form of friendship, ties to any terrorist organization, co-participation in training camps and/or wars, or co-participation in any previous terrorist attacks.

29) Manufacturing Company Employee Network (MFE; Cross et al., 2004): This is a network of 77 employees (nodes) from a research team in a manufacturing company; there exists an edge between two nodes if the two employees are aware of each other's knowledge and skills.

30) Social Networks Journal Co-authors (MSJ; McCarty & Freeman, 2008): This is a network of 475 authors (vertices) involved in the production of 295 articles for the Social Networks Journal since its inception until 2008; there is an edge between two vertices if the corresponding authors co-authored at least one paper published in the journal.

31) Author Facebook Network (AFB): This is a network of the 171 friends (vertices) of the author in Facebook. There exists an edge between two vertices if the corresponding people are also friends of each other.

32) Mexican Political Elite Network (MPN; Gil-Mendieta & Schmidt, 1996): This is a network of 35 Mexican presidents and their close collaborators (vertices); there exists an edge between two vertices if the corresponding two people have ties that could be either political, kinship, friendship or business ties.

33) ModMath Network (MMN; Batagelj & Mrvar, 2006): This is a network of 30 school superintendents (vertices) in Allegheny County, Pennsylvania, USA during the 1950s and early 1960s. There exists an edge between two vertices if at least one of the two corresponding superintendents has indicated the other person as a friend in a research survey conducted to see which superintendents (who are in office for at least a year) are more influential to effectively spread around some modern Math methods among the school systems in the county.

34) US Politics Books Network (PBN; Krebs, 2003): This is a network of 105 books (vertices) about US politics sold by Amazon.com around the time of the 2004 US presidential election. There exists an edge between two vertices if the corresponding two books were co-purchased by the same buyer (at least one buyer).

35) Primary School Contact Network (PSN; Gemmetto et al., 2014): This is a network of children and teachers (238 vertices) used in the study published by an article in BMC Infectious Diseases, 2014 [40]. There exists an edge between two vertices if the corresponding persons were in contact for at least 20 seconds during the observation period.

36) Prison Friendship Network (PFN; MacRae, 1960): This is a network of 67 prison inmates (vertices) surveyed by John Gagnon in the 1950s regarding their sociometric choice. There exists an edge between two vertices if an inmate corresponding to at least one of them has listed the inmate corresponding to the other vertex as one of his/her closest friends.

37) San Juan Sur Family Network (SJN; Loomis et al., 1953): This is a network of 75 families (vertices) in San Juan Sur, Costa Rica, 1948. There exists an edge between two vertices if at least one of the corresponding families has visited the household of the family corresponding to the other vertex once or more.

38) Scotland Corporate Interlocks Network (SDI; Scott, 1980): This is a network of multiple directors (a director who serves on multiple boards) and companies (a total of 230 vertices) during 1904-05 in Scotland. There exists an edge between two vertices v_i and v_j if any of the following are true: (i) both v_i and v_j correspond to two different multiple directors who are in the board of at least one company; (ii) one of the two vertices corresponds to a multiple director and the other vertex corresponds to one of the companies in whose board the person serves.

39) Senator Press Release Network (SPR; Grimmer, 2010): This is a network of 92 US senators (vertices) during the period from 2007 to 2010. There exists an edge between two senators if they issued at least one joint press release.

40) Slovenian Magazine Network (SMN; Batagelj & Mrvar, 2006): This is a network of 126 different magazines (vertices); there exists an edge between two vertices if at least one reader (among a total of 100,000 readers) indicated that s/he reads the corresponding two magazines as part of a survey conducted in 1999 and 2000.

41) Soccer World Cup 1998 Network (SWC; Batagelj & Mrvar, 2006): This is a network of 35 teams (vertices) that participated in the 1998 edition of the Soccer World Cup. A player for a national team could sometimes have contract with one or more other countries. In this network, there is an edge between two vertices if the national team corresponding to at least one of them has contracted players from the country represented by the national team corresponding to the other vertex.

42) Sawmill Strike Communication Network (SSM; Michael, 1997): This is a network of 24 employees (vertices) in a sawmill who planned a strike against the new compensation package proposed by their management. There exists an edge between any two vertices if the corresponding employees mutually admitted discussing about the strike with a frequency of three or more (on a 5-point scale).

43) Taro Exchange Network (TEN; Schwimmer, 1973): This is a network of 22 families (vertices) in a Papuan village. There exists an edge between two vertices if the corresponding families were seen exchanging gifts during the observation period.

44) Teenage Female Friendship Network (TWF; Pearson & Michell, 2000): This is a network of 47 female teenage students (vertices) who studied as a cohort in a school in the West of Scotland from 1995 to 1997. There exists an edge between two vertices if the corresponding students reported (in a survey) that they were best friends of each other.

45) UK Faculty Friendship Network (UKF; Nepusz et al., 2008): This is a network of 83 faculty (vertices) at a UK university. There exists an edge between two vertices if the corresponding faculty are friends of each other.

46) US Airports 1997 Network (APN; Batagelj & Mrvar, 2006): This is a network of 332 airports (vertices) in

the US in the year 1997. There is an edge between two nodes if there is a direct flight connection between the corresponding airports.

47) US States Network (USS): This is a network of the 48 contiguous states in the US and the District of Columbia (DC). Each of the 48 states and DC is a node and there is an edge involving two nodes if the corresponding states (or DC) have a common border between them.

48) Residence Hall Friendship Network (RHF; Freeman et al., 1998): This is a network of 217 residents (vertices) living at a residence hall located on the Australian National University campus. There exists an edge between two vertices if the corresponding residents are friends of each other.

49) Windsurfers Beach Network (WSB; Freeman et al., 1989): This is a network of 43 windsurfers (vertices) on a beach in southern California during Fall 1986. There exists an edge between two vertices if the corresponding windsurfers were perceived to be close to each other (determined based on a survey).

50) World Trade Metal Network (WTN; Smith & White, 1992): This is a network of 80 countries (vertices) that are involved in trading miscellaneous metals during the period from 1965 to 1980. There exists an edge between two vertices if one of the two corresponding countries imported miscellaneous metals from the country corresponding to the other vertex.

5. Results of Assortativity Analysis

We now present the *A. Index* values obtained for each of the 50 real-world network graphs (listed in Section 4) with respect to each of the four centrality metrics (introduced in Section 2). Table 4 lists the *A. Index* values and the values are color coded as per the range outlined in Table 2. One can easily see that for about 80% of the real-world networks analyzed (i.e., for 40 of the 50 real-world networks analyzed), the level of assortativity is not the same for all the four centrality metrics. For a majority (i.e., 56%) of the real-world networks (i.e., for 28 of the 50 real-world networks), we observe two different levels of assortativity and most of these are the neutral and weakly assortative levels. For very few real-world networks, the two different levels of assortativity represent levels whose ranges of assortativity index values are not contiguous (for example: neutral and strongly assortative). For about 24% of the real-world networks analyzed (i.e., 12 of the 50 real-world networks), we observe three levels of assortativity. For none of the real-world networks, we observe four different levels of assortativity (i.e., one assortativity level per centrality metric). Only 6-14% of the real-world networks are either weakly or strongly dissortative with respect to any centrality metric.

We also plot (Figures 7-10) the distribution of the *A. Index* values for each of the four centrality metrics. We estimate the probability of observing a network to be at a particular level of assortativity with respect to a centrality metric as the fraction of the total number of real-world networks exhibiting the particular level of assortativity with respect to the centrality metric. These empirically estimated probability values are also listed in Figures 7-10. As a high-level conclusion, we could say that there is at least a 50% chance for a real-world network to be neutral (neither assortative nor dissortative) with respect to the degree centrality and betweenness centrality metrics. On the other hand, we observe that there is at least a 50% chance for a real-world network to be assortative (either strongly assortative or weakly assortative) with respect to the closeness centrality and eigenvector centrality metrics.

More specifically: we observe a real-world network to be neutral with respect to the BWC and DegC metrics with a probability of 0.72 and 0.58 respectively. When considered with respect to the EVC metric, we observe a real-world network to be weakly assortative with a probability of 0.38 and strongly assortative with a probability of 0.28. When considered with respect to the ClC metric, we observe a real-world network to be strongly assortative with a probability of 0.38 and weakly assortative with a probability of 0.28. Note that though both BWC and ClC are shortest path-based centrality metrics, we observe that they are poles apart with respect to assortativity. While a real-world network is more likely to be neutral (neither assortative nor dissortative) with respect to the BWC metric, we observe a real-world network to be more likely to be strongly assortative or weakly assortative with respect to the ClC metric. Table 5 summarizes these empirically estimated probability values for all the five levels of assortativity and all the four centrality metrics. Figure 11 presents a pictorial view of the empirically estimated probability values for observing a real-world network at a particular level of assortativity with respect to a centrality metric.

Table 4. Fundamental Properties of the Real-World Network Graphs used for Assortativity Analysis

#	Net.	BWC	DegC	EVC	ClC	#	Net.	BWC	DegC	EVC	ClC
1	ADJ	-0.10	-0.10	0.04	0.13	26	LMN	-0.02	-0.08	0.43	0.21
2	AKN	-0.08	-0.08	0.09	0.12	27	MDN	-0.10	-0.05	-0.02	-0.05
3	JBN	-0.04	0.03	0.35	0.18	28	MTB	0.25	0.73	0.79	1.00
4	CEN	-0.06	-0.09	0.22	0.22	29	MCE	0.05	0.72	0.79	0.94
5	CLN	-0.12	-0.11	0.06	0.06	30	MSJ	0.24	0.35	0.94	1.00
6	CGD	0.07	0.14	0.59	1.00	31	AFB	0.09	0.35	0.89	1.00
7	CFN	-0.07	-0.17	-0.09	-0.09	32	MPN	-0.12	-0.16	0.13	0.09
8	DON	0.12	-0.04	0.64	0.53	33	MMN	0.00	0.10	0.50	0.47
9	DRN	0.30	0.35	0.62	1.00	34	PBN	0.04	-0.02	0.54	0.37
10	DLN	-0.08	0.07	0.34	0.33	35	PSN	0.10	0.22	0.29	0.26
11	ERD	0.05	0.18	0.40	1.00	36	PFN	0.23	0.59	0.67	0.96
12	FMH	0.39	0.65	0.84	1.00	37	SJN	0.03	-0.14	0.51	0.41
13	FHT	0.25	0.60	0.69	1.00	38	SDI	0.22	0.08	0.95	1.00
14	FTC	-0.07	-0.03	0.45	0.23	39	SPR	-0.06	0.02	0.14	0.16
15	FON	0.06	0.19	0.69	0.31	40	SMN	-0.20	-0.23	-0.22	-0.23
16	CDF	-0.10	-0.11	-0.10	-0.12	41	SWC	-0.23	-0.17	-0.02	-0.02
17	GD96	-0.24	-0.32	-0.03	0.47	42	SSM	0.04	-0.02	0.50	0.33
18	MUN	0.04	0.14	0.64	1.00	43	TEN	-0.16	-0.36	0.26	0.23
19	GLN	-0.16	-0.13	0.30	1.00	44	TWF	0.55	0.84	0.93	1.00
20	GD01	-0.92	-0.98	-0.75	-0.54	45	UKF	-0.08	0.00	0.22	0.12
21	HTN	-0.10	-0.12	-0.10	-0.12	46	APN	-0.15	-0.21	-0.02	0.06
22	HCN	0.01	0.03	0.18	1.00	47	USS	0.23	0.23	0.62	0.65
23	ISP	0.14	0.29	0.56	0.77	48	RHF	0.00	0.10	0.38	0.25
24	KCN	-0.36	-0.48	-0.24	-0.08	49	WSB	0.02	0.45	0.50	0.89
25	KFP	0.17	0.24	0.53	0.73	50	WTN	-0.26	-0.39	-0.37	-0.35

An interesting and significant observation from the color-coded Table 3 is that for real-world networks with two or three levels of assortativity with the centrality metrics: the level of assortativity typically exhibited a transition from dissortative to neutral (or) neutral to weakly assortative to strongly assortative when the centrality metrics are considered in this order: BWC, DegC, EVC and ClC. We also notice from Figures 7-10 that the distribution of the *A. Index* values gradually drifts from a predominantly neutral-level distribution (corresponding to the BWC and DegC metrics) to a predominantly assortative-level distribution (corresponding to the EVC and ClC metrics). Such observations further vindicate our conclusions (in the previous paragraphs) regarding the probability of observing a real-world network to be neutral, weakly assortative and strongly assortative with respect to the centrality metrics.

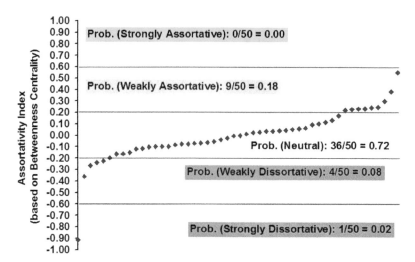

Figure 7. Distribution of Assortativity Index Values for Real-World Networks (based on Betweenness Centrality)

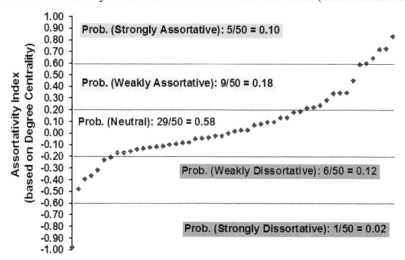

Figure 8. Distribution of Assortativity Index Values for Real-World Networks (based on Degree Centrality)

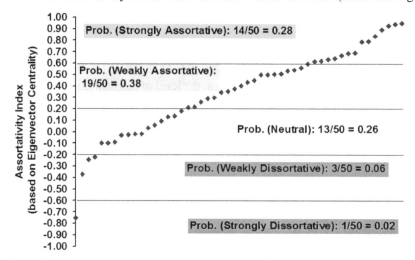

Figure 9. Distribution of Assortativity Index Values for Real-World Networks (based on Eigenvector Centrality)

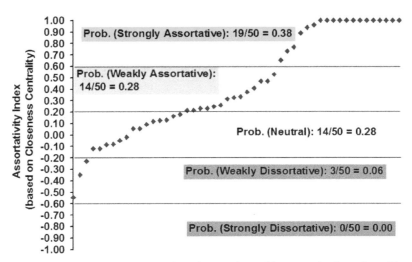

Figure 10. Distribution of Assortativity Index Values for Real-World Networks (based on Closeness Centrality)

Table 5. Empirically Estimated Probability Values for the Assortative Level of a Real-World Network with respect to the Centrality Metrics

Centrality Metric	Strongly Dissortative	Weakly Dissortative	Neutral	Weakly Assortative	Strongly Assortative
Betweenness	0.02	0.08	0.72	0.18	0.00
Degree	0.02	0.12	0.58	0.18	0.10
Eigenvector	0.02	0.06	0.26	0.38	0.28
Closeness	0.00	0.06	0.28	0.28	0.38

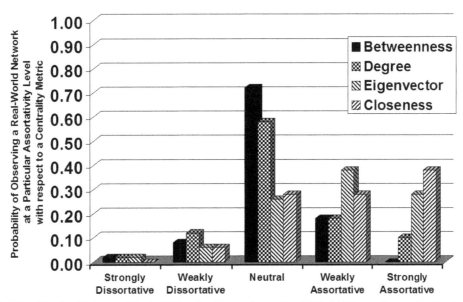

Figure 11. Empirically Estimated Probability for Observing a Real-World Network at a Particular Level of Assortativity with respect to a Centrality Metric

6. Related Work

To the best of our knowledge, all the results reported in the literature (e.g., Newman, 1999; Newman & Girvan, 2003; Noldus & Van Mieghem, 2015) on assortativity of real-world network graphs is based on the degree centrality metric. Ours is the first effort to study the assortativity of real-world network graphs based on the other commonly used centrality metrics such as betweenness centrality, eigenvector centrality and closeness centrality. We analyze the assortativity of a large collection of real-world network graphs (with a broad range of variation in node degree) and empirically propose the likelihood of observing a real-world network graph to be neutral or assortative with respect to a centrality metric. In this section, we discuss results from the most related work on assortativity and centrality metrics in the literature.

Traditionally, based on the degree centrality metric, social networks have been found to be assortative (high degree nodes tend to attach to high degree nodes); whereas, the technological and biological networks have been observed to be dissortative (i.e., low degree nodes tend to attach to high degree nodes and vice-versa; Newman, 2003). The networks generated from theoretical models such as the Erdos-Renyi random networks (Erdos & Renyi, 1959), Barabasi-Albert scale-free networks (Barabasi & Albert, 1999) and the Watts-Strogatz small-world networks (Watts & Strogatz, 1998) have also been observed to be neutral (neither assortative nor dissortative) with respect to the degree centrality metric (Newman, 1999). In addition, networks that evolve with time without any constraints have been observed to reach a maximum entropy state (entropy is a quantitative measure of robustness; Demetrius & Manke, 2005) with heterogeneous connectivity distribution and in such a state, networks have been usually dissortative (Johnson et al., 2010) with respect to the degree centrality metric. On the other hand, networks that evolved with constraints (with respect to the number of links a node can maintain) tend to transition from being dissortative to assortative with time (Konig et al., 2010). Also, synthetic social network graphs generated using the Monte Carlo Metropolis–Hastings type algorithms (Chib & Greenberg, 1995) were observed to quickly evolve to a giant component if edge distribution (based on *remaining degree*: one less than the degree centrality; Newman, 1999) follows assortative matching (rather than dissortative matching; Newman, 2003).

Iyer et al. (2013) analyzed the robustness of networks due to targeted removal of vertices that are ranked higher with respect to centrality metrics. It has been observed that dissortative networks degrade more rapidly due to the removal of vertices with higher degree; whereas, assortative networks degrade more rapidly due to the removal of vertices with higher betweenness (at least for the first 25% of the vertices) as the high degree vertices in assortative networks tend to form a concentrated interconnected core that would be difficult to break due to the removal of few vertices. For neutral networks (with assortativity index close to 0), targeted node removal based on degree has been observed to be the most effective method to degrade the network and targeted removal based on eigenvector centrality has been observed to be the least effective (Iyer et al., 2013). The findings from this paper could be considered complementary to the above research results as we observe real-world network graphs to be more likely assortative with respect to the EVC metric; hence, removal of vertices with higher EVC is more likely to have a relatively less degrading effect on the assortativity of networks.

Zhang et al. (2012) argued that assortativity level of the different communities with their neighborhood need not be the same as the assortativity level of the entire network. This could be attributed to the differences in the connectivity of the vertices in the various communities to their respective outside world. In this regard, Zhang et al. (2012) proposed an alternate metric called the Universal Assortativity Coefficient (UAC) defined for a community (sub graph) of vertices as the sum of the local assortativity indices of edges (Newman, 1999) emanating from the vertices that are part of the community. The local assortativity index of an edge is calculated as per the *remaining degree* based formulation proposed by Newman (1999): Edges with positive local assortativity index are referred to as assortative and edges with negative local assortativity index are referred to as dissortative. Zhang et al. (2012) claimed that a globally assortative network could still have majority of its edges to be locally dissortative and vice-versa. Similar to local edge assortativity, a measure called local node assortativity (Piraveenan et al., 2008) based on the remaining degree of a node has also been proposed in the literature; the sum of local node assortativity values is equal to the network assortativity. It has been shown by Piraveenan et al (2009) that distribution profiles of the local assortativity of nodes vs. their degrees could be used to identify assortative hubs in social and biological networks and dissortative hubs in scale-free networks such as the Internet. All of the above analyses has been based on only the degree centrality metric and is heavily based on the concept of remaining degree.

Joyce et al. (2010) proposed the notion of *leverage centrality* to capture the assortative or dissortative neighborhood of a node. The range of values for leverage centrality is (-1, ..., 1): positive values indicating an assortative neighborhood and negative values indicating a dissortative neighborhood. A node has a positive leverage centrality if it is connected to more nodes than its neighbors (assortative neighborhood); a node connected to fewer nodes than its neighbors has a negative leverage centrality (dissortative neighborhood). Nodes having higher leverage centrality are perceived to be important for facilitating information flow to and from its neighbors. Leverage centrality of a node is estimated simply based on the degree of the node and that of its neighbors; the centrality metric has been observed to be strongly correlated with betweenness centrality and weakly correlated with eigenvector centrality metric. Per the trends observed in this paper, we expect a real-world network to be more likely to be neutral (neither assortative nor dissortative) with respect to the leverage centrality metric (as is also observed for the betweenness centrality metric).

Meghanathan (2015) observed the degree centrality and betweenness centrality metrics to be highly correlated for real-world network graphs: we opine such a correlation is justified with the real-world network graphs exhibiting almost similar levels of assortativity with respect to both these centrality metrics in this paper. Meghanathan (2016) showed that a maximal assortative matching of vertices (with the objective of maximizing the assortativity index) in real-world network graphs (with respect to the degree centrality metric) cannot maximize the number of matched vertices and vice-versa. We attribute such a phenomenon to the relatively neutral levels of assortativity of the edges with respect to the degree centrality metric and its closely correlated betweenness centrality metric. As we observe the closeness centrality metric to exhibit stronger levels of assortativity, we opine that a maximal assortative matching of vertices based on closeness centrality would relatively increase the number of vertices matched (compared to the degree centrality metric).

7. Conclusions and Future Work

We have shown that the assortativity classification of real-world network graphs is dependent on the node-level centrality metric used to compute the assortativity index values of the edges. As part of this analysis, we formally propose five levels of assortativity and their associated ranges in the space of assortativity index values from -1 to 1. We computed the assortativity index values for a suite of 50 real-world network graphs (with spectral radius ratio for node degree ranging from 1.01 to 3.48) with respect to each of the four commonly used centrality metrics: degree centrality (DegC), eigenvector centrality (EVC), betweenness centrality (BWC) and closeness centrality (ClC). We observe about 80% of the real-world network graphs to exhibit more than one assortativity level (depending on the centrality metric used to compute the assortativity index values): 56% exhibiting two assortativity levels and 24% exhibiting three assortativity levels. We notice for a majority of these real-world network graphs, the level of assortativity exhibited a transition from dissortative to neutral (or) neutral to weakly assortative to strongly assortative when the centrality metrics are considered in this order: BWC, DegC, EVC and ClC. Using the results of the assortativity analysis, we also estimated the empirical probability for a real-world network graph to exhibit a particular level of assortativity: We claim that a real-network graph is more likely (probability of 0.72) to be neutral (neither assortative nor dissortative) with respect to the BWC metric and is more likely to be assortative (strongly or weakly assortative: probability of 0.38 + 0.28 = 0.66) with respect to the EVC and ClC metrics.

We have thus unraveled significant information about the assortativity of real-world network graphs with respect to the other commonly used centrality metrics such as betweenness, closeness and eigenvector centrality. As part of future work, we plan to analyze the centrality-based assortativity of complex network graphs generated from theoretical models (such as the Erdos-Renyi random network model (Erdos & Renyi, 1959), Barabasi-Albert scale-free network model (Barabasi & Albert, 1999) and the Watts-Strogatz small-world network model; Watts & Strogatz, 1998). We also plan to investigate the use of centrality metrics (other than degree centrality) to compute maximal assortative matching and maximal dissortative matching (Meghanathan, 2016) for real-world network graphs.

Acknowledgments

The research is financed by the NASA EPSCoR sub award (#: NNX14AN38A) from University of Mississippi.

References

Barabasi, A. L., & Albert, R. (1999). Emergence of Scaling in Random Networks. *Science, 286*(5439), 509-512. http://dx.doi.org/10.1126/science.286.5439.509

Batagelj, V., & Mrvar, A. (2006). *Pajek Datasets*. Retrieved from http://vlado.fmf.uni-lj.si/pub/networks/data/

Bernard, H. R., Killworth, P. D., & Sailer, L. (1980). Informant Accuracy in Social Network Data IV: A Comparison of Clique-level Structure in Behavioral and Cognitive Network Data. *Social Networks, 2*(3), 191-218. http://dx.doi.org/10.1016/0378-8733(79)90014-5

Biedl, T., & Franz, B. J. (2001). *Graph-Drawing Contest Report*. Paper presented at the 9th International Symposium on Graph Drawing, Vienna, Austria. http://dx.doi.org/10.1007/3-540-45848-4_60

Bonacich, P. (1987). Power and Centrality: A Family of Measures. *American Journal of Sociology, 92*(5), 1170-1182. http://dx.doi.org/10.1086/228631

Brandes, U. (2001). A Faster Algorithm for Betweenness Centrality. *The Journal of Mathematical Sociology*, *25*(2), 163-177. http://dx.doi.org/10.1080/0022250X.2001.9990249

Chib, S., & Greenberg, E. (1995). Understanding the Metropolis-Hastings Algorithm. *American Statistician*, *49*(4), 327-335. http://dx.doi.org/10.1080/00031305.1995.10476177

Cormen, T. H., Leiserson, C. E., Rivest, R. L., & Stein, C. (2009). *Introduction to Algorithms*. (3rd Ed.) MIT Press.

Cross, R. L., Parker, A., & Cross, R. (2004). *The Hidden Power of Social Networks: Understanding How Work Really Gets Done in Organizations*. (1st Ed.) Harvard Business Review Press.

Demetrius, L., & Manke, T. (2005). Robustness and Network Evolution - An Entropic Principle. *Physica A*, *346*, 682-696. http://dx.doi.org/10.1098%2Frsif.2006.0140

Erdos, P., & Renyi, A. (1959). On Random Graphs I. *Publicationes Mathematicae*, *6*, 290-297.

Evans, J. D. (1995). *Straightforward Statistics for the Behavioral Sciences*. (1st Ed.) Brooks Cole Publishing Company.

Freeman, L. (1977). A Set of Measures of Centrality based on Betweenness. *Sociometry*, *40*(1), 35-41. http://dx.doi.org/10.2307/3033543

Freeman, L. (1979). Centrality in Social Networks Conceptual Clarification. *Social Networks*, *1*(3), 215-239. http://dx.doi.org/10.1016/0378-8733(78)90021-7

Freeman, L., Webster, C. M., & Kirke, D. M. (1998). Exploring Social Structure using Dynamic Three-Dimensional Color Images. *Social Networks*, *20*(2), 109-118. http://dx.doi.org/10.1016/S0378-8733(97)00016-6

Freeman, L., Freeman, S. C., & Michaelson, A. G. (1989). How Humans See Social Groups: A Test of the Sailer-Gaulin Models. *Journal of Quantitative Anthropology*, *1*, 229-238.

Geiser, P., & Danon, L. (2003). Community Structure in Jazz. *Advances in Complex Systems*, *6*(4), 563-573. http://dx.doi.org/10.1142/S0219525903001067

Gemmetto, V., Barrat, A., & Cattuto, C. (2014). Mitigation of Infectious Disease at School: Targeted Class Closure vs. School Closure. *BMC Infectious Diseases*, *14*(695), 1-10. http://dx.doi.org/10.1186/s12879-014-0695-9

Gil-Mendieta, J., & Schmidt, S. (1996). The Political Network in Mexico. *Social Networks*, *18*(4), 355-381. http://dx.doi.org/10.1016/0378-8733(95)00281-2

Girvan, M., & Newman, M. (2002). Community Structure in Social and Biological Networks. *Proceedings of the National Academy of Sciences USA*, *99*(12), 7821-7826. http://dx.doi.org/10.1073/pnas.122653799

Gleiser, P. M. (2007). How to become a Superhero. *Journal of Statistical Mechanics: Theory and Experiments*, P09020. http://dx.doi.org/10.1088/1742-5468/2007/09/P09020

Grimmer, J. (2010). A Bayesian Hierarchical Topic Model for Political Texts: Measuring Expressed Agendas in Senate Press Releases. *Political Analysis*, *18*(1), 1-35. http://dx.doi.org/10.1093/pan/mpp034

Hayes, B. (2006). Connecting the Dots. *American Scientist*, *94*(5), 400-404. http://dx.doi.org/10.1511/2006.61.3495

Hummon, N. P., Doreian, P., & Freeman, L. C. (1990). Analyzing the Structure of the Centrality-Productivity Literature created between 1948 and 1979. *Science Communication*, *11*(4), 459-480. http://dx.doi.org/10.1177/107554709001100405

Isella, L., Stehle, J., Barrat, A., Cattuto, C., Pinton, J. F., & Van den Broeck, W. (2011). What's in a Crowd? Analysis of Face-to-Face Behavioral Networks. *Journal of Theoretical Biology*, *271*(1), 161-180. http://dx.doi.org/10.1016/j.jtbi.2010.11.033

Iyer, S., Killingback, T., Sundaram, B., & Wang, Z. (2013). Attack Robustness and Centrality of Complex Networks. *PLoS One*, *8*(4), e59613. http://dx.doi.org/10.1371/journal.pone.0059613

Johnson, S., Torres, J. J., Marro, J., & Munoz, M. A. (2010). Entropic Origin of Dissortativity in Complex Networks. *Physical Review Letters*, *104*, 108702.

Joyce, K. E., Laurienti, P. J., Burdette, J. H., & Hayasaka, S. (2010). A New Measure of Centrality for Brain Networks. *PLoS One*, *5*(8), e12200. http://dx.doi.org/10.1371/journal.pone.0012200

Knuth, D. E. (1993). *The Stanford GraphBase: A Platform for Combinatorial Computing.* (1st Ed.) Addison-Wesley.

Konig, M. D., Tessone, C. J., & Zenou, Y. (2010). From Assortative to Dissortative Networks: The Role of Capacity Constraints. *Advances in Complex Systems, 13*(4), 483-500. http://dx.doi.org/10.1142/S0219525910002700

Krackhardt, D. (1999). The ties that torture: Simmelian tie analysis in organizations. *Research in the Sociology of Organizations, 16*(1), 183-210.

Krebs, V. (2003). Proxy Networks: Analyzing One Network to Reveal Another. *Bulletin de Méthodologie Sociologique, 79,* 61-70.

Lee, J. S. (2004). Generating Networks of Illegal Drug Users using Large Samples of Partial Ego-Network Data. *Intelligence and Security Informatics, Lecture Notes in Computer Science, 3073,* 390-402. http://dx.doi.org/10.1007/978-3-540-25952-7_29

Loomis, C. P., Morales, J. O., Clifford, R. A., & Leonard, O. E. (1953). *Turrialba Social Systems and the Introduction of Change.* (1st Ed.) The Free Press.

Lusseau, D., Schneider, K., Boisseau, O. J., Hasse, P., Slooten, E., & Dawson, S. M. (2003). The Bottlenose Dolphin Community of Doubtful Sound Features a Large Proportion of Long-lasting Associations. *Behavioral Ecology and Sociobiology, 54*(3), 396-405. http://dx.doi.org/10.1007/s00265-003-0651-y

MacRae, D. (1960). Direct Factor Analysis of Sociometric Data. *Sociometry, 23*(4), 360-371.

McCarty, C., & Freeman, L. (2008). *Network Datasets.* Retrieved from http://moreno.ss.uci.edu/data.html

Meghanathan, N. (2014). *Spectral Radius as a Measure of Variation in Node Degree for Complex Network Graphs.* Paper presented at the 3rd International Conference on Digital Contents and Applications, Hainan, China. http://dx.doi.org/10.1109/UNESST.2014.8

Meghanathan, N. (2015). Correlation Coefficient Analysis of Centrality Metrics for Complex Network Graphs. Paper presented at the 4th Computer Science Online Conference. http://dx.doi.org/10.1007/978-3-319-18503-3_2

Meghanathan, N. (2016). Maximal Assortative Matching for Complex Network Graphs. *Journal of King Saud University – Computer and Information Sciences, 28*(2), 230-246. http://dx.doi.org/10.1016/j.jksuci.2015.10.004

Michael, J. H. (1997). Labor Dispute Reconciliation in a Forest Products Manufacturing Facility. *Forest Products Journal, 47*(11-12), 41-45.

Moreno, J. L. (1960). *The Sociometry Reader.* (1st Ed.) The Free Press.

Nepusz, T., Petroczi, A., Negyessy, L., & Bazso, F. (2008). Fuzzy Communities and the Concept of Bridgeness in Complex Networks. *Physical Review E, 77*(1), 016107.

Newman, M. (2010). *Networks: An Introduction.* (1st Ed.) Oxford University Press.

Newman, M. (1999). Assortative Mixing in Networks. *Physical Review Letters, 89*(20), 208701. http://dx.doi.org/10.1103/PhysRevLett.89.208701

Newman, M. (2006). Finding Community Structure in Networks using the Eigenvectors of Matrices. *Physical Review E, 74*(3), 036104. http://dx.doi.org/10.1103/PhysRevE.74.036104

Newman, M. (2003). Mixing Patterns in Networks. *Physical Review E, 67*(1), 026126, http://dx.doi.org/10.1103/PhysRevE.67.026126

Newman, M., & Girvan, M. (2003). Mixing Patterns and Community Structure in Networks. *Statistical Mechanics of Complex Networks: Lecture Notes in Physics, 625,* 66-87. http://dx.doi.org/10.1007/978-3-540-44943-0_5

Noldus, R., & Van Mieghem, P. (2015). Assortativity in Complex Networks. *Journal of Complex Networks, 3*(4), 507-542. http://dx.doi.org/10.1093/comnet/cnv005

Nooy, W. (1999). A Literary Playground: Literary Criticism and Balance Theory. *Poetics, 26*(5-6), 385-404. http://dx.doi.org/10.1016/S0304-422X(99)00009-1

Pearson, M., & Michell, L. (2000). Smoke Rings: Social Network Analysis of Friendship Groups, Smoking and Drug-taking. *Drugs: Education, Prevention and Policy, 7*(1), 21-37. http://dx.doi.org/

10.1080/dep.7.1.21.37

Piraveenan, M., Prokopenko, M., & Zomaya, A. Y. (2008). Local Assortativeness in Scale-Free Networks. *Europhysics Letters*, *84*(2), 28002. http://dx.doi.org/10.1209/0295-5075/84/28002

Piraveenan, M., Prokopenko, M., & Zomaya, A. Y. (2009). Local Assortativity and Growth of Internet. *Interdisciplinary Physics: The European Physical Journal B*, *70*(2), 275-285. http://dx.doi.org/10.1140/epjb/e2009-00219-y

Resnick, M. D., Bearman, P. S., Blum, R. W., Bauman, K. E., Harris, K. M., Jones, J., Tabor, J., Beuhring, T., Sieving, R. E., Shew, M., Ireland, M., Bearinger, L. H., & Udry, J. R. (1997). Protecting Adolescents from Harm. Findings from the National Longitudinal Study on Adolescent Health. *Journal of the American Medical Association*, *278*(10), 823-832. http://dx.doi.org/10.1001/jama.1997.03550100049038

Rogers, E. M., & Kincaid, D. L. (1980). *Communication Networks: Toward a New Paradigm for Research.* (1st Ed.) The Free Press.

Schwimmer, E. (1973). *Exchange in the Social Structure of the Orokaiva: Traditional and Emergent Ideologies in the Northern District of Papua.* (1st Ed.) C Hurst and Co-Publishers Ltd.

Scott, J. P. (1980). *The Anatomy of Scottish Capital: Scottish Companies and Scottish Capital.* (1st ed.) Croom Helm.

Smith, D. A., & White, D. R. (1992). Structure and Dynamics of the Global Economy: Network Analysis of International Trade 1965-1980. *Social Forces*, *70*(4), 857-893. http://dx.doi.org/10.1093/sf/70.4.857

Strang, G. (2006). *Linear Algebra and its Applications.* (4th Ed.) Brooks Cole.

Takahata, Y. (1991). *Diachronic Changes in the Dominance Relations of Adult Female Japanese Monkeys of the Arashiyama B Group.* (1st Ed.) Albany: State University of New York Press.

Watts, D. J., & Strogatz, S. H. (1998). Collective Dynamics of Small-World Networks. *Nature*, *393*, 440-442. 509-512.

White, J. G., Southgate, E., Thomson, J. N., & Brenner, S. (1986). The Structure of the Nervous System of the Nematode *Caenorhabditis Elegans*. *Philosophical Transactions B*, *314*(1165), 1-340. http://dx.doi.org/10.1098/rstb.1986.0056

Zachary, W. W. (1977). An Information Flow Model for Conflict and Fission in Small Groups. *Journal of Anthropological Research*, *33*(4), 452-473.

Zhang, G. Q., Cheng, S. Q., Zhang, G. Q. (2012). A Universal Assortativity Measure for Network Analysis. *arXiv: 1212.6456* [physics.soc-ph].

18

Technology Aspects of E-Government Readiness in Developing Countries: A Review of the Literature

Mustafa Omar M. Baeuo[1], Nor Zairah Binti Ab. Rahim[1] & Asma Ali Mosa Alaraibi[1]

[1] Advanced Informatics School, Universiti Teknologi Malaysia (UTM), Malaysia

Correspondence: Mustafa Omar M. Baeuo, Advanced Informatics School, Universiti Teknologi Malaysia (UTM), Kuala Lumpur, Malaysia. E-mail: mustafaomar12@yahoo.co.nz

Abstract

The rapid global growth of the Internet and information technology has inspired many governments to transform their traditional services into electronic ones. Many governments are now developing, implementing and improving their strategies to transform government services using information and communication technologies (ICTs). E-Government, as it is known, has become a popular focus of government efforts in many developed countries and, more recently, in several developing countries. Further, e-government services have become a significant and active means for interaction among government, citizens and businesses. E-government comprises several dimensions, one of the main ones being e-government readiness. To put technology to effective use, a government must be "ready". E-government readiness helps a government to measure its stages of readiness, identify its gaps, and then redesign its government strategy. One of the aspects of e-government readiness is that of technological readiness, which plays an important role in implementing an effective and efficient e-government project. This paper explores the gaps in current knowledge relating to the technological aspects of e-government readiness through the conduct of a literature review. In particular, the review focuses on the models and frameworks that have been developed to assess e-government readiness.

Keywords: e-government readiness, technological aspects, assessment, developing countries

1. Introduction

Government services are provided through a variety of channels such as banks, post offices and so on. In these situations, technology plays a key role in the services in order to improve government infrastructure. E-government, or the use of technology in government services, has become a global issue having a significant influence upon all public sectors and economies; hence, there is a need for global cooperation as well as knowledge and experience exchange in the area. Currently, all countries are seeking to meet user expectations, but few of them have the knowledge required for these expectations. Encouraging citizens to participate in the public sector development has created an unprecedented recognition among governments of the whole public-sector need to deliver services in a different way (OECD, 2008). E-Government adoption requires a high level of satisfaction from both citizens and businesses. A high satisfaction level will succeed in increasing the e-government adoption rate. It will also ensure transparency in government operations and restore trust in governments (Othman & Razali, 2013). However, the adoption of e-government needs significant requirements to be met, such as that of technological readiness.

Having introduced the concept of e-government in Section 1, the remainder of this paper is structured as follows: Section 2 presents the definition of e-government; Section 3 discusses the barriers to and challenges for e-government adoption; Section 4 indicates the degree of e-government readiness; Section 5 discusses technology readiness aspects of e-government; Section 6 presents technological aspects relating to e-government readiness and the gap; while Section 7 presents the conclusion and future directions for our work.

2. E-Government Definition

In recent years, the revolution of Information Communication Technology (ICT) has changed the way in which governments around the world interact with their citizens, businesses, government agencies and employees (Joseph, 2014). In other words, in the current information age, the basic principles of government services changes markedly. All countries now seek to deliver their services through ICT facilitation. In this regard, and according to Joseph (2014), the phenomenon of electronic government (henceforth called e-government) is derived from the desire for efficient service delivery. E-government services have become a significant and active means for interaction among government, citizens and businesses. However, there is as yet no commonly accepted definition (Solli, 2010), despite many definitions existing in literature. Some of them focus only on using ICT (especially the Internet) to deliver high quality government services. Other definitions view e-government as a wide and all-encompassing effort for transforming government and governance (Grant & Chau, 2006). Following is a list of some of the e-government definitions:

•   E-government refers to "government systems of ICT to transform relations with citizens, the private sector and other government agencies in order to enhance empowerment of citizens, government efficiency and delivery of service, increased transparency and accountability" (Karokola, Kowalski, & Yngstrom, 2013).

•   The World Bank defined e-government as "government agencies' use of ICT, such as mobile computing and Internet, which have the capability to change relations with citizens, businesses, and other government arms" (Othman & Razali, 2013; Mollah, Islam, & Islam, 2012; Alghamdi, Goodwin, & Rampersad, 2011).

•   According to Mollah et al. (2012), and UNESCO defined e-government as "the public sector's use of ICT to improve delivery of information and service, encourage participation of citizens in the decision-making process and provide increased transparency and effectiveness of government".

•   The common definition of e-government means "use of ICTs to enhance government business related to the provision or enhancement of public services or the management of internal operations of government" (Novakouski & Lewis, 2012).

•   According to Almarabeh and AbuAli (2010) most researchers agreed that electronic government denotes government use of ICT to interact with various stake holders and to conduct business with government agencies by use of the Internet and other various electronic media.

•   E-government refers to the capability of various government agencies to provide government information and services at any time to citizens using electronic means speedily and properly, resulting in less costs and effort via a single Internet site (Odat, 2012).

•   Zhang and Hou (2011) defined e-government as "the information technology use (particularly the Internet) by government to enhance operations of government, enhance citizens' participation, and provide services".

All of the above definitions indicate that e-government refers to the information and services delivery by governments via the Internet or other digital media to various stakeholders. The definitions also refer to the technological capability for improving various sectors of government; thereby transforming the relations between governments and various stakeholders. Further, this results in an increase in their interaction in such a manner as to significantly improve the lives of their citizens.

Using ICT to facilitate interaction between government and other stakeholders has been manifested in four e-government types, specifically: Government-to-citizen (G2C); government-to-business (G2B); government-to-employee (G2E) and government-to-government (G2G) (Gant, 2008; Qaisar & Khan, 2010; Jouzbarkand et al., 2011; Odat, 2012; Fgee & Alkallas, 2013). Governments should seek to enhance these interactions so as to simplify and improve all democratic aspects of government related to citizens and businesses alike.

In summary, it can be perceived that the most important feature which has been shown in the definition of e-government is the use and implementation of ICT in government services. In general, e-government refers to the concept of performing activities related to government matters through the use of ICT. In this regard, it refers to the concept of very new and innovative approaches by which to solve a country's problem and issues. However, the e-government concept is something more than utilizing ICT and Internet merely for information access; rather, it is about transforming the fundamental relationship between government and the people.

3. E-Government Barriers and Challenges

Most electronic government projects in developing countries have failed due to the gap existing between e-government systems design and reality. Many developing countries simply implement e-government systems designs from developed countries without taking into consideration the differences in historical and cultural aspects, infrastructure, people, as well as economic and government structures (Mkude & Wimmer, 2013).

Designing and sustaining e-government systems requires rigorous consideration of political, economic, technological, social, and cultural issues in addition to the legal status of the country. Such prerequisites impose significant design challenges, which have to be faced by developing countries. Most developing countries suffer from problems relating to emerging economies, high levels of corruption, political instabilities, unclear legal structures and diverse social and cultural norms, all of which greatly contribute to the challenges involved in designing e-government projects. According to Mkude and Wimmer (2013), the challenges involved in designing e-government systems in developing countries could be summarized as, specifically: political and organizational leadership; formulation of strategy and policy; prioritization of initiatives; availability of financial resources; public-private partnership; ICT literacy levels of public sector employees; ICT literacy levels of end users; formulation of legal framework; formulation of security and privacy guidelines; cultural factors; infrastructure issues; integration of backend processes; and finally, awareness of opportunities.

In order to provide practical experiences and to facilitate successful e-government adoption in developing countries, governments should encourage more and varied publications relating to experiences illustrating frameworks, challenges faced, failures, risks and proposed remedies. Such collaboration will result in reduction of failures, encourage application of innovative solutions among governments and enhance empirical learning (Mkude & Wimmer, 2013).

The governments of developing countries confront significant constraints in building e-Government services. These constraints completely shape the difference in adoption levels and e-Government usage in developed countries (Gant, 2008). Almarabeh and AbuAli (2010) summarized the expected challenges that face e-government program implementation during development of successful e-government as follows:

- *Development of Infrastructure*: It is essential for those states using electronic government practices to have the necessary infrastructure to be able to benefit from modern technologies. However, many developing countries lack the required infrastructure for prompt implementation of e-government services.

- *Law and Public Policy*: Use of ICT by government could result in policy or legal barriers. Legislative assemblies must guarantee the update of laws related to e-documents and transactions.

- *Digital Divide*: This refers to the gap between individuals who have access to the Internet and those who lack access. Those who lack access do not have the opportunity to learn basic computer literacy skills and cannot access information that could produce improved economic prospects. Thus, they cannot take advantage of electronic government services.

- *E-Literacy Accessibility*: E-Literacy accessibility highlights the plight of marginalized groups who cannot benefit from ICT because they lack computer abilities and skills. E-government has the capability to balance access to government services or increase the difficulty for users.

- *Accessibility*: Governments must provide services to all people regardless of their physical capabilities (impediments posed by blindness, deafness, etc.). Therefore, it is essential that e-services be designed with proper interfaces.

- *Trust*: To ensure success, e-government must build trust with and between government agencies, as well as with business and citizens.

- *Privacy*: Governments gather huge amounts of data on their citizens every day; therefore, they have a duty of care to protect the personal information they hold. It is a vital and significant issue to protect the confidentiality of the personal information stored in the government database while at the same time facilitating and enhancing their use.

- *Security*: In spite of the costs involved, security should be considered in the design phase because its violation may damage the trust of people in e-government. Trust is a fundamentally imperative part of e-government. Lack of trust could push some individuals who may be cautious about the use of technology to hesitate or avoid using online services that request personal information.

- *Transparency*: It is difficult for citizens to see and understand how decisions of government are made. Transparency absence hinders people from effective sharing in government and from protesting against inequitable decisions. A transparency absence can also hide official favoritism and graft.

- *Interoperability*: Putting incongruent record formats online will not be streamlined nor will it decrease the workload forced on individuals and government authorities. Dependable e-government has an obligation for thorough redesign of legacy systems.

- *Records Management*: Good management of information can assist authorities to distinguish barriers to more effective government practices. A framework for information management is important by which to understand available data and to help policy makers conclude useful analysis rapidly enough to be able to respond to social and financial developments.

• *Permanent availability and Preservation*: Governments consider that the historic documentation significance of ICT ensures quick and cheap data dissemination, in addition to ensuring compact and proper storage.

• *Education and Marketing*: E-services of government can be helpful if people have knowledge about them; thus, there is a need for education and awareness programs.

• *Public/Private Competition/Collaboration*: An important inquiry relates to the question of where government controls end and when the private sector assumes control in e-government endeavors.

• *Workforce Issues*: Human resources must be organized and trained in e-government objectives. A motivated and well-trained work force is basic to achievement of e-government objectives.

• *Cost Structures*: Governments should attempt to invest in suitable programs that can produce savings in spite of difficulties encountered in planning and budgeting in a changing environment.

• *Benchmarking*: Governments must conduct an orderly assessment of development and efficacy of their investments in e-government in order to determine if expressed objectives and targets are being met on schedule.

Based on these challenges, Odat (2012) developed a general framework concerning challenges and opportunities that confront e-government project implementation in developing countries. This is shown in Figure 1 following.

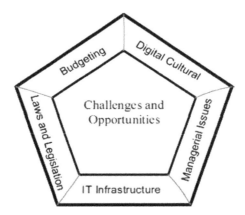

Figure 1. Challenges and Opportunities Framework (Odat, 2012)

The details concerning the challenges and opportunities framework are as follows:

• *IT Infrastructure*

This concerns a lack of technological skills among leaders, employees and citizens, as well as a paucity of hardware and software and knowledge as to their update or maintenance. In addition, there is a lack of communication systems, as well as a lack of digital information. This includes a scarcity of databases with different formats and capacity to archive various document types.

• *Managerial Issues*

Top management and administration should be in support of e-government programs. They also should have the competency to handle issues such as: workforce turnover and resistance to change; increased transparency in addition to collaboration and coordination among the e-government parties.

• *Digital Cultural*

This includes issues such as: digital divide; e-literacy; lack of awareness; trust; security and privacy.

• *Laws and Legislation*

Legislative assemblies must be able to guarantee that laws are upgraded to perceive e-documents and transactions. Although there has been a rapid advance in the development of systems and applications, there is at the same time an absence of legislations and laws that back the electronic systems.

• *Budgeting*

Any e-government project is a mega project that needs budgeting at all stages. However, developing countries are faced with problems such as: absence of funds; lack of availability of resources management; as well as widespread corruption and misuse of public money.

The barriers and challenges to e-government in developing countries are numerous and difficult and they relate to all organizational, technological, economic, social and legal aspects. It is not easy to overcome the effect of all these obstacles since great efforts are needed from both governments and citizens. ICT is considered as being a major challenge to the implementation of e-government in developing countries, but it offers significant opportunities for developing e-government practices. These remain limited because its potential benefits are not exploited effectively and efficiently in most of these countries. The e-government is the economic basis for organizational and political reformation and countries which have successfully developed e-government foundations have achieved excellent development outcomes.

The main objective of this part of the literature review was to identify barriers and challenges to e-government implementation. As mentioned above, there are some barriers and challenges to e-government readiness which have been reviewed and explained in this part of the study. A further and comprehensive review of the literature indicates that there are still more barriers and challenges existing than those mentioned above. There are many barriers that affect the success of e-government readiness. The researcher has summarized these in Table 1 follow

Table 1. Comparison between E-government Barriers and Challenges

Barriers and Challenges of E-government \ Author/s	Conklin (2007)	Abdelkader (2015)	Dada (2006)	Alshehri & Drew (2010)	Ahmed et al. (2013)	AlSuwaidi & Rajan (2013)	Ebrahim & Irani (2005)	Ashaye & Irani (2014)	Lam (2005)	Almarabeh, & AbuAli (2010)	Mouzakitis & Askounis (2010)	Ndou (2004)	Brown & Thompson (2011)	AlNuaimi et al. (2011)	Wang & Hou (2010)	Jouzbarkand et al. (2011)	Ziaie (2013)	Monyepao and Weeks (2012)	Total
Infrastructure					√	√	√			√			√	√	√	√		√	9
Privacy and security risk barriers		√		√		√	√	√		√				√	√	√			9
Legislative Barriers		√				√		√	√				√	√					6
Administrative Barriers	√	√		√		√		√	√	√						√	√		9
Technological Barriers	√	√		√	√		√	√	√	√						√	√	√	11
Cultural Barriers		√		√	√					√									4
Resistance		√														√			2
Hard-soft gap			√																1
Private-public gap			√							√									2
Country-context			√																1
Collaboration				√			√			√			√						4
Lack of Qualified people				√		√		√				√		√					5
Personnel and Training				√		√		√		√									4
Social (Digital Divide)				√	√					√			√	√	√		√		7

Author/s — Barriers and Challenges of E-government	Conklin (2007)	Abdelkader (2015)	Dada (2006)	Alshehri & Drew (2010)	Ahmed et al. (2013)	AlSuwaidi & Rajan (2013)	Ebrahim & Irani (2005)	Ashaye & Irani (2014)	Lam (2005)	Almarabeh, & AbuAli (2010)	Mouzakitis & Askounis (2010)	Ndou (2004)	Brown & Thompson (2011)	AlNuaimi et al. (2011)	Wang & Hou (2010)	Jouzbarkand et al. (2011)	Ziaie (2013)	Monyepao and Weeks (2012)	Total
Financial				√		√	√									√		√	5
Organizational					√	√		√	√					√					5
Skills							√			√	√								3
Lack of awareness														√					1
Lack of Information	√										√						√		2

Table 1 highlights the important fact that most of the barriers and challenges of e-government adoption can be related to technology factors. These include: infrastructure; security; technological/ technical issues; hard/soft gap; digital divide; internet use; and skills related to technology. Hence, it can be concluded that technology is one of the components that needs to be given more attention in this paper.

4. E-Government Readiness

In this part of the review, it is time to pay attention to the issue of e-government readiness. As an introduction to the topic, it can be said that government services are provided through a variety of channels including post offices, radio transmission and radar bands, as well as via other public services. Due to the recent advances in technology, most of the government organizations have implemented this technology in their public services. This type of service will henceforth be known as e-government services. In this regard, e-government has several dimensions. One of the main dimensions is that of e-government readiness. To put technology to effective use, a government must be "ready". This is the simple definition of e-government readiness. Joseph (2014) indicates that e-government readiness is the ability of the government to use technology so as to shift traditional services into new services.

A review of literature showed that e-government is vitally important to a country since e-government readiness can help a government to measure its stages of readiness, identify its gaps, and then redesign its government strategy respectively (Joseph, 2014). E-government readiness is not only related to government bodies but is also significant to society, frameworks of government institutions, human resources, interdepartmental relationships, national infrastructure, education as well as any issues that are related to e-government (Ahmed & Hussein, 2006).

According to Joseph (2014); Mkude & Wimmer (2013); Almarabeh & Abuali (2010), the primary reason for e-government failure is a lack of assessment of readiness for e-government, where this lack brings challenges and does not guarantee successful implementation of e-government (Joseph, 2014; Mkude & Wimmer, 2013). The comparison in Table 1 shows that the majority of barriers and challenges of e-government relate to technology. This result attracted our attention and motivated us to learn more about the technological aspects of e-government readiness.

5. Technology Readiness of E-Government

One of the challenges confronting governments that need to be considered is the willingness of people to use technology. Parasuraman (2000) in his research used the term technology readiness". He defined technology readiness as being "people's propensity to embrace and use new technologies for accomplishing goals in home life and at work" (Parasuraman, 2000). From a different point of view, readiness of e-government can be seen as the preparedness of a country to develop and adopt e-government in terms of its technology infrastructure, development of human resources, as well as telecommunication infrastructure. It also denotes the willingness of a government to use advanced technology to improve the lives of its citizens (Mundy & Musa, 2010). Although studies have been conducted on the significance of technology readiness in organizations, they lack robust foundations for empirical analysis (Choucri et al., 2003; Alghamdi et al., 2011). Alghamdi et al. (2011) indicated that there is deficient research connecting technology readiness and implementation of e-government in a country. They recommended that an organizational strategy of ICT and a national program relating to e-government ought to be considered as vital parts of the readiness assessment criteria.

Intake of existing technology and skipping over stages of local technological development is very difficult. The actual technology in use is often limited due to issues such as: the nature of technology; the availability of known technology; and how to make the correct selection from among the available technologies. Less-developed countries never acquire whole technical knowledge. Moreover, technical assistance fails to include technology's implicit steps. Acquiring and learning technology does not depend on buying, producing, selling, and using this technology, but needs an effective search to assess the existing procedures for possible changes (Hamed, 2009).

Regrettably, in spite of the availability of resources and technologies, developing countries face many challenges in developing and implementing e-government projects (Othman & Razali, 2013). The use of technology is the key to a successful e-government; however, the Internet usage in many developing countries is in its initial stage, which impedes e-government implementation (Kayani et al., 2011).

Developing countries should consider that building telecommunications infrastructure is costly and, in many cases, will need foreign investment in order to develop their infrastructure. Often, developing countries do not have suitable infrastructure for supporting the development of IT. Furthermore, they do not have the ability to invest in the IT field due to poor financial resources and lack of IT knowledge (Hamed, 2009). Information and communication technology can speed the country's development if it is adopted and adapted properly; otherwise, it can frustrate developmental efforts considerably and waste time and scarce resources. A systematic approach of assessing e-readiness forms a correct principle by which to identify and prioritize needs such as technology through proper planning & organization. Maximizing the benefits of technology needs government support (Colwell & Hewitt, 2015).

6. Technological Aspects of E-Government Readiness and the Gap

Nowadays, the issue of e-government has become a potential imperative at both a national and an international level for the majority of governments. In this situation, according to Azab et al. (2009), e-government is predicated on leveraging the power of technology to deliver services provided by governments. However, e-government is still in an early stage and has not achieved many of the expected outcomes such as cost savings and downsizing, amongst other issues (Azab et al., 2009). Moreover, according to UNDESA (2003) reports, the e-government projects failure rate reached somewhere between 60-80%. Due to the important role of technology, it is necessary to investigate the technological factors influencing e-government readiness especially in the developing countries. In order to find the gap of the study, a comprehensive review of literature was undertaken. It has been found that some technology-related factors have been studied from previous researches. However, there was no comprehensive study which could fulfill all components and factors.

Lau (2003) found that the digital divide can be one of the main factors which influence technological readiness of governments, especially in developing countries. Digital divide means that people who do not have access to the Internet will be unable to benefit from e-government services. In the developing countries, a growing number of individuals are trying to obtain access to the Internet, but there are still large numbers of other people who do not have any internet connection. In this regard, governments in developing countries are trying to improve services to citizens through other channels, since the inability to provide e-government services to all citizens can hold back e-government projects. Lau (2003) also found that security can be identified as another component of technological readiness. It is clear that the use of e-government services without a guarantee of privacy and security is not possible. This is particularly so nowadays due to advances in all fields of human life. In another study, (Belanger & Carter, 2006) explored the potential effects of the digital divide on e-government by surveying a diverse group of citizens to identify the demographic characteristics that impact upon use of e-government services.

In a further study, Hazlett and Hill (2003) examined the manner in which e-government is being used in the delivery and improvement of services in order to determine actual and potential problems faced by the UK government. Through the study, they found that issues of ICT infrastructure, hardware and software are the main factors of technological readiness which affect e-government services.

Ahmed and Hussein (2006) present a framework model for E-Government Readiness Assessment. They state that there are six necessary key factors to be assessed before launching the e-government program to guarantee the right implementation in the right direction and these are: organizational readiness; governance and leadership readiness; customer readiness; competency readiness; technology readiness and legal readiness. According to them, technology readiness includes all necessary technologies to enable the e-government initiative. These comprise applications such as hardware, software, communication and networks infrastructure and Internet penetration respectively.

Azab et al. (2009) developed an e-government appraisal framework encompassing several components such as people, technology, processes, and strategic planning. Technology in this framework comprises information system structure, hardware, as well as technical support and development.

Karunasena et al. (2011) found that the effectiveness of government programs are related to some e-government readiness factors such as financial and technological readiness. From the perspective of technological readiness, ICT infrastructure and security have been identified as key factors which influence e-government. They are working for the improvement of government and public service deliveries. Availability of communication technologies is another main technological factor affecting e-government readiness.

A study by Bakry (2004) introduced the STOPE model in order to provide a base for the development of an international framework related to e-government readiness. The model identified five dimensions (strategy, technology, organization, people and environment). As indicated, one of the components of the model is technology. From the technology perspective, ICT facilities, infrastructure, and support have been identified as e-government readiness factors. Bakry (2004) highlighted that the STOPE model can be useful in decision-making at different stages. Moreover, countries need to consider all dimensions if they are willing to become developed.

A further study Ebrahim and Irani (2005), investigated e-government readiness from a technological perspective. They found five dimensions needed for e-government success. Ebrahim & Irani (2005) believe that benefits associated with e-government should be considered as factors that influence the implementation process. ICT infrastructure, security, privacy and IT skills are the factors that are related to and associated with e-government readiness from a technological perspective. AlSuwaidi & Rajan (2013) found that technical support, ICT infrastructure and security are the key factors of an e-government implementation.

A study by Kurdi and Randles (2011) examined the technological factors of e-government readiness including the following factors: infrastructure of ICT; infrastructure of network; security infrastructure for data exchange; as well as infrastructure of information system (system, information, and quality of services). In addition, Zaied, Khairalla, & Al Rashid (2007) explored the e-readiness assessment models so as to assess the readiness of e-government in the State of Kuwait. Three main variables (human skills, infrastructure and connectivity) have been used.

Alghamdi et al. (2011) proposed an e-government framework for assessing the ICT readiness of government agencies in public sector organizations in developing countries. The proposed e-government framework comprises seven dimensions of ICT readiness assessment for government organizations including: e-government organizational ICT strategy; user access; e-government program; ICT architecture; business process and information systems; ICT infrastructure; and human resources. The dimension of ICT infrastructure includes, namely: hardware; software; connectivity; security; and operations.

The factors that previous researchers have focused on are summarized in Table 2. The table illustrates the technology factors that have been found to be influential (significant) on e-government readiness by previous scholars. Moreover, the factors investigated in the present study are presented in the last column.

Table 2. Comparison between Factors of Technology Readiness of E-government

Technology Factors of E-government Readiness \ Author/s	Zaid et al. (2007)	Azab et al. (2009)	Karunasena et al. (2011)	Alghamdi et al. (2011)	Lau (2003)	Al-Omari & Al-Omari (2006)	Hazlett and Hill (2003)	Kurdi and Randles(2011)	Ebrahim & Irani (2005)	Bakry (2004)	Total
Operations				√							1
Application						√					1
Skills									√		1
Internet						√					1
Infrastructure of Information system								√			1
Digital Divide				√							1
Connectivity	√			√							2
Technical support		√								√	2
Communication		√				√		√			3
Software			√			√	√				3
Network Infrastructure			√			√		√			3
Hardware		√		√		√	√				4
Security			√	√	√			√	√		5
ICT Infrastructure	√		√				√	√	√	√	6

It can be observed from Table 2 that there are several technology factors that influence the overall readiness of adopting and implementing e-government. The comparison of these technology factors indicate that factors such as ICT infrastructure, security, hardware, software, network infrastructure and communication are commonly emphasized in all of the studies examined. On the other hand, a few studies have placed an emphasis on operations, application, skills, internet, digital divide, technical support and connectivity. Thus, it can be concluded from the results in Table 2 that readiness of technology factors was not considered in every framework; there are certain factors missing from some studies, but reported in other studies. For example, communication factors, network infrastructure factors and software factors have been identified by three studies as being necessary factors for technology readiness to have a successful implementation of e-government; while these factors are missing from the seven other studies. In addition, the security factor is mentioned by five studies as being a necessary factor of e-government readiness, while this factor is missing from five other studies. Further, digital divide, operations, application, skills, internet and infrastructure of information system are other factors that are mentioned by one study in which they have been identified as technological components of e-government readiness; while these factors are missing from the other nine studies. Hardware is another factor that was mentioned by four studies as being an important factor for e-government implementation, while this factor is missing from six other studies. Moreover, connectivity and technical support are other factors mentioned by two studies as being necessary factors for assessing the readiness of e-government, while these two factors are missing from the remaining eight studies. Finally, the ICT infrastructure factor was mentioned by six studies as being a main component of technological factors related to e-government readiness; while this factor is missing from the other four studies. Thus, the comparison made between the eleven studies in Table 2 shows that there is a lack of identification of the necessary factors to assess technology readiness for e-government implementation.

7. Conclusion

The term e-government refers to the utilization of information and communication technology (ICT) by government agencies in order to provide services to citizens. The e-government services enhance government effectiveness and efficiency and change its relationship with the public. E-government readiness studies provide statistics that define the legal, financial, physical, social and technological attributes of infrastructure required by developing countries in order to become a fully networked society. Therefore, it is important to assess e-government readiness, including the technological aspects of readiness, in order for the implementation and adoption of e-government to be successful. The goal of this paper is to explore the gaps in knowledge regarding the technological aspects of e-government readiness. This paper has presented a review of the studies for assessing e-government implementation. The review showed that there is a lack of investigation and agreement about the factors that shape the technological aspects of e-government readiness; hence, a clear gap is identified as existing in the current knowledge on the technological aspects of e-government readiness. This work indicates a useful direction which can be taken in future research to investigate the factors related to the technological aspects of e-government readiness.

Hence, future research will be conducted in order to generate a list of the factors shaping the technological aspects of e-government readiness. It is anticipated that this list will be able to assist governments in developing countries to identify and understand the technological aspects that should be considered when assessing the readiness to adopt an e-government project. In addition, the list of technological readiness factors can be used by designers and developers as a guideline for identifying the necessary technological requirements for e-government implementation.

Acknowledgements

Author would like to thank his family members for their support in the completion of this paper. He also would like to thank the reviewers and editor for their helpful comments.

References

Abdelkader, A. (2015). A Manifest of Barriers to Successful E-Government: Cases from the Egyptian Programme. *International Journal of Business and Social Science, 6*(1).

Ahmed, A. M., Mehdi, Q. H., Moreton, R., & Elmaghraby, A. (2013). *E-government services challenges and opportunities for developing countries: The case of Libya.* Paper presented at the Second International Conference on Informatics and Applications (ICIA), 133-137. IEEE. http://dx.doi.org/10.1109/ICoIA.2013.6650243

Aisuwaidi, M., & Rajan, A. (2013). *E-Government Failure and Success Factors Rank Model an Extension of Heeks Factor Model.* Paper presented at the International Conference on Current Trends in Information Technology (CTIT), 161-165. IEEE. http://dx.doi.org/10.1109/CTIT.2013.6749495

Ahmed, A. O., & Hussein, A. O. (2006). E-government readiness assessment model. *Journal of Computer Science, 2*(11), 841-845. Retrieved from http://thescipub.com/PDF/jcssp.2006.841.845.pdf

Alghamdi, I. A., Goodwin, R., & Rampersad, G. (2011). *A suggested e-government framework for assessing organizational e-readiness in developing countries.* In International Conference on Informatics Engineering and Information Science. Springer Berlin Heidelberg. http://dx.doi.org/10.1007/978-3-642-25453-6_41

Almarabeh, T., & AbuAli, A. (2010). A general framework for e-government: definition maturity challenges, opportunities, and success. *European Journal of Scientific Research, 39*(1), 29-42.

AlNuaimi, M., Shaalan, K., Alnuaimi, M., & Alnuaimi, K. (2011). *Barriers to Electronic Government Citizens' Adoption: A case of Municipal Sector in the Emirate of Abu Dhabi.* Paper presented at the Developments in E-systems Engineering (DeSE), 398-403. IEEE. http://dx.doi.org/10.1109/DeSE.2011.65

Alshehri, M., & Drew, S. (2010). E-government Principles: Implementation, Advantages and Challenges. *International Journal of Electronic Business, 9*(3), 255-270.

Ashaye, O., & Irani, Z. (2014). E-government Implementation Benefits, Risks and Barriers in Developing Countries: Evidence from Nigeria. *International Journal of Information Technology & Computer Science (IJITCS),* 92-105.

Azab, N. A., Kamel, S., & Dafoulas, G. (2009). A suggested framework for assessing electronic government readiness in Egypt. *Electronic Journal of E-Government, 7*(1), 11-28.

Bakry, S. H. (2004). Development of e‑government: a STOPE view. *International Journal of Network Management, 14*(5), 339-350. http://dx.doi.org/10.1002/nem.529

Belanger, F., & Carter, L. (2006). *The Effects of the Digital Divide on E-Government: An Emperical Evaluation.* Paper presented at Proceedings of the 39th Annual Hawaii International Conference on System Sciences (HICSS'06). IEEE. http://dx.doi.org/10.1109/HICSS.2006.464

Brown, D. H., & Thompson, S. (2011). Priorities, Policies and Practice of E-government in A developing Country Context: ICT Infrastructure and Diffusion in Jamaica. *European Journal of Information Systems,*

20, 329-342. http://dx.doi.org/10.1057/ejis.2011.3

Choucri, N., Maugis, V., Madnick, S., Siegel, M., Gillet, S., Zhu, H., ... Haghseta, F. (2003). *Global e-Readiness–for What? Center for eBusiness at MIT.* Retrieved from http://web.mit.edu/polisci/nchoucri/publications/articles/G-7_Choucri_Global_eReadiness_for_What.pdf

Colwell, R., & Hewitt, M. (2015). *Teaching of instrumental music.* Routledge.

Conklin, A. (2007). *Barriers to Adoption of E-Government.* Paper presented at the 40th Hawaii International Conference on Systems Sciences, 1-8. IEEE. http://dx.doi.org/10.1109/HICSS.2007.102

Dada, D. (2006). The Failure of E-government in Developing Countries: A Literature Review. *The Electronic Journal on Information Systems in Developing Countries, 26*(1), 1-10.

Ebrahim, Z., & Irani, Z. (2005). E-government Adoption: Architecture and Barriers. *Business Process Management Journal, 11*(5), 589-611.

Fgee, E. B., & Alkallas, M. I. (2013). *E-government in Libya: Constraints, potentials and implementation.* Paper presented at International Conference on Computer Applications Technology (ICCAT), 1-7. IEEE. http://dx.doi.org/10.1109/ICCAT.2013.6521992

Gant, J. P. (2008). *Electronic government for developing countries.* International Telecommunication Union (ITU), Geneva.

Grant, G., & Chau, D. (2006). Developing A generic Framework for E-government. *Advanced Topics in Global Information Management, 5*, 72-101. http://dx.doi.org/10.4018/jgim.2005010101

Hamed, A. (2009). *E-commerce and Economic Development in Libya.* PhD thesis, University of Wales.

Hazlett, S. A., & Hill, F. (2003). E-government: the Realities of Using IT to Transform the Public Sector. *Managing Service Quality: An International Journal, 13*(6), 445-452. http://dx.doi.org/10.1108/09604520310506504

Joseph, S. (2014). *Development and Validation of A framework for E-government Readiness Measurement.* Durban University of Technology, Durban, South Africa.

Jouzbarkand, M., Khodadadi, M., & Keyvani, F. S. (2011). *Conceptual approach to e-government, targets and barriers facing its.* Paper presented at the 5th International Conference on Application of Information and Communication Technologies (AICT), 1-5. IEEE. http://dx.doi.org/10.1109/ICAICT.2011.6110903

Karokola, G., Kowalski, S., & Yngstrom, L. (2013). *Evaluating a Framework for Securing E-Government Services-A Case of Tanzania.* Paper presented at the 46th Hawaii International Conference on System Sciences (HICSS), 1792-1801. IEEE. http://dx.doi.org/10.1109/HICSS.2013.208

Karunasena, K., Deng, H., & Singh, M. (2011). Measuring the public value of e-government: a case study from Sri Lanka. *Transforming Government: People, Process and Policy, 5*(1), 81-99. http://dx.doi.org/10.1108/17506161111114671

Kayani, M. B., Ul Haq, M. E., Iqbal, M., & Humayun, H. (2011). *Assessing the e-Government Capabilities for Obstacle Identification within Pakistan.* Paper presented at the International Conference on Information Society (i-Society), 171-175. IEEE.

Kurdi, R., & Randles, M. (2011). *An Investigation into E-government Information Systems: Analysis and Review of the Literature.* Paper presented at Proceedings of the 13th Annual PostGraduate Symposium on The Convergence of Telecommunications, Networking and Broadcasting.

Lam, W. (2005). Barriers to E-government Integration. *Journal of Enterprise Information Management, 18*(5), 511-530. http://dx.doi.org/10.1108/17410390510623981

Lau, E. (2003). *Challenges for E-government Development.* Paper presented at the 5th Global Forum on Reinventing Government, 1-18. Mexico City.

Mkude, C. G., & Wimmer, M. A. (2013). *Strategic Framework for Designing E-Government in Developing Countries.* Paper presented at International Conference on Electronic Government, 148-162. Springer. http://dx.doi.org/10.1007/978-3-642-40358-3_13

Mollah, M. B., Islam, K. R., & Islam, S. S. (2012). *E-police system for improved e-government services of developing countries.* Paper presented at 25th IEEE Canadian Conference on Electrical & Computer Engineering (CCECE). IEEE. http://dx.doi.org/10.1109/CCECE.2012.6335057

Monyepao, M. D., & Weeks, R. V. (2012). *Case study: Assessing and Evaluating the Readiness of the ICT Infrastructure to Provide E-government Services at A local Government Level in South Africa.* Paper presented in the Proceedings of PICMET '12: Technology Management for Emerging Technologies (PICMET). 2778 - 2784. IEEE.

Mouzakitis, S., & Askounis, D. (2010). A knowledge-based Framework for Measuring Organizational Readiness for The Adoption of B2B Integration Systems. *Information Systems Management, 27*(3), 253-266. http://dx.doi.org/10.1080/10580530.2010.493842

Mundy, D., & Musa, B. (2010). Towards A framework for E-government Development in Nigeria. *Electronic Journal of E-Government, 8*(2), 148-161.

Ndou, V. (2004). E-government for Developing Countries: Opportunities and Challenges. *The Electronic Journal of Information Systems in Developing Countries, 18.*

Novakouski, M., & Lewis, G. A. (2012). *Interoperability in the e-Government Context.* Dtic Document. Carnegie-Mellon Univ Pittsburgh Pa Software Engineering Inst.

Odat, A. M. (2012). *E-Government in developing countries: Framework of challenges and opportunities.* Paper presented at International Conference for the Internet Technology And Secured Transactions, 578-582. IEEE.

OECD. (2008). *Future of E-government-Agenda 2020.* OECD E-Leaders Conference 2008.

Othman, M., & Razali, R. (2013). *Key contributing factors towards successful Electronic Government systems interoperability.* Paper presented at International Conference on Research and Innovation in Information Systems (ICRIIS), 302-307. IEEE. http://dx.doi.org/10.1109/ICRIIS.2013.6716726

Parasuraman, A. (2000). Technology Readiness Index (TRI) a multiple-item scale to measure readiness to embrace new technologies. *Journal of service research, 2*(4), 307-320. http://dx.doi.org/10.1177/109467050024001

Qaisar, N., & Khan, H. G. A. (2010). E-Government challenges in public sector: A case study of Pakistan. *International Journal of Computer Science Issues (IJCSI), 7*(5), 310-317.

Solli, S. H. (2010). *Analytical framework for e-government interoperability.* Paper presented at the eChallenges e-2010 Conference, 1-9. IEEE.

UNDESA. (2003). *E-government at the Crossroads.* World Public Sector Report 2003. United Nations Department of Economic and Social Affairs. United Nations, New York.

Wang, H., & Hou, J. (2010). *Perspectives, Skills and Challenges for Developing A successful E-government.* Paper presented at International Conference on Advanced Management Science (ICAMS), 3, 242-245. IEEE. http://dx.doi.org/10.1109/ICAMS.2010.5553248

Zaied, A. N. H., Khairalla, F. A., & Al Rashid, W. (2007). Assessing e-readiness in the Arab countries: Perceptions towards ICT environment in public organisations in the State of Kuwait. *Electronic Journal of E-government, 5*(1), 77-86.

Zhang, N., & Hou, X. (2011). *Government Process Management under electronic government and its application.* Paper presented at International Conference on E-Business and E-Government (ICEE), 1-4. IEEE. http://dx.doi.org/10.1109/ICEBEG.2011.5881951

Ziaie, P. (2013). *Challenges and issues of ICT Industry in Developing Countries Based on A case Study of the Barriers and the Potential Solutions for ICT Deployment in Iran.* Paper presented at the International Conference on Computer Applications Technology (ICCAT), 1-6. IEEE. http://dx.doi.org/10.1109/ICCAT.2013.6521973

19

Simulating the Performance Characteristic of Passband Modulation Techniques in MATLAB Environment

Saed Thuneibat[1], Abdallah Ijjeh[1], Huthaifa Al_Issa[1] & Mousa Ababneh[2]

[1] Department of Electrical Engineering, Al-Balqa Applied University, Jordan

[2] Department of Finance and Administrative Sciences, Al-Balqa Applied University, Jordan

Correspondence: Saed Thuneibat, Department of Electrical Engineering, Al-Balqa Applied University, Jordan. E-mail: Thuneibat@hotmail.com

Abstract

Now days, digital communication systems become complex and sophisticated. Not all vendors, if any, can understand the system and components of system that represent different modulation techniques, line and block coding, multiplexing and multiple access.

They need the conclusion about which of modulation techniques is the suitable for transmission and in the same time can save the power and bandwidth.

Engineers can study and analyze the modulation techniques and then compare between them to give such conclusion using modeling and simulation.

MATLAB is a high level mathematical language for technical computing.

In this paper we use MATLAB environment as simulation software to give on display a clear result that used to compare between two digital Passband modulation techniques BPSK and QPSK, and pinpoint the performance of the two techniques over selected parameters.

Keywords: simulation, modulation, performance parameters, MATLAB

1. Introduction

Nowadays, digital modulation techniques are the most widely used in communication systems. We need to achieve higher data rates in limited bandwidth of spectrum to improve the performance of transmission.

A great deal of interest for a digital Passband digital transmission system that is bandwidth efficient with low signaling rate and high data rate and provide low Bit Error Rate (BER) at a relatively low Signal to Noise Ratio (SNR). Various digital modulation schemes are well described in different literatures but cannot fulfill actual requirement in different kind of varying environment until studded and analyzed.

Recently, a large number of research papers which study the modulation techniques were published. In (Masud, 2010), authors have investigated the performance analysis of M-ary modulation techniques when the digital communication system is subjected to Additive White Gaussian Noise (AWGN) and multipath Rayleigh fading in the channel. The study has been performed by using MATLAB program for the simulation and evaluation of BER and SNR for W-CDMA system models. It shows that the analysis of quadrature phases shift key and 16-ary quadrature amplitude modulations which are being used in wideband CDMA system, Therefore, the system could go for more suitable modulation technique to satisfy the channel quality, thus can deliver the optimum data rate to mobile user.

The paper (Samson, 2013) analyzed the performance of different passband modulation techniques in AWGN channel and multipath fading channel. This study examined the inherent attributes of the digital modulation to overcome the channel impairments and was carried out to understand the contributions of channel characteristics to effective wireless communication and made comparison between the two channels. The BER for simulated modeled channels agreed with the theoretical results. It was found that the performance of 64-QAM is better compared to other passband modulation schemes in AWGN Channel. It was also observed that the BER is higher in frequency selective channel as compared to the AWGN channel and was also observed that multipath fading channel characteristic limits the data rate in wireless communication.

Authors in (Hemant, 2014) have presented the impact of various modulation parameters towards the modulation and demodulation processes. In addition, it has been proven that MATLAB simulation environment can play an important role towards the understanding of subject matter.

In (Rashmi, 2011), a general theoretical approach in studding various M-ary modulation schemes using MATLAB taking the BER as the measure of performance when the system is affected by AWGN and multipath Rayleigh fading channel is developed. Based on these performances a desirable modulation scheme is simulated that provides low BER at low received SNR, performs well in multipath and fading conditions, occupies a minimum of bandwidth and is easy and cost effective to implement in modern communication system.

In (Virendrakumar, 2014), (Tharakanatha, 2013), (Xiaolong, 2008), authors are implementing various binary and M-ary modulation schemes in MATLAB by using different SIMULINK tool boxes.

An efficient and effective methodology for teaching digital and analog modulation types to undergraduate students enrolled in an Information Technology program which does not require a strong foundation in mathematics as in the case of engineering program is provided in (Boulmalf, 2010). The implemented approach utilizes MATLAB program, SIMULINK, and Communication Blockset to simulate digital modulation techniques avoiding the derivation of mathematics formulations and without complex coding.

Research paper contains introduction to the subject with literature review. Section 2 introduces MATLAB software and environment. 3^d section presents the simulation of modulation and demodulation process in BPSK and QPSK using MATLAB environment. Sections 4-7 devoted for the performance parameters, data rate, bit error rate, capacity, PSD respectively. Finally, conclusion and literature references are included.

2. MATLAB Software and Environment

MATLAB is a mathematical computing environment with 4th generation programming language and interactive environment that enables engineers to perform intensive calculations based tasks very simply. Developed by Math works (http://www.mathworks.com), MATLAB allows matrix manipulation, plotting of functions and data in tables and curves, implementation of algorithms, creation of user interfaces, and interfacing with programs in other languages. MATLAB has been widely adopted in the academic community, industry and research centers. It was originally written to provide easy access to LINPACK and EISPACK software packages (Gilat, 2004), (www.mathworks.com/products/simulink), (Quarteroni, 2006), (Ferreira, 2009), (Leon, (2001). The MATLAB software provides the researchers with a large collection of toolboxes and modules for a variety of applications in many fields of interest.

Figure 1 demonstrates the basic MATLAB work environment and commands.

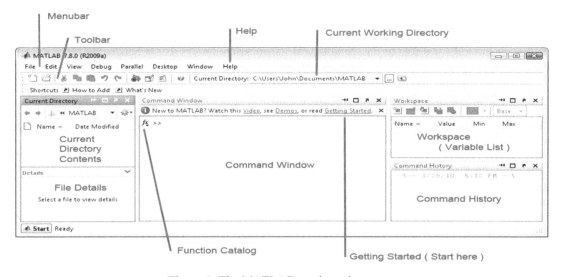

Figure 1. The MATLAB work environment

3. Simulation of Modulation and Demodulation

Here, to demonstrate the simulation using MATLAB environment we compare two will-known and basic passband modulation techniques BPSK and QPSK. These methods are still used in different modern communication systems.

3.1 BPSK Technology

BPSK modulation is a basic technique used in various wireless standards such as CDMA, Imax (16d, 16e), WLAN 11a, 11b, 11g, 11n, Satellite, DVB and cable modem. BPSK considered to be more robust among all the modulation schemes due to the 180° difference between two constellation points. Hence it can with stand severe amount of channel conditions or channel fading. It is used in OFDM and OFDMA to modulate the pilot subcarriers used for channel control.

Different channels are used for specific data transmission in cellular systems. The channels used to transmit system related information which are very essential are modulated using BPSK modulation.

BPSK is less susceptible to error than ASK, also is more efficient to use of bandwidth (higher data rate is possible). BPSK modulation and demodulation code was written in MATLAB environment. The result of running this program is shown in figure 2.

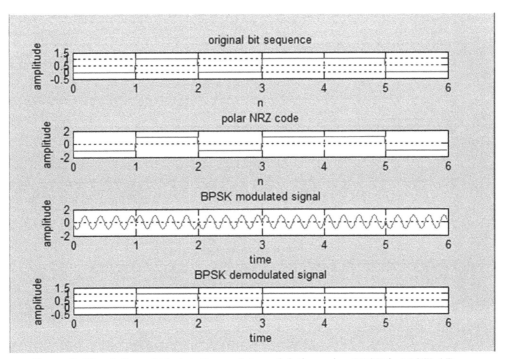

Figure 2. Simulation of Modulation and demodulation using BPSK in MATLAB

3.2 QPSK Technology

QPSK used widely in applications including CDMA cellular phone, wireless local loop, Iridium (a voice/data satellite system) and DVB-S (Digital Video Broadcasting — Satellite). QPSK is used for satellite transmission of MPEG-2 video also used in video conferencing.

With four phases, QPSK can encode two bit per symbol, to minimize the required bandwidth, twice the rate of BPSK in the same bandwidth. This may be used either to double the data rate compared to a BPSK system while the maintaining the bandwidth of the signal or to maintain the data rate of BPSK but half bandwidth needed.

As with BPSK, there are phase ambiguity problems at the receiver and differentially encoded QPSK is more normally used in practice. Another advantage of QPSK is the use of differential DQPSK. Here the phase shift is not relative to a reference phase of a signal but relative to the phase of previous two bit. The receiver does not need the reference signal but only compares two signals to reconstruct the original data.

The phase shift can always be relative to reference signal. If this scheme used, phase shift of 0 means that the signal is in phase with reference signal. QPSK signal will then exhibit a phase shift of $45°$ for the data 11, $135°$ for 10, $225°$ for 00 and 315^0 for 01, with all phase shifts being relative of the reference signal.

Inter channel interference (ICI) is significantly large in QPSK. To avoid ICI QPSK requires filtering which can change amplitude and phase of QPSK waveform. QPSK requires a round 8 times its bandwidth to transmit the same power.

The disadvantage of QPSK relative to BPSK is that it is more sensitive to phase variation. Transmitter and receiver have to be synchronized very often, example by using special synchronization patterns before user data arrives or via pilot frequency as reference.

QPSK modulation and demodulation code was written in MATLAB environment. The result of running this program is shown in figure 3.

We enter [0 0 0 1 1 1 0] as an original sequence to the simulation program and taking in to account the Gray code we got the result as shown in figure 3.

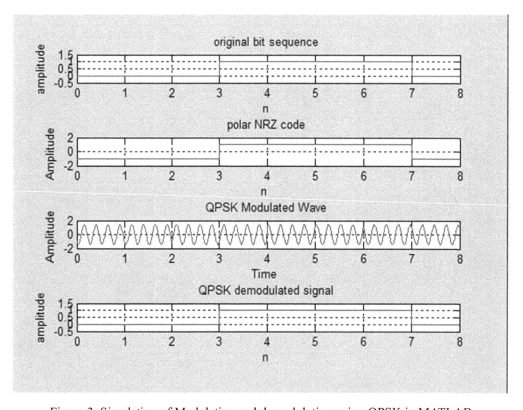

Figure 3. Simulation of Modulation and demodulation using QPSK in MATLAB

4. Nyquist Data Rate

Data rate is a parameter associated with the rate of data transferred between two or more computing or telecommunicating devices. Bit rate describes how much binary digits or bits can be transferred in a given time, normally in one second. Mostly data rate is measured in Mbps. Data rate is proportional to the bandwidth of communication channel not to information signal bandwidth. If the bandwidth is high, data rate will be also high.

In our situation we assume that the bandwidth is the same for BPSK and QPSK channels. According to the formula $R_b = 2B \times \log_2 L$, where L is the number of levels. In QPSK L is larger than the in BPSK, this leads to make the bit rate of QPSK larger than BPSK.

The Data Rate code of QPSK and BPSK was written in MATLAB environment, a part of which shown below. The result of running this program confirms the above idea and shown in figure 4.

```
BW=1:30
Rb_B=log2(2)/2.*BW*10^6
Rb_Q=log2(4)/2.*BW*10^6
plot(BW,Rb_B,'-rs')
hold on
plot(BW,Rb_Q,'-b*')
grid on
legend('BPSK','QPSK')
xlabel('BW (MHz)')
ylabel('Rb (bps)')
title('Bandwidth Vs. Data rate')
```

From figure 4, we can see that at the same bandwidth for example at 10 MH$_Z$, QPSK shows twice superiority on BPSK in data rate

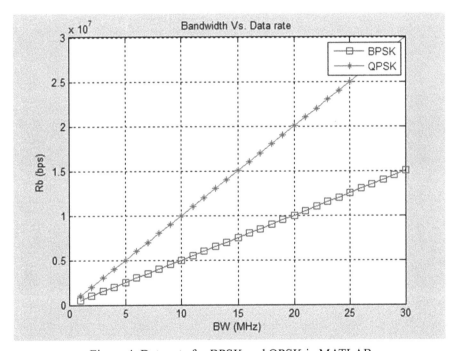

Figure 4. Data rate for BPSK and QPSK in MATLAB

5. Bit Error Rate

In digital transmission, the number of bit errors is the number of received bits of over a communication channel that have been altered due to noise, interference, distortion or bit synchronization errors.

BER is the number of bit errors divided by the total number of transferred bits during a studied time interval.

Also the definition of bit error rate can be presented in a simple formula; the equation below is the ratio of energy consumed in bit E_b to the signal spectral noise N_0 and represent bit error rate in BPSK $BER = 0.5\ erfc\sqrt{E_b/N_0}$. For QPSK using Q parameter $BER = Q\sqrt{E_b/N_0}$. Based on these BER formulas, a code was written in MATLAB environment. The result of running this program is shown in figure 5.

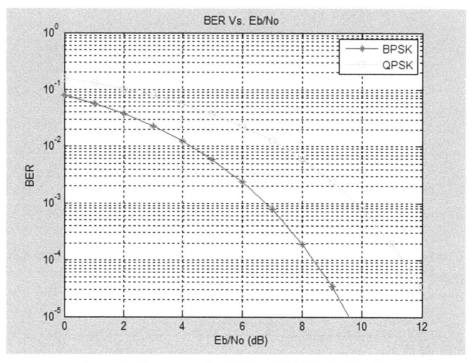

Figure 5. Bit error rate for BPSK and QPSK in MATLAB

To achieve the same BER, for example 10^{-4}, BPSK needs less energy as 8.5 dB, while QPSK needs 11.4 dB.

6. Capacity and Signal to noise ratio

Signal to noise ratio is expressed as $SNR = P_{signal}/P_{noise}$. The SNR for BPSK is very low means that it provides high immunity to noise as compare to the signal floating through the medium. The capacity is calculated as $c = B \times \log_2(SNR + 1)$. Figure 6 represents SNR of BPSK and QPSK as result of running MATLAB code.

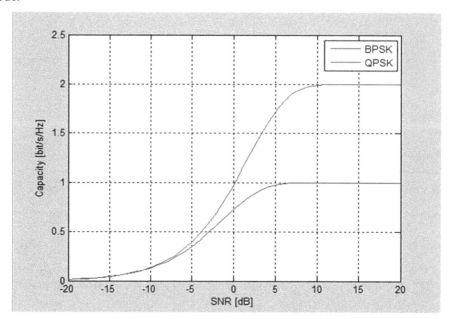

Figure 6. Capacity versus SNR for BPSK and QPSK

The capacity of QPSK is twice of BPSK at the same SNR.

7. Power Spectral Density

Power spectral density function (PSD) shows the power as a function of frequency. PSD shows at which frequencies variations are strong and at which variations are weak. Computation of PSD is done by fast Fourier transform.

The formula of PSD for BPSK modulation is $S_B\left(f\right)=2E_b Sinc^2\left(T_b f\right)$ and for QPSK modulation is

$$S_B\left(f\right)=4E_b Sinc^2\left(T_b f\right).$$

Figure 7 represents PSD for BPSK and QPSK as result of MATLAB code.

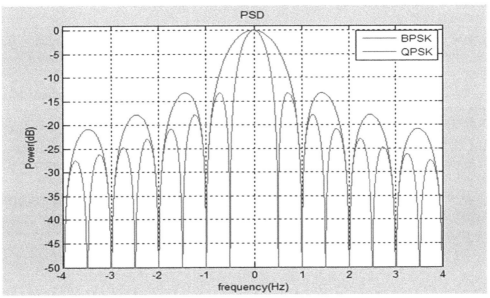

Figure 7. PSD for BPSK and QPSK

8. Conclusion

In this paper, we had presented two kinds of digital modulation techniques BPSK and QPSK which are widely used in wireless communication system.

We used MATLAB for the simulation and comparison between BPSK and QPSK over a set of performance parameters. We can conclude that:

- Bandwidth and data rate of QPSK is better than BPSK.
- Bit error rate is less occurred in BPSK unlike QPSK.
- Signal to noise ratio of QPSK is better than BPSK.
- Power spectral density of BPSK and QPSK are the same.

All of these expected and theoretical results prove the suggested idea of using MATLAB environment for the simulation of passband modulation techniques.

References

Boulmalf, M., Semmar, Y., Lakas, A., & Shuaib, K. (2010). *Teaching Digital and Analog Modulation to Undergraduate Information Technology Students Using Matlab and Simulink*, IEEE EDUCON 2010 Conference, the future of global learning engineering education, 685-691. http://dx.doi.org/10.1109/EDUCON.2010.5492513

Ferreira, A. J. M. (2009). *MATLAB Codes for Finite Element Analysis*, Springer. ISBN 978-1-4020-9199-5.

Gilat, A. (2004). *MATLAB: An Introduction with Applications 2nd Edition*, John Wiley & Sons. ISBN 978-

0-471-69420-5.

Hemant, D., & Ravindra, P. (2014). *Performance Analysis of Digital Modulation Techniques under Simulation Environment*, Journal of Emerging Technologies and Innovative Research (JETIR), Volume 1 Issue 5 JETIR (ISSN-2349-5162) JETIR1405013 Retrieved from http://www.mathworks.com/access/helpdesk_r13/help/toolbox/commblks/ref/simref-7.html#611864

Leon, W. C. (2001). *Digital and Analog Communication Systems*. Prentice Hall, New Jersey, sixth edition.

Li, X. L. (2008). Simulink-based Simulation of Quadrature Amplitude Modulation (QAM) System. Proceedings of The 2008 IAJC-IJME International Conference ISBN 978-1-60643-379-9.

Masud, M. A., Samsuzzaman, M., & Rahman, M. A. (2010). Bit Error Rate Performance Analysis on Modulation Techniques of Wideband Code Division Multiple Access. *Journal of Telecommunications, 1*(2), Retrieved from http://sites.google.com/site/journaloftelecommunications/

Quarteroni, A., & Fausto S., (2006). *Scientific Computing with MATLAB and Octave*, Springer. ISBN 978-3-540-32612-0.

Rashmi, S., Sunil, J., & Navneet, A. (2011). *Performance Analysis of Different M-ARY Modulation Techniques in Cellular Mobile Communication*, IP Multimedia Communications A Special Issue from IJCA – Retrieved from http:// www.ijcaonline.org

Samson, A., Oyetunji, A., & Akinninranye, A. (2013). Comparing Performances of Bandpass Modulation in Wireless Communication Channels. *Journal of Environmental Engineering and Technology, 2*(2). ISSN: 2165-8315 (Print) http://www.researchpub.org/journal/jeet/jeet.html

Tharakanatha, G. S. K., Mahaboob, K. B., & Vijay, B. C. (2013*). Implementation and Bit Error Rate analysis of BPSK Modulation and Demodulation Technique using MATLAB*, International Journal of Engineering Trends and Technology (IJETT), 4(9). ISSN: 2231-5381. http://www.ijettjournal.org

Virendrakumar, V., & Raut, J. (2014). IMPLEMENTATION OF DIGITAL MODULATION TECHNIQUES IN MATLAB. *International Journal of Advanced Technology in Engineering and Science, 2*(7). http://www.ijates.com

Permissions

List of Contributors

Zahurin Mat Aji and Nor Iadah Yusop
Public Enterprise Computing Research Platform, School of Computing, Universiti Utara Malaysia, Malaysia

Faudziah Ahmad, Azizi Ab. Aziz and Zaid M. Jawad
Human Centred Computing Group, Artificial Intelligence Research Platform, School of Computing, Universiti Utara Malaysia, Malaysia

Sarra Roubi and Mohammed Erramdani
High School of Technology, Mohammed First University, Oujda, Morocco

Samir Mbarki
Computer Science Department, Ibn Tofail University, Kenitra, Morocco

Hussain Mohammad Abu Dalbouh
Computer Science Department, Qassim University, Al-Qassim, Kingdom of Saudi Arabia

Xi Xie, Wei-zhong Jiang and Jun-hao Chi
Electrical and Information School, Jinan University, Zhuhai 519070, China

He Nie
College of Economics, Jinan University, Guangzhou 510632, China

Natarajan Meghanathan
Department of Computer Science, Jackson State University, USA

Dibaj Al Rosyada, Misbah and Eliyani
Electrical Engineering Program, Faculty of Engineering, Universitas Muhammadiyah Gresik, Indonesia

Mohamed Askali, Idriss Chana and Mostafa Belkasmi
MohammedV-Souisi University, SI2M Labo, ENSIAS, Rabat, Morroco

Fouad Ayoub
CRMEF, Kenitra, Morroco

Samir Mbarki
Departement of Computer Science, Faculty of Science, Ibn Tofail University, Kenitra, Morocco

Mohamed El Aroussi and Mohammed Wahbi
Department of Electrical Engineering, Hassania School of Public Works, Casablanca, Morocco

Khadija Jamali and Azz El Arab El Hossaini
Department of Computer Science, Faculty of Science, Ibn Tofail University, Kenitra, Morocco
Department of Electrical Engineering, Hassania School of Public Works, Casablanca, Morocco

Huang-Cheng Kuo and Shih-Hao Chen
National Chiayi University, Taiwan

Robert Goodwin and Giselle Rampersad
School of Computer Science, Engineering and Mathematics, Flinders University, Adelaide, Australia

Amal Alshardan
School of Computer Science, Engineering and Mathematics, Flinders University, Adelaide, Australia
Faculty of Computer and Information Sciences, Princess Nourah University, Riyadh, Saudi Arabia

Oluwatobi, A. Ayilara, Anuoluwapo, O. Ajayi, Kudirat and O. Jimoh
Computer Science and Engineering, Obafemi Awolowo University, Nigeria

Raoul Vallon and Thomas Grechenig
Research Group for Industrial Software, Vienna University of Technology, Vienna, Austria

M. M. MohieEl Din, Neveen I. Ghali, Mohamed S. Farag and O. M. Hassan
Department of Mathematics, Facility of Science Al-Azhar University Cairo, Egypt

Saed Thuneibat, Huthaifa Al Issa and Abdallah Ijjeh
Department of Electrical Engineering, Al-Balqa Applied University, Jordan

Mustafa Omar M. Baeuo, Nor Zairah Binti Ab. Rahim and Asma Ali Mosa Alaraibi
Advanced Informatics School, Universiti Teknologi Malaysia (UTM), Malaysia

Saed Thuneibat, Abdallah Ijjeh and Huthaifa Al_Issa
Department of Electrical Engineering, Al-Balqa Applied University, Jordan

Mousa Ababneh
Department of Finance and Administrative Sciences, Al-Balqa Applied University, Jordan

Index

Printed in the USA
CPSIA information can be obtained
at www.ICGtesting.com
JSHW051433221024
72173JS00006B/1461